THE ORGANIZATIONAL FRONTIERS SERIES

The Organizational Frontiers Series is sponsored by the Society for Industrial and Organizational Psychology (SIOP). Launched in 1983 to make scientific contributions to the field, the series has attempted to publish books on the cutting edge of theory, research, and theory-driven practice in industrial organizational psychology and related organizational science disciplines.

Our overall objective is to inform and to stimulate research for SIOP members (students, practitioners, and researchers) and people in related disciplines, including the other subdisciplines of psychology, organizational behavior, human resource management, and labor and industrial relations. The volumes in the Organizational Frontiers Series have the following goals:

1. Focus on research and theory in organizational science, and the implications for practice
2. Inform readers of significant advances in theory and research in psychology and related disciplines that are relevant to our research and practice
3. Challenge the research and practice community to develop and adapt new ideas and to conduct research on these developments
4. Promote the use of scientific knowledge in the solution of public policy issues and increased organizational effectiveness

The volumes originated in the hope that they would facilitate continuous learning and a continuing research curiosity about organizational phenomena on the part of both scientists and practitioners.

The Nature of Organizational Leadership

Understanding the
Performance Imperatives
Confronting Today's
Leaders

Stephen J. Zaccaro

Richard J. Klimoski

Editors

Foreword by Neal Schmitt

JOSSEY-BASS
A Wiley Company
San Francisco

Jossey-Bass books and products are available through most bookstores. To contact Jossey-Bass directly, call (888) 378-2537, fax to (800) 605-2665, or visit our website at www.josseybass.com.

Substantial discounts on bulk quantities of Jossey-Bass books are available to corporations, professional associations, and other organizations. For details and discount information, contact the special sales department at Jossey-Bass.

 Manufactured in the United States of America on Lyons Falls Turin Book. This paper is acid-free and 100 percent totally chlorine-free.

Library of Congress Cataloging-in-Publication Data

The nature of organizational leadership: understanding the performance imperatives confronting today's leaders / Stephen J. Zaccaro, Richard J. Klimoski, editors; foreword by Neal Schmitt. — 1st ed.

    p.   cm. — (The Jossey-Bass business & management series)

    ISBN 0-7879-5290-7

    1. Leadership. 2. Organization. I. Zaccaro, Stephen J. II. Klimoski, Richard J.

III. Series.

HD57.7 .N38 2001

658.4'092—dc21

00-011638

FIRST EDITION

HB Printing 10 9 8 7 6 5 4 3 2 1

The Jossey-Bass
Business & Management Series

The Organizational Frontiers Series

SERIES EDITOR

Sheldon Zedeck
University of California at Berkeley

EDITORIAL BOARD

Walter C. Borman
University of South Florida

Ann Howard
Leadership Research Institute and
Development Dimensions International

Daniel R. Ilgen
Michigan State University

Allen I. Kraut
Baruch College
City University of New York

Elaine D. Pulakos
HumRRO International

Denise M. Rouseau
Carnegie Mellon University

Contents

Foreword

This is the fourteenth book in a series published by Jossey-Bass and initiated by the Society for Industrial and Organizational Psychology (SIOP) in 1983. Originally published as the Frontiers of Industrial and Organizational Psychology Series, the series name was changed in 2000 to the Organizational Frontiers Series in order to clarify the identity and mission of the series.

The purpose of the series has been to promote the scientific status of the field. Raymond Katzell first edited the series. He was followed by Irwin Goldstein and Sheldon Zedeck, who proposed and developed this book. As usual, the topics and the book editors are chosen by the editorial board. The series editor and the editorial board then work with the book editor in planning the book and, occasionally, in suggesting and selecting chapter authors and content. During the writing of the book, the series editor works with the editor and the publisher to bring the manuscript to completion.

The success of the series is evident in the high number of sales (now nearly forty thousand). The series books have received excellent reviews, and individual chapters as well as entire books have been cited frequently. A recent symposium at the SIOP annual meeting examined the impact of the series on research and theory in industrial and organizational psychology. And although influence is difficult to track and the books have varied in intent and perceived centrality to the discipline, most participants concluded that the books in this series have exerted a significant impact on research and theory in the field and are regarded as being representative of the best the field has to offer.

This book, edited by Stephen Zaccaro and Richard Klimoski, seeks to move the field forward by integrating literature on the nature of organizational leadership from the strategic management area and the psychological literature. The psychological literature has often failed to consider the context of leadership and has typically focused on leadership at relatively low levels in organizations. The management literature has focused on leadership as a function of organizational structure and context-producing models of executive and organizational leadership and well-developed descriptions of how effective leadership behavior varies as a function of organizational level and environmental complexity. The management literature often seems to ignore the cognitive, social, and affective processes that vary as a function of the demands or imperatives on the leader, which typically are most interesting to psychologists. This book provides an integration of these perspectives into a single theoretical framework. We hope this theoretical integration will lead to a better understanding of leadership behavior and process, as well as stimulate future collaborative efforts between researchers in the strategic management area and those whose primary disciplinary focus is psychology.

The editors have done an excellent job in providing the integrative framework for this book, recruiting and selecting a diverse group of authors and then working with them to produce a focused set of chapters. We believe that this book will initiate a dialogue and future fruitful research collaboration. The editors and chapter authors deserve our gratitude for pursuing this challenging integrative effort.

The production of a book such as this one involves the hard work and cooperative effort of many individuals. The book editors, the chapter authors, and the editorial board all played important roles in this endeavor. Because all royalties from the series are used to help support SIOP financially, none of them received any remuneration. They deserve our appreciation for engaging a difficult task for the sole purpose of furthering our understanding of organizational science.

We also express our sincere gratitude to Cedric Crocker, Julianna Gustafson, and the entire staff at Jossey-Bass. Over many years and several books, they have provided support during the planning, development, and production of the series.

January 2001   NEAL SCHMITT
Ann Arbor, Michigan   *Series Editor, 1998–2003*

Preface

Leadership has been part of the lexicon of industrial and organizational psychology for a long time. Nonetheless, this book grew out of a vague sense of frustration that we felt when defining and modeling organizational leadership. Most of the prominent theories in our literature seem to miss the mark in describing the drivers and processes of leadership that occur within organizations. We felt this more keenly when our focus turned specifically to leadership at the top of organizations. Indeed, the field of industrial and organizational psychology has little to say exclusively about executive leadership, ceding the topic to strategic management scholars. When this domain gets treated at all, typically theories and models of generic leadership are stretched to fit the unique features of organizational and executive leadership.

In contrast, this book reflects a key assumption that understanding organizational leadership requires a careful specification of the contextual dynamics underlying and driving this phenomenon. Situating leadership within the organizational context means more than specifying moderators. Contextual variables act also as determinants of leadership moments, as well as drivers of leadership processes. Leadership moments refer to those critical periods within organizational life when the intervention of leadership processes is necessary for organizational effectiveness. Note our assumption that leadership does not reside in the routine minutiae of organizational flow but rather in the places where key decisions, choices, and actions need to occur. The leader performance imperatives that follow from contextual dynamics give rise to these leadership moments.

The chapters in this book describe in detail the nature of these performance imperatives. However, as a starting point, we defined seven leadership performance imperatives: cognitive, social, personal, political, technological, financial, and staffing. The chapter authors elucidate the key dynamics underlying one or more of the leadership imperatives. At most, existing perspectives of executive and organizational leadership typically have been grounded in only one or two of these imperatives. This book explores a fuller set of these imperatives, as they might contribute to an integrated framework that captures the contextual nature of organizational leadership.

Furthermore, although most chapters in this book include implications for leadership practice, questions related to senior leader selection, assessment, development, and effectiveness are the subjects of chapters in their own right. Finally, another key feature of this book is that we have selected several strategic management scholars as chapter authors because the data and models within this perspective literature tend to be underrepresented in traditional I/O leadership research.

Our intention here is not to present a new theory or conceptual framework of leadership. We believe that additional inductive and descriptive research that considers more fully the role of performance imperatives in executive work will be necessary before we can successfully model the dynamics of organizational leadership. Nonetheless, this book provides a description of these imperatives with the intention of stimulating further conceptual modeling.

Several basic assumptions flow through the chapters. First, leadership processes are important drivers of organizational effectiveness. Several theorists have argued with this viewpoint, but we believe the evidence favors the side of substantial influence by top leaders on organizational performance. This assumption means that it is critical to delineate how contextual influences determine what processes are key in a leadership moment and how these processes influence organizational performance.

A second assumption is that key leader attributes are those that foster the delivery of necessary leadership processes at critical leadership moments. Thus, in addition to our taking a contextual view of leadership, we argue for the importance of individual difference variables in explaining significant variance in leadership. We recognize that there has been considerable debate in the leadership literature over the past fifty years about this point, but we believe the weight of the evidence has favored the importance of certain personal qualities of the leader as instrumental in leader success. Accordingly, several chapters in Part One devote some attention to the specification of these qualities.

A final assumption is that the human resource functions of selection, training, and development should target key leadership processes and leader attributes. This seems indisputable as it is at the core of most selection and training models in I/O psychology. Yet we suspect that a survey of leadership research, particularly on executive leadership, would document the lack of validity evidence for many leader selection and training programs. Several of the authors in Part One address such concerns in their chapters. Also, the chapters in Part Two are devoted specifically to these topics.

The exercise of preparing this book and writing our own respective chapters has broadened our awareness of the challenges of modeling executive leadership. By bringing together scholars from different leadership domains, this book has also helped us develop a broader picture of such leadership. We hope that it will stimulate your thinking too.

January 2001   STEPHEN J. ZACCARO
Fairfax, Virginia   RICHARD J. KLIMOSKI

The Contributors

STEPHEN J. ZACCARO is an associate professor of psychology at George Mason University, Fairfax, Virginia. He has also held positions on the faculties of Virginia Tech and Holy Cross College. He received his M.A. (1980) and Ph.D. (1981) degrees from the University of Connecticut, specializing in social psychology. He has written numerous articles, book chapters, and technical reports on such topics as leadership, group dynamics, team performance, and work attitudes. He coedited *Occupational Stress and Organizational Effectiveness* (1987). He has also coedited three special issues of *Leadership Quarterly* and is on its editorial board. He has directed funded projects in the areas of team performance and shared mental models, leadership training, cognitive and metacognitive leadership capacities, and executive leadership.

RICHARD J. KLIMOSKI is professor of psychology, director of the Center for Behavioral and Cognitive Studies, director of the A-E Area Program in Psychology in the Department of Psychology, and associate dean, College of Arts and Sciences, at George Mason University in Fairfax, Virginia. His teaching and research interests revolve around the areas of organizational control systems in the form of performance appraisal and performance feedback programs and team performance. His research has appeared in the *Journal of Applied Psychology, Personnel Psychology, Academy of Management Journal, Journal of Management, Administrative Science Quarterly,* and *Journal of Conflict Resolution.* He is coauthor of *Research Methods in Human Resources Management.* He is on the editorial review board of *Human Resource Management Review* and *Organizational Research Methods* and has served on the editorial boards of the *Academy of Management Journal* (1985–1987), *Journal of Applied Psychology* (1988–1994), *Personnel Psychology* (1977–1989), and *Administrative*

Science Quarterly (1978–1988). He was senior editor of the *Academy of Management Review* from 1990 to 1993.

DEANNA J. BANKS is a doctoral student in industrial/organizational psychology at George Mason University. A graduate of Guilford College, her research interests are in the areas of leadership and team adaptability. She is particularly interested in the role of work experiences and stretch assignments in executive leader development.

DANIEL J. BRASS holds the J. Henning Hilliard Chair in Innovation Management at the University of Kentucky and is serving as associate editor of *Administrative Science Quarterly*. He received his Ph.D. degree in business administration from the University of Illinois-Urbana. His research focuses on the antecedents and consequences of social networks in organizations. He has published articles in such journals as *Administrative Science Quarterly, Academy of Management Journal, Academy of Management Review, Journal of Applied Psychology, Organizational Science, Organizational Behavior and Human Decision Processes, Human Relations, Business Horizons, Organizational Behavior Teaching Review, Research in Personnel and Human Resources Management, Research in Politics and Society,* and *Research in Negotiation in Organizations,* as well as numerous book chapters.

CATHERINE M. DAILY is the John and Marilyn Kosin Faculty Fellow of Strategic Management and Associate Professor of Strategic Management in the Kelley School of Business, Indiana University. She received her Ph.D. degree in strategic management from the Kelley School of Business. Her research interests include corporate governance, strategic leadership, the dynamics of business failure, ownership structures, and research methods. She is an associate editor of the *Academy of Management Journal.* Her research has appeared in the *Academy of Management Journal, Strategic Management Journal, Decision Sciences, Personnel Psychology, Journal of Management,* and *Academy of Management Executive,* among others.

DAN R. DALTON is dean and Harold A. Poling Chair of Strategic Management at the Kelley School of Business, Indiana University. He received his Ph.D. degree from the University of California. His research interests include corporate governance, managerial ethics, research methods, and corporate social responsibility. His research has appeared in the *Academy of Management Journal, Strategic Management Journal, Academy of Management Review, Administrative Science Quarterly, Decision Sciences, Personnel Psychology, Journal of Management,* and *Academy of Management Executive,* among others.

KEVIN DANIELS is reader in organizational behavior at Sheffield University Management School, United Kingdom. He received his Ph.D. degree in applied psychology from Cranfield Institute of Technology. His research interests encompass links between emotion, cognition, and organization. He is an associate editor of the *Journal of Occupational and Organizational Psychology* and is on the editorial board of the *Journal of the Australia* and *New Zealand Academy of Management.*

DEEPAK K. DATTA is professor of strategic management and Charles W. Oswald Faculty Fellow at the University of Kansas. He earned his Ph.D. degree (1986) in strategic management at the University of Pittsburgh. He has also taught in the M.B.A. programs at the École Supérieure de Commerce in Toulouse, France, and the China-Europe International Business School in Shanghai, China. His research interests include mergers and acquisitions, chief executive officer selection, top management demography, strategic decision processes, and international entry strategies. He has published in the *Academy of Management Journal, Strategic Management Journal, Journal of Management Studies, Journal of Management, Management International Review,* and *Long Range Planning.* He is a member of the Academy of Management, Strategic Management Society, and the Academy of International Business. He has been the codirector of the Center for International Business and is the founding director of the International Business Resource Center at the University of Kansas.

DAVID V. DAY is an associate professor of psychology at Penn State University. He received his Ph.D. degree (1989) in industrial and organization psychology from the University of Akron. Day's research interests are mainly in the areas of personality influences in organizations, as well as leadership and leadership development. He is currently investigating factors associated with the development of human and social capital as part of leadership development programs in organizations. He serves on the editorial board of the *Journal of Management* and is an associate editor of *Leadership Quarterly*.

ROBERT HOOIJBERG is professor of organizational behavior at the International Institute for Management Development in Lausanne, Switzerland. He received his B.A. and M.A. degrees from the University of Nijmegen, the Netherlands, and his Ph.D. degree in organizational psychology from the University of Michigan. His research focuses on leadership and 360-degree feedback, diversity, organizational culture, and decision making. His research has appeared in such journals as *Leadership Quarterly, Journal of Management, Human Relations, Organization Science, Human Resource Management*, the *Journal of Organizational Behavior.* He has consulted widely.

ANN HOWARD is manager of assessment technology integrity for Development Dimensions International, a provider of human resource programs and services. She received her Ph.D. degree from the University of Maryland (1976) and her M.S. degree from San Francisco State University (1967), both in industrial/organizational psychology. She holds an honorary doctor of science degree from Goucher College, where she earned a B.A. degree in psychology. She is president of the Leadership Research Institute, a nonprofit organization that she cofounded in 1987. She is the author of more than eighty-five publications on topics such as assessment centers, management selection, managerial careers, and leadership. She is the senior author (with Douglas W. Bray) of *Managerial Lives in Transition: Advancing Age and Changing Times* (1988), which received the George R. Terry Award of Excellence from the Academy of Management in 1989. She is a past president and fellow of the Society for Industrial and Organizational Psychology and served as its secretary-treasurer, editor of *Industrial-Organizational Psychologist,* and chair or member of several other committees. She received the society's Distinguished Service Contributions Award in 1994. She is a Fellow of the American Psychological Association and the American Psychological Society and past president of the Society of Psychologists in Management.

ANNE HUFF is professor of strategic management at the University of Colorado, Boulder, with a joint appointment at Cranfield School of Management in the United Kingdom. She received her Ph.D. degree from Northwestern University. Her research interests focus on strategic change, both as a dynamic process of interaction among firms and as a cognitive process affected by the interaction of individuals over time. In addition to articles on topics related to strategic change, her publications include *Mapping Strategic Change* (1990). She is on the editorial board of the *Strategic Management Journal,* the *Journal of Management Studies,* and the *British Journal of Management* and is the strategy editor for the book series Foundations in Organization Science. In 1998–1999 she served as president of the Academy of Management.

T. OWEN JACOBS is Leo Cherne Distinguished Visiting Professor of Leadership and Strategic Decision Making at the Industrial College of the Armed Forces, National Defense University. He retired as chief of the Strategic Leadership Technical Area (SLTA) of the Army Research Institute in 1994. Jacobs received his B.A. and M.A. degrees from Vanderbilt University and his Ph.D. degree from the University of Pittsburgh (1956). He is the author of *Leadership and Exchange in Formal Organizations,* as well as eight book chapters, twenty-eight reports, and journal articles.

PHYLLIS JOHNSON is a visiting research fellow at Strathclyde University Business School in Scotland and a chartered psychologist. She received her Ph.D. degree from Cranfield University School of Management in the United Kingdom. Her research interests, in the area of strategic organizational behavior, encompass top team decision making, managerial cognition, organizational therapy, and diversity in the boardroom. She reviews for a series of journals, consults for several organizations, and is completing therapy training.

K. LEE KIECHEL KOLES is a doctoral student in the industrial/organizational psychology program at George Mason University. A graduate of Williams College, her research interests are in the area of team dynamics, with a special emphasis on team learning and team leadership.

ROBERT G. LORD received his Ph.D. degree (1975) in organizational psychology from Carnegie-Mellon University. He has been at the University of Akron since that time and is currently professor and chair of the Department of Psychology. He is a fellow of the Society for Industrial and Organizational Psychology and a founding fellow of the American Psychological Society. He has published extensively on topics related to motivation, self-regulation, social cognition, leadership processes, leadership perceptions, and information processing. He coauthored *Leadership and Information Processing: Linking Perceptions and Performance* (1991) with Karen J. Maher. He has served as associate editor of the *Journal of Applied Psychology* and is editing the Jossey-Bass Organizational Frontiers series book *Emotions at Work* with Richard Klimoski and Ruth Kanfer.

JOHN E. MATHIEU is a professor of management and organization at the University of Connecticut. He received his Ph.D. degree (1985) in industrial/organizational psychology from Old Dominion University. His current research interests include models of training effectiveness, team and multiteam processes, and cross-level models of organizational behavior. He has published over fifty articles and chapters on a variety of topics, mostly in the areas of micro- and meso-organizational behavior. He is a member of the Academy of Management and a fellow of the Society of Industrial Organizational Psychology and the American Psychological Association.

CYNTHIA D. MCCAULEY is vice president of new initiatives at the Center for Creative Leadership. She received her B.A. degree (1980) from King College and her M.A. (1982) and Ph.D. (1984) degrees from the University of Georgia, all in psychology. Her research has examined various management development strategies: 360-degree feedback, training programs, challenging job assignments, and developmental relationships. She has published articles in a variety of professional journals and books and is the author of several management development tools, including Benchmarks (a 360-degree feedback instrument) and the Job Challenge Profile (an assessment of on-the-job learning opportunities). She is coeditor with Russ Moxley and Ellen Van Velsor of the *Center for Creative Leadership Handbook of Leadership Development* (1998).

MICHAEL L. MCGEE is a doctoral candidate at George Mason University in the field of industrial/organizational psychology. He received his B.A. degree in history from Texas Tech University

(1972), an M.B.A. degree in organizational design and behavior from the University of Texas (1981), and a master's degree in industrial/organizational psychology from George Mason University (1996). He was commissioned as a Distinguished Military Graduate from Texas Tech University in 1972 and served for over twenty-five years in the U.S. Army as an infantry officer. He is a member of the American Psychological Association, the American Psychological Society, the Society of Industrial and Organizational Psychologists, and the Academy of Management.

NANDINI RAJAGOPALAN is an associate professor of management and organization at the Marshall School of Business, University of Southern California. She received her Ph.D. degree from the University of Pittsburgh. Her research on executive compensation, chief executive officer succession, strategic change, and strategic decision processes has been published in leading management journals, including the *Academy of Management Journal, Academy of Management Review, Strategic Management Journal, Journal of Management, Journal of Management Studies,* and *Advances in Strategic Management.* She serves on the editorial boards of the *Academy of Management Journal, Strategic Management Journal,* and *International Journal of Organizational Analysis.* She has received several awards for her scholarly contributions, including the Western Academy of Management's Ascendant Scholar Award (1996).

MARGUERITE SCHNEIDER recently received her Ph.D. degree in organization management from Rutgers University. She is assistant professor of management and international business at the School of Business, College of New Jersey. Prior to her academic career, she worked in corporate strategic planning in the financial services industry and in program development in academic administration. Her primary areas of research are governance, leadership, and public sector organizations. Her work will soon be published in the *Journal of Management and Governance.* She has presented several papers related to her research interests at various conferences, including the Academy of Management.

YAN ZHANG is a Ph.D. candidate in the department of management and organization at the Marshall School of Business, University of

Southern California. Her research interests include CEO succession, top management teams, international strategic alliances, and new venture strategy in transitional economies. She has presented several research papers on these topics at annual conferences of the Academy of Management (AOM) and the Strategic Management Society. Her work has also been published in the AOM's Best Paper Proceedings (2000). She has received several academic honors and awards, including the 2000 James S. Ford/Commerce Associate Doctoral Fellowship, which is awarded to the best doctoral candidate by the Marshall School of Business, University of Southern California.

PART 1

Defining Leadership Imperatives

CHAPTER 1

The Nature of Organizational Leadership
An Introduction

Stephen J. Zaccaro
Richard J. Klimoski

Leadership has been a major topic of research in psychology for almost a century and has spawned thousands of empirical and conceptual studies. Despite this level of effort, however, the various parts of this literature still appear disconnected and directionless. In our opinion, a major cause of this state of the field is that many studies of leadership are context free; that is, low consideration is given to organizational variables that influence the nature and impact of leadership. Such research, especially prominent in the social and organizational psychology literatures, tends to focus on interpersonal processes between individuals, nominally leaders and followers. Studies that explicitly examine leadership within organizational contexts, particularly from the strategic management literature, seem incomplete for other reasons. They typically ignore the cognitive, interpersonal, and social richness of this phenomenon, in that they fail to come to grips with processes that would explain or account for outcomes. While model building in the strategic management literature is typically focused on the examination of leadership occurring at upper organization levels, any insights offered regarding the selection, development, and training of potential leaders are not often grounded in strong conceptual frameworks having significant empirical support. These observations sometimes leave the student of leadership with the feeling that many wheels are spinning in a deepening rut.

One reason for the lack of progress in developing an integrated understanding of organizational leadership is that theorists of all stripes have sought to offer generic leadership theories and models that use many of the same constructs to explain leadership across different organizational levels. Such an approach assumes that leadership at the top of the organization reflects the same psychological and sociological dynamics as leadership at lower organizational levels. This lack of consideration to organizational level and other structural factors has contributed to a dearth of good empirical research on organizational leadership, particularly at the executive level.

Some writers have argued for qualitative shifts in the nature of leadership across organizational levels (Day & Lord, 1988; Hunt, 1991; Jacobs & Jaques, 1987; Katz & Kahn, 1978; Zaccaro, 1996). This view recognizes that dimensions of organizational structure, specifically hierarchical level, degree of differentiation in function, and place in organizational space, moderate the nature of organizational leadership as well as its antecedents and consequences. Thus, performance demands on leaders change across organizational levels. This also means changes in the critical competencies and work requirements that form the basis for selection policies and that leader training and development programs must target. If leadership were to be studied in situ, researchers could then fully appreciate how the antecedents, dynamics, consequences, and criteria of leadership change as a function of such variables as organizational level, organizational structure, environmental complexity, and cultural and societal parameters.

In our view, a situated approach that examines the contextualized influences on organizational leadership is more likely to produce accurate, defensible, and ultimately more successful models and midrange theories of this phenomenon. If such an approach were to include a focus on top managers, this would culminate in fuller and more generalizable models of organizational leadership, including a better understanding of how executive leadership differs from lower-level leadership. There would also emerge from such efforts a more integrated conceptual framework for the specification and development of leader assessment, selection, training, and development programs.

This book presents a contextualized perspective of leadership that we hope will serve as a starting point for subsequent model building and theory development. An essential question is addressed across the chapters of this book: what does the organizational context imply for the problems to be confronted and the requisite behaviors, attributes, and outcomes of top leaders? We have chosen to focus primarily on executive leadership, because research and models on this aspect of leadership are particularly lacking in the industrial/organizational (I/O) literature.

The focus of this book is on the performance demands and problematics that chief executive officers (CEOs) need to manage or otherwise address if they and their organizations to be successful. We have derived these imperatives both inductively from reviews of case studies and work description studies (Hemphill, 1959; Isenberg, 1984; Kaplan, 1986, Kotter, 1982; Kraut, Pedigo, McKenna, & Dunnette, 1989; Levinson & Rosenthal, 1984; Luthans, Rosenkrantz, & Hennessey, 1985; Tornow & Pinto, 1976; Zaccaro, 1996) and deductively from several models and perspectives of organizational leadership (Day & Lord, 1988; Hunt, 1991; Jacobs & Jaques, 1987, 1990, 1991; Katz & Kahn, 1978; Lord & Maher, 1993; Zaccaro, 1996). These reviews suggest seven fundamental performance imperatives in the life space of organizational leaders: cognitive, social, personal, political, technological, financial, and staffing demands and requirements that define the nature of organizational leadership work.

The next section of this chapter presents some central elements that can be used to describe organizational leadership. Our intention is not to try to develop the "best" definition of leadership; we agree with other observers (Bass, 1990; Stogdill, 1974; Yukl, 1994) that this is not a useful direction to take. However, we will identify some defining qualities that are important, at least from the perspective of this book. We then briefly review and summarize major themes in the study of leadership to be found in the existing literature. Once again, this is not an end in and of itself, but is directed to sharpening the focus of this book for readers. Following this, we provide a more detailed description of the logic for the above-mentioned leadership performance imperatives that are central to the rest of this book. In a sense, this contextualizes the approach that we have adopted. Finally, as is customary, we provide an overview of the chapters themselves.

Some Defining Elements of Organizational Leadership

Stogdill (1974, p. 259) noted that "there are almost as many definitions of leadership as there are persons who have attempted to define the concept." We do not wish to add still another; indeed, we suspect that what we might offer would not satisfy all of the chapter authors, much less the entire community of leadership scholars. However, there are central defining elements of organizational leadership that have some consensus in the literature and provide a unifying perspective for the ideas offered here. For the purposes of our discussion, we make the following arguments:

- Organizational leadership involves processes and proximal outcomes (such as worker commitment) that contribute to the development and achievement of organizational purpose.
- Organizational leadership is identified by the application of nonroutine influence on organizational life.
- Leader influence is grounded in cognitive, social, and political processes.
- Organizational leadership is inherently bounded by system characteristics and dynamics, that is, leadership is contextually defined and caused.

Leadership and Organizational Purpose

Positions of leadership are established in work settings to help organizational subunits to achieve the purposes for which they exist within the larger system. Organizational purpose is operationalized as a direction for collective action. Leadership processes are directed at defining, establishing, identifying, or translating this direction for their followers and facilitating or enabling the organizational processes that should result in the achievement of this purpose. Organizational purpose and direction becomes defined in many ways, including through mission, vision, strategy, goals, plans, and tasks. The operation of leadership is inextricably tied to the continual development and attainment of these organizational goal states.

This perspective of leadership is a functional one, meaning that leadership is at the service of collective effectiveness (Fleishman et al., 1991; Hackman & Walton, 1986; Lord, 1977). Describing a similar approach to team leadership, Hackman and Walton (1986, p. 75) argued that the leader's "'main job is to do, or get done, whatever is not being adequately handled for group needs' (McGrath, 1962, p. 5). If a leader manages, by whatever means, to ensure that all functions critical to both task accomplishment and group maintenance are adequately taken care of, then the leader has done his or her job well." These assertions can be made whether leaders are leading groups, multiple groups combined into a department or a division, the organization as a whole, or conglomerates of multiple organizations. This defining element of organizational leadership also means that the success of the collective as a whole is a (if not the) major criterion for leader effectiveness.

It should also be noted that functional leadership is not usually defined by a specific set of behaviors but rather by generic responses that are prescribed for and will vary by different problem situations. That is, the emphasis switches from "what leaders *should do*" to "what *needs to be done* for effective performance" (Hackman & Walton, 1986, p. 77). Thus, leadership is defined in terms of those activities that promote team and organizational goal attainment by being responsive to contextual demands (Mumford, 1986).

Senior organizational leaders generally carry the construction of organizational purpose and direction. The leadership performance imperatives that derive from the organizational context become entwined in this obligation as well as in the content of organizational directions (see Chapter Seven, this volume). For example, the complexity of the senior leader's operating environment requires considerable cognitive resources to build the frame of reference that provides the rationale for organizational strategy (see Chapter Two, this volume). Similarly, organizational goals and strategies need to be responsive to the requirements of multiple stakeholders and constituencies, indicating the social imperatives confronting senior leaders (see Chapter Four, this volume). Finally, a little-noted observation about organizational goal setting is that when such directions are created, they reflect in part the senior leader's personal and self-defined (career) imperatives. Thus, when leaders develop and implement organizational strategies, they do so from and within the context of these and the other imperatives discussed here.

Leadership as Nonroutine Influence

Leadership does not reside in the routine activities of organizational work. Instead, it occurs in response to, or in anticipation of, nonroutine organizational events. This defining element was suggested by Katz and Kahn (1978), who considered "the essence of organizational leadership to be the influential increment over and above mechanical compliance with the routine directives of the organization" (p. 528).

Nonroutine events can be defined as any situation that constitutes a potential or actual hindrance to organizational goal progress. Thus, organizational leadership can be construed as large- (and small-)scale social problem solving, where leaders are constructing the nature of organizational problems, developing and evaluating potential solutions, and planning, implementing, and monitoring selected solutions within complex social domains (Fleishman et al., 1991; Zaccaro et al., 1995). This is not to suggest that leadership (as social problem solving) is necessarily reactive. The boundary management obligations widely assigned to organizational leaders (Katz & Kahn, 1978) require that leaders be attuned to environmental events, interpreting and defining them for their followers, anticipating the emergence of potential goal blockages, and planning accordingly. Thus, successful organizational leadership is quite proactive in its problem solving.

This defining element of leadership as involving nonroutine influence reflects two other points. First, critical organizational leadership is more likely to be reflected in responses to ill-defined problems (Mumford, 1986; Fleishman et al., 1991), defined as those for which the starting parameters, the permissible solution paths, and the solution goals are unspecified (Holyoak, 1984). In such situations, leaders need to construct the nature of the problem, as well as the parameters of potential solution strategies, before they can begin to devise resolutions to the problem. In well-defined problems, solutions are grounded mostly in the experience of the leaders in prior similar situations. Such solutions are also not likely to require significant large-scale change in organizational routine.

The second point is that leadership typically involves discretion and choice in what solutions are appropriate in particular problem domains (Hunt, Osborn, & Martin, 1981; Jacobs & Jaques, 1990; Zaccaro et al., 1995). Thus, as Jacobs and Jaques (1990, pp. 281–282) argue, "Leadership must be viewed as a process which occurs only in situations in which there is decision discretion. To the extent discretion exists, there is an opportunity for leadership to be exercised. If there is no discretion, there is no such opportunity."

Team or organizational actions that are completely specified by procedure or practice or are fully elicited by the situation do not usually require the intervention of leaders. Such actions are likely to be encoded as part of the organizational rule or normative structures (although, leadership is involved in the evolution of these structures). Instead, leadership is necessitated by organizationally relevant events that present alternative interpretations and by problems in which multiple solution paths are viable or requisite solutions need to be implemented. Individuals in leadership roles are then responsible for making the choices that define subsequent collective responses.

In this sense, the performance imperatives we highlight can be construed as representing a cluster of ill-defined discretionary problems or obligations requiring collective action for organizational success. For example, the nature and rate of technological change can pose a number of challenges to organizational leaders: how information is to be gathered and distributed, how to interpret the resulting flood of data, and how to gain competitive advantages from technological advances in both production and human resource systems are just a few of these. In the same way, financial imperatives challenge executives to make and integrate a variety of long- and short-term strategic decisions. Senior staffing imperatives follow these challenges as executives strive to create the right human resource combinations for their strategic choices. Thus, a functional or social problem-solving perspective of leadership is necessarily grounded in a contextual framework that presents fundamental performance imperatives demanding organizational choices.

Leadership as Managing Social and Cognitive Phenomena

Most definitions of leadership stress social or interpersonal influence processes as key elements. Thus, persuasion, the management of social and political processes, and the use of social power are ubiquitous constructs in the leadership literature. In addition, as suggested by the problem-solving perspective, the execution of effective cognitive processes is equally critical to leader effectiveness. To illustrate, cognitive requirements include interpreting and modeling environmental events for organizational members, determining the nature of problems to be solved, and engaging in long-term strategic thinking. In general, models of leadership, particularly those in the psychological literature, have focused on social processes directed toward the implementation of solutions to organizational problems. A full exposition of leadership must also include the cognitive processes leaders use to plan collective action.

Some researchers in the organizational and management literatures have indeed emphasized the role of leaders in organizational sense making, where collective actions are given meaning through the leader's interpretation and cognitive modeling of environmental events (Huff, 1990; Jacobs & Jaques, 1987; Thomas, Clark, & Gioia, 1993). Along these lines, Jacobs and Jaques (1991, p. 434) noted:

> Executive leaders "add value" to their organizations in large part by giving a sense of understanding and purpose to the overall activities of the organization. In excellent organizations, there almost always is a feeling that the "boss" knows what he is doing, that he has shared this information downward, that it makes sense, and that it is going to work.

Such understandings, defined as frames of reference by Jacobs and Jaques (1987, 1990; see also Chapter Two, this volume), become crucial mediators of leadership influence in organizations.

An organizational frame of reference is a cognitive representation of the elements and events that comprise the leader's operating environment. Such models contain the pattern of relationships among these events and elements. Accordingly, the logic and rationale for an articulated organization strategy become grounded in the causal relationships interpreted by top executives as existing among the critical events in organizational space.

These frames of referen[ce] [are a re]sponsibility of senior leaders. [They define the op]erating environment and c[onstrain lower-level] constituencies. However, Jac[obs and Jaques] 1992), relying on the notion [of complexity, ar]gued that the complexity of t[he leader must] respond to the complexity [of the environment as] patterned. Therefore, the fr[ames of reference that] senior leaders develop must [be far richer than lead]ers at lower organizational le[vels. These frames] must accommodate many m[ore elements and rela]tions among these elements [than those at lower] levels (Jacobs & Jaques, 198[7). Such a de]velopment of increasingly c[omplex frames at higher] organizational levels compel[s more complex cog]nitive processes.

We do not mean to argue that the use of cognitive and social leadership processes is entirely independent. In many instances of effective leadership, these processes become inextricably entwined. For example, functionally diverse teams (where members have varied specializations within the organization) can help leaders interpret environmental ambiguity and reduce uncertainty. This is particularly true in top management teams, where environmental complexity is typically stronger than for lower-level leaders (Zaccaro, 1996). If the top executive team is constructed with individuals of varying functional expertise, the team as a whole has considerably more resources to develop more complex representations of the organization's operating environment. However, team members will often stay silent and defer to the CEO unless social processes permit them to contribute to environmental interpretation (Jacobs & Jaques, 1987; see Chapters Three and Eight, this volume).

Leadership and the Organizational Context

Most theories of organizational leadership in the psychological literature are largely context free. For example, leadership is typically considered without adequate regard for the structural considerations that affect and moderate its conduct. We maintain, however, that organizational leadership cannot be modeled effectively without attending to such considerations.

One particularly strong influence is the organizational level at which leadership occurs. Not only do the fundamental demands and work requirements of leaders change at different levels (Jacobs & Jaques, 1987; Katz & Kahn, 1978; Zaccaro, 1996); the hierarchical context of leadership has profound effects on the personal, interpersonal, and organizational choices that can be made, as well as the import that a given choice might have. Clearly a CEO's stating a preference for a site for a new factory is different from the case of a department manager's stating his or her preferences. Organizational level matters profoundly yet, surprisingly, has been ignored in all but a few leadership models in the literature.

What has been argued about leadership at different organizational levels? Katz and Kahn (1978) specified three distinct patterns of organizational leadership. The first pattern concerns the administrative use of existing organizational structures to maintain effective organizational operations. If problems arise to disrupt these operations, existing organizational mechanisms and procedures are used to resolve them. Indeed, Katz and Kahn note that "such acts are often seen as so institutionalized as to require little if any leadership" (p. 537). This leadership pattern occurs at lower organizational levels. The second leadership pattern, occurring at middle organizational levels, involves the embellishment and operationalization of formal structural elements. Such actions require a two-way orientation by the leader (that is, toward both superiors and subordinates), as well as significant human relations skills. The third pattern of organizational leadership, which occurs at the top of organizations, concerns structural origination or change in the organization as a reflection of new policy formulations. Taken together, the distribution of separate leadership patterns across organizational levels that Katz and Kahn proposed suggests significant qualitative differences between the nature of junior and senior leadership. Similar models specifying differences across levels of organizational leadership have been proposed in separate theoretical formulations by Jacobs and Jaques (1987), Mumford, Zaccaro, Harding, Fleishman, and Reiter-Palmon (1993), and Bentz (1987).

In our view, a contextual model of leadership would be different from approaches that emphasize context as implying situational moderators (Fiedler, 1967, 1971, 1978; Gupta, 1984, 1988; Howell & Dorfman, 1981). In the latter, the situation is viewed as determining which leadership response (and sometimes which leaders; Fiedler, 1967, 1971) is likely to be the most effective. Generally, these models produce classifications of leader-situation matches that produce effectiveness. Such conceptualizations are important and do contribute to understanding organizational leadership. However, they tend to understate the role of the organizational context in influencing and mediating the fundamental nature of leadership work, including those forces that animate or retard leader initiatives or behaviors, themselves. This context shapes the performance imperatives that both stimulate and define the parameters of appropriate leadership action. It implies qualitative shifts in the ways that leaders acquire information in their roles and go on to make sense of this information. It changes if and when (and then how and what) leaders plan appropriate collective responses. It changes the nature and role of key processes such as how leaders influence and manage their followers. It clearly affects the range and scope of their influence. The organizational context even changes the mechanisms by which leaders acquire their role and develop their legitimacy. These effects extend beyond those typically modeled in situational contingency approaches in the current leadership literature. Thus, unlike the situation as moderator, we view situation or context as boundary conditions for theory building and model specification.

Major Conceptual Approaches to Leadership

These defining elements and the contextual perspective of organizational leadership were our guiding principles when we planned this book with the chapter authors. As such, we are promoting an alternative view in this book, or perhaps more accurately, we are angling for a more holistic perspective in modeling organizational leadership, albeit at one level of the organization. By way of contrast, we have abstracted from a survey of leadership research four established traditions: social and interpersonal exchange, strategic management, organizational systems theory, and performance effectiveness models of leadership. We examine each of these briefly and highlight their major limitations. We do this not to discredit established traditions in research on leadership but to argue for the value of the approach we have chosen to follow in this book.

Social and Interpersonal Exchange

The social exchange approach to leadership is perhaps the most popular and pervasive perspective in the literature. The major unit of analysis in this approach is the relationship between the leader and his or her followers: leaders provide direction, guidance, and activity structuring to a collective; members of the collective in turn grant the leader permission to influence them (therefore conferring legitimacy), as well as reverence and respect. Leader effectiveness is defined as a function of the dynamic that occurs between leader and followers.

As might be expected, models from this approach focus on one or more of three elements: characteristics of the leader, characteristics of the followers, and characteristics of their relationship. In defining key leader characteristics that contribute to a successful exchange, researchers have focused mainly on the leader's predominant interaction style. Specifically, leaders vary in terms of their primary tendency to adopt a structuring task-oriented style toward their subordinates or a considerate, socioemotional style. For example, Fleishman and his colleagues defined initiating structure and consideration as key leadership behaviors (Fleishman, 1953, 1973; Fleishman & Harris, 1962, Halpin & Winer, 1957; Hemphill & Coons, 1957; Stogdill & Coons, 1957). Likert (1961) argued for task-oriented and relationship-oriented behaviors as differentiating effective from ineffective managers. In his contingency model, Fiedler (1964, 1971) used his least-preferred coworker (LPC) scale to define a similar task (low LPC) versus group-oriented (high LPC) dimension. Similar stylistic differences have been proposed by Blake and Mouton (1964), House and Dessler (1974), Katz, Maccoby, and Morse (1950), and Hersey and Blanchard (1969).

Other leadership theorists within the social exchange tradition have focused heavily on characteristics of the subordinate. Hollander (1958, 1979; Hollander & Julian, 1970) examined the role of followers in granting "legitimacy" to the leader to be innovative. Lord and his colleagues (Cronshaw & Lord, 1987; Lord, Foti, & Phillips, 1982; Lord, Foti, & De Vader, 1984; Lord & Maher, 1993; Rush, Thomas, & Lord, 1982) have taken these notions further to describe the leadership schemas that followers develop and use to bestow leadership status on individuals. Hersey and Blanchard (1969, 1982) argue that the maturity level of subordinates determines what behavioral style the leader should adopt when seeking to influence a group. Leadership substitutes theory (Kerr & Jermier, 1978; Howell & Dorfman, 1981) cites the experience, ability, and commitment of subordinates as moderating the efficacy of leadership influence.

The characteristics of leader-subordinate relationships that have been investigated include their overall quality (Fiedler, 1964, 1971), the degree to which they are mutually influential (Vroom & Jago, 1974, 1978, 1995), their variability across individual subordinates (Dansereau, Graen, & Haga, 1975; Graen & Cashman, 1975; Graen & Scandura, 1987), and the sense of empowerment they engender (Bass, 1985, 1996; Bass & Avolio, 1990, 1993; House, 1977; House & Shamir, 1993). Fiedler conditioned the situational favorability for leadership influence on whether the leaders and followers experienced good versus poor relations. Vroom and his colleagues examined the factors that determined whether the exchange between leader and follower was a participative one, where influence flows in both directions, or a directive/autocratic one, where influence flows solely from leader. While most of these models emphasize an average leadership behavioral style displayed across subordinates, Dansereau, Graen, and their colleagues argued that the quality of leader-follower relationships varied across members within the same collective unit. Some relationships were participative, close, and characterized by a high level of trust, while others were more formal, directive, and less trustful. Finally, research on inspirational leadership by Bass and his colleagues has focused on a dynamic established between leader and follower that reflects an intense reverence and loyalty to the leader and a strong sense of empowerment in the follower.

Taken together, these models and theories constitute a huge proportion of research in the leadership literature. They have contributed to a broad and deep understanding of the following topics:

- What constitutes an effective exchange between leaders and subordinates
- How leader qualities and behaviors facilitate subordinate and small group effectiveness
- How the contributions of various leadership styles to subordinate effectiveness are moderated by a variety of situational factors
- How the characteristics and information processing of subordinates contribute to effective leadership

The social exchange approach has greatly enhanced our fundamental knowledge about leadership. Nonetheless, this approach has several limitations that constrain an understanding of organizational leadership. Social exchange models and theories emphasize individual, small group, and direct leadership. The focus is on the direct interaction of leader and followers. Such leadership does reside at all levels of the organization, but other forms of indirect or mediated leadership also exist. For example, middle-level managers are typically tasked with providing meaning and direction to subordinates several levels down whom they rarely see face-to-face. At the top of the organization, executives are engaged in sense making and direction setting for followers they may never meet. Most of the theories noted do not attempt to model or explain this form of influence. Indeed, these theories do not fundamentally explain executive leadership very well. Day and Lord (1988) observed of the existing leadership literature that "the topic of executive leadership . . . has not been a major concern of leadership researchers or theorists. Their focus has been primarily lower-level leadership" (p. 458).

Although several of the social exchange theories do provide what can be called a contingent or contextual perspective (Fiedler, 1964, 1971; House & Dessler, 1974; House & Mitchell, 1974), they do not significantly account for organizational contextual variables. For example, none of these theories explicates how the processes and relationships they model would (must) change at different organizational levels. Along this line, Zaccaro (1995, 1998) argued that the postulates of Fiedler's contingency model and his cognitive resources model do not apply easily to the executive leader effectiveness.

As a final illustration, the functional leadership behaviors and processes that are necessary for effectiveness at different organizational levels and in different kinds of organizations are broader than the stylistic approaches typical of this tradition (Day & Lord, 1988). Thus, the social exchange models either do not consider, or obscure in their theorizing, the importance of such leadership processes as information acquisition, sense making, sense giving, systematic social networking, boundary spanning, and long-term and long-range strategic decision making (Fleishman et al., 1991).

Strategic Management

Models of strategic decision making and management argue that organizational effectiveness emerges from a coalignment between the organization and its environment; the role of senior organizational leaders is to create and manage this fit (Bourgeois, 1985; Lawrence & Lorsch, 1967; Thompson, 1967; Wortman, 1982). The major unit analysis in this leadership research tradition is the strategic decision-making activities of top executives. Thus, strategic management models describe how executives make the strategic decisions that are intended to facilitate organization-environment coalignment. Researchers in this approach focus on key leadership processes: environment scanning, sense making and sense giving, the specification of strategic choices, and the selection and implementation of appropriate strategies.

Some models within the strategic management tradition actually deemphasize the contributions of top executives to organizational effectiveness (Hannan & Freeman, 1977; Pfeffer & Salancik, 1978), arguing that organizational and environmental parameters (such as resource availability, the fit of the organization with its environmental niche, and the strategic predisposition of the organization) primarily account for organizational outcomes. Other theorists have adapted a contingency model (Gupta, 1984, 1988) in which effectiveness is a product of the fit between the organization's strategic orientation and the characteristics of its top managers. Thus, this approach defines strategy as a determinant rather than a consequence of executive selection and action. For example, Gupta (1988, p. 160) noted:

> By definition, the notion that matching executives to organizational strategies enhances organizational performance assumes that strategies get specified prior to executive selection; in other words, for most CEOs, strategies are assumed to be a given and the CEO's primary task is assumed to consist of the implementation rather than formulation of strategies.

Other leadership models have placed a more central role on the thought processes and characteristics of top leaders. Rational and normative models argue that the responsibility of executives is to make strategic decisions based on a careful analysis of environmental contingencies and organizational strengths and weaknesses and an application of objective criteria to strategic choices to determine the most appropriate organizational strategy (Bourgeois, 1984, 1985; Hitt & Tyler, 1991; Pearce, 1981). Thus, strategic leaders are viewed as mostly rational and optimizing informational processors.

An alternate or augmenting view suggests that the personal qualities and characteristics of top leaders play an inordinate role in strategic decision making. For example, Hambrick (1989, p. 5) noted:

> In the face of the complex, multitudinous, and ambiguous information that typifies the top management task, no two strategists will identify the same array of options for the firm; they will rarely prefer the same options; if, by remote chance, they were to pick the same options, they almost certainly would not implement them identically. Biases, blinders, egos, aptitudes, experiences, fatigue, and other human factors in the executive ranks greatly affect what happens to companies.

Recent work has also focused on the top management team processes and characteristics that influence strategic decision making (Amason, 1996; Hambrick, 1994). Such research adds team processes and demographics to executive values and belief systems as primary determinants of executive decision-making processes.

The strategic management approach has greatly increased our understanding of organizational and executive leadership. Unlike the social exchange perspective, the emphasis here is primarily on the cognitive and planning processes of executives. In particular, researchers in this tradition consider environmental scanning and analysis as key leadership processes, a point not readily apparent in most leadership literatures (Fleishman et al., 1991; Zaccaro et al., 1995). Further, this body of research deals with large-scale leadership, that is, leadership of large collectives and organizations. Thus, it showcases indirect or mediated leadership processes that are prominent in any but small-sized organizations. In addition, several of the models in this tradition feature a contextual perspective that specifies the environmental and organizational forces shaping strategic decisions. As such, this perspective is represented within several chapters in this book.

Despite these strengths, several limitations are clear. Strategic management models do not describe the direct interpersonal processes, so prominent in the social exchange tradition, but still vitally important in strategic implementation. This is readily apparent in the research on top management teams, where much of the focus is team demographics and their meaning for strategic outcomes. Few studies have examined team processes in these settings (see Amason, 1996; Smith, Smith, Olian, & Sims, 1994, as exceptions), and even fewer explore the role of top executives in shaping these processes.

Organizational Systems

In common with the strategic management approach, the models in this leadership research tradition emphasize the boundary spanning and internal coordination responsibilities of leaders within open social systems. However, unlike the strategic management approach, these models postulate guiding principles that apply to leaders at different organizational levels, but also describe the differences in performance requirements at successive levels.

This perspective is grounded heavily in the work of Katz and Kahn (1978), who described organizations as open systems in close transactional relationship with their resource-providing environments.

Organizations convert environmental inputs into usable outcomes through a set of interlocking throughput processes. These processes become the basis of connected subsystems within the organization—in particular, the production subsystem that is most directly responsible for resource conversion. The production subsystem is buttressed by two other subsystems, supportive and maintenance, that are responsible for procuring material and personnel resources, respectively. Adaptive subsystems are established to look outward, providing environmental outreach and input for the organization. Managerial subsystems overlay all of these patterned activities.

Katz and Kahn (1978) noted two critical aspects of social behavior patterns that are particularly defining for managerial subsystem roles. First, the system character of organizations means that "movement in one part leads in predictable fashion to movement in other parts" (p. 3). Further, discrete patterns of functional responses are collectively interconnected to define the responses of larger units and subsystems. An essential function of management is to coordinate the activities of integrated units. Although this requirement exists in fundamental form at all organizational levels, the complexity of such coordination increases at successive levels as the number and variability of interacting social units also increases.

The second aspect of social behavior patterns is their susceptibility to shifting environmental dynamics. The embedding environments of organization are rarely in stasis, and their fluctuations can have profound implications for resource procurement and output receptivity. Accordingly, a major responsibility of organizational leaders is to monitor the external environments of their units and promote system adaptation to critical changes. Again, this responsibility extends to leaders at all organizational levels. However, the "external environment" for the first-line supervisor is the larger organization, whereas the top executive needs to span the boundary between the entire organization and more complex and unstructured environment. Nevertheless, both are responsible for facilitating system responsiveness.

For top executives, the responsibility for facilitating system coordination extends to other organizations that are linked in a partnering arrangement with their constituent companies. Such "interorganizational relationships" (Hall, 1991; Van de Ven & Ferry, 1980) also reflect a systemic response to environmental demands that operate on all members of a particular niche. A response by one organization in such an arrangement clearly has implications for the activities of other linked organizations. Their actions also often require careful coordination to gain industry-wide advantages (such as political lobbying efforts)

The organizational systems approach, then, emphasizes the role of the leader in coordinating and maintaining system interconnectiveness and promoting system adaptiveness to external change. This perspective places a premium on both the unity and distinctiveness of leadership functions across organizational levels. Earlier, we provided a brief summary of models that describe qualitative differences in upper- and lower-level organizational leaders (Bentz, 1987; Jacobs & Jaques, 1987, 1990, 1991; Hunt, 1991; Katz & Kahn, 1978; Mumford et al., 1993; Zaccaro, 1996). After reviewing the executive leadership literature, primarily from the organizational systems perspective (but including models from social exchange and strategic management traditions), Zaccaro (1996, pp. 357, 360) offered the following conclusions:

- Leader performance requirements can be described in terms of three distinct levels in organizational space.
- All organizational leaders engage in direction setting (such as goal setting, planning, strategy making, and envisioning) for their constituent units. Such direction setting incorporates an increasingly longer time frame at higher organizational levels.
- All organizational leaders engage in boundary-spanning activities, linking their constituent units with their environments. At lower organizational levels, this environment is the broader organization. At upper levels, boundary spanning and environmental analysis occur increasingly within the organization's external environment.
- All organizational leaders are responsible for operational maintenance and coordination within the organization. At upper levels, operational influence becomes increasingly indirect.
- The effective accomplishment of executive performance functions facilitates organizational performance and success.
- Characteristics of the operating environment influence the nature and quality of executive performance requirements.

These conclusions reflect the leader's responsibility at all levels to maintain system effectiveness and viability. They also highlight the dual external and internal systemic perspective of the leader's requisite functions (Katz & Kahn, 1978).

This approach is a significant addition to the other traditions. It provides an organization-wide perspective, while denoting how leadership changes at successfully higher organizational levels. Thus, it can speak to both small group and large-scale leadership. Organizational systems models describe contextual influences on leadership by virtue of specifying key environmental dynamics that alter system requirements (Aldrich, 1979, Hall, 1991; Katz & Kahn, 1978). As such, this perspective is reflected in several chapters in this book.

Nonetheless, like the others, this approach too has some limitations. Although it does provide a contextual perspective, models in this approach rarely distinguish the range of performance imperatives in the leader's operating environment that influence leadership activity. Further, these imperatives are often systematically linked, just as are the organizations they influence. That is, the intensity and quality of one imperative (say, technological) can have reverberations that alter the intensity and quality of other imperatives (say, cognitive, social, and staffing). The nature of this interconnectiveness also changes across organizational levels. The strategic management tradition attends more closely than the systems approach to these dynamics (although not in a thorough, finely grained sense), but does not specify how they change across levels. The systems approach provides some fundamental constructs for cross-level model building but needs to attend specifically to the nature of contextual imperatives that impinge on organizations' systems.

Finally, the organizational systems approach emphasizes the importance of leadership processes for organizational effectiveness. This assumption is also apparent in several of the models within the strategic management perspective. Nonetheless, despite some well-articulated exceptions (Katz & Kahn, 1978; Jacobs & Jaques, 1987, 1990, 1991), there has not been sufficient attention given to the links among leader attributes, the leadership functions articulated by systems models, and organizational effectiveness. Further, the models do not consider systematically leader training, development, and selection systems that have as their ultimate end the improvement of organizational functioning. That is the focus of the last leadership research tradition described here.

Leader Effectiveness

A central assumption in organizational leadership research is that leaders and leadership processes make a difference in organizational effectiveness. Although a number of theorists and researchers have offered countering notions or evidence (Aldrich, 1979; Bourgeois, 1984; Calder, 1977; Hannan & Freeman, 1977; Lawrence & Lorsch, 1967; Lieberson & O'Connor, 1972; Meindl, 1990; Meindl & Ehrlich, 1987; Meindl, Ehrlich, & Dukerich, 1985; Miles & Snow, 1978; Romanelli & Tushman, 1986; Salancik & Pfeffer, 1977; Starbuck, 1983), the predominant view, supported by empirical findings, is that "top executives matter" (Hambrick & Mason, 1984, p. 194; see Barrick, Day, Lord, & Alexander, 1991; Day & Lord, 1988; Hitt & Tyler, 1991; Weiner & Mahoney, 1981). Accordingly, some perspectives of organizational leaders emphasize the connections between leader attributes and organizational effectiveness. A result of this tradition is a focus on leader assessment, selection, training, and development systems that enhance these attributes.

Zaccaro (1996) defined executive attributes as personal qualities that facilitate the successful accomplishment of executive performance requirements, which in turn drive organizational success. These attributes also provide a framework for the construction of measures and tools that can be used for executive selection and assessment and training and development programs that target one or more of them. Thus, a key focus in this research tradition is identifying and validating personal qualities linked to indexes of leadership and organizational effectiveness.

Perhaps the oldest tradition in leadership research is the search for critical leader traits. Early forms of this research, although prodigious, did not yield consistent evidence for particular attributes, and hence researchers moved in other directions (see early reviews by Bird, 1940; Stogdill, 1948; Mann, 1959, although the conclusions of these reviews have often been misinterpreted). More recent efforts have renewed the argument for leader attributes by correcting for earlier methodological and statistical limitations (Kenny & Zaccaro, 1983; Lord, De Vader, & Alliger, 1986), updating reviews of this literature and highlighting consistent patterns (Kirkpatrick & Locke, 1991; Lord et al., 1986; Zaccaro, 1996), and by offering conceptual models linking key attributes to leadership performance processes required for organizational effectiveness (House, 1988; Hunt, 1991; Mumford et al., 1993). Unfortunately, research that validates the connections between particular attributes and key leadership processes and organizational effectiveness, respectively, has lagged behind this theoretical interest.

The performance effectiveness approach emphasizes leader assessment and development. Two examples of this focus are the longitudinal assessment center research conducted at American Telephone & Telegraph (ATT) (Bray, 1982; Bray, Campbell, & Grant, 1974; Howard & Bray, 1988) and the investigations of leader development by the Center for Creative Leadership (CCL). The ATT research developed assessment center procedures in which a number of exercises and tasks are used to identify managerial characteristics that purportedly predict career advancement. In a longitudinal research program, these researchers associated scores from assessment centers with managers' rate and level of promotion over a twenty-year span. They found that such characteristics as need for power, interpersonal and cognitive skills, and motivational orientations were significant predictors of attained level. Although this research has been important for identifying characteristics relevant for one index of leader effectiveness, it also provided a viable means of leader assessment, albeit one that has been fraught with debate (Klimoski & Strickland, 1977).

Research by CCL has focused on identifying the characteristics of top executives who succeed versus those who derail in their career (McCall & Lombardo, 1983). They found that managers who were emotionally unstable and not able to handle high pressure were defensive, and those who put personal advancement ahead of personal integrity, had weak interpersonal skills, and were narrowly focused in terms of technical and cognitive skills were more likely to fail after reaching higher levels of management. Note that these were managers who were as successful at lower organizational levels as those executives who tended to succeed in their careers. Their shortcomings emerged, presumably as critical predictors of effectiveness, only when they attained top executive positions. This research therefore argues for different effectiveness models at successive levels of the organization.

The development of executives is a difficult task. Research by McCauley and others at CCL has focused on the role of work experiences and developmental relationships as key antecedents and mediators of executive growth (McCauley, Ruderman, Ohlott, & Morrow, 1994; McCauley, Moxley, & Van Velsor, 1998). A consistent premise in this work and in related research (Hooijberg & Quinn, 1992) is that the complex cognitive and social competencies required for effective executive work emerge from training and work experiences that push the leader to the limits of his or her retained schemas and ways of behaving. When these comfortable patterns of thinking and behaving no longer suffice in completing required work assignments, individuals who are likely to succeed at higher levels of organizational leadership can develop new functional schemas and behavior patterns.

In sum, the performance effectiveness approach has promoted research on the attributes linked to leader and organizational success, as well as the means of assessing and developing these attributes. Nonetheless, it has not yet contributed a level of understanding commensurate with the conceptual advances in the other traditions described. One limitation has been a lack of consideration given to the diversity of organizational imperatives that will influence the leader's performance efforts. Such imperatives create a rich operating environment for the leader that renders as insufficient narrowly defined leader assessment and development systems. Validation research, so vital to affirming leader performance effectiveness models, has consistently lagged behind the conceptual models that have emerged in this tradition (Zaccaro, 1996).

Summary

These four research traditions in leadership have made tremendous contributions to our understanding of leadership; nevertheless, each has limitations, particularly in terms of modeling, assessing, and developing executive leadership. We believe that a more thorough specification of the performance imperatives that operate for organizational leaders, particularly at the top, will begin to address some of these limitations and perhaps promote a greater integration of these research approaches.

Performance Imperatives for Organizational Leadership

As used in this book, an operational imperative is analogous to a functional requirement, derived from factors or forces that coexist in the context or operating environment of a senior leader. Our list of imperatives has been gleaned from the descriptive, theoretical, and inferential literatures in the area (Zaccaro, 1996). Although there may be alternative ways of characterizing them, we believe the following are a reasonably complete set.

Cognitive Imperative

This imperative refers to the complex information processing and problem-solving demands that organizational leaders, particularly executives, need to confront to be successful. These demands derive from the multiplicity and interconnectiveness of causal factors operating to affect corporate success. In addition, the recent rapidly burgeoning advances in information technology have resulted in exponential increases in the data flowing to executive decision makers. Attending to, processing, and interpreting these factors are central to resolving such problems as organizational sense making and charting long-term strategic directions. Moreover, the environment for executive leaders is typically unstructured and ill defined; thus, successful performance in such environments requires qualitatively different cognitive skills and capacities than leadership at lower levels.

Social Imperative

This imperative reflects the behavioral complexity that is required of organizational leaders. Such complexity results from the social complexity (that is, the number, nature, and variability of relationships) in the leader's operating environment. For example, executives need to coordinate and supervise the activities of multiple (or even all) units within the organization. This leads to greater social complexity because leaders need to integrate these units, even when their members have conflicting goals and demands. Executives are also required to adopt multiple organizational roles simultaneously when relating to constituencies, with many of these roles specifying competing behavioral requirements. Further, executive leaders have the responsibility for maintaining relationships, even while implementing organization-wide change, a responsibility that involves the development and nurturance of large social networks and the acquisition of social capital. These social imperatives suggest that the social skills and competencies required for executive leadership also differ qualitatively from those required for lower-level leadership. At lower levels, social demands are less complex because leaders are typically in charge of fewer subordinates and organizational units, and they supervise more functionally homogeneous units.

Personal Imperative

This imperative refers to demands on leaders for the timely and skillful execution of such activities as career and reputation management and the acquisition of power. This is especially true as executives seek to place their own stamp on the organization. These imperatives become critical forces during periods of executive succession and CEO transitions. They are also reflected in the personal values that executives bring to organizational visioning and strategic decision making. Some crucial questions reflect personal imperatives: How does a new CEO develop or staff a new top management team without disrupting important and functional dynamics that carry over from previous CEO tenures? How does the nature of departure by the previous CEO influence the selection, entry, and tenure of the new CEO? What are the critical reputation and impression management techniques that contribute to successful CEO succession and transition?

Political Imperative

Closely related to the personal imperative is pressure coming from the political environment within which most organizational leaders need to operate. Such pressures stem from the role that power plays in organizations. The acquisition of power, the timely and judicious use of power, and even the appropriate application of power sharing are part of the story. A special aspect of the political imperative has to do with the routine need for building and maintaining coalitions. Thus, paradoxically, the operation of executive leadership is often described as more collegial and less authoritative than at lower levels. Such leadership requires more persuasion as an influence tactic and coalition building among top decision makers. The use of power inevitably gives rise to a significant amount of conflict at top organizational levels. How CEOs confront and resolve these dynamics plays an important role in organizational performance and adaptation. Finally, most, if not all, of the strategic and tactical decisions made by organizational leaders, particularly those in top executive teams, will be influenced in part by the political network within which the organization is embedded. That is, organizational strategic decisions are determined not only by internal political dynamics but external ones as well.

This last point means that political imperatives are also driven by the interorganizational relationships executives need to establish and maintain on behalf of their organizations. Well-constructed interorganizational relationships are highly instrumental for organizational success. The acquisition of resources and political advocacy are two critical reasons for the development of interorganizational relationships (Galaskiewicz, 1985), and power plays a crucial role here as well. Top executives need to apply the judicious use of power and persuasion to position their organization close to the center of interorganizational networks, where links are strongest to resource bases. Effective political advocacy also requires the welding together of diverse and common interests into a powerful coalition. This imperative will drive much of the strategic implementation efforts of top executives.

Technological Imperative

Today's organizations operate in the context of an information age in which technology has revolutionized the operating environment of organizational leaders. This technology, with its corresponding impact on organizational information flow, presents leaders with challenges and opportunities that can fundamentally restructure how they accomplish the tasks of organizational leadership and change. Key questions regarding technological imperatives need to be considered in a theory of organizational leadership. How does information technology change the strategic decision processes of leaders, particularly top executives? What kinds of support systems (such as decision support systems and control systems) are available to assist in leadership and decision making? How do executives use technology in the service of organizational transformation and change? How does technology operate to change or deny traditional leadership roles or functions.

Financial Imperative

This imperative is perhaps the most fundamental source of pressures on senior organizational leaders. Financial and industry factors in an executive's operating environment may prompt an orientation toward short-term thinking, in which decisions regarding acquisitions and mergers are made in the context of fairly immediate gain rather than long-term organizational investment and adaptation. Competitive dynamics in the organizational environment also provide financial imperatives that may force a short-term perspective on top organizational executives. Most theories of executive leadership promote the idea that effective leaders adopt a long-term perspective—one that is strategic and visionary. However, such theories need to consider the financial and competitive imperatives that shorten this perspective. Thus, executive compensation as well as investor pressures interact here. Furthermore, the links among such imperatives, executive actions, and organizational decline need to be noted.

Senior Staffing Imperative

The previous imperatives imply a set of forces that would require that the staffing of senior organizational positions be done with individuals who possess a particular set of skills, dispositions, and capabilities. This, in turn, demands that renewed attention be given to the traditional staffing concerns of recruitment, assessment for selection, training and development, and performance assessment as they are applied to senior organizational leaders. More specifically, given that the nature of work at the top is problematic in the ways so described, just how should we go about measuring and preparing organizational leaders of the future? Thus, whereas the previous imperatives can be used to describe the context of the modern senior leader, this last imperative represents, in the abstract, pressure on the organization to respond appropriately in its senior staffing demands.

Staffing imperatives also embrace the CEO's management of the executive team. Much of the popular literature and current models and theories in organizational studies tend to treat senior organizational leadership as a solitary phenomenon. However, much of the CEO's work is collective work emphasizing the coordinated contributions of multiple executives. Although some of the forces that operate here reflect social imperatives, the CEO's management of this process represents another aspect of staffing imperatives. Thus, key questions associated with this imperative include how staffing decisions contribute to and shape top-level human resource management concerns and how the senior leader is responsible for, interacts with, and indeed is affected by the top management team.

Summary

Our basic premise for this book is that these imperatives define the context of executive leadership action and its effects on organizational effectiveness. Figure 1.1 illustrates how we view the influence and operation of leader performance imperatives. The model specifically links executive characteristics with executive performance requirements and executive performance with organizational success. Executive characteristics are also the foundation for leader assessment and development. We would argue that performance imperatives act as direct influences, mediators, and moderators of these phenomena; they create the boundary conditions theory building and model specification regarding the linkages in Figure 1.1.

Plan of This Book

This book addresses these imperatives more thoroughly and weaves them into postulates for effective leadership at the top of the or-

Figure 1.1. Performance Imperatives and Executive Leadership.

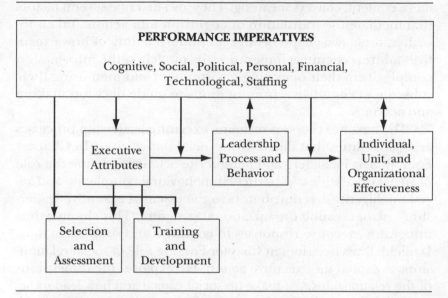

Source: Adapted from Zaccaro (1996). Used with permission.

ganization. One edited book cannot fully explicate or capture the complex role of organizationally contextual factors on leadership. Our hope, rather, is to initiate this discussion with an eye toward enriching and augmenting other existing research traditions, because they all have merit at some level.

This book is divided into three parts. Part One presents definitional information about the performance imperatives and describes leadership attributes and processes that are engaged by the presence of these demands. Part Two explores issues related to the identification and growth of effective executives. Part Three provides some integrative conclusions regarding the chapters and some principles to guide future leadership research.

In Chapter Two, T. Owen Jacobs and Michael L. McGee describe an organizational stratification model that specifies changes in cognitive demands as a function of organization level. They also describe the conceptual skills and abilities required at each successive level to address the cognitive imperative operating at that level. Phyllis Johnson, Kevin Daniels, and Anne Huff follow in

Chapter Three with a description of managerial mental maps and, in particular, how their animation into action, rather than their mere content, conveys meaning. They also describe several factors that mediate the translation of cognition into action. Taken together, these two chapters offer an understanding of how executives address cognitive imperatives by modeling the information complexity in their operating environment and then using their subsequent cognitive representations to guide decision making and action.

The next two chapters examine executive leadership processes and capabilities that derive from social imperatives. In Chapter Four, Robert Hooijberg and Marguerite Schneider define the role of social capabilities, in particular, behavioral complexity and social intelligence, as contributors to the essential executive leadership task of creating organizational structure. This chapter thus integrates executive responses to cognitive and social demands. Daniel J. Brass describes in Chapter Five the role of social relationships as capital for executive action. He explores the dimensions of the relationships that make up social capital and how leaders acquire social capital. Together, these chapters provide a framework for defining executive responses to social imperatives through linked individual and social terms. The leader attributes that Hooijberg and Schneider put forth influence the construction of the elaborated and far-flung social networks that Brass describes. We would speculate perhaps along with these authors that executives with these attributes are also likely to use social capital in more effective and organizationally beneficial ways.

Catherine M. Daily and Dan R. Dalton explore in Chapter Six the political and power dynamics that characterize the contest for corporate control, particularly between CEOs and boards of directors. They describe and contrast two models of this relationship, agency theory and stewardship theory, and argue that firm performance acts as a prime mediator determining corporate control. Thus, they capture several aspects of political and financial leadership imperatives.

In Chapter 7, Stephen J. Zaccaro and Deanna Banks describe the nature and influence of executive visions. Although all of the performance imperatives are implicated in vision formation and articulation, personal imperatives have a particular role. Visions are grounded in the personal values that executive visionaries bring to organizational work. Values influence how executives scan the environment, what factors they attend to, what opportunities they seek and employ, whom they select as their managers, and the emotional appeal behind vision communication. In Chapter Eight, Richard J. Klimoski and K. Lee Kiechel Koles examine the role of leader performance imperatives in the top management teams. CEOs manage corporations through their top management teams. Formation of the team recalls staffing and personal imperatives, and the management of team processes implicates social and political imperatives. The strategic decision-making requirements of the top management team define the cognitive imperatives confronting these teams, while financial imperatives provide the boundaries for such decisions. Both Chapters Seven and Eight examine phenomena common to executive leadership and describe how the various performance imperatives contextualize how these phenomena play out.

Although financial imperatives are implicated in several chapters, Chapter Nine, by Yan Zhang, Nandini Rajagopalan, and Deepak K. Datta, examines these themes more closely. These authors focus on strategic choices and their link to firm performance. They review the influences of executives' demographic characteristics and executive compensation, respectively, on strategic choices and firm performance and conclude with an integrated model linking these variables.

Chapters Ten through Twelve extend the ideas in this book to several human resource management practices. As such, they cover themes that are of particular relevance to I/O psychologists. Ann Howard in Chapter Ten examines best practices in the selection of organizational executives. Cynthia D. McCauley follows in Chapter Eleven by examining issues related to the development of executives. In Chapter Twelve, David V. Day describes themes related to the assessment of leadership outcomes.

We have asked Robert G. Lord to examine all of the chapters in this book and provide concluding commentary in Chapter Thirteen. We also feel that we would be remiss if we did not include a chapter that examines methodological issues related to the executive leadership research. Accordingly, Chapter Fourteen by John E. Mathieu offers several guiding principles for conducting such research.

References

Aldrich, H. E. (1979). *Organizations and environments.* Upper Saddle River, NJ: Prentice Hall.

Amason, A. C. (1996). Distinguishing the effects of functional and dysfunctional conflict on strategic decision making: Resolving a paradox for top management teams. *Academy of Management Journal, 39,* 123–148.

Ashby, W. (1952). *Design for a brain.* New York: Wiley.

Barrick, M. R., Day, D. V., Lord, R. G., & Alexander, R. A. (1991). Assessing the utility of executive leadership. *Leadership Quarterly, 2,* 9–22.

Bass, B. M. (1985). *Leadership and performance beyond expectations.* New York: Free Press.

Bass, B. M. (1990). *Bass and Stogdill's handbook of leadership: Theory, research, and managerial applications* (3rd ed.). New York: Free Press.

Bass, B. M. (1996). *A new paradigm of leadership: An inquiry into transformational leadership.* Alexandria, VA: U.S. Army Research Institute for the Behavioral and Social Sciences.

Bass, B. M., & Avolio, B. J. (1990). The implications of transactional and transformational leadership for individual, team, and organizational development. In R. W. Woodman & W. A. Passmore (Eds.), *Research in organizational change and development.* Greenwich, CT: JAI Press.

Bass, B. M., & Avolio, B. J. (1993). Transformational leadership: A response to critiques. In M. M. Chemers & R. Ayman (Eds.), *Leadership theory and research.* Orlando, FL: Academic Press.

Bentz, V. J. (1987). *Explorations of scope and scale: The critical determinant of high-level effectiveness.* Greensboro, NC: Center for Creative Leadership.

Bird, C. (1940). *Social psychology.* New York: Appleton-Century-Crofts.

Blake, R. R., & Mouton, J. S. (1964). *The managerial grid.* Houston: Gulf.

Bourgeois, L. J., III. (1984). Strategic management and determinism. *Academy of Management Review, 9,* 586–596.

Bourgeois, L. J., III. (1985). Strategic goals, perceived uncertainty, and economic performance in volatile environments. *Academy of Management Journal, 28,* 548–573.

Bray, D. W. (1982). The assessment center and the study of lives. *American Psychologist, 37,* 180–189.

Bray, D. W., Campbell, R. J., & Grant, D. L. (1974). *Formative years in business: A long-term AT&T study of managerial lives.* New York: Wiley.

Calder, B. J. (1977). An attributional theory of leadership. In B. M. Staw & G. R. Salancik (Eds.), *New directions in organizational behavior.* Chicago: St. Clair Press.

Cronshaw, S. F., & Lord, R. G. (1987). Effects of categorization, attribution, and encoding processes on leadership perceptions. *Journal of Applied Psychology, 72,* 97–106.

Dansereau, F., Graen, G., & Haga, W. J. (1975). A vertical dyad linkage approach to leadership within formal organizations. *Organizational Behavior and Human Performance, 13,* 46–78.

Day, D. V., & Lord, R. G. (1988). Executive leadership and organizational performance: Suggestions for a new theory and methodology. *Journal of Management, 14,* 453–464.

Fiedler, F. E. (1964). A contingency model of leadership effectiveness. In L. Berkowitz (Ed.), *Advances in experimental social psychology* (Vol. 1). Orlando, FL: Academic Press.

Fiedler, F. E. (1971). Validation and extension of the contingency model of leadership effectiveness: A review of the empirical findings. *Psychological Bulletin, 76,* 128–148.

Fiedler, F. E. (1978). The contingency model and the dynamics of the leadership process. In L. Berkowitz (Ed.), *Advances in experimental social psychology* (Vol. 11). Orlando, FL: Academic Press.

Fleishman, E. A. (1953). The description of supervisory behavior. *Personnel Psychology, 37,* 1–6.

Fleishman, E. A. (1973). Twenty years of consideration and structure. In E. A. Fleishman & J. G. Hunt (Eds.), *Current developments in the study of leadership.* Carbondale: Southern Illinois University Press.

Fleishman, E. A., & Harris, E. F. (1962). Patterns of leadership behavior related to grievances and turnover. *Personnel Psychology, 15,* 43–56.

Fleishman, E. A., Mumford, M. D., Zaccaro, S. J., Levin, K. Y., Korotkin, A. L., & Hein, M. B. (1991). Taxonomic efforts in the description of leader behavior: A synthesis and functional interpretation. *Leadership Quarterly, 2,* 245–287.

Galaskiewicz, J. (1985). Interorganizational relationships. *Annual Review of Sociology, 11.*

Graen, G., & Cashman, J. F. (1975). A role-making model of leadership in formal organizations: A developmental approach. In J. G. Hunt & L. L. Larson (Eds.), *Leadership frontiers.* Carbondale: Southern Illinois University Press.

Graen, G., & Scandura, T. (1987). Toward a psychology of dyadic organizing. *Research in Organizational Behavior, 9,* 175–208.

Gupta, A. K. (1984). Contingency linkages between strategy and general managerial characteristics: A conceptual examination. *Academy of Management Review, 9,* 399–412.

Gupta, A. K. (1988). Contingency perspectives on strategic leadership:

Current knowledge and future research directions. In D. C. Hambrick (Ed.), *The executive effect: Concepts and methods for studying top managers*. Greenwich, CT: JAI Press.

Hackman, J. R., & Walton, R. E. (1986). Leading groups in organizations. In P. S. Goodman et al., *Designing effective work groups*. San Francisco: Jossey-Bass.

Hall, R. H. (1991). *Organizations: Structures, processes, and outcomes* (5th ed.). Upper Saddle River, NJ: Prentice Hall.

Halpin, A. W., & Winer, B. J. (1957). A factorial study of the leader behavior descriptions. In R. M. Stogdill & A. E. Coons (Eds.), *Leader behavior: Its description and measurement*. Columbus: Ohio State University, Bureau of Business Research.

Hambrick, D. C. (1989). Guest editor's introduction: Putting top managers back in the strategy picture. *Strategic Management Journal, 10,* 5–15.

Hambrick, D. C. (1994). Top management groups: A conceptual integration and reconsideration of the "team" label. In *Research in organizational behavior* (Vol. 16). Greenwich, CT: JAI Press.

Hambrick, D. C., & Mason, P. A. (1984). Upper echelons: The organization as a reflection of its top managers. *Academy of Management Review, 9,* 195–206.

Hannan, M. T., & Freeman, J. (1977). The population ecology of organizations. *American Journal of Sociology, 82,* 926–963.

Hemphill, J. K. (1959). Job descriptions for executives. *Harvard Business Review, 37,* 55–67.

Hemphill, J. K., & Coons, A. E. (1957). Development of the Leader Behavior Description Questionnaire. In R. M. Stogdill & A. E. Coons (Eds.), *Leader behavior: Its description and measurement*. Columbus: Ohio State University, Bureau of Business Research.

Hersey, P., & Blanchard, K. H. (1969). *Management of organizational behavior: Utilizing human resources*. Upper Saddle River, NJ: Prentice Hall.

Hitt, M. A., & Tyler, B. B. (1991). Strategic decision models: Integrating different perspectives. *Strategic Management Journal, 12,* 327–351.

Hollander, E. P. (1958). Conformity, status, and idiosyncrasy credit. *Psychological Review, 65,* 117–127.

Hollander, E. P. (1979). Leadership and social exchange processes. In K. Gergen, M. S. Greenberg, & R. H. Willis (Eds.), *Social exchange: Advances in theory and research*. New York: Winston/Wiley.

Hollander, E. P., & Julian, J. W. (1970). Studies in leader legitimacy, influence, and motivation. In L. Berkowitz (Ed.), *Advances in experimental social psychology* (Vol. 5). Orlando, FL: Academic Press.

Holyoak, K. J. (1984). Mental models in problem solving. In J. R. Anderson & K. M. Kosslyn (Eds.), *Tutorials in learning and memory*. New York: Freeman.

Hooijberg, R., & Quinn, R. E. (1992). Behavioral complexity and the development of effective managers. In R. L. Phillips & J. G. Hunt (Eds.), *Strategic leadership: A multiorganizational perspective*. Westport, CT: Quorum Books.

House, R. J. (1977). A 1976 theory of charismatic leadership. In J. G. Hunt & L. L. Larson (Eds.), *Leadership: The cutting edge*. Carbondale: Southern Illinois University Press.

House, R. J. (1988). Power and personality in organizations. In *Research in organizational behavior* (Vol. 10). Greenwich, CT: JAI Press.

House, R. J., & Dessler, G. (1974). The path-goal theory of leadership: Some post hoc and a priori tests. In J. G. Hunt & L. L. Larson (Eds.), *Contingency approaches to leadership*. Carbondale: Southern Illinois University Press.

House, R. J., & Mitchell, T. R. (1974). Path-goal theory of leadership. *Journal of Contemporary Business, 4*, 81–97.

House, R. J., & Shamir, B. (1993). Toward the integration of transformational, charismatic, and visionary leadership theories. In M. M. Chemers & R. Ayman (Eds.), *Leadership theory and research: Perspectives and directions*. Orlando, FL: Academic Press.

Howard, A., & Bray, D. W. (1988). *Managerial lives in transition: Advancing age and changing times*. New York: Guilford Press.

Howell, J. P., & Dorfman, P. W. (1981). Substitutes for leadership: Test of a construct. *Academy of Management Journal, 24*, 714–728.

Huff, A. (1990). *Mapping strategic thought*. New York: Wiley.

Hunt, J. G. (1991). *Leadership: A new synthesis*. Thousand Oaks, CA: Sage.

Hunt, J. G., Osborn, R. N., & Martin, H. J. (1981). *A multiple-influence model of leadership*. Alexandria, VA: U.S. Army Research Institute for the Behavioral and Social Sciences.

Isenberg, D. J. (1984). How senior managers think. *Harvard Business Review, 62*, 81–90.

Jacobs, T. O., & Jaques, E. (1987). Leadership in complex systems. In J. Zeidner (Ed.), *Human productivity enhancement*. New York: Praeger.

Jacobs, T. O., & Jaques, E. (1990). Military executive leadership. In K. E. Clark & M. B. Clark (Eds.), *Measures of leadership*. Greensboro, NC: Center for Creative Leadership.

Jacobs, T. O., & Jaques, E. (1991). Executive leadership. In R. Gal & A. D. Manglesdorff (Eds.), *Handbook of military psychology*. New York: Wiley.

Jacobs, T. O., & Lewis, P. (1992). Leadership requirements in stratified systems. In R. L. Phillips & J. G. Hunt (Eds.), *Strategic leadership: A multiorganizational-level perspective.* Westport, CT: Quorum Books.

Kaplan, R. E. (1986). The warp and woof of the general manager's job. In B. Schneider & D. Schoorman (Eds.), *Facilitating work effectiveness.* San Francisco: New Lexington Press.

Katz, D., & Kahn, R. L. (1978). *The social psychology of organizations* (2nd ed.). New York: Wiley.

Katz, D., Maccoby, N., & Morse, N. (1950). *Productivity, supervision, and morale in an office situation.* Ann Arbor: University of Michigan, Institute for Social Research.

Kenny, D. A., & Zaccaro, S. J. (1983). An estimate of variance due to traits in leadership. *Journal of Applied Psychology, 68,* 678–685.

Kerr, S., & Jermier, J. M. (1978). Substitutes for leadership. *Organizational Behavior and Human Performance, 22,* 375–403.

Kirkpatrick, S. A., & Locke, E. A. (1991). Leadership: Do traits matter? *Academy of Management Executive, 5,* 48–60.

Klimoski, R. J., & Strickland, W. J. (1977). Assessment centers: Valid or merely prescient? *Personnel Psychology, 33,* 543–555.

Kotter, J. P. (1982). *The general managers.* New York: Free Press.

Kraut, A. I., Pedigo, P. R., McKenna, D. D., & Dunnette, M. D. (1989). The role of the manager: What's really important in different management jobs. *Academy of Management Executive, 3,* 286–293.

Lawrence, P., & Lorsch, J. (1967). *Organization and environment.* Boston: Harvard Business School Division of Research.

Levinson, H., & Rosenthal, S. (1984). *CEO: Corporate leadership in action.* New York: Basic Books.

Lieberson, S., & O'Connor, J. F. (1972). Leadership and organizational performance: A study of large corporations. *American Sociological Review, 37,* 117–130.

Likert, R. (1961). *New patterns of management.* New York: McGraw-Hill.

Lord, R. G. (1977). Functional leadership behavior: Measurement and relation to social power and leadership perceptions. *Administrative Science Quarterly, 22,* 114–133.

Lord, R. G., De Vader, C. L., & Alliger, G. M. (1986). A meta-analysis of the relation between personality traits and leadership perceptions: An application of validity generalization procedures. *Journal of Applied Psychology, 71,* 402–410.

Lord, R. G., Foti, R. J., & De Vader, C. L. (1984). A test of leadership categorization theory: Internal structure, information processing, and leadership perceptions. *Organizational Behavior and Human Performance, 34,* 343–378.

Lord, R. G., Foti, R. J., & Phillips, J. S. (1982). A theory of leadership categorization. In J. G. Hunt, U. Sekaran, & C. Schriesheim (Eds.), *Leadership: Beyond establishment views.* Carbondale: Southern Illinois University Press.

Lord, R. G., & Maher, K. J. (1993). *Leadership and information processing.* New York: Routledge.

Luthans, F., Rosenkrantz, S. A., & Hennessey, H. W. (1985). What do successful managers really do? An observational study of managerial activities. *Journal of Applied Behavioral Science, 21,* 255–270.

Mann, R. D. (1959). A review of the relationship between personality and performance in small groups. *Psychological Bulletin, 56,* 241–270.

McCall, M. W., & Lombardo, M. M. (1983). *Off the track: Why and how successful executives get derailed.* Greensboro, NC: Center for Creative Leadership.

McCauley, C. D., Moxley, R. S., & Van Velsor, E. (Eds.). (1998). *Handbook of leadership development.* San Francisco: Jossey-Bass.

McCauley, C. D., Ruderman, M. N., Ohlott, P. J., & Morrow, J. E. (1994). Assessing the developmental components of managerial jobs. *Journal of Applied Psychology, 37,* 46–67.

Meindl, J. R. (1990). On leadership: An alternative to the conventional wisdom. In B. M. Staw & L. L. Cummings (Eds.), *Research in organizational behavior* (Vol. 12). Greenwich, CT: JAI Press.

Meindl, J. R., & Ehrlich, S. B. (1987). The romance of leadership and the evaluation of organizational performance. *Academy of Management Journal, 30,* 91–109.

Meindl, J. R., Ehrlich, S. B., & Dukerich, J. M. (1985). The romance of leadership. *Administrative Science Quarterly, 30,* 78–102.

Miles, R. E., & Snow, C. C. (1978). *Organizational strategy, structure, and process.* New York: McGraw-Hill.

Mumford, M. D. (1986). Leadership in the organizational context: Conceptual approach and its application. *Journal of Applied Social Psychology, 16,* 212–226.

Mumford, M. D., Zaccaro, S. J., Harding, F. D., Fleishman, E. A., & Reiter-Palmon, R. (1993). *Cognitive and temperament predictors of executive ability: Principles for developing leadership capacity.* Alexandria, VA: U.S. Army Research Institute for the Behavioral and Social Sciences.

Pearce, J. A., III. (1981). An executive-level perspective on the strategic management process. *California Management Review, 24,* 39–48.

Pfeffer, J., & Salancik, G. R. (1978). *The external control of organizations: A resource dependence perspective.* New York: HarperCollins.

Romanelli, E., & Tushman, M. L. (1986). Inertia, environments, and strategic choice: A quasi-experimental design for comparative-longitudinal research. *Management Science, 32,* 608–621.

Rush, M. C., Thomas, J. C., & Lord, R. G. (1982). Implicit leadership theory: A potential threat to the internal validity of leader behavior questionnaires. *Organizational Behavior and Human Performance, 20,* 93–110.

Salancik, G. R., & Pfeffer, J. (1977). Constraints on administrator discretion: The limited influence of mayors on city budgets. *Urban Affairs Quarterly, 12,* 475–498.

Smith, K. G., Smith, K. A., Olian, J. D., & Sims, H. P. (1994). Top management team demography and process: The role of social integration and communication. *Administrative Science Quarterly, 39*(3), 412–438.

Starbuck, W. H. (1983). Organizations as action generators. *American Sociological Review, 48,* 91–102.

Stogdill, R. M. (1948). Personal factors associated with leadership: A survey of the literature. *Journal of Psychology, 25,* 35–71.

Stogdill, R. M. (1974). *Handbook of leadership.* New York: Free Press.

Stogdill, R. M., & Coons, A. E. (Eds.). (1957). *Leader behavior: Its description and measurement.* Columbus: Ohio State University, Bureau of Business Research.

Thomas, J. B., Clark, S. B., & Gioia, D. A. (1993). Strategic sensemaking and organizational performance: Linkages among scanning, interpretation, action, and outcomes. *Academy of Management Journal, 36,* 239–270.

Thompson, J. D. (1967). *Organizations in action.* New York: McGraw-Hill.

Tornow, W. W., & Pinto, P. R. (1976). The development of a managerial job taxonomy: A system for describing, classifying, and evaluating executive positions. *Journal of Applied Psychology, 61,* 410–418.

Van de Ven, A. H., & Ferry, D. L. (1980). *Measuring and assessing organizations.* New York: Wiley.

Vroom, V. H., & Jago, A. G. (1974). Decision making as a social process: Normative and descriptive models of leader behavior. *Decision Sciences, 5,* 743–769.

Vroom, V. H., & Jago, A. G. (1978). On the validity of the Vroom-Yetton model. *Journal of Applied Psychology, 63,* 151–162.

Vroom, V. H., & Jago, A. G. (1995). Situation effects and levels of analysis in the study of leader participation. *Leadership Quarterly, 6,* 169–181.

Weiner, N., & Mahoney, T. A. (1981). A model of corporate performance as a function of environmental, organizational, and leadership influences. *Academy of Management Journal, 24,* 453–470.

Wortman, M. S. (1982). Strategic management and changing leader-follower roles. *Journal of Applied Behavioral Science, 18,* 371–383.

Yukl, G. A. (1994). *Leadership in organizations* (3rd ed.). Upper Saddle River, NJ: Prentice Hall.
Zaccaro, S. J. (1995). Leader resources and the nature of organizational problems: Commentary on *Cognitive resources and leadership* by Fred E. Fiedler. *Applied Psychology, 44*, 32–36.
Zaccaro, S. J. (1996). *Models and theories of executive leadership: A conceptual/empirical review and integration.* Alexandria, VA: U.S. Army Research Institute for the Behavioral and Social Sciences.
Zaccaro, S. J. (1998). The contingency model and executive leadership. In F. J. Yammarino & F. Dansereau (Eds.), *Leadership: The multiple-level approach.* Greenwich, CT: JAI Press.
Zaccaro, S. J., Mumford, M. D., Marks, M. A., Connelly, M. S., Threlfall, K. V., Gilbert, J., & Fleishman, E. A. (1995). *Cognitive and temperament determinants of Army leadership* (Tech. Rep. for U.S. Army Research Institute for the Behavioral and Social Sciences). Bethesda, MD: Management Research Institute.

CHAPTER 2

Competitive Advantage
Conceptual Imperatives for Executives

T. Owen Jacobs
Michael L. McGee

The thrust of this book is that organizational leadership makes a difference, but insufficient attention has been paid to a rigorous understanding of what organizational leadership actually is. That is, if top-level leaders are vitally important to their organizations, what is it they do that makes that much difference? As a second question, what can this book do that goes beyond Barnard's (1938) compelling and insightful description of executive work, Mintzberg's (1973) description of varied managerial roles, and the accurate differentiation of responsibilities by organizational level found in a host of sources (for example, Simon, 1977; Katz & Kahn, 1966). The answers to both questions may be found in the level of analysis brought to bear on the question of what constitutes organizational leadership and on insights generated about how to develop and improve it. Typically, generative insights come from bridging different disciplines, and that is what we do here.

This chapter focuses on conceptual skills and abilities. Its initial premise is that the skills required for effective performance are different at different organizational levels. The higher one goes in most organizations, the more complex the thinking skills need to be. Executives must be able to deal with abstract constructs that do not concern managers at lower levels, and they need to be more integrative in their thinking. We support this premise by logical analysis of executive responsibilities, observational analysis (Jaques, 1976, 1989; Jacobs & Jaques, 1987), and research findings (Jacobs & Jaques, 1990, 1991). A second premise is that although these skills tend to develop over time for most individuals (Jaques, 1976), growth is a function of more basic operations, and individual differences in growth rate are a function of the differential application of these operations. Clearly, native endowment plays a role, but there is some evidence that it is somewhat less important than may have been previously thought or that its influence is nonlinear, becoming somewhat less important above some threshold. This chapter thus invokes some constructs beyond undifferentiated native endowment to explain growth rate and offers suggestions about strategies for accelerating development.

Conceptual Capacity

Managerial tasks increase in complexity, and thus in difficulty, as one moves from the operations level to the strategic apex. That is hardly a significant discovery, nor is it particularly significant to observe that most managers develop the capacity to deal with increasing complexity. Those who do not eventually fail. Task complexity thus defines requisite conceptual complexity and mandates that conceptual complexity increase systematically as managers move higher in their organizations. Those who do not continue to develop will plateau or derail. A manager's capacity to continue developing thus becomes an extraordinarily important issue for all organizations concerned with executive development and succession.

Stratified Systems Theory (Jaques, 1989; Jacobs & Jaques, 1987; Jaques & Clement, 1991) speaks to conceptual capacity as both current capacity and potential capacity or mode. Current capacity is that level of complexity that can be mastered at the given time. Its measure is the maximum level of task complexity that, all other things equal, an incumbent can successfully deal with. Mode is the maximum level of task complexity that, all other things equal, can eventually be mastered. Jaques and Clement (1991) define a similar construct, cognitive power, as "the potential strength of cognitive processes in a person and is therefore the maximum level of task complexity that someone can handle at any given point in his or her development" (p. 49).

The concepts of cognitive power and potential capacity raise interesting measurement issues. How can one assess a future state? Stratified Systems Theory addresses this question empirically. In his early research, Jaques (1968) developed what he referred to as progression curves from a collection of cases he had followed in a large manufacturing company, and he used these curves in conjunction with a time span assessment (Jaques, 1964). With time span, he assessed current capability; given the progression curves, he could estimate potential. Later, Stamp (1988) developed an individual interview, the Career Path Appreciation (CPA), to assess current capability semi-independently of current occupation, and to serve as the basis for estimating potential. Jaques (1989, p. 50) describes these progression curves as "bands" that show the "rates of maturation of cognitive modes."

Of course, the question remains as to what capacity and power are, and what matures and why. Jacobs and Jaques (1990) speculated that these might be defined as the ability to develop cognitive maps, or mental models, pertinent to the causal dynamics of a given knowledge or experience domain. Research comparing experts to novices typically finds them differentiated by the ability of the experts to see patterns that permit rapid assessment of situations, their later recall (as in chess), and prediction of the likely subsequent flow of events from the point in time assessed. Jacobs and Jaques thought these mental models probably are developed through reflective thinking about experience. Reflective thinking would thus be a meaning-making activity, in which the elements of experience are placed in relationship with one another to form what might be termed an implicit decision support system. As in an explicit decision support system, the number of elements and their defined interconnections would define its complexity; the accuracy with which the model reflects the actual experience domain would define its utility for situation diagnosis and decision making. They speculated that significant effort would be required for the development of these mental models, and therefore they thought it likely that significant individual differences would be found in the proclivity (intrinsic motivation) to build them. Proclivity, perhaps in conjunction with native ability, would be the source of individual differences in capacity to deal with complexity given the same background development. That is, mental model complexity and veridicality should increase as more work is done to incorporate elements and test postulated interconnections. Complexity and veridicality could be limited by an inability to incorporate more elements or test their interconnections. It could also be limited by proclivity.

This argument points toward the importance of understanding these development processes in order to know how to develop complexity independent of the specific work experiences that otherwise would be required. Said another way, a fundamental understanding of these processes might enable the design of developmental experience that would accelerate the growth of strategic capacity. In particular, Streufert and Swezey (1986) make the point that capacity for complexity generated in one content domain may not generalize to another. So, of even greater potential worth, a fundamental understanding of these developmental processes might inform developmental experience that would achieve cross-domain complexity development—for example, generalization of complexity gained in one environment, such as a training environment, to another, such as a top-level managerial position.

The Role of Leadership: Competitive Advantage

Organizations, like other complex systems, take in resources and operate on them to produce some kind of output. They therefore depend on a continuing flow of resources for their existence and thus find themselves in an endless competition with other organizations that need the same resources.[1] Except in very unusual situations, resources are finite, so the competition has real meaning. It is to some extent zero sum. Organizations that compete more effectively get a larger portion of available resources, which means that those that compete less effectively get fewer resources. Organizations act much like other systems that have intelligence. They have goals and long-term strategies for achieving them. By the same token, they also have strategies for how they are going to compete with other organizations to obtain the resources they need.

Donaldson and Lorsch (1983) provide an excellent description of decision making and strategy formulation in a sample of Fortune 500 companies. In each organization, decisions are made and strategies are formulated on the basis of a fundamental set of assumptions and beliefs of long standing. Typically, these sets of assumptions and beliefs differ from organization to organization; so, consequently, do the decisions and strategies. However, there are some commonalities. One, in particular, is a drive for resources independence. To the extent an organization must depend on some specific source for a given resource, that source gains some degree of control over the options available to the organization. That is, resources dependence limits the options, and therefore the long-term adaptability, of the organization. The managers whom Donaldson and Lorsch studied recognized the impact of external dependencies on their own decision discretion and sought to limit it in various ways. Among them were market diversification (to limit dependency on one specific consumer group), capital independence (to limit dependency on the financial markets), and vertical integration (to limit dependency on specific sources of material resources). A second is a drive to be a dominant supplier, that is, to develop a product or service for which there is no competition. Some companies (not the ones Donaldson and Lorsch studied) become niche players, providing specialized products or services that others do not. Others seek to dominate their market. In the early 1980s, the General Electric chairman set an objective for all divisions of the company to be either first or second in their fields. If they were not, they were to be fixed, sold, or shut down.

The dynamics are the same for both drives. Control over resources needed by others creates resources dependency, and thus some degree of control over the decision options that managers can exercise in the dependent organization. If available decision options can be viewed as a resource, then this is also a competition. There consequently is a drive to gain some measure of control over the resources that a competitor needs, thereby gaining power to control that competitor's options, and there is a drive to reduce one's own resources dependency, thereby reducing the power of others to control one's own options. We suggest that this autonomy motive is probably culture free; it is probably found in virtually any organization in any country.[2] Of course, ability to achieve autonomy is not culture free. However, we think the motive is. And we think the defining measure of managerial value-added is the extent to which the manager is able to enhance the competitive advantage of his or her organization, thereby enhancing its autonomy.[3]

Clearly, the contribution of a top-level manager will differ from that of a first-line supervisor, as will the specific managerial actions that make up that contribution. In a well-structured organization, the contributions of different levels of management will be purposefully additive and nonoverlapping, and the different levels of management will in themselves represent meaningful growth stations for management development. That is, a fundamental premise of good organizational design ought to be that each level of management and supervision adds value to each adjacent level higher and lower, and the degree of complexity that must be mastered in each upward step is just within the capacity of the rising manager to achieve. All other things being equal, such an organization will make very good use of its human resources and will by its nature provide an excellent context for human resource development.[4]

Levels of Complexity in Organizations

Organization theorists have long recognized three organizational layers and their functions. Large-scale organizations typically have a foundation layer, dedicated to operations of one sort or another. In the divisional form (Mintzberg, 1979), the production of manufactured goods occurs in this layer, which may itself have several additional sublayers of "real" supervision. (A "real" supervisor, according to Jaques, 1989, can hire and fire and can unilaterally assign work duties.) The next layer, the middle line, is composed of midlevel managers whose responsibility is to establish operational goals for the division as a whole and to coordinate effort to achieve those goals. The midlevel sets the conditions, procedures, and standards for the production level and allocates resources so as to promote production efficiency and effectiveness. And it, as is true for the operations layer, may also have several levels of "real" management. The topmost layer is the strategic apex. It consists of the strategic management of the organization as a whole, which may consist of several or many divisions. The strategic apex establishes corporate vision, sets strategic objectives, and determines broad policy for organization-wide operations and management development. As was the case with the other layers, more than one level of management may be found here.

Although this formulation has widespread acceptance, it is of limited value for aggregating managerial tasks of relatively similar complexity (to create a parsimonious vertically differentiated structure) or for designing managerial development interventions. Nor is it particularly useful for understanding how to go about making judgments about what constitutes managerial potential or for its early identification. Of considerably greater value is a formulation that Jaques (1976) developed specifying parameters for a more finely graduated structure in which each level of management can add value uniquely. Based on nearly a generation of observations taken in heavy, capital-intensive industry, Jaques and his colleagues (Jaques, Gibson, & Isaac, 1978) then undertook to describe the complexity of work at each of the differentiated levels of his "well-structured" organization and to relate work complexity to human capability. Jacobs and Jaques (1987) continued this work by laying out critical tasks of managers by level.

Jaques (1976) specifies that a well-structured large-scale organization will probably have on the order of seven levels, with the exact number depending on size and scope of operations and the nature of the technology employed. Perhaps the more significant point is that an organization probably ought not to have more than seven levels, regardless of how large its scope and scale. Although Jaques did not originally group these levels, or strata, Jacobs and Jaques (1987) allocated them to three domains, as shown in Table 2.1, to conform to the larger body of organization theory and to emphasize similarities in functions that exist between strata.

Stratum I

In large scale, capital-intensive industry, the lowest domain is concerned with direct operations. Leaders here typically exercise influence on operations through direct interaction with those who are involved in their execution. Their units are aggregated on the basis of common function or process, and unit members typically know one another. As Jaques puts it, they operate on the basis of mutual recognition and mutual knowledge of subsystems. Leaders

Table 2.1. Stratified Systems Theory General Performance Requirements, by Level.

Stratum	Time Span	General Task Requirements	Title	Domain
VII	20–50 years	Creates complex systems; organizes acquisition of major resources; creates policy	CEO, corporation	Systems/strategic
VI	10–20 years	Oversees operation of subordinate systems; applies policy	Executive vice president, corporate headquarters	
V	5–10 years	Directs complex systems	President, division	General management
IV	2–5 years	Tailors resource allocations to independent subordinate programs or units	General manager, department	
III	1–2 years	Develops and executes plans to implement policy/missions	Manager, plant	
II	3–12 months	Directs performance of work; anticipates/solves current problems	Supervisor	Direct leadership
I	Less than 3 months	Hands-on work performance; uses practical judgment to solve ongoing problems	Production worker	

generally deal with concrete, relatively bounded problems with relatively few, generally linear solution paths and obvious desired end states. The decisions with which they are entrusted are usually near-term, with consequences that are apparent within a relatively short period of time. Their time span—the forward planning horizon—thus is also short. One reason that time span is an important construct in Stratified Systems Theory is that incumbents at all levels continuously make trade-off decisions about resources allocations. Most trade-offs involve balancing current needs against future needs. Current productivity is important, but future capability also is important. With finite resources, overinvestment in either one will jeopardize the other, so one way incumbents add value is by weighing one against the other so as to achieve the balance that will maintain best competitive advantage at that level.

For example, stratum I, the shop floor, consists of production workers. Stratified Systems Theory postulates a time span of discretion ranging out to approximately three months. Trade-off decisions here typically concern the day-to-day pacing of work; each individual must contribute to the work effort so as to make it successful, but not so much as to be unable to continue working effectively for the duration of a given job or production run. The present-future trade-off here is allocation of personal effort so as to be effective in the longer term (which here is weeks or months).

Stratum II

Working within a time span of discretion in excess of three months, leaders at stratum II exercise diagnostic judgment to overcome obstacles in a linear pathway. At the same time, they are accumulating experience and learning in order to diagnose emerging problems and initiate action to deal with identified problems. These leaders constitute the first level of true supervision. As such, they are responsible for planning the work flow for specific jobs or production runs, fitting personnel to work assignments so as to maximize their human resources net worth to the organization, and increasing the net value of human resources entrusted to their care.

Two kinds of trade-off decisions are quite important here. One has to do with smoothing production irregularities. When there are interruptions in the flow of product, for example, these leaders make the choice between using considerably more resources to "make up the deficiency" in the short run, or fewer resources to make it up in a longer time period. (The value trade-off is the utility of resources against the utility of immediate production; some perspective is required to make such trade-off decisions well.) The second interesting kind of trade-off has to do with maintaining human capability—human resource net worth—within the unit or group. A typical example is whether a unit member should be given needed training. Sending that person for training cuts into near-term unit effectiveness but produces greater long-term effectiveness. Again, this issue requires weighing the utility of one against the other.

Stratum III

Stratum III leaders manage interdependencies among similar subunits in the operation of one major function. To solve problems, they find a path that has a chance of coping with short-term requirements while simultaneously providing the initial stages of progress toward more long-term goals. Their time span of discretion is beyond one year.

These leaders constitute the first level of general management, and their responsibilities typically involve, for the first time, the management of a budget of expendable resources against major production objectives extending beyond the near-term. The longer term of responsibility adds both greater uncertainty and risk to the trade-offs that must be decided and greater discretion in the options available. It also adds demands in the conceptual skills and experience base required to make good trade-off decisions. For example, mastery of the skills required for interpreting and extrapolating trends is essential for intermediate-term management of stocks and flows. Similarly, mastery of dynamic linear systems probably is also required for an understanding of how to restore observed experience to the desired trend lines from which it is deviating—in other words, fundamental quality control. At this level, the mechanisms are basically concrete and extant. That is, the fundamental mechanisms that must be dealt with in these dynamic linear systems are probably physically represented and thus available for inspection and direct manipulation.

Stratum IV

The organizational level, or the middle of the leadership hierarchy, requires that leaders begin to coordinate multiple differentiated subunits and manage less directly. At this stratum, leaders are typically responsible for a major subdivision of functions within the larger organization—production, sales, or research and development. They are responsible for formulating operational practices and procedures for lower levels (Mintzberg, 1979) that reflect business objectives and policies decided at higher levels. They are also responsible for allocating resources to subordinate elements according to priorities that are calculated to implement these business objectives and policies. Stratum IV managers thus can be considered not only leaders in their own right but also, in large organizations, crucially important translators who understand objectives and policies in their larger competitive context and formulate the more explicitly tangible and concrete objectives and plans necessary for those conducting operations. The translation process requires conversion of abstractions, the tools of higher echelons, into concrete mandates, the tools of the lower echelons, and thus requires the capacity to manipulate these abstractions analytically. The resources allocation process also requires analytic skills.

Stratum IV managers may be responsible for decisions about the technologies their departments use. They must be concerned with competitive advantage, and thus be investing in the current state-of-the-art, while at the same time maximizing the return on investment on existing technology. Technology investment and conversion decisions demand substantial analytic sophistication and are very much more complex than the trend management tasks at stratum III, typically demanding a time horizon extending more than two years, and perhaps as long as five years, according to Jaques. So the tasks at stratum IV appear to be qualitatively different from, and substantially more complex than, those at stratum III. It may well be that the minimum conceptual skills required for success are also qualitatively more complex in the level of abstraction of the constructs that must be manipulated and the rigor of the analysis skills needed to manipulate them.

Stratum V

Tasks required of stratum V managers are more complex yet. These managers are accountable not only for achieving their own business goals but also for formulating those goals within the context set by organizational vision established at higher (corporate) levels of the hierarchy. Incumbents operate bounded open systems that exist as entities within the larger corporate structure. The problems that they face are less defined than those at the production level, and their boundary-spanning activities involve a more diverse group of stakeholders. They are responsible for developing business strategies and product lines, and for establishing priorities that determine the resources allocated to the various departments in the organization. By adjusting these priorities, these managers can and do influence the direction of the organization over much longer time frames than is the case at stratum IV. For example, the decision to invest resources in R&D that will result in a new product may not be reflected positively in the bottom line for seven to ten years. These managers must also be much more concerned about competitive advantage than stratum IV managers are. The stratum V manager is typically the president of a division or the managing director of a relatively large free-standing enterprise.

These organizations typically exist in an environment that contains other similar organizations, with which they must compete to exist. So whereas a stratum V manager typically focuses attention primarily on running the business, considerable attention must also be paid to benchmarking the competition and understanding how to maintain the division's competitive advantage. At this level, the factors that influence competitive advantage are considerably more extensive and complex to manage. For example, these managers must balance the competing demands of strategic constituencies within their own organizations. To some extent, these demands may truly be mutually exclusive; for example, the demands of a production general manager for resources needed to outsource acquisition of a new production technology—legitimately needed to remain competitive—in the near term may make it impossible to provide resources to the R&D general manager for in-house development of that same technology. Such a decision requires the capacity to assess the relative utility of immediate enhancement of capability against that of longer-term enhancement, which might also create substantial enhancement of R&D capability as a second-order effect. (It might also make subtle changes in the internal power structure of the firm as a third-order effect.) The conceptual skills of stratum V managers would seem to be of again a different order from those of stratum IV managers. They deal with broader problems, within a wider context, and must be able to see indirect (second- and third-order) effects that may extend over substantial time periods.

Strata VI and VII

At the executive level, strata VI and VII, leaders are responsible for structural change, extensive external boundary spanning, and both horizontal and vertical integration of business units. Incumbents operate in global political, economic, sociocultural, and technological environments. They conceptualize feasible futures, build consensus about them, and develop the resource bases required to initiate movement toward them. These leaders set broad directions for the total organization and create strategic business units that, in sum, produce movement of the total system in those desired directions. They may also make the decision to spin off, sell, or close down business units that are unprofitable or are no longer on the main path envisioned. They work to establish a corporate culture that will support the goals of the organization. They also work proactively to influence strategic constituencies in the external environment, both to create support for the total organization's objectives and to strengthen the organization's competitiveness. These leaders are expected to be proactive in ensuring the continuing availability of needed resources; for this, they must create effective social networks in addition to the conventional business connections. The problems at this level are more complex and may be "wicked" as well. Incumbents must frame them in ways that facilitate their eventual solution. Leadership at this level is more complex, indirect, and persuasive than at any other level.

Working with a time horizon of ten to twenty years, stratum VI leaders (typically, executive vice presidents) contribute to long-term corporate success and survival by judging corporate investment strategies and enhancing the value of corporate assets. Among their many responsibilities, two stand out. First, they may well have broad supervisory responsibilities over the activities of several corporate divisions. In this role, they are responsible not only for approving division goals and performance, but also for integration across divisions that will enhance the competitive advantage of these divisions as a group. They also are typically responsible for ensuring that division operations reflect broad corporate policies and generally also monitor the flow of resources into and out of divisions as dictated by corporate strategic goals.

Second, corporate executive vice presidents typically constitute an executive decision team. The critical issues that can be resolved only at the corporate level are typically too complex to be fully encompassed by the frame of reference of a single executive, even the chief executive officer (CEO). An effective executive decision team brings diverse perspectives, talents, and backgrounds into the issue analysis and decision-making arena. One member may be expert on the national or international financial markets that are relevant to a given contingency. Another may be expert on basic technology relevant to that contingency, say, geology or marine biology. Yet others may be long-time members of the firm who have worked their way up in operations or sales. In really good executive decision teams, the meeting of diverse perspectives generates energy and insight to explore options that might not otherwise be seen and to discover long-term courses of action that otherwise would have remained hidden. The extent to which that happens is dependent on the skill of the CEO in harnessing, encouraging, supporting, and containing the flow of energy. (When the executive decision team is functioning well, the terminal offense is not disagreeing with the boss but rather failing to speak up to push forward knowledge critically relevant to the issue at hand.)

The responsibilities of stratum VII leaders are more complex still. These leaders leverage the complex talents of members constituting the executive decision teams at the corporate level. Drawing on international resources, they develop and pursue worldwide strategic plans and produce stratum V units through development, acquisition, merger, or joint ventures that mature over a time span of twenty to fifty years (Jaques, 1989). By virtue of their decisions about subsystems (such as personnel management, information, and quality control) and their beliefs and assumptions about how to do business (Donaldson & Lorsch, 1983), they maintain or reshape the cultures of their organizations as required and influence executive succession for decades beyond their own tenures. Perhaps even more important, their beliefs about how the business ought to operate guide decisions about corporate policies in the near term as well. For example, their beliefs about debt management, cash flow objectives, and other key concerns, typically reflected in corporate balance sheets rather than bottom-line profitability statements, have to do with their views about their strategic constituencies.

As Mintzberg (1973) and others have noted, top-level executives also are responsible for determining the image they want their corporations to project and then of ensuring that both public and private release of information is calculated to produce the desired results. In many cases, they are instrumental in the public projection of the corporate image. They also are members of extensive personal networks through which they seek and gain access to information about likely developments in the political, economic, sociocultural, and technological worlds that will have relevance to corporate well-being and also those developments that may be relevant. The networks to which they belong are networks of influential people—others like themselves who control and direct major resources. Membership in such a network is typically permitted only to those who add value to it. Value may be added by ability to commit resources (such as a financier), share precious information (such as a fellow CEO in a related but not competitive industry), or influence political outcomes (such as elected officials). These networks operate to enable sharing information important to all, finding potential partners in joint ventures, and forming coalitions to influence legislation (or other matters) deemed important to the future operating environments of coalition partners. Membership in such networks, and particularly the ability to influence other network members, may confer public influence that is critical to the continued existence of the firm. A prime example is the successful petitioning of the U.S. Congress by Lee Iacocca to guarantee loans to Chrysler, which otherwise would probably have either dissolved or been so badly damaged that it might not ever have recovered its capacity to compete.

The capacity to operate in these networks and to manage the other responsibilities of this level seem to require qualitatively more complex conceptual skills to handle a higher order of abstractions than at the midlevels and to be creatively proactive in guiding the organization through the application of integrative skills to generate concepts, vision, and objectives that span very long time intervals. But there is yet another reason that these complex conceptual skills are needed at the strategic level. The strategic environment is not only dynamic, complex, and ambiguous but also uncertain—and to some extent purposefully uncertain. We described competitive advantage as an attribute that enables more effective competition for needed resources. However, at that time, we did not deal with competitive strategies, nor will we do so here except in one respect. Many of the consequential decisions taken at the strategic level play out over very long time frames and require huge resource commitments. They may consequently demand significant lead time to implement. But in an intensely competitive environment, the lengthy time interval between the initial commitment of resources and the ultimate payoff usually puts the organization at risk. If a competitor can negate the resources investment by a competitive strategy, significant opportunity may be lost and, with it, significant competitive advantage. So the strategic world is full of strategy and counterstrategy. The executive who can enable the organization to encompass the strategies of its competitors, either by concealing its own winning strategy or by inferring theirs in time to counter them, will develop substantial competitive advantage. Dahl (1998) describes at length the perspective-taking and inference-making skills required, which include being able to understand and operate not only within the frame of reference of the adversary but also to take the adversary's perspective on one's own frame of reference. These are highly complex conceptual skills.

Time Span

Throughout this discussion, time spans of discretion have been given for the various strata as Jaques envisioned them. However, we think our concept of time horizon may differ somewhat from that of Jaques, in two ways. First, Jaques (1964) defined time span of discretion essentially as the longest interval of activity a boss will allow between reviews of progress. That is, if a subordinate is given a project to plan and accomplish, there will be reporting time lines. A job may be given that will require two years to accomplish, but the subordinate may be required to report progress each month and to adjust plans as directed at each reporting point. Jaques would say this time span of discretion is one month, not two years. Jaques thought that the incumbent's felt weight of responsibility is proportional to the time span of discretion. The longer the time span, the greater the level of responsibility the incumbent should feel. He also felt that job complexity is highly related to time span.

We depart from this formulation by noting, for reasons to be explained below, that a requirement to report progress may not necessarily define a time span. We also contend that complexity is defined by other factors, some of which may be related to time span but not unequivocally determined by it. That is, a given development or task may be highly complex but may have a very short half-life. Consider an example provided by a company developing software applications. The half-life of an application might be less than two years, but the decision to develop it and the development itself are probably an order of complexity exceeding stratum III. A second example is the current product development cycle of many U.S. automobile manufacturers. Through the use of integrated process teams, new product development times are now at least two years shorter than they were fifteen years ago, in response to the challenge introduced by Japanese manufacturers, but the process is no less complex. In fact, it may be more complex. What may have happened was that a more complex process involving mutual adjustment was adopted, replacing earlier processes that were more linear, thereby enabling alternative ways of getting it done.

We also diverge from Jaques's time span in another way. A fundamental notion in our understanding of Stratified Systems Theory is that of a frame of reference. We view a frame of reference as a dynamic decision support system, internally held by an incumbent, that allows this person to analyze an existing complex set of events, understand their significance, and also understand where the power levers are to influence outcomes. The perception of time must be an element in any such system. Just as Day and Lord (1988) found time lagging important in measuring the impact of executive succession, it would seem that an executive decision support system would need to be framed in such a way that its user would understand the time intervals over which events play out, and thus the time intervals that should be examined to look for effects. It seems useful to presume also that the spans of time over which an incumbent can look to seek effects will themselves grow with age and experience. Not only is this compatible with Jaques's concept of progression curves, which are growth curves over time, but also it appeals intuitively. That is, it would seem difficult for a ten-year-old child to have an accurate sense of what twenty years is like or how events play out over that kind of time span. There would be no experience base for such a time sense. Finally, it would seem reasonable to assume that time horizon, thus conceived, would be correlated with complexity of frame of reference. That is, such a sense of time would seem to require a representation of the events that flow over whatever time period is sensed. The more events there are and the greater the number of their interactions, the greater the complexity ought to be, all other things equal.

Frames of Reference

Implicit in the preceding discussion is the assumption that the growth of executive capacity is associated with growth in perspective. We would go further and assert that growth in perspective is a sine qua non for growth in executive capacity. The critical questions have to do with the nature of perspective and the role it plays, especially in the decision-making and strategic negotiation functions of the executive, the essential conditions for development of perspective, and the reason for individual differences in growth of perspective.

We define *frame of reference* as an integrated set of constructs, ordered according to some structure that imparts meaningfulness to them in some teleological sense. Several postulates are implicit in this definition. First, its elements are constructs, representations of processes, concepts, or sets of events in the external world. Our concept of construct is similar to the product of Kelly's (1955) process of construing. All constructs probably are abstractions by their very nature, but we would assert that the more meaningful ones are abstractions of abstractions, that is, symbolic representations of intangibles. Centralization is an example of such a construct, as is, indeed, frame of reference. To an organizational theorist, central-ization as a construct brings a rich set of associations, which in-clude some evaluative statements about its utility under differing circumstances.

Second, its structure is purposive. We assume that the work of constructing frames of reference is intrinsically satisfying and that at least some of this satisfaction derives from the increased under-standing of phenomena or events they provide. Given that ef-fectance is a human need, it seems reasonable also to assume that the meaning-giving structures are focused on real-world operations of some sort, in such a way that a good frame of reference provides its owner with some degree of competitive advantage in doing something of value. To some extent, the process would match Kolb's (Kolb & Fry, 1975) description of the learning cycle, which takes concrete experience through successive stages of observation and reflection, formation of abstract concepts and generalizations, and, finally, the testing of implications of concepts in new situa-tions. The point is that individual differences exist in need for ef-fectance, thus in the proclivity to do reflective thinking, and thus in the effort allocated to frame of reference construction. But the notion of effectance extends beyond simply understanding, and so does the notion of purposiveness in our understanding of frames of reference. If any of the executive's roles are more criti-cal than others, it would be their roles in diagnosing the complex and ill-structured problem situations that characterize the strate-gic world, and devising strategic goals around which consensus of stakeholders can be built. So we assume further that executive frames of reference are functional in dealing with the content do-mains specifically relevant to their responsibilities (that is, they are instrumentally valuable) and that the motivation to maintain and extend them arises in part from this instrumentality.

Finally, the structure gives meaning to the elements of which it is composed (and can be extended to include, and give mean-ing to, additional elements as they are derived from experience). We mean by this that the structure is probably more dynamic than taxonomic in the sense that it probably incorporates some sense of the flow of events over time, and thus permits inferences about causality. In this sense, a frame of reference could be compared to a model. Simple linear models would allow inferences of linear cause and effect. Presumably more complex models—those with more elements and with more pathways among elements—would allow inferences about multiple causality and thus would be more useful in addressing the kinds of complex issues that must be framed at the top levels of large-scale organizations. Perhaps equally important, it would be a tool for assessing the significance of observed events, as by a competitor, or for realizing that there ought to be more information than there is, and thus for understanding what questions to ask in order to fill out awareness of the situation.

In this sense, a frame of reference—a model—is like a template. Military intelligence analysts use a process called templating in intelligence analysis. By understanding how other forces configure and deploy their standard organizations, an analyst can record observations of enemy equipment and personnel, and by examining the emerging configurations in relation to known patterns, this person can make shrewd inferences as to what constitutes the other force. If there is uncertainty because insufficient information is available, these inferences permit targeted probes to gain more information. That is, the analyst may infer, but cannot be sure, that an organization of type X exists at point Y. By deduction, this person can state that if the organization is type X, then at point Z there will be another specific type of equipment, and so he or she can order a probe to find out whether that specific type of equipment is in fact at point Z. In other words, an understanding of typical ways in which the other force does things permits confident decision making and subsequent action based on less information than otherwise would be required. In the same way, a frame of reference permits more rapid understanding and more confident action than would otherwise be possible in the complex and ill-structured situations characterizing the strategic world.

Klein's (1993) recognition-primed decision-making model is a useful analogue. It has three broad sets of operating conditions. The first, simple match, describes a situation in which the problem is of a recurring type, and the problem solver recognizes the type. This would also be the simplest form of templating. Recognizing the problem type, the decision maker knows the appropriate response and executes it without further ado. A more complex situation is that of developing a course of action. Here, a prior solution does not necessarily come to mind, so the problem solver generates a plausible one. The next step is to envision a mental simulation in which the plausible action is played out—that is, tested. If it appears that it will work, it will be attempted. This follows Simon's (1955) formulation of satisficing as a strategy; the plausible action will not necessarily be the best one possible and probably will never be weighed in a classical sense against another option, but if it seems likely to work based on the mental simulation, it will be tried. If the mental simulation suggests it will not work, then it will be modified or another action entirely will be constructed.

The third condition is the most complex. Klein describes this as experiencing the situation in a changing context. It is not clear that this is intended to convey the sense of ill structured in the sense of strategic problems and issues, but it certainly is more complex than the previous two because of situational instability. (Rate of change in the situation is one of the elements of complexity.) The decision process is much the same as in the other two, however, with the exception of recognition that the situation may not be familiar and that more information may be required. There also is the question of whether the decision maker's expectations about the situation are violated by additional information, and the consequent need to reassess the situation if they are. Nonetheless, the model calls for testing the problem solution using mental imagery, much as is the case with the second condition.

Fundamental to all three conditions are four issues: plausible goals to be achieved in the situation, relevant cues, expectations about the situation (including diagnostic inferences) based on information available, and permissible actions. So Klein's model is frankly purpose oriented, as a problem-solving or decision-making model ought to be. And it involves evaluating a course of action or decision implementation in a mental simulation in which the action can be played out.

In form, our frame of reference concept is quite similar. We would assert that goals to be accomplished are important for the decision maker, but we would also assert that strategic leaders entertain more goals, and more distant goals, than just the immediate one.

Stratified Systems Theory suggests that managers at each organizational level must continually trade off short-term gains against potentially greater long-term gains that can be purchased only through the sacrifice of something in the short term. In theory, as leaders gain experience in making these trade-offs at one level, they develop the capacity for longer-term trade-offs at the next higher level. However, a more crucial point about time span may lie in its relation to frame of reference. Most decisions made and actions taken by a stratum V manager will not play out over a ten-year time frame. Most, in fact, will play out over a few weeks or months at most. The point about time frame is that these decisions should be made with reference to a context that is much longer in concept. To the extent a short-term action can facilitate a longer-term possible objective, a string of short-term actions can create a path to a much more significant set of outcomes. Kotter (1982) made this point in describing the agendas of his effective managers. These managers had longer-range objectives they were striving to achieve but could not reach because of obstacles of one sort or another. However, having defined these objectives, they were able to be situationally opportunistic, seizing the moment when opportunity presented itself. Streufert (Streufert & Swezey, 1986) makes a similar point in relating complexity theory to managerial action. His more effective managers in a free simulation much more frequently made decisions in the near term with the intent of creating greater latitude for subsequent decisions. That is, given a choice between two decisions, one of which would facilitate a subsequent decision under a certain contingency, the facilitating decision would be made. One could assume that the effective managers were future oriented in the sense of envisioning future contingencies as they formulated courses of action to respond to near-term events. Beach and Lipshitz (1993) make a similar point:

> In a rapidly changing world, . . . decision makers rely upon their own vision of what the future holds. . . . Strategic decisions are made in order to *act* upon the world, to make sure that the future does *not* look like the past. Decision makers go to great lengths to insure that they have the ability to control key future events, and controllability is factored into their decisions [p. 26].

The Content of Strategic Frames

The frames of reference that strategic leaders employ include many intangible elements that are not touched on in Klein's model, such as values, ethical mandates, and the degree of self-reference (subjectivity) that the decision maker exhibits. It also includes deeply held beliefs and assumptions about the nature of the organization and proper ways for the organization to conduct business (Donaldson & Lorsch, 1983). Many of these beliefs and assumptions may date from the time of the organization's founding, and they may well limit the options that are available to decision makers. Examples of limiting beliefs have to do with the nature of the organization's central competencies, whether the organization should diversify beyond these competencies, and the growth rate the organization should seek. In our view, beliefs and assumptions such as these are elements of a dynamic causal model that managers use to envision future possibilities and to calculate and minimize risk. They are relevant to decision making because they appear in if-then consequential linkages.

These assumptions and beliefs may or may not be empirically grounded. In fact, belief in the value of empirical tests probably differentiates among the frames that different managers hold. In addition, experience and training probably have strong effects on frame content. Organizations have strong socializing effects on their rising managers, as does professional training. Bolman and Deal (1991) describe four frames that to some extent are mutually exclusive, although each is a fragment of reality in large-scale formal organizations:

Structural—emphasizing the importance of formal roles and relationships

Human resources—emphasizing human needs, feelings, prejudices, skills, and limitations

Political—emphasizing conflict, that is, the competition for power and resources endemic to organizations

Symbolic—emphasizing the cultural aspects of organizations, particularly the fundamental assumptions and beliefs that influence decision making

The point that Bolman and Deal make is that "exemplars" can readily be found. Exemplars analyze issues and solve problems mainly within the boundaries of single frames. Structuralists are more inclined to rely on principles of scientific management and emphasize rationality in both organizational design and management.

Individual differences are controlled by procedures and work simplification. An extreme structural orientation is quite mechanistic and may produce organizational conditions that alienate its members, especially those at the lower levels. A human resource perspective is very nearly diametrically opposed, holding that organizations and their members are essentially partners and that organizational effectiveness depends to a large extent on the commitment of its members. An extreme human resource orientation is quite humanistic, holding organizations responsible for satisfaction of a broad range of human needs. On a somewhat different dimension, the political orientation is essentially adversarial, holding that organizational life is by its very nature a competition for finite resources. Power therefore is a precious commodity, opening the door to both resources and autonomy in assigning their uses. An extreme political orientation would, in theory, be quite Machiavellian. And finally, a symbolic orientation differs from the three others in the sense that it focuses on the meaning of events in addition to the events themselves. A strong symbolic orientation may facilitate the perception of second- and third-order effects.

We make no case here for the correctness or the comprehensiveness of these frames. There are, however, two important points to be made. The first is that frame exemplars can be found in everyday experience. These are individuals who act—though without awareness that they are doing so—as though most or all problems can be solved by application of a set of assumptions that are equivalent to those of a single frame. Everyday experience suggests that operation within a specific frame constitutes a constraint on capacity to diagnose problem situations and develop adaptive courses of action to deal with them. The growth of capacity therefore would seem to require integration of the multiple frames with all their inherent contradictions, in the sense of becoming capable of viewing situations from multiple perspectives and then understanding and accommodating the apparent contradictions thereby generated (Quinn, 1988). This would correspond to multidimensional integration, which Streufert (Streufert & Swezey, 1986) suggests is the highest level of conceptual complexity and the level of complexity required by top-level managers.

The second point is that while all of these frames contain intangible elements—assumptions and beliefs—that clearly influence perception and decision making, the formal aspects are still much like those that Klein proposed. That is, although the frames of reference—the mental models—may be different, the diagnosis and decision processes may be quite similar, differing primarily in the level of abstraction of frame elements and the complexity of their interrelationships. Again, we make no case for these particular frames, only that it is possible to generalize a concept such as Klein's recognition-primed decision-making model beyond the physically anchored contexts to which it is most frequently applied. In this particular case, it would appear that a mental model that integrates the multifold and often contradictory facets of organizational experience, as perhaps partially illustrated by the Bolman and Deal's (1991) frames, might enable one to apply processes like those of the recognition-primed decision-making model to understanding human interaction and decision processes within an organizational context. It is also possible to imagine that mental model as one functioning part of yet a larger mental model that integrates both human interaction and decision processes with systems processes influencing the interaction of organizations in the broader national and global surrounds.

Mental Model Construction and Conceptual Capacity

We have speculated that complexity is a function of the number of elements that mental models contain and the number of interconnections among the elements. Presumably, complexity increases with increasing numbers of both elements and interconnections. That is, it seems that complexity must involve both and that an increase in complexity might be nonlinear since the number of possible interconnections is a power function of the number of elements. This would have implications for understanding both the developmental tools and the effort needed to build complex models.

An apt illustration of complexity comes from work done by Forsythe (1992). He interviewed students and faculty at a senior service college (SSC)—the Army War College, Industrial College of the Armed Forces—and strategic leaders who had been invited to speak there. He asked them to speak in response to specific questions. The interviews were transcribed and graphically mapped. Figure 2.1 is a "map" from a student. Descriptively, it shows a listing of elements, with linear association chains for three of the elements. There are no interconnections among the main elements in the map. Presumably if this student were asked to formulate an action plan in response to that question, she or he would review the elements, perhaps choose one or another (or do a sequential cost-benefits trade-off among the elements under consideration, ultimately picking the "high" number), and proceed toward developing an implementation plan.

The chart depicted in Figure 2.2, done by an SSC faculty member, is somewhat more complex. It is clearly more organized than the student map, containing at least the beginning of parallel paths, alternative options, and linked associations. However, it still

Figure 2.1. Complexity Map, Senior Service College Student.

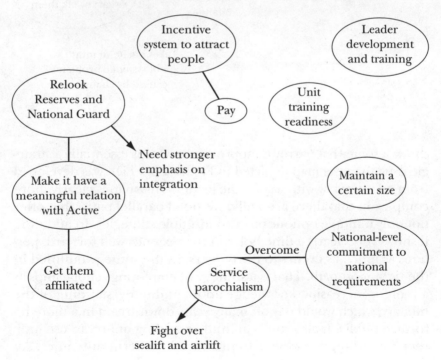

Actions: In response to issues of composition of the military force and the economy (threatens ability to expand and sustain war)

Figure 2.2. Complexity Map, Senior Service College Faculty Member.

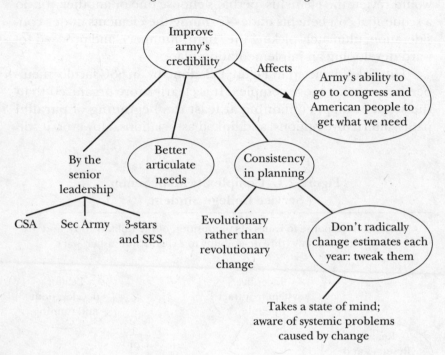

Actions: In response to issues of availability of manpower pool and integration of advanced technologies

shows a somewhat narrower approach to what is essentially a strategic issue than the map depicted in Figure 2.3, which was developed from an interview with a strategic leader. This map is clearly more complex in that there are well-developed parallel paths that offer not only multiple options but also multiple strategies. In addition, it shows very clearly a time horizon that extends well forward, perhaps as much as twenty to thirty years, in the strategy outlined in the right-most path. That is a strategy of employing scholarships as a tool for increasing knowledge about and understanding of the military, which would pay off many years downstream in a more informed public. It also shows an understanding of how to use indirect and intangible effects to produce long-term outcomes. An

Figure 2.3. Complexity Map, Strategic Leader.

Actions: In response to the issue of shaping the army of the future and civil-military integration

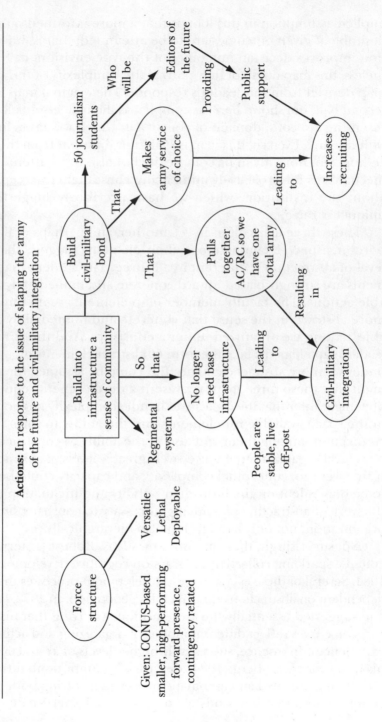

implicit assumption in this loop is that a more informed public is desirable if given outcomes are to be attempted; that is, information improves decision outcomes of the type envisioned. Nevertheless, this map does not fully portray the complexity of the actual map derived from this leader's response. The original map had a second half, not shown here, as complex as the first, essentially representing a second domain of constructs, which was cross-linked with the first. Even so, this map is strikingly different from the preceding two, not only in its complexity but also in its attention to mechanisms for proactively influencing constituency perceptions about the institution, which we have previously suggested is uniquely strategic.

These three maps differ in yet another, and perhaps vitally important, aspect. Examination of their elements suggests that the level of abstraction is different in all three. The student map elements are strongly biased toward concrete and immediately available actions. The faculty member map elements seem one step more abstract, in the sense that concrete and immediately available actions are organized under a construct. And the strategic leader map elements take the form of abstract elements organized under yet more abstract elements. If it could be assumed for a moment that these three maps represent a development sequence, one might infer that the capacity to handle complexity lies not only in the space available for elements and the ability to form interconnections among them, but also in the ability to construct a hierarchical organization of successively greater levels of abstraction. If that were so, conceptual complexity and capacity could be said to be dependent on the individual's ability and inclination to do the work of abstracting and linking necessary to construct such an organization, not only laterally but also hierarchically.

Not surprisingly, these are not new ideas. Robert J. Sternberg edited a sparkling collection of essays on cognitive development in 1984. Several of these essays suggest development processes that are dependent on abstraction and principles generation. In 1978, Jaques had suggested essentially the same notion, asserting that his progression curves reflect different modes of organizing and acting on experience—in essence, successively higher levels of abstraction. In his own essay, Sternberg (1984) describes a componential theory with both controlled and automatic processes involving both meta-components and other kinds of components. Expertise develops as a result of packing information into componential subsystems. He hypothesized that all elements of such a subsystem are of the same hierarchical order and thus are all equally available for processes relegated to the subsystem. The more information is packed into a subsystem, the more diversely capable the subsystem becomes. One is strongly tempted to compare his componential subsystem concept with the cognitive map concept.

Case (1984) asserts that higher-order processes involve "(1) the coordination of lower-order processes, (2) the differentiation of lower-order processes, and (3) the hierarchical integration of processes, or 'operations on operations'" (p. 41). However, Case differentiates his thinking from classical Piagetian concepts. In his view, stage transition "takes place by a set of processes that are oriented toward achieving particular results, in particular physical and social environments. These processes include problem solving, exploration, imitation, and mutual regulation" (p. 41). That is, development and stage transition are the result of purposeful activities.

Finally, Fischer and Pipp (1984) describe processes of mapping and system construction that produce a hierarchical structure of ten tiers, ranging from a single sensorimotor act at the bottom to a system of abstract systems, equivalent to a single principle, at the top. Key concepts in Fischer's theoretical formulation are optimal level, "the upper limit of a person's general information-processing capacity, the most complex type of skill that he or she can control"; optimal skill, which increases as a function of long age spans; hierarchically organized development levels; and transformation rules that specify how a particular skill can be transformed or rewritten to create a new skill. In form, these concepts look much like the Stratified Systems Theory concepts previously described.

If these pieces can all be accepted and interwoven, one might conclude that strategic capacity depends hugely on cognitive skills, and particularly on the development of systems of domain elements that, in our view, function as a kind of decision support system. These systems must develop purposefully, as Case suggests. They must develop through use of mechanisms that produce successively higher-order abstractions (Jaques, 1976; Fischer & Pipp, 1984). And in operation, they must be interlinked in some networked fashion, as the description of Sternberg's (1984) componential subsystem suggests.

However, if these analogies are correctly drawn, there are individual differences in the extent to which these processes operate. Stamp's CPA interview produces huge individual differences
among individuals who also show huge differences in upward mobility (and subjectively in their concreteness of thought). In a longitudinal study of some two hundred subjects, some of whom had
been followed for as long as fourteen years, she found a correlation of .71 between the organizational level to which her subjects
had risen and that predicted earlier from their interviews. The
question then becomes one of understanding the reason these individual differences exist and the extent to which development can
be accelerated by intervention. Not enough is known now to answer these questions, but some evidence can be cited if we assume
that the CPA is a surrogate or operational definition of the conceptual complexity and potential constructs of Stratified Systems
Theory.

First, we have suggested that breadth of perspective, and particularly the capacity to frame and reframe, are important. Kegan
(1982) suggests one methodology for assessing perspective taking.
Lewis (Lewis & Jacobs, 1982) employed Kegan's assessment procedure, and Jacobs did the Stamp interview on a sample of SSC students and found a correlation of .59 between the two assessments,
although range was restricted on both. This is an impressive correlation, given that both types of interviews were methodologically
prescribed and in theory related to different underlying constructs.
Kegan's theory is about how people develop increasingly broad
perspectives of themselves in relation to the world. Lewis concluded from the strong relationship between the two assessments
that "strategic leadership potential is, first and foremost, a function of the capacity for generating an independent perspective on
the strategic environment . . . and thinking using abstract conceptual models" (p. 134).

The CPA is related to a variety of other constructs as well. In a
later SSC sample (McGee, Jacobs, Kilcullen, & Barber, 1999), the
CPA correlated .49 with the Original scale of the Gordon Personal
Preference Inventory, .49 with the Myers-Briggs Type Indicator
Sensing-Intuiting scale, and .40 with the overall Kriton Adaptor-
Innovator Scale score. All of these are thought to reflect an orien-
tation toward creativity, conceptual orientation, conceptual ca-

pacity, and openness to new ideas. However, its correlation with a measure of crystallized intelligence, the Wonderlic Personnel Test, was only .21, that is, significant but relatively inconsequential. In the 1999–2000 class at the Industrial College of the Armed Forces, a major component of the CPA measure correlated .53 with a "New Ideas" score from a Team Roles instrument, .54 with the Gordon PPI Original scale, .42 with the Openness scale from the Mini-markers, and .62 with the Personality Profiler S-N scale. The stability of the correlations between the CPA (and its component in the second set of data) and indicators of creativity and openness to new ideas suggests that conceptual capacity must also be reliably related to these kinds of constructs.

One of us recently collected data of further interest. Early in a course on creative and critical thinking, students were asked to enter into their journals a "mind map" of critical and creative thinking. They were given no further elaboration as to what a mind map might be. These journal entries were then rated on a scale from 1 (a linear listing of elements) through 9 (a spatial and net-worked array of elements with interconnections). The resulting ratings correlated with the Personality Profiler S-N scale at .60, significant at $p = .05$ even with a small class (n = 15), and .57 with the major component of the CPA used in the previously cited research. So at least within this small sample, individuals who tend toward an N preference (reflective, open to new ideas) and score high on the CPA tend to organize concepts in a more spatial and inter-connected manner than those who tend toward an S preference (preferring objective reality).

Finally, in unpublished research, Berthold (1997) investigated the influence of SSC attendance on CPA assessments. She obtained a sample of students from two colleges and a control sample comprising members who had been selected to attend but had been delayed for a year. Presumably all were of equal conceptual ability initially, to the extent the selection system focuses on conceptual ability. The CPA was administered within the first three months of attendance and again at least one month before the nine-month course terminated. Jaques postulates that estimated potential is relatively stable, with current capacity maturing predictably over time. However, Berthold's two SSC groups scored significantly higher gains in the same amount of time than the control group on the second administration. This suggests that a concentrated experience focused on expanding perceptual limits, a primary objective of SSC, is effective in increasing current capability as measured by this instrument and that estimated potential therefore may not be relatively stable. By inference, improving the cognitive processes involved may also improve ultimate capacity.

These pieces of research are only fragments of the whole needed to fill in the entire picture. Nevertheless, they suggest that conceptual capacity is at least in part associated with reflective processing of experience, openness to new ideas, and the capacity to form and integrate multiple perspectives about one's environment and experience. It probably is also associated with how information is organized in cognitive maps. That is, a tendency to organize information in a networked or spatial fashion might be interactive with assessed capacity; similarly, a tendency toward linear organization might be a limiting factor rather than the result of a limiting factor. These are all questions that need research answers.

Conclusion

We have focused on the importance of conceptual skills for successful strategic leadership and decision making. This is not to deny, of course, the great importance of other attributes, such as behavioral and dispositional ones, which are also addressed in this book. As the integration will show, it is the combination that counts, and there probably are significant additivity effects in the combinations that can emerge. Nevertheless, it appears that conceptual skills are of unusual significance in the determination of success and failure in the rarified atmospheres found at the strategic apex of large-scale organizations.

The strategic world can be characterized as a system of systems that compete with one another for finite resources. The effectiveness with which an organization competes is an outcome of strategies implemented by its senior management in combination with special attributes that give it competitive advantage. The extent to which an organization has competitive advantage is significant for its continued prosperity and growth. By implication, strategic leadership and management add value by contributing to competitive advantage.

Organizational design influences the extent to which leadership and management can contribute to competitive advantage. All large-scale organizations must be concerned about the efficient utilization of their human resources, to include both current managerial value-added and development for managerial succession. We have used the model of requisite organization that Jaques suggested in his Stratified Systems Theory to examine both conceptual skill requirements and speculate about their development. Specifically, we have suggested that top-level leaders and managers have developed complex frames of reference—mental models—by reflective processing of experience, which involves successively higher orders of abstraction. The resulting mental models probably function like small decision support systems, in that they contain patterned representations of the real dynamic systems within which these top-level leaders and managers function. They probably are used in a fashion like that described by Klein as recognition-primed decisions. The broader the model and the richer the interconnections among its elements are, the greater the likelihood is that the model can be used to detect patterns in the complex flux of events in the strategic world.

We also speculated about the processes by which these models are constructed. In agreement with Jaques, but for different reasons, we conclude that time horizon is important, as is the individual's intrinsic motivation to construct them; the effort involved is probably substantial, so they must be seen by their builders as intrinsically worth the effort. We also reported previously unpublished research showing the amenability of cognitive capacity as defined by Jaques to change from intervention. And, finally, we attempted to show with some limited data a convergence of constructs relating to conceptual skills and the constellation of attributes now typically clumped together under the construct of intellectance. Although much additional research is needed, it appears that the importance of these constructs for developing top-level leaders and managers is substantial.

Notes

1. The following discussion appears to be drawn from capitalistic economic views in ignorance of other systems of economic thought. Based on the short term, this might be a valid criticism. However,

we would argue that over the long term, competition for similar scarce resources occurs between dissimilar systems, and competitive advantage remains a key element in long-term survival. This is not an endorsement of competition as desirable, but rather a description of competition for resources as a fact of systems life.

2. One might argue this point, citing the interlocking directorates that characterize Japanese industry. However, if one looks at what actually constitutes the system, one must conclude that the interlocking directorates themselves constitute a system that seemed effective (until recently) for promoting survival of the interdependent organizations and reducing external competition.

3. Competitive advantage is an attribute of an organization that enables it to compete more effectively for resources and thus to survive.

4. One necessary equal is a system for identifying potential so as to advance the right people. This sounds self-evident, yet surprisingly few organizations understand how to measure potential in any systematic way.

References

Barnard, C. (1938). *Functions of the executive*. Cambridge, MA: Harvard University Press.

Beach, L. R., & Lipshitz, R. (1993). Why classical decision theory is an inappropriate standard for evaluating and aiding most human decision making. In G. A. Klein, J. Orasanu, R. Calderwood, & C. E. Zsambok (Eds.), *Decision making in action: Models and methods*. Norwood, NJ: Ablex.

Bolman, L. G., & Deal, T. C. (1991). *Reframing organizations: Artistry, choice, and leadership*. San Francisco: Jossey-Bass.

Case, R. (1984). The process of stage transition: A neo-Piagetian view. In R. J. Sternberg (Ed.), *Mechanisms of cognitive development*. New York: Freeman.

Dahl, A. B. (1998). *Command dysfunction: Minding the cognitive war*. Maxwell Air Force Base, AL: Air University Press.

Day, D. V., & Lord, R. G. (1988). Executive leadership and organizational performance: Suggestions for a new theory and methodology. *Journal of Management, 14*, 453–464.

Donaldson, G., & Lorsch, J. W. (1983). *Decision making at the top*. New York: Basic Books.

Fischer, K. W., & Pipp, S. L. (1984). Processes of cognitive development: Optimal level and skill acquisition. In R. J. Sternberg (Ed.), *Mechanisms of cognitive development*. New York: Freeman.

Forsythe, G. B. (1992, Spring). The preparation of strategic leaders. *Parameters*, pp. 38–49.

Jacobs, T. O., & Jaques, E. (1987). Leadership in complex systems. In J. Zeidner (Ed.), *Human productivity enhancement* (Vol. 2). New York: Praeger.

Jacobs, T. O., & Jaques, E. (1990). Military executive leadership. In K. E. Clark & M. B. Clark (Eds.), *Measures of leadership*. West Orange, NJ: Leadership Library of America.

Jacobs, T. O., & Jaques, E. (1991). Executive leadership. In R. Gal & A. D. Manglesdorff (Eds.), *Handbook of military psychology*. New York: Wiley.

Jaques, E. (1964). *Time-span handbook*. Portsmouth, NH: Heinemann.

Jaques, E. (1968). *Progression handbook*. Carbondale: Southern Illinois University Press.

Jaques, E. (1976). *A general theory of bureaucracy*. Portsmouth, NH: Heinemann.

Jaques, E. (1989). *Requisite organization*. Arlington, VA: Cason Hall.

Jaques, E., & Clement, S. D. (1991). *Executive leadership*. Arlington, VA: Cason Hall.

Jaques, E., Gibson, R. O., & Isaac, D. J. (1978). *Levels of abstraction in logic and human action*. Portsmouth, NH: Heinemann.

Katz, D., & Kahn, R. L. (1966). *The social psychology of organizations*. New York: Wiley.

Kegan, R. (1982). *The evolving self*. Cambridge, MA: Harvard University Press.

Kelly, G. A. (1955). *The psychology of personal constructs: Vol. 1. A theory of personality*. New York: Norton.

Klein, G. A. (1993). A recognition-primed decision (RPD) model of rapid decision making. In G. A. Klein, J. Orasanu, R. Calderwood, & C. E. Zsambok (Eds.), *Decision making in action: Models and methods*. Norwood, NJ: Ablex.

Kolb, D. A., & Fry, R. (1975). Towards an applied theory of experiential learning. In C. L. Cooper (Ed.), *Theories of group processes*. New York: Wiley.

Kotter, J. P. (1982). *The general managers*. New York: Free Press.

Lewis, P., & Jacobs, T. O. (1982). Individual differences in strategic leadership capacity: A constructive/developmental view. In R. L. Phillips & J. G. Hunt (Eds.), *Strategic leadership: A multiorganizational-level perspective*. Westport, CT: Quorum Books.

McGee, M. L., Jacobs, T. O., Kilcullen, R. N., & Barber, H. F. (1999). Conceptual capacity as competitive advantage: Developing leaders for the new army. In J. G. Hunt, G. E. Dodge, & L. Wong (Eds.), *Out-of-the-box leadership: Transforming the twenty-first-century army and other top-performing organizations*. Greenwich, CT: JAI Press.

Mintzberg, H. (1973). *The nature of managerial work*. New York: Harper-Collins.

Mintzberg, H. (1979). *The structuring of organizations.* Upper Saddle River, NJ: Prentice Hall

Quinn, R. E. (1988). *Beyond rational management: Mastering the paradoxes and competing demands of high performance.* San Francisco: Jossey-Bass.

Simon, H. A. (1955). A behavioral model of rational choice. *Quarterly Journal of Economics, 69,* 99–118.

Simon, H. A. (1977). *The new science of management decision* (3rd ed.). Upper Saddle River, NJ: Prentice Hall.

Stamp, G. (1988). *Longitudinal research into methods of assessing managerial potential.* Alexandria, VA: U.S. Army Research Institute.

Sternberg, R. J. (1984). Mechanisms of cognitive development: A componential approach. In R. J. Sternberg (Ed.), *Mechanisms of cognitive development.* New York: Freeman.

Streufert, S., & Swezey, R. W. (1986). *Complexity, managers, and organizations.* Orlando, FL: Academic Press.

CHAPTER 3

Sense Making, Leadership, and Mental Models

Phyllis Johnson
Kevin Daniels
Anne Huff

The key function of a strategic leader (often the chief executive officer along with his or her top team) is to decide on and implement organizational strategy (Calori, Johnson, & Sarnin, 1994). The process of strategic decision making has been variously described as rational and planned (Ansoff, 1965), an emergent process of social negotiation (Eden & Ackerman, 1998), or an accumulation of a series of political maneuvers (Hickson, Butler, Cray, Mallory, & Wilson, 1986). However, there appears to be a degree of convergence around the idea that the process of strategic decision making encompasses scanning the organization's competitive environment, analyzing that environment, forming a strategy, and implementing that strategy (Milliken & Vollrath, 1991). Decisions that are strategic, and therefore the domain of the strategic leader, have been found to occur infrequently, be nonroutine, have few precedents, involve the commitment of major resources, and usually set off a wave of smaller internal decisions (Hickson et al., 1986).

It has been argued that a general means of making sense of the environment of the strategic decision maker is to assume that the decision maker is boundedly rational, that power usually wins battles about choice, and that in terms of eventual performance outcomes, chance does appear to matter (Eisenhardt & Zbaracki,

1992). The basic message is that strategy development within organizations is important and has major implications for organizational survival. It is also complex, to a large extent unpredictable, and a slave to the variable capabilities of those involved in it.

The Cognitive Approach to Understanding Organizational Leadership

Research in the field of managerial and organizational cognition (MOC) has contributed to the advance of a psychological account of strategic organizational behavior. In the cognitive perspective, the strategic leader is seen as a sense maker (Weick, 1995). This recognition brings with it a fascinating yet researchable paradox or core puzzle that is concerned with the cornerstone of our intelligent life (Rumelhart & Norman, 1990): the human ability to attend selectively to information, disregarding unimportant stimuli in favor of those that our preexisting store of knowledge indicates as important. This ability speeds and advances our capacity to remember, reason, solve problems, and act. However, it also presents us with a potential Achilles heel, by allowing predetermined expectations to exclude contradictory, novel, and unfamiliar pieces of information from entering our analysis of the world. In 1974, Tversky and Kahneman demonstrated how such heuristic processing can lead to systematic and repeated errors in basic information processing. The paradox of strategic sense making, then, resides in the recognition that our greatest information processing asset also has the potential to become our greatest handicap.

Within the strategy process literature, the existence of systematic errors in processing strategic information has been confirmed. For example, the work of Dutton and her colleagues (Dutton, Fahey, & Narayanan, 1983; Dutton & Jackson, 1989; Dutton, Walton, & Abrahamson, 1989) has demonstrated how threats and opportunities can be consistently misinterpreted during periods of strategic issue diagnosis. In fact, our ability is vast to reject as false that which does not fit what we think to be true. Exemplified as dissonance by Festinger (1957) and the perseverance effect by Fiske and Taylor (1991), the impact of this form of shortsightedness, or strategic myopia (Abrahamson & Fomburn, 1994), can be seen in the trends of strategic drift (Johnson, 1987) and nonresponse to environmental jolts identified in the strategy literature (Kiesler & Sproull, 1982; Murmann & Tushman, 1995), as well as in other more dramatic contexts, including two fatal aircraft crashes (Weick, 1990; Hughes & Harris, 1995) and a fire disaster (Weick, 1993).

The challenge of the cognitive approach has been to explore the way in which organizational leaders process and use strategic information. More specifically, it is to understand precisely how cognition contributes to strategy development and to highlight the variables that facilitate or bound the positive and negative effects of human information processing on strategy development processes and ultimately organizational performance.

Just as the strategic task of the organizational leader has been split into the stages of scanning, analysis, choice, and implementation (Milliken & Vollrath, 1991), the cognitive demands of strategic leadership can be characterized as attention, encoding, storage, and retrieval of strategic information in order to act (Corner, Kinicki, & Keats, 1994). At the group level, that is, within the top team, there are the additional collective cognitive processes of sharing meanings, constructing interpretive frames, and socializing processes for choosing and coordinating action. It has been argued that over and above these individual and collective cognitive demands of strategic information processing, the CEO has the additional pressure of collating and making sense of the entire top team's views. This is suggested to be manifest in the greater complexity of understanding embedded within the CEO's interpretation of information gained by scanning the strategic environment (Calori, Johnson, & Sarnin, 1994). This complexity argument mirrors cognitive explorations of the architecture of expertise (King, 1995; Day & Lord, 1992).

More broadly though (that is, within the entire top team), strategic leaders have been found to employ predominantly top-down processing of information. That is, driven by naive or lay theories or models of what is or what should be (Nisbett & Ross, 1985; Abelson & Black, 1986), they selectively attend to information that is consistent with their mental models when scanning and analyzing their strategic environment. This top-down processing may be especially prevalent when, for example, managers are pressured by time, have other cognitive demands, or feel they are already familiar with the issues (Dutton, Fahey, & Narayanan, 1983).

Dutton, Walton, and Abrahamson (1989) identified four dimensions generally used to sort strategic issues:

Analytic characteristics, such as the magnitude of the issue, whether it is positive or negative, and its complexity

Content, such as whether the issues arise from political, social, economic, or technological changes in the competitive environment

Action, such as the amount of payoff or controllability associated with the issue

Source, whether internal or external

Dutton and Jackson (1987) suggested and later demonstrated (Jackson & Dutton, 1988) that over and above selective attention, strategic leaders also showed a bias toward negative or threatening information. That is, they "subjectively value the avoidance of loss and the actualization of gain differently" (Dutton & Jackson, 1987, p. 84).

A final observation at a general level is that there appears to be considerable inertia in terms of the mental models that strategic leaders use to scan, analyze, and make sense of their competitive environment (Lyles & Schwenk, 1992; Hodgkinson, 1997; Reger & Palmer, 1996). Moreover, this inertia is not easy to combat. Barr and Huff (1997) found that only multiple impacts on firm performance and multiple events appear to reduce this inertia. This converges with research demonstrating strategic leaders' inability to attend to considerable but single jolts in their competitive environment (Murmann & Tushman, 1995).

Although the basic stages of a leader's strategic task ought to be completed in sequence (environmental scanning, analysis, choice, and implementation), the speed and way in which each of these stages is executed varies. It is the extent to which strategic leaders match appropriate variations to their particular strategic context that accounts for the effectiveness of the strategy development process in organizations. For instance, Eisenhardt (1989, 1992) argues that fast decision making is appropriate in high-velocity (fast-moving) competitive environments, such as information technology industries. Fast decision making means speeding up stages, not skipping them. Eisenhardt (1992) demonstrated that fast decision makers appear to attend to equal (if not more) strategic information. They gain assistance in analyzing that information from expert counsel. During their choice stage, they do not inject speed by avoiding conflict, as may be imagined. In fact, they appear to make use of conflict to identify individuals' positions quickly and then move to build consensus.

The strategic tasks of environmental scanning and analysis (that is, attending to and interpreting information) have been the focus of attention in MOC work on strategic leadership. However, the process of choice, that is, choosing from among strategic alternatives, is also of particular interest from a cognitive point of view. When members of top teams attend to and interpret strategic information from their environment, they do so as individuals. At a very fundamental level, we process information independently from one another (Resnick, 1993). Because individual heuristics (used to filter which information to attend to and process) are likely to be diverse, the resulting interpretations of competitive environments are also likely to be diverse (Daniels, de Chernatony, & Johnson, 1994; Hodgkinson & Johnson, 1995; Johnson, Daniels, & Asch, 1998). A major cognitive element of the process of strategic choice is to mediate this potential diversity in order to achieve consensus—in effect, to make cognition collective throughout the top team. Some authors have suggested that diverse mental models represented among the top team are not problematic because consensus can be created through the use of conflict resolution techniques such as devil's advocacy and dialectical inquiry (Schwenk, 1989). Others suggest that diversity is tolerable and does not impede the achievement of consensus in strategic choice as long as the top team has certain core aspects of their cognition that are homogeneous (Porac, Thomas, & Baden-Fuller, 1989) or overlap (Langfield-Smith, 1992). This core level of collective cognition is argued to be sufficient to facilitate the construction of shared ways of interacting as a team during successive periods of strategic choice and that these shared ways of interacting (heedful interaction, Weick & Roberts, 1993; behavioral routines, Johnson, 1998) override individual cognitive diversity.

A Critique of the Cognitive Approach

An important aim of the MOC approach has been to understand the particular ways that strategists make sense of and use information about their strategic environment. In so doing, researchers have sought to understand the content and structure of managers' knowledge and how managers use this knowledge, often by using cognitive mapping methods. *Cognitive mapping* is a term used to refer to a range of methods that seek to assess and re-represent an individual's mental model of a particular target subject (see Huff, 1990, for a discussion of methods of mapping strategic thought). Early research agendas were outlined in highly influential texts by Gioia and Sims (1989) and Huff (1990). Huff (1990) identified a number of exciting contributions that MOC research could make to the understanding of an organizational leader's strategic behavior. These included uncovering the CEO's corporate vision, interpreting the competitive environment, and examining the resulting interaction among the top management team. Stubbart and Ramaprasad (1990) focused on the notion of expertise in information processing at both the individual (that is, CEO) level and the collective institutional level as sources of competitive advantage.

The bias (a reflection of the developing nature of the field) in these agendas was toward how strategic leaders make sense of their competitive world as opposed to how they apply that knowledge. In fact, as Huff noted in later commentaries on the future of MOC (Fiol & Huff, 1992; Huff, 1997), the initial excitement with possible applications led to a rush to develop mapping methods, the emergence of too many similar concepts, and little empirical data. The result has been a vast array of research that in many ways is disparate and uncoupled and lacks a general theoretical framework for classification.

Weick (1985) has argued that the most useful aspect of cognitive interpretations of behavior in organizations (most frequently operationalized using cognitive maps) is its ability to tap into the processual—that is, that the maps purporting to represent strategists' mental models or cognitive schema that strategic leaders create of their world impose enough meaning on this highly complex environment to allow them to act. However, it is this animation, not the map or mental model per se, that actually imposes meaning and helps us make sense of the role of strategic leadership. In other words, the focus of attention in MOC ought to be on the interaction between thinking and behaving in strategy development. Consequently, to restrict research to mapping how managers make sense of their competitive worlds (described as content portraits by Walsh, 1995) and to develop elegant methods for doing so is to ignore the most important contribution that could made by MOC research.

Walsh's (1995) review of this research marked the beginning of a new phase of work. He demonstrated the lack of consistency that there had been on the nature of MOC. For example, he illustrated the variety of terms that had been used to describe mental models (well over seventy). He also helped to draw the field together and generate a coherent future agenda. He found a historical preference for individual-level content-based work, which he referred to as portraits of the contents of a manager's mental model regarding a specific target subject. He made four major proposals for future MOC work. First, he called for a moratorium on content portraits. He argued that their role as a first step in exploring the potential of the cognitive approach in management research is now clearly redundant because we know enough of the basics to move on to more challenging questions.[1] Second, he, along with many others (including Weick & Roberts, 1993, and Klimoski & Mohammed, 1994), called for MOC research to become more social and to move beyond individual minds. Weick makes the point effectively:

> Discussions of collective mental processes have been rare, despite the fact that people claim to be studying social cognition. The preoccupation with individual cognition has left organizational theorists ill-equipped to do much more with the so called cognitive revolution than apply it to organizations one brain at a time [Weick & Roberts, 1993, p. 358].

However, a move into the collective domain would demand simultaneous interest in individuals and collectives, as well as attention to broader social phenomena. This complexity is presumably a significant contributory factor in the paucity of work that moves beyond the individual mind.

The third and final point that Walsh makes is to isolate one particular area of the social cognition research that he sees as particularly promising. That is the emotional or affective aspect of the relationship between cognition and behavior within the organization. He describes this as one of the most important new directions the field can take. The role of emotion can have a huge impact on the decisions people make and the ways they choose to act, but to date many MOC researchers appear to have been reluctant to address emotions.

Differences Between MOC and Cognitive Science

The criticisms leveled at the MOC literature here are not necessarily universal criticisms that can be applied to cognitive psychology as a whole. For example, cognitive science, the discipline on which the MOC field was originally based, is not concerned centrally with overt behavior. Cognitive scientists make it clear that cognition is a legitimate topic in its own right (Anderson, 1985). Cognitive science in its pure form is really the science of how individuals develop knowledge, and for cognitive scientists behavior is operationalized as information search, processing, transfer to long-term memory, and so on—hence, the usefulness of the computational metaphor (Johnson-Laird, 1988). Other branches of psychology (such as social cognition) are concerned with overt behavior, but initially very few MOC researchers claimed to pin their work back into social cognition, referring instead to cognitive science.

Consequently, it is not valid to criticize cognitive science for not focusing on behavior per se. It may be more appropriate to criticize MOC research that has not been clear about exactly where it is basing itself in relation to the broad field of cognitive psychology (Huff, 1997) and the concomitant assumptions of taking that position. For instance, if it were to be assumed that cognition is a legitimate topic in its own right, then the study of cognition in the context of strategy development could also be legitimately operationalized as primarily cognitive activity, that is, as exploring an individual's own strategic planning and visioning. However, strategy development is much more than this, being a social as well as cognitive process. Consequently, any cognitive approach to strategic management also needs to have a strong behavioral element. In turn, this ought to lead to a greater concern with social cognition than cognitive science. Therefore, to come full circle, Walsh's criticism about the lack of focus on behavior could be valid when leveled at MOC work that lays claim to approximating cognitive science (by heavily citing cognitive science work and ignoring social cognition), but not cognitive psychology in general.

In addition, as Huff (1997) argued, the very fact that MOC is not cognitive science can open up new and different avenues of exploration useful to the management and leadership contexts. For instance, exploring the consequences for overt behavior of forgetting, misunderstanding, intuition, and serendipity may all have their place in an appreciation of the relationship between cognition and strategic leadership. However, these tend not to be central considerations (especially in terms of behavioral consequences) of cognitive scientists.

Cognition and Behavior in the Top Team Environment

We now turn to exploring the particular variables that may mediate the relationship between cognition and behavior in the top management team—in other words, those factors that animate leaders' mental models (Weick, 1985).

The Group Environment

It seems generally to be accepted that the aspect of leaders' cognition that is of interest is its animation: cognition in action. In terms of the strategy development process, it is highly unusual for decisions to be made in isolation. The strategy development process is designed and legislated (see the discussion of the legal responsibilities of directorship in Lorsch & McIver, 1989) to happen in concert among first the top team and then the corporate board. Consequently, the dynamics associated with a group environment are central to understanding the relationship between cognition and leadership behavior.

Group membership serves an important affective function in that it fulfills one of our basic desires and needs: to be included and feel affection (McClure, 1990). Individuals may act in ways that in terms of their own views of a particular issue (in the case of organizational leaders, a strategic issue) is counterintuitive so that they satisfy these basic desires to conform to group expectations. Simply being part of a group can significantly change an individual's normal pattern of behavior. Consider behavior in a crowd. In crowds, a person's sense of individuality and control of a situation can rapidly deteriorate; the person can be quite literally dragged along, finding it almost impossible to move in a different direction from the movement or opinion of the crowd. Zimbardo's (1970) prison experiments vividly demonstrated individuals' propensity to follow a pattern of extreme behavior that has been established among strangers.

A further example of individuals in groups acting outside the bounds of the explanations of the cognitive perspective alone is the phenomenon of social loafing (Williams, Harkins, & Latane, 1979), that is, that away from the gaze of responsibility, individuals will loaf (not contribute their maximum effort). In her empirical study of the emergence of collective cognition in small work groups in a French factory, Allard-Poesi (1997) found that social loafing interfered with the link between collective believing and collective behaving: some group members did not believe in the consensus but could not be bothered to contribute to change it. Mulvey, Vega, and Elass (1996) discuss several instances where "team mates raise the white flag" and withdraw their effort and attention from the group. Importantly, Williams and others (1979) stressed that social loafing is not the same concept as learned helplessness in the face of a dominant coalition; it is a distinct form of avoidance of behaving and contributing at all.

Finally, moving away from elements of group dynamics—that is, changes in behavior caused by the group context—it may be unreasonable to expect that all individuals will demonstrate consistency between what they think and how they behave all of the time. First, there is variability among individuals. In one context, a person may feel at liberty to act in line with his or her beliefs, whereas in another he or she may not. This is, in effect, a state- or context-dependent variability found among situations. However, there is also the possibility of trait interindividual variability in the relatedness of thinking and behaving. For example, some people have a higher propensity to express their ideas and opinions than others simply because their cognitive life has a more external orientation (they are extroverts). Others have a stronger tendency toward cognitive self-sufficiency, doing their thinking and feeling without the need for verbalization and external feedback or referencing (these are the introverts). Again, a vast amount of empirical data demonstrates differences in behavioral preference based on personality type (see Hampson, 1999, for a review).

The Top Team Environment

Those who have looked exclusively at top teams and boards of directors have found that senior managers seem especially prone to act in a fashion that is not reflective of their own views. Garratt's (1996) recent work explored the reasons that directors seem to be reticent to question and raise contentious issues that may disturb the equilibrium in their top team. These include the intense pressure to get things right, which promotes a powerful fear of failure and a determination not to ask for help (perhaps especially because of the public nature, long-term and far-reaching consequences, and usually irreversible nature of such decisions). In addition, the personal perquisites (a luxury company car, share options, salary, and first-class travel, for instance) combine to make their loss far too risky. And, finally, new directors are often told that they will pick things up as they go along and to accept the status quo; even boards in crisis appear to demand such compliance. These pressures can result in a level of group performance that is lower in top teams compared to other groups in the organization (Katzenbach, 1997).

In addition to the pressure of working at the top of an organization, power and political influence are added pressures that may go some considerable way to mediating the relationship between leaders' cognition and their behavior in the top team environment. Power has been interpreted in several ways: as an individual characteristic, an interpersonal construct, a commodity, and a philosophical construct (Cavanaugh, 1984). In terms of this research, it is the second interpretation that is important: power as an interpersonal construct. French and Raven (1959) produced a classification of five types of interpersonal power—reward power, coercive power, legitimate power, referent power, and expert power—to which Raven (1965) added information power. But perhaps the most important contribution that French and Raven made was to stress that influence is exerted only when A recognizes that he or she is influenced by B. Emerson (1962) extended this by pointing out that B too has to recognize that A is allowing himself or herself to be influenced and consequently act to maintain the ability to influence A. Emerson described this reciprocity a "tie of mutual dependence" (p. 32). These ties of mutual dependence could be expected to affect the relationships among individual cognition, collective cognition, and behavior in the top management team. Walsh, Henderson, and Deighton (1988) have argued that power affects the consensus achieved by a group, and in so doing represses the views of the least powerful members.

Other authors interested in power have focused on the skills of those employing it (Mangham, 1986). An appreciation of the use of power leads to political behavior—the mechanisms that individuals use to employ their influence. In their discussion of political behavior in organizations, Kakabadse and Parker (1984) pointed out the significant definitional problems associated with the concept of political behavior and that it is frequently perceived of extremely negatively instead of as a normal activity in organizational life. They argue that if political behavior is seen as the application of tactics and strategies of gamesmanship, then all behavior in organizations has the potential to be political.

In the top management team environment, Pettigrew and McNulty (1995) argue that nonexecutive directors have to draw on both will and political skill to bring their formal influence to bear. Brass and Burkhardt (1993) also found that the use of power in top management teams is dependent not only on position power but on the skilled application of it. Therefore, just as power can mediate the relationship between cognition and behavior, so too can the political skills that are employed to exert influence. In addition to the interpretation of political behavior as a mechanism to exert influence, political behavior can be interpreted in terms of self-advancement and protection. While some authors view senior managers as altruistic stewards of their organization's resources (Donaldson 1990a, 1990b; Kay & Silberston, 1995), operating without the motive of self-interest, others maintain a more Machiavellian view that once an individual has reached the top of an organization, it is a natural (and not necessarily negative) instinct to wish to seek to maintain that position (Garratt, 1996). Whatever the view of the characteristics of those who achieve progression to senior management, it is reasonable to assume that political behavior (interpreted as the advancement of one's own agenda) will have an impact on the relationship between cognition and behavior in the top management team.

Affect and Strategic Information Processing

Affect, an area Walsh (1995) highlighted as neglected by the MOC field, is the general term for emotions and moods. It influences and is influenced by cognitive and social processes (Parkinson, 1995). We might then expect affect to influence both cognitive and social processes of strategic management (Daniels, 1999). Although there has been little research on the role of affect in strategic management (but see Daniels, 1998), there is sufficient evidence to outline some general expectations. This evidence comes from laboratory studies and field research from other areas of organizational research.

Affect may influence managers' information processing during strategic decisions by influencing the information from the environment that is attended to or the recall processes involved in the top-down information processing that characterizes much top management cognition (Walsh, 1995). Laboratory evidence supports the existence of both paths (Mathews, 1993). Much of this research has examined the role of the negative affects of anxiety and sadness on the allocation of attention to stimuli and the recall of information (see Dalgleish & Watts, 1990; MacCleod, 1991; Mathews, 1993; Williams, Watts, MacLeod, & Mathews, 1997). The evidence indicates that anxiety acts directly on the processes of attention allocation, so that anxious individuals attend more to the threatening or negative aspects of a given situation (Dalgleish & Watts, 1990; MacCleod, 1991; Mathews, 1993). Sadness has been found to lead to recall of more negative information (Dalgleish & Watts, 1990; Matt, Vazquez, & Campbell, 1992, Mathews, 1993; Hartlage, Alloy, Vazquez, & Dykman, 1993).

Organizational research too has looked at the relationships between affect and information processing. The majority of these studies have examined the relationships between the perceived stressfulness of the immediate organizational environment and negative affectivity, a latent trait representing a pervasive cross-situational tendency to experience the negative emotions of anxiety and sadness (Watson & Clark, 1984; Watson & Tellegen, 1985). Spector and O'Connell (1994) found that negative affectivity was associated with subsequent reports of greater role ambiguity, role conflict, job constraints, and interpersonal conflict at work in a sample of recent graduates. Other organizational studies have examined relationships between situational (rather than dispositional) negative affect and appraisals of the immediate work environment. These longitudinal studies too have found that negative affect leads to subsequent self-reports of negative working environments (Wolpin, Burke, & Greenglass 1991; Firth-Cozens & Hardy, 1992; Daniels & Guppy, 1997).

One exploratory cross-sectional study has sought to generalize these findings to the area of strategic management by examining the relationship between negative affectivity and perceptions of the strategic environment (Daniels, 1998). In a small, heterogeneous sample of managers ($n = 59$), Daniels found significant relationships between negative affectivity and perceptions of poor organizational performance and greater industry complexity. In a larger heterogeneous sample of managers ($n = 272$), Daniels replicated these results and also found significant relationships among perceived industry decline, perceived industry competitiveness, and negative affectivity.

Together, these laboratory and field studies indicate that affect can have a significant effect on cognition in organizational contexts. More specifically, the Daniels study indicates that affect influences how managers process information about the strategic environment. One conclusion from this study might be that managers with high negative affect may consider strategies that reflect pessimistic interpretations of the strategic environment to be more appropriate. Conversely, managers with low negative affect, biased toward perceiving the positive aspects of the strategic environment, may consider strategies that reflect optimistic interpretations of organizational and industry activity to be appropriate.

Affects other than anxiety and sadness may also influence information processing. Daniels (1999) discusses how anger may influence managers to allocate more resources to current strategies or reposition strategies against perceived sources of frustration such as competitors; how positive affect may lead managers to consider initiating radical strategic change; and how fatigue depletes cognitive resources, perhaps making managers less likely to consider fully all strategic options toward the end of lengthy top team meetings.

Looking specifically at affect in the team environment, the social element of affect may also make more complex the relationships among affect, cognition, and behavior of senior managers. Daniels (1999) considers the affective tone of the top team to be the most likely process through which affect can influence social processes in the top team. Insofar as there is consistency of affect within groups (George, 1990), then others' affect may influence an individual manager's information processing, and hence the strategic options considered appropriate. The process of emotion contagion may be relevant here. This is where one person's affective state induces that state in another by unconscious signals (Hatfield, Cacioppo, & Rapson, 1992). In turn, this may influence that person's information processing.

A common affective state spread by emotional contagion may then lead to information processing that is biased collectively toward or away from negative information. This may lead to convergence among individual managers in interpretations of the strategic environment. For example, a common state of negative affect may lead a management team collectively to attend closely to a new but small entrant into the industry, recall that in the past their own company was slow to respond to the competitive moves of other new entrants, or interpret the market positioning of the entrant as a direct competitive threat to their own market position.

Research into the cognitive and social aspects of affect in top teams is only just beginning. To date, any predictions must be speculative and informed by research in other areas of psychology. Nevertheless, the strength of this other evidence and the pervasiveness of emotional experience in organizations (Fineman, 1993) indicate that affect can have an important influence on how senior managers, as individuals and groups, process and use information about their strategic environments.

Conclusion

This chapter has discussed aspects of the MOC field and its development that are relevant to the topic of organizational leadership and examined a range of issues that can mediate the relationship between cognition and behavior in the top team environment.

In discussing the past, present, and future agendas of the MOC field, we have noted that MOC researchers have moved beyond simply reporting the contents and structure of a manager's knowledge related to specific organizational issues. The agenda, initially expressed by Weick in 1985, has now become to appreciate the animation of managers' and, in particular, organizational leaders' knowledge. This shift of focus toward cognition in action presents the MOC field with the challenge of looking at behavior and factors that mediate the relationship between cognition and behavior. Developments have been made with this new agenda (Weick & Roberts, 1993; Allard-Poesi, 1995; Johnson, 1998; Tomicic, 1998), but it has yet to be accepted as the dominant paradigm. There is still a considerable amount of portrait work being presented.

In illustrating the range of variables that can mediate the relationship between cognition and action, we discussed general issues relating to the group environment and the more specific issues of high pressure and risk, power and political influence, and affect in the top team environment. We illustrated that the mediation of the relationship between thinking and behaving, that is, the animation of cognition, is especially great in the top team environment. Empirical evidence also suggests this to be the case (Johnson, 1998). Such findings seem to suggest that our understanding of organizational leadership from a cognitive perspective needs to be supplemented by a broader understanding of the pressures and relational dynamics of the leader's task in order to put cognition into its social and affective context and give it the animation that Weick described as the major contribution of the MOC perspective.

The complexity and dynamic nature of top team cognition and action mean that research methods are required that can capture power dynamics, affective change, and cognition in action in real situations and real time. In-depth ethnographic and case methods may provide one route for developing research along these lines (Weick & Roberts, 1993, Johnson, 1998), although more structured longitudinal diary methods might also capture the relationships between senior managers' behavior, affect, and cognition. The complexity and relatively nascent nature of the subject areas preclude firm recommendations on what constitutes effective top team cognition in action, although from our discussion, we may suggest issues of which senior managers should be aware:

• Mental models, influenced by past functional and other management experience, can hasten decision making but can also lead to misdiagnosis of strategic issues. Senior managers should be aware that simple top-down processing may be effective only when quick decisions are needed in stable conditions and that well-considered judgments, aided by thorough strategic analysis, should be pursued wherever possible to less complex and dynamic environments (Daniels & Henry, 1998). Senior managers should also be aware that time pressures, information overload, and affect can encourage using top-down processing (Dutton, 1993; Daniels, 1998; Sparrow, 1999), and that they should develop the discipline to ask whether other demands or their moods are forcing them to decide and act too quickly.

• Where quick decisions are needed in dynamic environments, the most successful managers may be the ones who are most insightful—those who have the cognitive flexibility to reconfigure mental models to suit new and changing circumstances (Daniels & Henry, 1998). Nevertheless, insight might be encouraged by removing management teams from everyday surroundings (for strategic retreats) or using external consultants to surface and challenge assumptions and received mental models (Daniels & Henry, 1998). Managers may even be able to surface and challenge their own assumptions, perhaps through the use of the cognitive mapping techniques (Huff, 1990) developed by researchers in the MOC field (see Johnson & Johnson, forthcoming, for a case study account of such self-reflection).

• Social dynamics and affective dynamics in the management team can be used to promote open discussion to surface convergence and divergence of views. It may be fruitful to seek divergence during the earlier stages of decision making (Eisenhardt, 1992), so that any later consensus is based on reasoned opinion rather than shallow discussion of issues where the top team members have convergent views in any case (Larson, Christensen, Abbott, & Franz,

1996). This suggests making strategic decision making a more interactive process in which dissenting views are encouraged (Quinn, 1980). Teams of managers who base decision making solely on areas of cognitive convergence may risk acting on "impoverished views of the world" (Weick, 1979, p. 68).

These suggestions raise questions for the assessment, selection, and development of top teams. Is it possible to assess the strategic competencies of creativity, flexibility, social, and emotional awareness? If so, can these competencies be developed, or is it more sensible to select for them?

Note

1. For instance, we know that managers simplify their information environment, and we know that individual differences in heuristic processing (Tversky & Kahneman, 1974) can lead to individual differences in knowledge structures created by closely associating managers (Hodgkinson & Johnson, 1995). Conversely, we know that individuals who associate with each other can share common elements of understanding (Allard-Poesi, 1997; Fiol, 1994; Weick & Roberts, 1993; Larson & Christensen, 1993; Langfield-Smith, 1992), and the antecedents of this cognitive similarity and diversity would seem to include some or all of the following: functional background (Bowman & Daniels, 1995; Schilit & Paine, 1987), management level (Johnson, Daniels, & Asch, 1998), organizational membership (Daniels, de Chernatony, & Johnson, 1994), degree of expertise (Day & Lord, 1992; Lurgio & Carroll, 1985; King, 1995; Schoenfeld & Herrmann, 1982), and nationality (Calori, Lubatkin, & Very, 1998; Calori, Johnson, & Sarnin, 1992; Schneider & de Meyer, 1991; Shaw, 1990).

References

Abelson, R. P., & Black, J. B. (1986). Introduction. In J. A. Galambos, R. P. Abelson, & J. B. Black (Eds.), *Knowledge structures*. Mahwah, NJ: Erlbaum.

Abrahamson, E. C., & Fomburn, C. (1994). Macro cultures: Determinants and consequences. *Academy of Management Review, 19,* 728–755.

Allard-Poesi, F. (1997, September). *Understanding collective representations in working groups: A comparison of three case studies.* Paper presented at the Fifth International Workshop on Managerial and Organizational Cognition, Brussels, Belgium.

Anderson, J. R. (1985). *Cognitive psychology and its implications* (2nd ed.). Pittsburgh, PA: Carnegie Mellon University.

Ansoff, I. (1965). *Corporate strategy.* New York: McGraw-Hill.

Barr, P. S., & Huff, A. S. (1997). Seeing isn't believing: Understanding diversity in the timing of strategic response. *Journal of Management Studies, 34,* 337–370.

Bowman, C., & Daniels, K. (1995). The influence of functional experience on perceptions of strategic priorities. *British Journal of Management, 6,* 157–168.

Brass, D. J., & Burkhardt, M. E. (1993). Potential power and power use: An investigation of structure and behavior. *Academy of Management Journal, 36,* 441–470.

Calori, R., Johnson, G., & Sarnin, P. (1992). French and British top managers' understanding of the structure and the dynamics of their industries: A cognitive analysis and comparison. *British Journal of Management, 3,* 61–78.

Calori, R., Johnson G., & Sarnin, P. (1994). CEOs' cognitive maps and the scope of the organization. *Strategic Management Journal, 15,* 437–457.

Calori, R., Lubatkin, M., & Very, P. (1998). The development of national collective knowledge in management. In C. Eden & J. C. Spender (Eds.), *Managerial and organizational cognition.* Thousand Oaks, CA: Sage.

Cavanaugh, M. S. (1984). A typology of social power. In A. Kakabadse & C. Parker (Eds.), *Power, politics, and organizations.* New York: Wiley.

Corner, P., Kinicki, A. J., & Keats, B. W. (1994). Integrating organizational and individual processing perspectives on choice. *Organization Science, 5,* 294–308.

Dalgleish, T., & Watts, F. N. (1990). Biases of attention and memory in disorders of anxiety and depression. *Clinical Psychology Review, 10,* 589–604.

Daniels, K. (1998). Toward integrating emotions into strategic management research: Trait affect and the perception of the strategic environment. *British Journal of Management, 9,* 163–168.

Daniels, K. (1999). Emotion and strategic decision making. *Psychologist, 12,* 24–28.

Daniels, K., de Chernatony, L., & Johnson, G. (1994). Differences in cognitions of competition. *British Journal of Management, 5,* 21–29.

Daniels, K., & Guppy, A. (1997). Stressors, locus of control, and social support as consequences of psychological well-being. *Journal of Occupational Health Psychology, 2,* 156–174.

Daniels, K., & Henry, J. (1998). Strategy: A cognitive perspective. In S. Segal-Horn (Ed.), *Readings on strategy.* New York: Macmillan.

Day, D. V., & Lord, R. G. (1992). Expertise and problem categorization: The role of expert processing in organization sense-making. *Journal of Management Studies, 29,* 35–47.

Donaldson, L. (1990a). The ethereal hand: Organizational economics and management theory. *Academy of Management Review, 15,* 369–381.

Donaldson, L. (1990b). A rational basis for criticisms of organizational economics: A reply to Barney. *Academy of Management Review, 15,* 394–401.

Dutton, J. E. (1993). Interpretations on automatic: A different view of strategic issue diagnosis. *Journal of Management Studies, 30,* 339–357.

Dutton, J. E., Fahey, L., & Narayanan, V. K. (1983). Understanding strategic issue diagnosis. *Strategic Management Journal, 14,* 307–323.

Dutton, J. E., & Jackson, S. (1987). Categorizing strategic issues: Links to organizational action. *Academy of Management Review, 12,* 76–90.

Dutton J. E., Walton, E. J., & Abrahamson, E. (1989). Important dimensions of strategic issues: Separating the wheat from the chaff. *Journal of Management Studies, 26,* 379–396.

Eden, C., & Ackerman, F. (1998). *Making strategy: The journey of strategic management.* London: Sage.

Eisenhardt, K. M. (1989). Making fast strategic decisions in high-velocity environments. *Academy of Management Journal, 32,* 543–576.

Eisenhardt, K. M. (1992). Speed and strategic choice: Accelerating decision making. *Planning Review, 20,* 30–34.

Eisenhardt, K. M., & Zbaracki, M. J. (1992). Strategic decision making. *Strategic Management Journal, 13,* 17–37.

Emerson, R. M. (1962). Power-dependency relations. *American Sociological Review, 27,* 31–41.

Festinger, L. (1957). *A theory of cognitive dissonance.* Stanford, CA: Stanford University Press.

Fineman, S. (Ed.). (1993). *Emotion in organizations.* Thousand Oaks, CA: Sage.

Fiol, M. (1994). Consensus, diversity, and learning in organizations. *Organization Science, 5,* 403–420.

Fiol, M., & Huff, A. S. (1992). Maps for managers: Where are we? Where do we go from here? *Journal of Management Studies, 29,* 267–285.

Firth-Cozens, J., & Hardy, G. E. (1992). Occupational stress, clinical treatment, and changes in job perceptions. *Journal of Occupational and Organizational Psychology, 65,* 81–88.

Fiske S. T., & Taylor, S. E. (1991). *Social cognition.* New York: McGraw-Hill.

French, J.R.B., Jr., & Raven, B. (1959). The bases of social power. In D. Cartwright (Ed.), *Studies in social power.* Ann Arbor: University of Michigan Press.

Garratt, B. (1996). *The fish rots from the head: The crisis in our boardrooms.* New York: HarperCollins.

George, J. M. (1990). Personality, affect, and behavior in groups. *Journal of Applied Psychology, 75,* 107–116.

Gioia, D. A., & Sims, H. P. (1986). *The thinking organization: Dynamics of organizational social cognition.* San Francisco: Jossey-Bass.

Hampson, S. (1999). State of the art: Personality. *Psychologist, 12,* 284–288.

Hartlage, S., Alloy, L. B., Vazquez, C., & Dykman, B. (1993). Automatic and effortful processing in depression. *Psychological Bulletin, 113,* 247–278.

Hatfield, E., Cacioppo, J. T., & Rapson, R. (1992). Primitive emotional contagion. In M. S. Clark (Ed.), *Review of personality and social psychology: Vol. 14. Emotion and social behavior.* Thousand Oaks, CA: Sage.

Hickson, D. J., Butler, R. J., Cray, D., Mallory, G., & Wilson, D. C. (1986). *Top decisions: Strategic decision making in organizations.* Cambridge, MA: Blackwell.

Hodgkinson, G. (1997). Cognitive inertia in a turbulent market: The case of U.K. residential estate agents. *Journal of Management Studies, 34,* 921–947.

Hodgkinson, G., & Johnson, G. (1995). Exploring the mental models of competitive strategists: The case for a processual approach. *Journal of Management Studies, 31,* 525–551.

Huff, A. S. (Ed.). (1990). *Mapping strategic thought.* New York: Wiley.

Huff, A. S. (1997). A current and future agenda for cognitive research in organizations. *Journal of Management Studies, 34,* 947–952.

Hughes, P., & Harris, D. (1995). *Illustration of confirmatory bias in high-risk complex information processing.* Unpublished teaching case, Cranfield School of Management, Bedfordshire, U.K.

Jackson, S. E., & Dutton, J. E. (1988). Discerning threats and opportunities. *Administrative Science Quarterly, 33,* 370–387.

Johnson, G. N. (1987). *Strategic change and the management process.* Cambridge, MA: Blackwell.

Johnson, P. (1998). *A study of cognition and behavior in top management team interaction.* Unpublished doctoral dissertation, Cranfield University, Bedfordshire, U.K.

Johnson, P., Daniels, K., & Asch, R. (1998). Mental models of competition. In C. Eden & J. C. Spender (Eds.), *Managerial and organizational cognition: Theory, methods, and research.* Thousand Oaks, CA: Sage.

Johnson, P., & Johnson, G. (forthcoming). Facilitating group cognitive mapping. In A. S. Huff & M. Jenkins (Eds.), *Mapping strategy.* Thousand Oaks, CA: Sage.

Johnson-Laird, P. N. (1988). *The computer and the mind.* London: Fontana Press.

Kakabadse, A., & Parker, C. (1984). Toward a theory of political behavior in organizations. In A. Kakabadse & C. Parker (Eds.), *Power, politics, and organizations*. New York: Wiley.

Katzenbach, J. (1997, November). The myth of the top management team. *Harvard Business Review*, pp. 83–91.

Kay, J., & Silberston, A. (1995, August). Corporate governance. *National Institute Economic Review*, pp. 84–95.

King, I. W. (1995, July). *The potential of expertise in organizations*. Paper presented at the European Group Organisational Scholars conference, Istanbul.

Kiesler, S., & Sproull, L. (1982). Managerial response to changing environments: Perspective on problem sensing from social cognition. *Administrative Science Quarterly, 27*, 548–570.

Klimoski, R. J., & Mohammed, S. (1994). Team mental model: Construct or metaphor? *Journal of Management, 20*, 403-437.

Langfield-Smith, K. (1992). Exploring the need for a shared cognitive map. *Journal of Management Studies, 29*, 349–367.

Larson, J. R., Jr., & Christensen, C. (1993). Groups as problem-solving units: Toward a new meaning of social cognition. *British Journal of Social Psychology, 32*, 5–30.

Larson, J. R., Jr., Christensen, C., Abbott, A. S., & Franz, T. M. (1996). Diagnosing groups: Charting the flow of information in medical decision-making teams. *Journal of Personality and Social Psychology, 71*, 315–330.

Lorsch, J. W., & McIver, E. A. (1989). *Pawns or potentates? A study of corporate governance*. Boston: Harvard Business School Press.

Lurgio, A. J., & Carroll, J. S. (1985). Probation officers' schemata of offenders: Content, development, and impact on treatment decisions. *Journal of Personality and Social Psychology, 48*, 1112–1126.

Lyles, M. A., & Schwenk, C. R. (1992). Top management, strategy, and organizational knowledge structures. *Journal of Management Studies, 29*, 153–174.

MacCleod, C. (1991). Clinical anxiety and the selective encoding of threatening information. *International Review of Psychiatry, 3*, 279–292.

Mangham, I. (1986). *Power and performance in organizations*. Cambridge, MA: Blackwell.

Mathews, A. (1993). Biases in processing emotional information. *Psychologist, 6*, 493–499.

Matt, G. E., Vazquez, C., & Campbell, W. K. (1992). Mood-congruent recall of affectively toned stimuli: A meta-analytic review. *Clinical Psychology Review, 12*, 227–255.

McClure, B. A. (1990). The group mind: Generative and regressive groups. *Journal for Specialists in Group Work, 15*, 159–170.

Milliken, F. J., & Vollrath, D. A. (1991). Strategic decision-making tasks and group effectiveness: Insights from theory and research on small group performance. *Human Relations, 44*, 1229–1253.

Mulvey, P. W., Vega, J. F., & Elass, P. M. (1996). When team-mates raise the white flag. *Academy of Management Executive, 10*, 40–50.

Murmann, J. P., & Tushman, M. L. (1995). *The effects of executive team characteristics and organizational context on organization responsiveness to environmental jolts.* Paper presented at the Academy of Management Conference, Vancouver, Canada.

Nisbett, R. E., & Ross, L. (1985). *Human inference: Strategies and shortcomings of social judgment.* Upper Saddle River, NJ: Prentice Hall.

Parkinson, B. (1995). *Ideas and realities of emotion.* New York: Routledge.

Pettigrew, A. M., & McNulty, T. (1995). Power and influence in and around the board room. *Human Relations, 48*, 845–873.

Porac, J., Thomas, H., & Baden-Fuller, C. (1989). Competitive groups as cognitive communities: The case of the Scottish Knitwear Manufacturers. *Journal of Management Studies, 26.*

Quinn, J. B. (1980). *Strategies for change.* Burr Ridge, IL: Irwin.

Raven, B. H. (1965). Social influence and power. In I. D. Steiner & M. Fishbein (Eds.), *Current studies in social psychology.* Austin, TX: Holt, Rinehart and Winston.

Reger, R. K., & Palmer, T. B. (1996). Managerial categorization of competitors: Using old maps to navigate new environments. *Organization Science, 7*, 22–39.

Resnick, L. B. (1993). Shared cognition: Thinking as social practice. In L. B. Resnick, J. M. Levine, & S. D. Teasley (Eds.), *Perspectives on socially shared cognition.* Washington, DC: American Psychological Association.

Rumelhart, D. E., & Norman, D. A. (1990). Representation of knowledge. In A. M. Aitkenhead & J. M. Slack (Eds.), *Issues in cognitive modeling.* Mahwah, NJ: Erlbaum/Open University Press

Schilit, W. K., & Paine, F. T. (1987). An examination of the underlying dynamics of strategic decisions subject to upward influence activity. *Journal of Management Studies, 24*, 161–187.

Schoenfeld, A. H., & Herrmann, D. J. (1982). Problem perception and knowledge structure in expert and novice mathematical problem solvers. *Journal of Experimental Psychology, 8*, 484–494.

Schwenk, C. (1989). Research notes and communications: A meta-analysis on the comparative effectiveness of devil's advocacy and dialectical inquiry. *Strategic Management Journal, 10*, 303–306.

Shaw, J. B. (1990). A cognitive categorization model for the study of inter-cultural management. *Academy of Management Review, 15,* 626–645.

Sparrow, P. S. (1999). Strategy and cognition: Understanding the role of management knowledge structures, organizational memory, and in-formation overload. *Creativity and Innovation Management, 8,* 140–148.

Spector, P. E., & O'Connell, B. J. (1994). The contribution of personality traits, negative affectivity, locus of control, and type A to subsequent reports of job stressors and job strains. *Journal of Occupational and Organizational Psychology, 67,* 1–12.

Stubbart, C., & Ramaprasad, A. (1990). Comments on the empirical ar-ticles and recommendations for future research. In A. S. Huff (Ed.), *Mapping strategic thought.* New York: Wiley.

Tomicic, M. (1998). *A top team's cognitive structure: Homogeneity, heterogene-ity, and change* [in Swedish]. Unpublished master's thesis, Linköping University, Sweden.

Tversky, A. T., & Kahneman, D. (1974). Judgments under uncertainty heuristics and biases. *Science, 185,* 1124–1131.

Walsh, J. P. (1995). Managerial and organizational cognition: Notes from a trip down memory lane. *Organization Science, 6,* 280–321.

Walsh, J. P., Henderson, C. M., & Deighton, J. (1988). Negotiated belief structures and decision performance: An empirical investigation. *Organizational Behavior and Decision Processes, 42,* 194–216.

Watson, D., & Clark, L. A. (1984). Negative affectivity: The disposition to experience aversive emotional states. *Psychological Bulletin, 96,* 465–490.

Watson, D., & Tellegen, A. (1985). Toward a consensual structure of mood. *Psychological Bulletin, 98,* 219–235.

Weick, K. E. (1979). Cognitive processes in organizations. In B. M. Staw (Ed.), *Research in organizational behavior* (Vol. 1). Greenwich, CT: JAI Press

Weick, K. E. (1985). Sources of order in underorganized systems: Themes in recent organizational theory. In Y. S. Lincoln (Ed.), *Organiza-tional theory and inquiry.* Thousand Oaks, CA: Sage.

Weick, K. E. (1990). The vulnerable system: An analysis of the Tenerife air disaster. *Journal of Management, 16,* 571–593.

Weick, K. E. (1993). The collapse of sensemaking in organizations: The Mann Gulch disaster. *Administrative Science Quarterly, 38,* 628–652.

Weick, K. E (1995). *Sensemaking in organizations.* Thousand Oaks, CA: Sage.

Weick, K. E., & Roberts, K. H. (1993). Collective mind in organizations: Heedful interrelating on flight decks. *Administrative Science Quar-terly, 38,* 357–381.

Williams, J.M.G., Watts, F. N., MacLeod, C., & Mathews, A. (1997). *Cognitive psychology and emotional disorders* (2nd ed.). New York: Wiley.

Williams, K., Harkins, S. G., & Latane, B. (1979). Many hands make light the work: The cause and consequences of social loafing. *Journal of Personality and Social Psychology, 37,* 822–832.

Wolpin, J., Burke, R. J., & Greenglass, E. R. (1991). Is job satisfaction an antecedent or a consequence of psychological burnout? *Human Relations, 44,* 193–209.

Zimbardo, S. (1970). The human choice: Individuation, reason, and order versus de-individuation, impulse, and chaos. In W. J. Arnold & D. Levine (Eds.), *Nebraska Symposium on Motivation* (Vol. 16). Lincoln: University of Nebraska Press.

CHAPTER 4

Behavioral Complexity and Social Intelligence

How Executive Leaders Use Stakeholders to Form a Systems Perspective

Robert Hooijberg
Marguerite Schneider

Researchers have asserted that executive leadership differs qualitatively from lower-level leadership, but few have theoretically or empirically examined the implications of these qualitative differences (Day & Lord, 1988). Despite some work that indicates that the responsibility and style of leadership of top-level executives differ qualitatively from that of lower-level leaders, most leadership researchers seem to assume that findings at the lower and middle levels of organizations also apply to leaders at the highest levels. There is a need, then, to clarify how executive leadership differs from leadership at middle and lower levels and discuss the implications of the differences. That is what we do in this chapter. We use the work of Katz and Kahn (1978), Hamel and Prahalad (1994), Selznick (1957), and Jaques (1989) to identify how the work of executive leaders differs qualitatively from that of leaders at lower levels. We examine research on behavioral complexity and social intelligence as leadership approaches that are potentially useful to understanding the skills that executive leaders need to address these qualitative differences and then link behavioral complexity and social intelligence to key characteristics of executive-level leadership. Our overarching framework is presented in Figure 4.1.

Key Characteristics of Top Management Work

Katz and Kahn (1978) distinguish among the responsibilities of upper-, middle-, and lower-level managers by examining how they use organizational structure. They argue that upper-level managers create structure, middle managers interpret structure, and lower-level managers use structure. Creating structure refers to such decisions as mergers with and acquisitions of other organizations, the addition or deletion of product lines, being first with a new manufacturing process or waiting until others attempt it, and geographical location of company sites. Executive leaders should make these decisions about the structure of their organizations on the basis of their assessment of the environment external to their organization. In adapting to the external environment, they also need to take

Figure 4.1. Executive Skills and Executive Work.

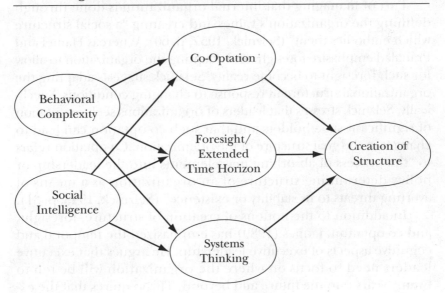

into consideration the internal resources of their organization, such as the relationships among the subsystems, the culture of the organization, and the competencies of their employees.

Hamel and Prahalad (1994) extend the notion of the creation of structure by also emphasizing that executive leaders need to have a vision of the future—what they refer to as foresight. Leaders need foresight about the needs and types of customers the organization will serve in the future. Hamel and Prahalad discuss ways in which top management can develop foresight skills, including learning to forget old practices, hiring from the outside, seeking out and rewarding unorthodox ideas, asking which customers and needs the organization is not serving, and being "willing to move beyond issues on which one can claim expert status" (p. 94). This is best accomplished by conceiving of the company as "a portfolio of core competencies rather than a portfolio of business units" (p. 83) and by focusing on functionality rather than functions. In addition to emphasizing the importance of foresight, they stress the need to get the entire organization involved in understanding what the future holds and how it can capitalize on that future. They discuss how managers need to manage the internal organization by creating a sense of destiny and meaning and by setting challenges.

Part of managing that internal organization is done through defining the organization's values and creating "a social structure which embodies them" (Selznick, 1957, p. 60). Whereas Hamel and Prahalad emphasize foresight and adapting the organization to allow for such foresight to become reality, Selznick suggests adapting the organizational structure in response to changing conditions. Specifically, Selznick stresses that leaders of organizations seek co-optation of significant stakeholders and that such co-optation can lead to changes in the goal structure of the organization. Co-optation refers to "the process of absorbing new elements into the leadership or policy-determining structure of an organization as a means of averting threats to its stability or existence" (Selznick, 1948, p. 31).

In addition to the notions of creation of structure, foresight, and co-optation, Jaques (1989) has emphasized the temporal and cognitive aspects of executive leadership. He argues that executive leaders need to focus on where the organization will be ten to twenty years into the future and beyond. This requires that the executive leader examine trends and changes in society at large and have the ability to see important connections between those trends and changes and the organization. There may be only two or three decisions each year that involve the entire organization and its future ten to twenty years hence, but these critical decisions (Selznick, 1957) are crucial for the long-term survival of the organization and require the conceptual skills Jaques and others stress (Mann, 1964). A key component of those conceptual skills is the ability to see the organization within the larger industry and society, or what has been called systems thinking (Senge, 1990). Because the notion of extended time horizon seems to fit closely with the notion of foresight, we will refer only to the notion of foresight in the remainder of this chapter.

The notions of creation of structure, foresight, co-optation of important stakeholders, and systems thinking are the key characteristics of the work of top-level leaders that seem to be most distinct from the work of lower-level leaders. Although these characteristics have received some attention, little attention has been paid to the actual skills that executive leaders need if they are to choose the right structure, develop accurate foresight, decide on which stakeholders to co-opt, and develop sound systems thinking. We examine the behavioral and social skills that allow executive leaders to do so.

Executive Leader Skills

Mann (1964) argued that as one moves up the organization, conceptual skills become more important and human relations and technical skills less important. Although we still agree with Mann's assertion of diminished importance of technical skills, we believe human relations skills remain highly important. However, the reason for their importance changes as one moves up the organizational hierarchy. At the lower levels, human relations skills are important for managing conflict, creating loyalty and commitment, getting people to exert extra effort, and so on; at the executive leadership level, human relations skills are important for fostering positive, constructive relationships with the stakeholders of the organization. We assert that executive leaders develop their systems perspective, foresight, and conceptual skills through their interactions with diverse stakeholder groups.

We also believe that in order to maximize the benefits of these interactions, executive leaders need to demonstrate behavioral complexity (Hooijberg, Hunt, & Dodge, 1997; Hooijberg & Quinn, 1992) and social intelligence (Zaccaro, Foti, & Kenny, 1991). Behavioral complexity refers to the ability of leaders to perform a wide array of leadership roles in the organizational arena. Social intelligence refers to their cognitive representations of social elements (for example, organizational members, organizational stakeholders, and expected interaction rituals) in their environment. We propose that leaders with requisite social intelligence and behavioral complexity will be better able to meet the needs of their stakeholders than will those lower in social intelligence and behavioral complexity. They will use their stakeholder relationships to discern changes in the needs and types of customers and translate that knowledge into appropriate organizational responses.

Behavioral Complexity

The concept of behavioral complexity addresses three problems of behavioral approaches to leadership: the impossibility of specifying the appropriate leadership role for all possible contingencies, the implicit assumption that all followers are subordinates, and the need for leaders, especially in organizational settings, to meet the expectations of stakeholders other than the followers. Researchers who have investigated behavioral complexity (Denison, Hooijberg, & Quinn, 1995; Hart & Quinn, 1993; Hooijberg, 1996; Hooijberg, Bullis, & Hunt, 1998; Hooijberg, Hunt, & Dodge, 1997; Hooijberg & Quinn, 1992) distinguish two key components: behavioral repertoire and behavioral differentiation.

Behavioral Repertoire

Behavioral repertoire refers to the portfolio of leadership roles a leader can perform. A broad portfolio of leadership roles makes it more likely that a leader can perform the appropriate leadership role for a given situation and meet the expectations of a variety of stakeholders. Research supports the idea that leaders who perform multiple leadership roles score higher on leadership effectiveness than those who do not. Quinn, Spreitzer, and Hart (1992), in a study of leaders from a Fortune 50 company, found that leaders who balance competing demands well by performing multiple leadership roles do better than leaders who focus on one demand over another. Denison, Hooijberg, and Quinn (1995) studied effective and ineffective leaders from the public utility industry and found that effective leaders perform more leadership roles than ineffective leaders do.

Hart and Quinn (1993) and Bullis (1992) found that behavioral repertoire not only affects managerial but also organizational effectiveness. Hart and Quinn (1993) studied chief executive officers (CEOs) from a large metropolitan area in the industrial Midwest and found that those who scored in the top third on the four leadership roles under study had significantly more impact on firm performance than those who scored in the bottom third on all four roles and those who scored high on some roles and low on others. Bullis (1992) examined the behavioral complexity of company commanders who participated in combat training exercises at the army's National Training Center on both leader and company effectiveness. Although he found that behavioral complexity had a positive effect on leader effectiveness, he did not find a direct effect on company effectiveness. Rather, the impact of behavioral complexity on company effectiveness was indirect, through leader effectiveness.

The research indicates that leaders with large behavioral repertoires are more effective than those with smaller behavioral repertoires. None of the research cited, however, has assessed effectiveness other than through general impressions of either subordinates or superiors of the focal leaders. Pfeffer and Salancik (1975) and Tsui and her colleagues (Tsui, 1984; Tsui & Gutek, 1984; Tsui & Ohlott, 1988) have shown that criteria for leader effectiveness differ depending on the organizational role relationship that respondents have with the focal leader.

Hooijberg (1996) expanded the research on behavioral complexity by examining the impact of the performance of the leadership roles that Quinn (1988) described on the perceptions of effectiveness by the leaders' subordinates, peers, and superiors. He found strong support for the notion that leaders who have a broad repertoire of leadership roles and perform those roles frequently are seen as more effective by subordinates, peers, and superiors.

Various researchers have prescribed a variety of roles for leaders to perform. However, the implicit assumption has been that once leaders identify the characteristics of a situation, they then pick the appropriate leadership role for that situation. That assumption, however, implies rather static, unidimensional situations rather than a wide variety of stakeholders in multiple and rapidly changing settings. For that reason, we must not only concern ourselves with a leader's behavioral repertoire but also address how such leaders achieve effective functioning across a variety of situations. That is, a leader needs not only the "ability to perceive the needs and goals of a constituency [but also the ability] to *adjust* one's personal approach to group action accordingly" (Kenny & Zaccaro, 1983, p. 678, emphasis added). The concept of behavioral differentiation captures that notion.

Behavioral Differentiation

Behavioral differentiation refers to the ability of leaders to perform the leadership roles they have in their behavioral repertoire differently (more adaptively, more flexibly, more appropriately, more individually, and more situation specifically) depending on the organizational situation. Research conducted at the lower and middle levels of the organizational hierarchy has emphasized the need for leaders to take into consideration the characteristics of their subordinates and the structure and clarity of the task when performing their leadership roles (Dansereau, Graen, & Haga, 1975; Fiedler, 1967; Hersey & Blanchard, 1982; House, 1971; Vroom & Yetton, 1973).

The literature on influence attempts provides support for the idea that individuals vary their downward, lateral, and upward influence processes (Yukl & Falbe, 1990; Yukl & Tracey, 1992). Similar to the importance of choosing the right influence tactics, leaders must carefully select the appropriate leadership role for their interactions with subordinates, peers, and superiors. The concept of behavioral differentiation suggests that leaders who vary the performance of their leadership roles depending on the relationship they have with the people with whom they interact will function more effectively than those who do not. The various members of these leaders' organizational role sets may have different expectations regarding the extent to which they think focal leaders ought to perform various leadership roles (Pfeffer & Salancik, 1975) and effective leaders will try to meet these expectations.

Hooijberg (1996) studied how behavioral differentiation affected the perceptions of effectiveness in two managerial samples.

He operationalized behavioral differentiation as the variation in the performance of leaders' roles in their interactions with their subordinates, peers, and superiors. He found that the results were quite mixed. Behavioral differentiation seemed to have a positive impact on perceptions of effectiveness by the leaders' superiors but a negative impact on the perceptions of effectiveness by the subordinates. As one conceivable explanation for the results, Hooijberg (1996) offered the possibility that the leaders' superiors interpreted the behavioral differentiation as appropriate to the situational demands, whereas the subordinates interpreted the behavioral differentiation as inconsistency (Staw & Ross, 1980). Another possible explanation is that leaders who vary their behaviors depending on which members of their organizational role set they interact with are seen as lacking in integrity (Hooijberg, Bullis, & Hunt, 1999). Research on behavioral complexity, then, has shown that leaders who have large behavioral repertoires and vary the application of the roles in their repertoire depending on whether they interact with their subordinates, peers, or superiors function more effectively than leaders who do not.

Although we believe that the general notion of behavioral complexity applies to the highest-level organizational leaders, some important modifications to the application of the concept need to be made. At the upper levels of the organization, leaders are concerned not only with the internal functioning of the organization but also with the larger marketplace and the role of the organization in the community and society. Interacting with the members of the community and government may well require a different set of behaviors from those needed within the organization (Osborn, Hunt, & Jauch, 1980). For example, executive leaders often serve on the boards of directors of other companies, as has been documented in the large management literature on interlocking directorates (Mizruchi, 1982). They may be selected as outside directors to represent shareholders interested in monitoring management (Fama & Jensen, 1983; Zahra & Pearce, 1989) or for their instrumentality in serving the organization by helping it acquire necessary resources (Pfeffer, 1981) such as financial resources (Sterns & Mizruchi, 1993). We discuss the importance of behavioral complexity for the creation of structure, co-optation, foresight, and systems thinking later in the chapter. Because executive leadership requires interacting with stakeholders over whom they have no formal authority, executive leaders need to have an accurate understanding of social relationships. In the psychological literature, this has been discussed under the heading of social intelligence, and it has also received some attention in the leadership literature.

Social Intelligence

Most leadership researchers agree that leaders need to have important interpersonal skills such as empathy, motivation, and communication. What has received considerably less attention than the skills is that appropriate application of these skills requires a thorough understanding of one's social setting, or social intelligence. Social intelligence has been defined in a variety of ways. For example, Gardner (1985) speaks of being able "to notice and make distinctions among other individuals . . . in particular, among their moods, temperaments, motivations, and intentions" (p. 239), and Sternberg (1985) defines social intelligence as being able to understand and act on one's understanding of others. Cantor and Kihlstrom (1987) define social intelligence as the multifaceted, domain- and task-specific expertise required to accomplish social goals. Salovey and Mayer (1989–1990) focus on the emotional dimension of social intelligence, which they define as "the ability to monitor one's own and others' feelings and emotions, to discriminate among them and to use this information to guide one's thinking and actions" (p. 189).

Zaccaro, Gilbert, Thor, and Mumford (1991) argue that leaders need to have accurate perceptions of social requirements and the ability to respond appropriately to social stimuli and that such capability results from "well-organized social knowledge structures representing the typical social elements in the organizational context confronting leaders" (p. 318). Zaccaro et al. (1991) further note that accurate social perception has a triple orientation: (1) acquisition and interpretation of social information regarding problems that impede organizational progress, (2) acquisition and interpretation of social information regarding personnel dynamics that may constrain or impede certain solution paths, and (3) acquisition and interpretation of social information regarding goal-related opportunities for organizational growth. Under the last point, leaders are acting in a proactive capacity by perceiving and attending to opportunities in the organizational environment. Leaders who have high social intelligence are able to make more finely grained distinctions among types of persons, situations, and social episodes, and they apply "a more elaborate social information store to the interpretation of social stimuli" (Zaccaro et al., 1991, p. 327).

Preliminary research indicates a difference between purely general intelligence and social intelligence. Rosnow, Skleder, Jaeger, and Rind (1994) found no substantial relationships between interpersonal acumen (that is, social differentiation) and linguistic and logical capacities tapped in IQ, Scholastic Aptitude Test, and other traditional measures of intelligence. Similarly, Sternberg and his colleagues (Sternberg, 1985; Sternberg, Wagner, Williams, & Horvath, 1995) studied types of intelligence not measured by IQ tests. They found that effective leaders are able to assimilate tacit (nonarticulated) information in the workplace rapidly and that this ability was not related to traditional psychometric measures of intelligence. (See Herrnstein & Murray, 1994, for a discussion of measures of *g* intelligence and a counterview.)

Each of the definitions of social intelligence emphasizes social aspects of relationships. We find that important because we believe that it is these social skills that allow leaders to interact effectively with a wide variety of internal and external organizational stakeholders, acquire organization-relevant information, and identify opportunities for their organizations. More specifically, the ability to distinguish moods, temperaments, motivations, and intentions of stakeholders is important because decision-making processes, implementation of planned solutions, organizational progress, and emerging social problems are rarely emotion free. In fact, the majority of emotion experienced in life is evoked in the context of social relationships (Averill, 1982; Clark, Pataki, & Carver, 1995; de Rivera, 1984; Scherer, Wallbott, & Summerfield, 1986; Schwartz & Shaver, 1987), and people can manipulate emotions to increase organizational effectiveness (Hochschild, 1983).

The general notion is that expressed positive (or negative) emotions are a tool of social influence because encounters with a friendly person are positively reinforcing. People are then disposed to reciprocate an upbeat person's kindness by complying with his or her requests (Cialdini, 1984) and to trust that requests made by the likable person are credible. While Hochschild (1983) primarily studied how flight attendants use good cheer to deal with passengers, Rafaeli and Sutton (1990, 1991) show how cashiers, criminal interrogators, and bill collectors use positive and negative emotions to obtain desired responses from their customers. Gardner (1992) discusses how employees can use a variety of impression management techniques to create desired self-images. The notion of using emotion to elicit desired organizational responses is also implicit in the charismatic and transformational leadership literature (Conger & Kanungo, 1987; Gardner & Avolio, 1998).

In addition to assessing social relationships with stakeholders accurately, executive leaders need to know what their values are and how these values affect their ability to differentiate social contexts. Values can be thought of as strong, enduring preferences for courses of action and outcomes (Hunt, 1991). They may affect leaders' fields of vision, their selective perceptions, their interpretations, and ultimately their choices and behaviors (Finkelstein & Hambrick, 1996). Values therefore can have a significant impact on how executive leaders form social knowledge structures.

Social intelligence can also allow the leader to develop and use social capital (Coleman, 1988; Brass, 1996). Social capital is potential influence or increased understanding that is available to a leader solely as a function of the characteristics and structure of a social setting (Brass, 1996). It allows the leader to establish and enforce norms, achieve trust and reputation, and accomplish instrumental objectives. Understanding how the resources of one relationship or context can be brought to bear on others to achieve operational closure on an issue or problem, and grasping how social relationships created for one purpose can be appropriated for other purposes, are results of leaders' accurate estimations of the social capital available within their social contexts. Effective use of idiosyncrasy credits (Hollander, 1979; Yukl, 1994), social exchanges, obligations, and expectations also depends on an integrated understanding of the social condition (Dienesch & Liden, 1986).

Behavioral Complexity and Social Intelligence and Executive Leadership

At the middle and lower levels of leadership in organizations, researchers have expounded primarily on the need for task and people orientation and somewhat on a variety of other leadership roles, such as innovation, brokering, monitoring, and building a vision. We examine to what extent findings at the lower and middle levels apply to the executive leaders' work of co-optation, foresight, systems thinking, and the creation of structure.

Behavioral Complexity and Co-Optation, Foresight, and Systems Thinking

Co-optation refers to "the process of absorbing new elements into the leadership or policy-determining structure of an organization as a means of averting threats to its stability or existence" (Selznick, 1948, p. 31). One of the ways in which executive leaders co-opt stakeholders is through their relationships with the members of their boards of directors. Researchers on board of directors have argued, for example, that "the composition of an organization's board is a conscious response to the critical contingencies of an external environment" (Boeker & Goodstein, 1991, p. 808). Pfeffer (1974) studied the composition of the boards of electric utilities and found that the representation of various economic interests (such as agricultural and manufacturing interests) was correlated with the representation of those sectors in a state's economy. Other researchers have found correlations between composition and the extent to which members of the boards can provide access to capital and financial resources for the organization (Mizruchi & Stearns, 1988; Palmer, 1983).

The primary official function of the board of directors, however, is the legal obligation to serve as an internal control on management. Through this monitoring role, boards honor their fiduciary responsibility to shareholders to protect their interests. This function can create tension for the executive leadership of the organization because it also has to deal with stakeholders who do not evaluate the organization on financial performance alone. Mintzberg (1983) provides yet another view of the role of the board of directors. He argues that the members of the board provide service to the organization through their advice to the executive leadership and by expanding the network of contacts for the executive leadership.

Thus, the relationship between executive leaders and their boards of directors indicates an interesting reciprocal interdependence. On the one hand, the board members evaluate the performance of the executive leadership, provide advice to the executive leadership, and have the authority to fire the CEO; on the other hand, they may be dependent on the firm's executive leadership for contracts for their own organizations. Thus, board members who are external to an organization may have a business or professional affiliation with it that potentially reduces their ability to function as independent members (Daily & Dalton, 1994; Pearce & Zahra, 1991).

This relationship of reciprocal interdependence also exists with other stakeholders, such as government officials, pension funds, mutual funds, public interest groups, unions, trade associations, and charitable organizations. Although these stakeholders do not hold the same formal authority as the board of directors, they can exercise substantial influence on the actions of the executive leadership through their wielding of legitimacy, power, and urgency with the organization (Mitchell, Agle, & Wood, 1997). Unions can use their members to put pressure on the executive leadership to increase salaries, benefits, and nonfinancial incentives. The pension and mutual funds in turn can pressure the executive leadership not to give in to the demands of the unions and instead make the organization leaner for the benefit of owners. We posit that executive leaders require behavioral complexity to deal with this wide range of stakeholders, conflicting pressures, and dependency relationships.

Although executive leaders need behavioral complexity if they are to be effective, the leadership roles that they require in their portfolios will differ substantially in substance and level of specificity. Researchers previously assessed the extent to which leaders use consideration and initiation of structure behaviors with quite specific items covering a broad range of behaviors. Consideration, defined as "the extent to which an individual is likely to have job relationships characterized by mutual trust, respect for subordinates' ideas, and consideration for their feelings" (Fleishman & Peters, 1962), is assessed with such items as "He treats all members of his group as equals," "He is friendly and approachable," and "He does personal favors for group members." Initiation of structure is defined as "the extent to which an individual is likely to define and structure his role and those of his subordinates toward goal attainment" (Fleishman & Peters, 1962), and it is assessed with such items as "He schedules work to be done," "He maintains definite standards of performance," "He emphasizes the meeting of deadlines," and "He lets group members know what is expected of them." Consideration and initiation of structure still represent important criteria for evaluation, but we expect that the content of these roles will be less specific for executive leaders, reflecting the unique qualities of work at the top level. For the role of consideration, we might emphasize more the values with which the executive leadership imbues the organization, how well they maintain relationships with their customers and their suppliers, and how responsive they are to requests from Wall Street (or others) for information. For the role of initiation of structure, we may examine the vision and mission statements of the executive leaders, the quality of the products, the overall profit margins, the extent of market penetration of the organization's products, and so on.

One of the key requisite skills of the executive behavioral portfolio is the ability to convey a similar message in many different ways, so that it makes sense to many different stakeholders. In conversations with Wall Street representatives, executive leaders need to emphasize return on investments and other financial indicators. In conversations with consumer advocacy groups, they need to emphasize quality, price, and safety. In conversations with government representatives, they need to bring forth the governmental and societal benefits of legislation and regulation that are also beneficial to their organizations. In some cases, favorable legislation and regulation may not mean less legislation and regulation. In the pharmaceutical industry, for example, the large, established companies may want to keep existing regulations (such as the approval process by the Food and Drug Administration for new drugs) because they have devoted significant resources to having structures in place to deal with the regulations. This gives them a competitive advantage over less well-established companies and makes new companies think seriously about entering their market, given this barrier to entry. Executive leader conversations with unions will emphasize productivity and cooperation. The conversations with the unions need not be antagonistic in nature, as the case of Saturn so well demonstrates. In all of these interactions, leaders have to vary the extent to which they act directively versus submissively, controlling versus participatively, friendly versus unfriendly, and so on. Through interactions with the board of directors and conversations with the various stakeholders, executive leaders can improve the predictability of changes in the external environment and be subject to fewer incidents of damaging moves by stakeholders (such as strikes, boycotts, bad press, and hampering regulations) (Harrison & St. John, 1996). Harrison and St. John (1996) suggest a wide variety of partnering tactics that executive leaders can engage in that will co-opt stakeholders and improve organizational flexibility.

The points just noted primarily pertain to the variables of co-optation and systems thinking. Executive leaders, however, can and should use their interactions with their stakeholders to explore long-term changes in the organization's environment of the organization. That is, they should look at interacting with stakeholders not only for the purpose of reducing the uncertainty currently facing the organization. They should also explore the long-term agendas of public interest groups, political leaders, consumer advocacy groups, and the strategic plans of other organizations in their own and related industries. Through a thorough examination of those agendas, executives can develop part of their foresight. For example, the automobile industry closely follows the actions of environmental groups and the state legislature in California to anticipate future regulations on car emissions and fuel efficiency. The executive leaders in the automobile industry most likely also closely followed the 1999 international conference in Japan on global warming. Although that conference does not affect car sales in the immediate future, it does provide executive leaders with the opportunity to develop insight into the current thinking of international political leaders. They can then start incorporating some of the outcomes of the conference into their foresight, which will come to be reflected in their organizations' plans over the next ten to twenty years.

The notion that executive leaders can develop part of their foresight through an exploration of long-term agendas of a wide variety of stakeholders also has implications for their behavioral repertoires. Such explorations by executive leaders with their stakeholders may result in expanded role repertoires, achieved through contemplating the potential behaviors that could be made in response to a realm of potential environmental scenarios. The exploration of long-term ideas is analogous to a series of if-then propositions followed by challenges and discussion of implications. For example, an automobile executive leader could engage an environmental activist leader in an if-then discussion about the reduction in emission standards and the introduction of electric cars in California: "If emission standards become stricter and the California state legislature mandates that 20 percent of all cars sold have to be electric cars, then what would be next on your agenda?" The executive might then discern a series of potential behavioral responses to the activist's agenda, make judgments regarding the outcomes they would respectively yield, and appraise the outcomes in terms of their favorableness to the organization and its stakeholders.

Finally, executive leaders develop and refine foresight by trying out ideas on their peers at a variety of social events associated with nonprofit and charitable organizations. Executive leaders from different organizations may serve, for example, on the board of trustees of a university, a business school, or an orchestra. In addition to their contributions to the performance and functioning of these institutions, these social activities allow the leaders to meet some of their peers in nonbusiness situations and thereby obtain others' opinions regarding their foresight for their own organizations. Executive leaders may feel reluctant to share rough or preliminary foresight ideas with internal members of the management team or the board of directors for fear of negative reputational effects, but they may share such ideas with peers external to their organization. A former CEO of a computer services company indicated that this was one of the primary reasons he attended roundtable discussions on computer technology and other mostly symbolic events. Testing preliminary ideas on knowledgeable, external parties provides, in effect, a peer review of the idea. Of course, judgment and caution need to be exercised in the exposure of preliminary vision ideas because they may be potentially appropriated by the peer or leaked to others.

Social Intelligence and Co-Optation, Foresight, and Systems Thinking

Executive leaders need to be sensitive to the emotions and values of the stakeholders of the organization as well as to the emotions of employees in their direct interactions with customers. For example,

Waddock and Graves (1997) point out that the strategic management literature now associates the broader notion of corporate social performance with financial performance of the organization, and many of these social performance issues have strong emotional content. Corporate social performance refers to such issues as investments in pollution control equipment and other environmental strategies, treatment of women and minorities, nature of products produced, types of customers served, community relations, and philanthropic programs. These at first may seem tangential to the operation of the organization, but they indirectly affect the organization's external environment through the favorableness or unfavorableness of resulting issues, such as government scrutiny, ability to attract human resources, lawsuits against the company, sales, the local tax environment, and overall public opinion of the company.

Social intelligence regarding sensitivity to corporate social performance issues relates directly to Selznick's (1948) notion of co-optation. Executive leaders high in social intelligence understand that environmental interest groups will do more than pressure their organization to improve its pollution prevention activities. These groups will simultaneously pressure politicians to take a stand, urge voters to call their political representatives, and attempt to convince the organization's distributors and buyers to go elsewhere. This understanding of the network of social relationships and the potential emotional reactions will encourage executive leaders to seek input from community organizations regarding the creation and operation of facilities or from environmental interest groups regarding pollution issues. In this manner, executive leaders not only show sensitivity to the concerns of their many stakeholder groups and work toward cooperative rather than hostile relationships with them, but they also increase the likelihood that the values of their organizations start to reflect the values of the interest groups. The organization comes to reflect in part the diverse perspectives of its stakeholder groups as its executive leaders' vision becomes more informed and their values are affected by the experience.

Besides demonstrating sensitivity to important stakeholder concerns, cooperative engagement with stakeholders should also shape the image of the organization. Personal involvement in philanthropic programs, serving on blue ribbon committees, and serving on boards of charitable institutions represent ways in which executive leaders can promote the overall image of their organization. Executive leaders high on social intelligence will more accurately assess the potential importance and impact of these social relationships than will executive leaders low on social intelligence. Just as Nike tries to enhance its image by associating its sneakers with famous athletes, so can executive leaders enhance the image of their organization by participating in charitable events. In addition, executive leaders high in social intelligence will realize that their peers from other organizations will attend these same functions, which provides them with the opportunity to ascertain informally what their peers are doing and thinking and test some of their own thoughts and ideas on their peers.

Besides engaging stakeholders on social issues, Lenway and Rehbein (1991) show that organizations have become active in managing the political uncertainty stemming from an increase in legislative and federal regulatory activity (Keim & Baysinger, 1988). Executive leaders try to manage the political uncertainty by establishing offices in Washington, D.C., hiring lobbyists, and forming political action committees. These tactics focus on gaining access to Congress and are important for influencing legislation that directly or indirectly affects the organization. For example, executive leaders from organizations that provide supplies to the military probably expended many resources on keeping military bases in various regions of the country open. Certainly influencing state and federal legislation is important, but Lenway and Rehbein (1991) argue as well that organizations also try to influence regulatory agencies directly, and they provide the example of how organizations try to influence the functioning of the U.S. International Trade Commission (ITC). The actions of this commission have great importance to organizations involved in the import and export of goods. Again, we propose that executive leaders high in social intelligence will sense the importance of the social and regulatory relationships among organizations in the United States and abroad, the members of the ITC, and their own organization. Even if their organization currently has no pressing business before the ITC, it is still advantageous to maintain good working relationships with the commission so that future issues will receive their due, and, hopefully, organizationally favorable attention.

By exploring and improving their understanding of the social relationships among the stakeholders in their organization's environment, executive leaders enhance their opportunities for co-opting relevant stakeholders, forming more informed foresight, and improving their understanding of the larger system within which their organization operates.

Co-Optation, Foresight, Systems Thinking, and the Creation of Structure

Senge (1990) poses the interesting question of who is the leader of a ship. Most of the participants in his workshops answer captain, some the steersman, and even fewer the owner. Few think of the architect as the leader of the ship. Yet it is the architect whose design determines the parameters within which the captain and the steersman can exercise leadership. Similarly it is the executive leaders who determine such issues as which products and markets to focus on, which major suppliers and distributors to use, and where to locate operations. Most important, it is the executive leaders who have a large impact on the organization's values and culture that influence its current practices and shape its future.

It is our contention that behavioral complexity and social intelligence have an indirect impact on these decisions through co-optation, foresight, and systems thinking (see Figure 4.1). Executive leaders cannot possibly personally motivate all of their employees. Rather, they enable their employees to go beyond mere compliance with the routine directives of the organization (Katz & Kahn, 1978) through their design of the organizational "ship." If the legitimate, powerful, and urgent stakeholders (Mitchell et al., 1997) have been identified and co-opted by executive leaders, foresight has been informed not only by the experts within the executive leaders' organization but also through extensive interactions with a wide variety of stakeholders. Foresight can also be informed through executive leadership interaction with peers through service on corporate boards of directors, nonprofit boards of trustees, and other social interaction opportunities. In the process, a solid understanding of the organization's external environment and its linkages with the environment is gained. This enables executive leaders to design an organization that can successfully weather today's and tomorrow's storms, rain, sleet, and currents, as well as one that is ready to sail in uncharted waters toward new destinations.

Executive leaders in the public utility industry who are high in behavioral complexity and social intelligence most likely started to adjust their organizations for deregulation long before most leaders even considered deregulation a realistic possibility. While preparing their organizations, they also actively sought to influence the implementation of the deregulation by sharing their concerns, opinions, and ideas with state and federal policymakers (Al Koeppe, Public Service Electric & Gas, personal communication, 1997). These executive leaders started to change the value structure of their organizations from one focused on monitoring use and setting rates to one of customer service and cost containment.

Executive leaders of engineering companies that had one sole customer, the U.S. Department of Defense, long ago faced the need to recognize that the budget for defense was shrinking, and that meant that they had to reorient the company, co-opt new stakeholders, seek nondefense contracts, and reconceptualize and reconfigure the system within which their organization operated. It meant that the rules governing bidding for contracts changed, they no longer needed to comply with a wide variety of government regulations in the execution of their contracts, and the executive leaders had to find new customers. Such transitions can devastate organizations. We believe that executive leaders high in behavioral complexity and social intelligence ascertained these trends well before most other leaders and well before their revenue streams ran dry. Through foresight, they began to prepare their organizations for the transition by changing their organizations' structures well in advance of their peers at other defense firms. In some cases, executive replacement was necessary for organizational survival; new leaders who had foresight and could create new structure had to be designated (Thompson, 1995).

It may seem that we are saying that executive leaders create structures commensurate with a single coherently formulated foresight and systems understanding, but that is not the message we want to convey. Executive leaders may place a relatively larger emphasis in their design and activities on one dominant view of the future and organizational system, but we expect that they also create a flexible organizational system that is equipped to respond to a myriad of possible futures. For example, executive leaders in the automotive industry seem to have designated a substantial part of their organizational structure to the design and introduction of electrical cars. Even if they believe that electrical cars may become a mainstay, they will also continue to devote substantial resources to improving the fuel efficiency of gas-fueled cars, and perhaps even to other options.

Conclusion

The four key qualities of executive leadership work—co-optation of stakeholders, foresight, systems thinking, and the creation of structure—significantly differentiate executive leadership work from leadership work at lower levels. Two areas of leadership research—behavioral complexity and social intelligence—are particularly relevant for the study of executive leaders; findings from that research can be applied to the four characteristics of executive leader work. Although research on behavioral complexity and social intelligence has concentrated on the middle and lower levels of organizations, we have asserted that they are equally, if not more, important concepts at the highest levels of the organization

Executive leaders require behavioral complexity and social intelligence in their interactions with the stakeholders of their organizations and other important associations and organizations, so that they can co-opt stakeholders for their organizations, and develop informed foresight and accurate systems thinking. As illustrated in Figure 4.1, the mediating variables of co-optation, foresight, and systems thinking influence the creation of organization structure. We note that while structure reflects executives' commitment to their dominant views of the current and future organizational systems, it must also be flexible and adaptable to respond to other realities that may emerge (Allaire & Firsirotu, 1989). There is a fluidity to this structure, reflecting that even informed foresight may be surprised by uncontrollable, unpredictable, and possibly previously unimaginable events.

Many researchers and practitioners have emphasized the need for executive leaders to formulate a coherent vision for the organization, but few have provided insight into how to do so, as have Hamel and Prahalad (1994). By examining the relevance of behavioral complexity and social intelligence research for these executive leadership skills, we contribute to identifying the process by which executive leaders may develop informed foresight and work toward bringing it to fruition. The model we present does much more than suggest placating stakeholders or neutralizing their threats; it recognizes their potential to be a source of strategic input with new ideas, new values, and refinement of existing organizational values. It brings stakeholders into the strategic process early on and stresses that doing so may result in productive, cooperative relationships with them rather than antagonistic ones. The model thus bridges the leadership literature in management and psychology to the strategy literature by identifying some strategic implications associated with behavioral complexity and social intelligence for vision development and stakeholder management.

We have posited that executive leaders who are high in behavioral complexity and social intelligence have sufficiently developed behavioral repertoires, behavioral differentiation, social perception, and ability to use emotion for social influence. They are able to develop a vision that reflects the perspectives of various stakeholders and rally their support toward it. More specifically, we propose that executive leaders who are high in behavioral complexity and social intelligence will be more effective in developing informed foresight, co-opting internal and external stakeholders, and viewing the organization within its larger social systems. We also propose that they will be more effective in developing an organizational structure that both reflects and is responsive to internal stakeholders such as middle managers, lower-level managers, professionals, and line employees. Accordingly, leader behavioral complexity and social intelligence will tend to have a positive relationship with leader effectiveness and a less direct but positive relationship with organizational effectiveness.

The second proposition about internal stakeholders reflects the importance of strategic implementation for organizational effectiveness, which has traditionally been relatively neglected in both the strategy literature and practice because of previous undue emphasis on strategic planning (Bourgeois & Brodwin, 1984; Mintzberg, 1994). We propose that executive leaders high in behavioral complexity and social intelligence will tend to view planning and implementation as intertwined, rather than as disparate components of strategy, and will tend to be more successful as strategists.

The linkage of behavioral complexity and social intelligence with executive work that is established here promotes much additional research. We believe there is great applicability of the two notions to corporate strategy, specifically regarding executive or strategic leadership and its relationship to vision development, stakeholder management, strategy implementation, and organizational effectiveness. Although there are undoubtedly many existing models for each of these constructs, and many variables have been identified that potentially affect each, the behavioral and social skills of strategic leaders have been relatively unexplored in current research. This presents a wealth of research opportunities for those interested in the study of leadership within the psychology, management, and strategy fields.

References

Allaire, Y., & Firsirotu, M. E. (1989). Coping with strategic uncertainty. *Sloan Management Review, 30*(3), 7–16.

Averill, J. R. (1982). *Anger and aggression: An essay on emotion.* New York: Springer-Verlag.

Boeker, W., & Goodstein, J. (1991). Organizational performance and adaptation: Effects of environment and performance on changes in board composition. *Academy of Management Journal, 34,* 805–826.

Bourgeois, L., & Brodwin, D. R. (1984). Strategic implementation: The applicability of current theory. *Strategic Management Journal, 5,* 241–264.

Brass, D. J. (1996, March). *The social capital of twenty-first century leaders.* Paper presented at the Army Leadership in the Twenty-First Century symposium, Chicago.

Bullis, R. C. (1992). *The impact of leader behavioral complexity on organizational performance.* Unpublished doctoral dissertation, Texas Tech University.

Cantor, N., & Kihlstrom, J. F. (1987). *Personality and social intelligence.* Upper Saddle River, NJ: Prentice Hall.

Cialdini, R. B. (1984). *Influence: The new psychology of modern persuasion.* New York: Quill.

Clark, M. S., Pataki, S. P., & Carver, V. H. (1995). Some thoughts and findings on self-presentation of emotions in relationships. In G. J. O Fletcher & J. Fitness (Eds.), *Knowledge structures in close relationships.* Mahwah, NJ: Erlbaum.

Coleman, J. S. (1988). Social capital in the creation of human capital. *American Journal of Sociology, 94,* 95–120.

Conger, J., & Kanungo, N. (1987). Toward a behavioral theory of charismatic leadership in organizational settings. *Academy of Management Review, 12,* 637–647.

Daily, C. M., & Dalton, D. R. (1994). Bankruptcy and corporate governance: The impact of board composition and structure. *Academy of Management Journal, 3,* 1603–1617.

Dansereau, G., Graen, G., & Haga, W. J. (1975). A vertical dyad linkage approach to leadership with formal organizations: A longitudinal investigation of the role-making process. *Organizational Behavior and Human Performance, 13,* 46–78.

Day, D. V., & Lord, R. G. (1988). Executive leadership and organizational performance: Suggestions for a new theory and methodology. *Journal of Management, 14,* 453–464.

de Rivera, J. (1984). The structure of emotional relationships. In P. Shaver (Ed.), *Review of personality and social psychology: Emotions, relationships, and health.* Thousand Oaks, Calif.: Sage.

Denison, D. R., Hooijberg, R., & Quinn, R. E. (1995). Paradox and performance: A theory of behavioral complexity in managerial leadership. *Organization Science, 6,* 524–541.

Dienesch, R. M., & Liden, R. C. (1986). Leader-member exchange model of leadership: A critique and further development. *Academy of Management Review, 11,* 618–634.

Fama, E. F., & Jensen, M. C. (1983). Separation of ownership and control. *Journal of Law and Economics, 26,* 301–325.

Fiedler, F. E. (1967). *A theory of leadership effectiveness.* New York: McGraw-Hill.

Finkelstein, S., & Hambrick, D. C. (1996). *Strategic leadership: Top executives and their effects on organizations.* St. Paul, MN: West.

Fleishman, E. A., & Peters, D. R. (1962). Interpersonal values, leadership attitudes, and managerial "success." *Personnel Psychology, 15,* 127–143.

Gardner, H. (1985). *The mind's new science: A history of the cognitive revolution.* New York: Basic Books.

Gardner, W. L. (1992). Lessons in organizational dramaturgy: The art of impression management. *Organizational Dynamics, 20,* 33–46.

Gardner, W. L., & Avolio, B. J. (1998). The charismatic relationship: A dramaturgical perspective. *Academy of Management Review, 23,* 32–58.

Hamel, G., & Prahalad, C. K. (1994). *Competing for the future.* Boston: Harvard Business School Press.

Harrison, J. S., & St. John, C. H. (1996). Managing and partnering with external stakeholders. *Academy of Management Executive, 10*(2), 46–60.

Hart, S. L., & Quinn, R. E. (1993). Roles executives play: CEOs, behavioral complexity, and firm performance. *Human Relations, 46,* 543–574.

Herrnstein, R. J., & Murray, C. (1994). *The bell curve: Intelligence and class structure in American life.* New York: Free Press.

Hersey, P., & Blanchard, K. H. (1982). *Management of organization behavior: Utilizing human resources* (4th ed.). Upper Saddle River, NJ: Prentice Hall.

Hochschild, A. L. (1983). *The managed heart.* Berkeley: University of California Press.

Hollander, E. P. (1979). Leadership and social exchange processes. In K. Gergen, M. S. Greenberg, & R. H. Willis (Eds.), *Social exchange: Advances in theory and research.* New York: Wiley.

Hooijberg, R. (1996). A multidirectional approach toward leadership: An extension of the concept of behavioral complexity. *Human Relations, 49,* 917–946.

Hooijberg, R., Bullis, R. C., & Hunt, J. G. (1999). Behavioral complexity and the development of military leadership for the twenty-first century. In J. G. Hunt, G. E. Dodge, & L. Wong (Eds.), *Out-of-the-box leadership: Transforming the twenty-first-century army and other top-performing organizations.* Greenwich, CT: JAI Press.

Hooijberg, R., Hunt, J. G., & Dodge, G. E. (1997). Leadership complexity and development of the leaderplex model. *Journal of Management, 23,* 375–408.

Hooijberg, R., & Quinn, R. E. (1992). Behavioral complexity and the development of effective managerial leaders. In R. L. Phillips & J. G. Hunt (Eds.), *Strategic management: A multiorganizational-level perspective.* Westport, CT: Quorum.

House, R. J. (1971). A path-goal theory of leader effectiveness. *Administrative Science Quarterly, 16,* 321–338.

Hunt, J. G. (1991). *Leadership: A new synthesis.* Thousand Oaks, CA: Sage.

Jaques, E. (1989). *Requisite organization.* Arlington, VA: Cason Hall.

Katz, D., & Kahn, R. L. (1978). *The social psychology of organizing.* New York: Wiley.

Keim, G., & Baysinger, B. (1988). The efficacy of business political activity: Competitive considerations in a principal-agent context. *Journal of Management, 14,* 163–180.

Kenny, D. A., & Zaccaro, S. J. (1983). An estimate of variance due to traits in leadership. *Journal of Applied Psychology, 68,* 678–685.

Lenway, S. A., & Rehbein, K. (1991). Leaders, followers, and free riders: An empirical test of variation in the corporate political environment. *Academy of Management Journal, 34,* 893–905.

Mann, F. C. (1964). Toward an understanding of the leadership role in formal organizations. In R. Dubin, G. Homans, & D. Miller (Eds.), *Leadership and productivity.* San Francisco: Chandler.

Mintzberg, H. (1983). *Power in and around organizations.* Upper Saddle River, NJ: Prentice Hall.

Mintzberg, H. (1994). *The rise and fall of strategic planning.* New York: Free Press.

Mitchell, R. K., Agle, B. R., & Wood, D. (1997). Toward a theory of stakeholder identification: Defining the principle of who and what really counts. *Academy of Management Review, 22,* 853–886.

Mizruchi, M. S. (1982). *The American corporate network, 1904–1974.* Thousand Oaks, CA: Sage.

Mizruchi, M. S., & Stearns, L. B. (1988). A longitudinal study of the formation of interlocking directorates. *Administrative Science Quarterly, 33,* 194–210.

Osborn, R. N., Hunt, J. G., & Jauch, L. R. (1980). *Organization theory: An integrated approach.* New York: Wiley.

Palmer, D. (1983). Broken ties: Interlocking directorates and intercorporate coordination. *Administrative Science Quarterly, 28,* 40–55.

Pearce, J. A., & Zahra, S. A. (1991). The relative power of CEOs and boards of directors: Associations with corporate performance. *Strategic Management Journal, 12,* 135–153.

Pfeffer, J. (1974). Cooptation and the composition of electric utility boards of directors. *Pacific Sociological Review, 17,* 333–363.

Pfeffer, J. (1981). *Power in organizations.* Marshfield, MA: Pittman.

Pfeffer, J., & Salancik, G. R. (1975). Determinants of supervisory behavior: A role-set analysis. *Human Relations, 28,* 139–164.

Pfeffer, J., & Salancik, G. R. (1978). *The external control of organizations: A resource dependence perspective.* New York: HarperCollins.

Quinn, R. (1988). *Beyond rational expectations.* San Francisco: Jossey-Bass.

Quinn, R. E., Spreitzer, G. M., & Hart, S. (1992). Challenging the assumptions of bipolarity: Interpenetration and managerial effectiveness. In S. Srivastva & R. E. Fry (Eds.), *Executive and organizational continuity: Managing the paradoxes of stability and change.* San Francisco: Jossey-Bass.

Rafaeli, A., & Sutton, R. I. (1990). Busy stores and demanding customers: How do they affect the expression of positive emotion? *Academy of Management Journal, 33,* 623–637.

Rafaeli, A., & Sutton, R. I. (1991). Emotional contrast strategies as means of social influence: Lessons from criminal interrogators and bill collectors. *Academy of Management Journal, 34,* 749–775.

Rosnow, R. L., Skleder, A. A., Jaeger, M. E., & Rind, B. (1994). Intelligence and the epistemics of interpersonal acumen: Testing some implications of Gardner's theory. *Intelligence, 19,* 93–116.

Salovey, P., & Mayer, J. D. (1989–1990). Emotional intelligence. *Imagination, Cognition, and Personality, 9,* 185–211.

Scherer, K. R., Wallbott, H. G., & Summerfield, A. B. (1986). *Experiencing emotion: A cross-cultural study.* New York: Cambridge University Press.

Schwartz, J. C., & Shaver, P. R. (1987). Emotions and emotion knowledge in interpersonal relationships. In W. Jones & D. Perlman (Eds.), *Advances in personal relationships.* Greenwich, CT: JAI Press.

Selznick, P. (1948). Foundations of the theory of the organization. *American Sociological Review, 13,* 25–35.

Selznick, P. (1957). *Leadership in administration.* New York: HarperCollins.

Senge, P. (1990). *The fifth discipline: The art and practice of the learning organization.* New York: Doubleday.

Staw, B. M., & Ross, J. (1980). Commitment in an experimental society: A study of the attribution of leadership from administrative scenarios. *Journal of Applied Psychology, 65,* 249–260.

Sternberg, R. J. (1985). *Beyond IQ.* Cambridge, U.K.: Cambridge University Press.

Sternberg, R. J., Wagner, R. K., Williams, W., & Horvath, J. (1995). Testing common sense. *American Psychologist, 50,* 912–927.

Sterns, L. B., & Mizruchi, M. S. (1993). Board composition and corporate financing: The impact of financial institution representation on borrowing. *Academy of Management Journal, 36,* 603–618.

Thompson, R. (1995, October 11). Harsco is recharged by scrap metal, hazardous waste. *Wall Street Journal,* p. B4.

Tsui, A. S. (1984). A multiple-constituency framework of managerial reputational effectiveness. In J. G. Hunt, D. M. Hosking, C. A. Schriesheim, & R. Stewart (Eds.), *Leaders and managers: International perspectives on managerial behavior and leadership.* New York: Pergamon Press.

Tsui, A. S., & Gutek, B. A. (1984). A role-set analysis of gender differences in performance, affective relationships, and career success of industrial middle managers. *Academy of Management Journal, 27,* 619–635.

Tsui, A. S., & Ohlott, P. (1988). Multiple assessments of managerial effectiveness: Interrater agreement and consensus in effectiveness models. *Personnel Psychology, 41,* 779–803.

Vroom, V. H., & Yetton, E. W. (1973). *Leadership and decision making.* Pittsburgh, PA: University of Pittsburgh Press.

Waddock, S. A., & Graves, S. B. (1997). The corporate social performance-financial performance link. *Strategic Management Journal, 18,* 303–319.

Yukl, G. (1994). *Leadership in organizations* (3rd ed.). Upper Saddle River, NJ: Prentice Hall.

Yukl, G., & Falbe, C. M. (1990). Influence tactics in upward, downward, and lateral influence attempts. *Journal of Applied Psychology, 75,* 132–140.

Yukl, G., & Tracey, B. (1992). Consequences of influence tactics used with subordinates, peers, and the boss. *Journal of Applied Psychology, 77,* 525–535.

Zaccaro, S. J., Foti, R. J., & Kenny, D. A. (1991). Self-monitoring and trait-based variance in leadership: An investigation of leader flexibility across multiple team situations. *Journal of Applied Psychology, 76,* 308–315.

Zaccaro, S. J., Gilbert, J. A., Thor, K. K., & Mumford, M. D. (1991). Leadership and social intelligence: Linking social perceptiveness to behavioral flexibility. *Leadership Quarterly, 2,* 317–347.

Zahra, S. A., & Pearce, J. A. (1989). Boards of directors and corporate social performance: A review and integration. *Journal of Management, 15,* 291–334.

CHAPTER 5

Social Capital and Organizational Leadership

Daniel J. Brass

People have always been fascinated by the personal characteristics of great leaders. In the popular press as well as academic research, the focus on leadership has persistently been a focus on human capital: the knowledge, skills, personality, and behavioral styles of leaders. We believe that individuals become leaders in corporate America because they are smarter, more charismatic, better educated, or more skilled than others (Brass & Krackhardt, 1998; Burt, 1997). Yet we define leadership as the ability to accomplish work through others: bringing together the right people at the right time in order to get the job done. As Mintzberg (1973) has noted, the myth of managerial work is that it occurs in isolation. The observational analyses of managers indicate that they spend a large portion of their time communicating and interacting with others (Mintzberg, 1973; Luthans, Rosenkrantz, & Hennessey, 1985). All evidence indicates that leaders are embedded within networks of relationships with others (Geletkanycz & Hambrick, 1997). Despite this acknowledgment, a brief history of leadership research indicates that trait, behavioral, and situational approaches, as well as the more recent attributional, charismatic, and transformational paradigms (Bass, 1990; Meindl, 1993; Yukl, 1994), largely ignore the role of social relationships in leadership. The emphasis has been on finding the elusive human capital explanation for leadership. The goal of this chapter is to nudge the study of leadership toward a closer look at the social capital of leaders.

Social Capital

Just as human capital refers to the skills and abilities that may be potentially beneficial to individuals, social capital refers to social relationships that can potentially confer benefits to individuals and groups (Bourdieu, 1977; Burt, 1992, 1997; Coleman, 1988, 1990; Fukuyama, 1995; Gabbay, 1997; Putnam, 1995). The term *social capital* was first used by community sociologists in noting that neighborhood networks of strong personal relationships could provide the cooperation, trust, and ability to act collectively to enhance the community (Loury, 1977; Jacobs, 1965). For example, Putnam (1995) has lamented the decline of membership in associations in the United States (such as church-related groups, labor unions, parent-teacher associations, and bowling leagues) and suggests that America is losing its social capital. The concept of social capital has been applied in a variety of ways since its early use, but the central principle linking these applications is that networks of relationships can be a valuable resource for both groups and individuals.

Social capital may be contrasted with human capital (personal attributes), financial capital (money), and physical capital (physical property such as land, buildings, machinery). Whereas human capital is an individual quality, social capital is an opportunity or potential benefit created by relationship with others. It is owned jointly by the parties in the relationship and is less easily transferred than physical, financial, or human capital.

In focusing on social capital, I do not mean to suggest that leaders cannot be identified on the basis of human capital: their skills and abilities and their willingness to use them. Human capital and individual agency are acknowledged, along with the social capital that may enhance or constrain a leader's ability to make use of his or her other forms of capital. The ability to profit from one's human, financial, and physical capital comes through relationships with friends, acquaintances, suppliers, customers, and others.

The social capital perspective begins with the assumption that actors are embedded in a complex web (or network) of interrelationships with other actors. This network includes everyone the actor, or potential leader, knows and, indirectly, everyone these friends, acquaintances, neighbors, and colleagues of the leader know. It is this intersection of relationships that defines a leader's role in the social structure of organizations, or simply a leader's position within a social network of potentially beneficial relationships. The social capital perspective focuses on the relationships rather than the actors (the links in the network rather than the nodes). It is these networks of relationships that provide the opportunities and constraints that, in combination with other forms of capital, may be the causal forces of leadership.

Examples of Social Capital

Coleman (1988, 1990) notes three examples of social capital, that is, three benefits that may result from social relationships. First, obligations and expectations, and the trust that facilitates them, arise when actors are willing to do something for other actors because they expect and trust that the recipients will honor the obligation to reciprocate in the future. The second example of social capital, norms and sanctions, is similar to the first. Norms and sanctions allow for the reduction of costs involved in transactions between people. For example, merchants in the New York City diamond exchange transact millions of dollars in business without formal or legal contracts; a handshake seals a deal (Coleman, 1988). The strong norms and sanctions prevent any fraud or misconduct. Coleman was focusing on cooperative behavior and benefits for the collective, but he does note that norms may infringe on individual autonomy. However, he further notes that individuals may also benefit by sharing in the social capital of the group.

The third example of social capital that Coleman noted refers to actors' obtaining information that may be useful to them from others, indirectly taking advantage of others' knowledge, skills, and other forms of human capital. Burt (1992, 1997) focuses his writing on the information benefits of social capital, primarily at the individual level of analysis. Social networks act as conduits of information. According to Burt (1992), information benefits result from access, timing, and referrals. Because humans have limited information processing capabilities, relationships provide access to the human capital of others. Relationships can also affect timing, that is, when one learns about a piece of information is important. As Burt (1992, p. 14) notes, "It is one thing to find out that the stock market is crashing today. It is another to discover that the price of your stocks will plummet tomorrow." Finally, relationships can provide the benefits of referrals. Personal contacts can refer you to others and can provide references for you. In this case, information about you is transferred to others through their network connections.

In suggesting that relationships have benefits, researchers have found that one's social network relates to such outcomes as job attainment, job satisfaction, power, and promotions in organizations (Brass, 1984; Krackhardt & Brass, 1994; Burt, 1992). The underlying assumption is that an employee's friends and acquaintances help the employee obtain promotion by providing such forms of social capital as critical information, mentorship, and good references.

Opportunity Costs

The process of developing social capital may include opportunity costs as well as benefits. For example, developing strong, trusting relationships may interfere with the opportunities for bridging diverse groups through weak ties (Gargiulo & Benassi, 1999). As Granovetter (1985) noted, the obligations and expectations of strong, long-lasting relationships may prevent a person from realizing greater economic opportunities by constraining the search for and development of new training partners. Gabbay (1997) has noted that some actors may be constrained by the same social structure that benefits other actors.

Social Liabilities

Labianca and Brass (1997) have expanded the notion of social capital by adding to it the role of negative relationships— relationships in which at least one person has a negative affective judgment of the other. For example, it is likely that an employee's negative relationships with others in an organization might prevent promotion if those others withhold critical information or provide bad references. Thus, Labianca and Brass (1997) argue that it may be equally important to consider the negative side of the social ledger: social liabilities as well as social capital. Just as a financial ledger records financial assets and liabilities, the social ledger is an accounting of social assets (social capital) and social liabilities (negative relationships).

Labianca and Brass (1997) distinguish between social liabilities (negative relationships) and the opportunity costs of building social capital. Social liabilities are the opposite of social capital. They do not represent lost opportunities or the indirect cost of accruing social capital by having some positive relationships rather than other positive relationships, or pursuing weak ties rather than strong ties. Rather, they represent potential liabilities that can result from negative relationships.

Perceptions of Relationships

It is important to note that people observe the relationships of others and have cognitive maps that represent those relationships. For example, Kilduff and Krackhardt (1994) argue that individuals are known by the relationships they keep. As an illustration, they note that when the wealthy and successful baron de Rothschild was asked for a loan, he reportedly replied, "I won't give you the loan myself; but I will walk arm-in-arm with you across the floor of the Stock Exchange, and you soon shall have lenders to spare" (Kilduff & Krackhardt, 1994, p. 87). Thus, relationships may confer benefits, such as legitimacy, depending on how they are perceived by others. Leaders may bask in the reflected glory of their associates— or they may be guilty by association.

Types of Relationships

Strong Ties

In social network terms, strong ties are differentiated from weak ties on the basis of duration, emotional intensity, intimacy, and reciprocity (Granovetter, 1973). Strong ties are often characterized as friendships, while weak ties are often said to connect acquaintances. Strong tie relationships involve actors who may be more credible and trusted sources of information (or other resources), more motivated to provide the resources in a timely fashion, and more readily available than weak tie relationships. For example, valuable information is more likely to be shared with close friends than with acquaintances. One's attitudes and opinions also are more likely affected by close friends than by casual acquaintances (Krackhardt, 1992). Thus, strong ties may be the primary medium for social influence. Strong links to others also provide social and emotional support. For example, mentoring relationships in organizations involve strong ties. Strong ties are also exemplified in Coleman's notion that social capital is found in the trust and mutual expectations and obligations of relationships.

The functional, beneficial consequences of strong ties have often been extolled (at least indirectly) in leadership and management. These are the types of ties that build loyalty, trust, mutual respect, and emotional attachment between "leaders and his men." For example, Sparrowe and Liden (1997) have noted that strong ties are similar to the type of relationship between a supervisor and employees advocated by the leader-member exchange (LMX) approach to leadership. High-LMX relationships, characterized by trust and mutual reciprocation, have been shown to relate to follower satisfaction, performance, and turnover (Graen & Uhl-Bien, 1995).

Despite the advantages of strong ties, there are also important opportunity costs, or disadvantages. Strong ties require time and energy to maintain, they are difficult to break, and they may prevent access to new opportunities. For example, a leader may be reluctant to choose a more cost-effective supplier when the relationship with the current supplier is long term and trusting.

In addition, people who are linked to an individual by strong ties are likely to be linked themselves (Granovetter, 1973, 1982). That is, friends of an individual also are likely to be friends. For example, we invite our friends to dinner, introduce them to each other, and they subsequently become friends. Two friends are likely to be in the same social circle and subject to the same information and resources. Thus, an important disadvantage of strong ties is that they may provide redundant information. Nonredundant information is more likely provided by weak ties.

Weak Ties

Casual acquaintances, represented by infrequent interaction and indifferent affect, are characterized by weak ties. As opposed to strong ties, people who are linked to you through weak ties are not likely to be linked themselves. An individual's acquaintances are much less likely to be linked than an individual's friends. The "strength of weak ties" (Granovetter, 1973, 1982) lies in the fact that such ties often act as bridges between groups. As such, these weak relationships often are key sources of novel, divergent, nonredundant information or resources. Weak ties can be a useful source of information about job opportunities and consequently income attainment (Granovetter, 1982; Boxman, De Graaf, & Flap, 1991; Lin, Ensel, & Vaughn, 1981). Other research has emphasized and modified the strength of weak ties (see Wegener, 1991, for a review).

Weak ties often bridge otherwise unconnected groups, acting as conduits for the flow of information between groups. Although the dense connections of strong ties within a group can foster trust and loyalty, common expectations and obligations, and norms, a lack of weak ties outside the group can foster density-induced prejudice and mistrust of outsiders. The social psychology literature is rich with examples of biases and stereotypes regarding in-groups and out-groups. Ties that cross unit boundaries may facilitate cooperation (Krackhardt & Stern, 1988). Weak ties require less time and energy to maintain, but the cost of weak ties is that acquaintances may not be motivated to provide you with information in a timely fashion. Weak ties also fail to provide the trust and mutual expectations and obligations that Coleman (1988) noted.

Negative Ties

Negative ties are defined as relationships in which at least one person has a negative affective judgment of another person (Labianca & Brass, 1997); they represent the opposite end of the continuum of strong and weak ties. The importance of considering the social liabilities of negative relationships is based on negative asymmetry: the possibility that negative ties may have greater explanatory power than positive ties in organizations. For example, in an organizational field study, Labianca, Brass, and Gray (1998) found that negative relationships increased perceptions of intergroup conflict, but strong positive relationships had no counterbalancing effect.

Taylor (1991) summarizes a diverse psychological literature indicating that negative events elicit greater physiological, affective, cognitive, and behavioral activity and lead to more cognitive analysis than neutral or positive events. In seeking to explain negative asymmetry, Skowronski and Carlston (1989) summarize a number of theories (see Labianca & Brass, 1997, for a review). For example, negative events dominate social judgment because of the contrast effects with positive and moderate events that people typically experience and expect. Since people expect positive, moderate information, negative, extreme information is weighted more heavily in impression formation. Negative information is also attended to because it is more unambiguous than positive information; it allows people to make social judgments more easily.

In addition to direct social information, indirect social information can result in negative relationships. Secondhand information is filtered and simplified so as to be unambiguous, and amplification of negative aspects is often more pronounced than positive information (Burt & Knez, 1995). Dislike of another person can result from negative gossip about that person.

Multiplex Relationships

Relationships can also be characterized by multiplexity, that is, the degree to which two actors are linked by more than one type of relationship (such as friend, business associate, and neighbor) (Burt, 1983). Typically, multiplex relationships are strong ones, although strength is not necessary for multiplexity to occur, and vice versa. Multiplex relationships provide the flexibility of exchanging different kinds of resources in relationships. For example, a leader may obtain information in exchange for friendship. Uzzi (1997) illustrated the advantages of multiplex embedded (strong) relationships. Although such relationships may prevent access to new, more cost-effective opportunities, the multiplexity of the relationship may allow for the exchange of different resources. For example, although a long-term, trusted supplier may not offer the best price, the supplier may provide other resources, such as valuable information or better scheduling of deliveries.

Multiplex ties allow network relationships that were built for one reason to be used for another reason. As the Girl Scouts of the USA knows, your friends and neighbors are more likely than strangers to buy cookies from your daughter. Friendship relationships are used for economic transactions. At the network level of analysis, Coleman (1988) notes that social capital inherent in an established network can be appropriated for other purposes.

Structure of Relationships

The characteristics of strength, negative affect, and multiplexity describe the relational content of dyadic ties. However, dyadic interactions seldom occur in isolation; relationships within organizations almost always involve other parties. The addition of relationships among multiple parties requires consideration of the structure of relationships. One advantage of the network perspective is its focus on the structure of the entire network in addition to the dyadic ties. To illustrate the effects of the structure of relationships, we consider the degree to which these other people are connected within the network.

Density

The total number of network ties divided by the total number of possible ties in a group is referred to as density (Scott, 1991). It is a measure of the extent to which people in a network are interconnected. From the perspective of the group, dense interconnections may be necessary for the establishment of norms, mutual expectations and obligations, and (when these ties are strong) trust (Coleman, 1988, p. 107, refers to "closure in the network"). That is, people must interact with each other to establish norms and mutual expectations. Coleman (1988), Granovetter (1985), and Burt and Knez (1995) arrive at a similar conclusion regarding density and trust in the New York City diamond exchange. The closely knit community of diamond merchants can easily monitor behavior in a business where reputation is critical to success. In addition, these dense network relations provide for the rapid dissemination of any instances of unethical behavior (Brass, Butterfield, & Skaggs, 1998).

Centrality

In addition to considering the overall density of relationships, we can assess the extent to which individuals or leaders are central to the overall structure. Centrality is not an individual attribute; it is contingent on the structure of relationships.

The results of small group laboratory studies in the 1950s (see Shaw, 1964, for a review) indicate that one's position in the social network structure of task-performing groups was a powerful predictor of perceptions of leadership. Although these studies are limited in their generalizability, certain network structures resulted in more than 90 percent of the subjects listing the same name when asked, "Did your group have a leader? If so, who?" (Leavitt, 1951). These leaders occupied central positions in the network.

More recently, social network studies in a variety of settings have consistently found that centrality is related to influence and power (see Brass, 1992, for a review). If, as Yukl (1994, p. 223) has argued, "influence is the essence of leadership," then we can anticipate that centrality will be significantly associated with leadership in organizations.

Increasing one's social capital by gaining a position of centrality and leadership in a social network can be accomplished in three slightly different ways. First, for anyone who has the time and energy, simply making lots of connections can be effective, if not always efficient. If we think of central players as having lots of connections, we could measure a leader's centrality by the number of links that person has in the network. Other things being equal, larger networks are better than smaller ones (Brass & Burkhardt, 1992). However, as the size of the network increases, the costs of time and energy become more pronounced. In addition, the number of links may become less important as information technologies allow one to make connections with an almost infinite set of actors. Thus, rather than randomly building lots of relationships, two other methods for becoming central in a network are proposed.

Connecting to Central Others

Assuming a limit to the number of direct links that a leader can maintain, building ties to highly connected, central others is more efficient than links to peripheral others who are not well connected. This second method of gaining centrality allows a leader to be central by virtue of a few direct links to others who have many direct links. The leader has indirect access to resources such as information through the links of the highly connected other. However, the reliance on indirect links creates a dependency on the highly connected other to mediate the flow of resources. Thus, this method of gaining centrality and social capital probably requires the trust of a strong tie (a close, frequent relationship) with the highly connected other.

Connecting to highly central others can result in "basking in the reflected glory" of the other, but some caution is required. Because we are known by the company we keep, it is important that the highly central other be respected, liked, or admired by others. In addition, it may appear that the leader is "riding the coattails" or "playing second fiddle" to the highly central other. The difference in perceptions may be the result of the stage of one's career. Early in one's career, strong connections to a mentor are perceived as an indication of potential success. This mentor provides access to the network. However, later in one's career, one is expected to perform successfully on one's own and to mentor others, especially if one is to obtain leadership status.

Connecting to powerful others may be an important means of gaining social capital for women, minorities, or newcomers who may face barriers to entry in established networks (Ibarra, 1992, 1993), as Burt's (1992) analyses suggest. Using the criterion of early promotions, Burt (1992) found that connecting to powerful others was an effective strategy for women and newly hired managers. Brass (1985) found that for a sample of nonsupervisors, links to the dominant coalition (a small group of top executives in the company) were related to promotions for women as well as men.

Connecting Others Who Are Not Themselves Connected

A leader can also gain social capital by mediating the flow of resources between others who are otherwise not connected. This third method of gaining centrality involves the leader's becoming the central link or bridge between different individuals or groups. As such, these bridging relationships often are key sources of novel, divergent, nonredundant information or resources (similar to the "strength of weak tie" argument). "Structural hole" is the term Burt (1992) used to refer to the absence of a link between two actors; a structural hole exists when the leader is connected to two people who are not themselves connected. Burt (1992) suggests that entrepreneurial leaders take advantage of structural holes. He argues that the strength of the tie is less important than whether it bridges diverse, unconnected groups (for example, not all weak ties necessarily bridge otherwise unconnected groups). The leader is in a position to control the information flow between the two (that is, broker the relationship), mediating synergistic exchanges or playing the two off against each other. The leader is central by virtue of being the hub of activity; all resource exchanges flow through the leader.

This third centrality strategy may be particularly effective when leaders are judged by their ability to bring together otherwise disconnected individuals or groups. Ties that cross unit boundaries have been shown to facilitate cooperation between groups (Krackhardt & Stern, 1988). Connecting otherwise disconnected others may be particularly important in rapidly changing environments where the leader is required to create and improvise as new opportunities arise. Leadership during rapid change may involve identifying, locating, and organizing the necessary competencies across organizational and international boundaries. Effective leaders become human resource brokers, bringing together the right mix of people and technology to offer a product or service successfully. And that mix may be used only temporarily as environments and technologies rapidly change (Brass, 1995b).

Connecting otherwise disconnected others may also be important in transformational leadership. The transformational leadership paradigm has resurrected interest in visionary, inspirational, charismatic leadership, emphasizing the personal attributes and activities of leaders (Bass, 1996; House, Spangler, & Woycke, 1991; Kuhnert & Lewis, 1987; Yammarino & Bass, 1990). Rather than appealing to the self-interests of followers, the transformational leader motivates followers to transcend their own self-interests for the sake of the larger group. Recognizing the need for revitalizing the organization, the transformational leader inspires followers with a vision of a better future (Tichy & Devanna, 1986). Although the focus of transformational leadership has been on the content of the vision and the personal attributes, values, and personality (the human capital) of the leader (Kuhnert & Lewis, 1987; Larwood, Falbe, Kriger, & Miesing, 1995; Westley & Mintzberg, 1989), Tichy and Devanna (1986) suggest that the transformational leader develops extensive external networks to a diverse set of contacts. Similarly, Bennis and Nanus (1985) found that top-level organizational leaders did not develop these transformational visions in isolation. Rather, these top executives reported extensive contact, both within and outside their organizations, and attention to a diversity of viewpoints from others. Thus, when innovation and vision are required of leaders, they will be effective in developing visions when they bridge diverse groups, acquiring novel, innovative, nonredundant information. The acquisition of creative ideas (Brass, 1995a) may require contacts with a scattered, disconnected group of actors, including actors in different functional areas and actors outside the organization.

Developing network paths for transmitting transformational visions throughout the organization may require a different strategy. The diffusion of such information might be efficiently and effectively accomplished through connections with central players. The transformational leader contacts central actors in each clique, or work group, allowing those central actors to translate the vision to others. Such a strategy transmits the vision to the greatest number of others in the shortest amount of time.

It is important to note that Geletkanycz and Hambrick (1997) found that the external links of top executives were related to organizational performance when these links were within the executives' industry. External links outside the primary industry of the executives did not relate to organizational performance. Thus, connecting those who are not connected and gaining novel, nonredundant information may not always produce benefits. As Geletkanycz and Hambrick note, the executives with intra-industry links may have acquired less novel information, but they may have had very good, reliable information about trends in their own industry.

Centrality and Power

Leaders can acquire social capital by gaining centrality in three ways: building large networks of direct contacts; building connections with highly central others, thus gaining indirect access to the resources of those people connected to the highly central others; and building connections with individuals or groups who are not themselves connected. Research (Brass, 1984; Brass & Burkhardt,

1992, 1993) has shown that these three types of centrality are interrelated and that each is positively associated with intraorganizational influence and promotions. From a resource dependence or exchange theory perspective (Emerson, 1962; Pfeffer & Salancik, 1978), social capital and power result from access to and control over important organizational resources such as information. People who have access to resources decrease their dependence on others. People who control relevant resources increase others' dependence on them, thereby acquiring power (Pfeffer, 1981). These types of centrality capture both access to others through a great number of direct and indirect links and control through mediating the flow of resources between otherwise disconnected others.

In discussing centrality, only nonnegative links have been considered. Being central in a network of negative affective ties (being directly or indirectly disliked by many others) will likely destroy any chance for assuming a leadership role. Potential leaders must also be careful not to link to others who are disliked or not trusted to avoid any perceptions of guilt by association. On the other hand, it is common to hear that leaders disregard others on their way up, or, conversely, that "nice guys finish last." More research is needed to investigate the effects of negative ties on leadership.

Combining Relationship Types and Structure

The structure of relationships is not completely independent of the types of relationships that exist between the actors. For example, although all weak ties do not necessarily bridge diverse groups, the strategy of connecting those who are not themselves connected likely involves weak ties and overlaps with the potential advantages and disadvantages of weak ties.

In addition, the density of the network will affect opportunities for bridging structural holes. Thus, there may be trade-offs between the social capital of the collective and the social capital of the individual. Densely connected networks of nonnegative ties may result in the common norms, expectations, and trust that facilitate collective action and individual transactions within a group. Dense ties provide for the rapid transmission of enforcement of norms. At the same time, dense connections may prevent individuals from taking advantage of structural holes within the group. There will be fewer disconnected others in a dense network. However, the relatively large size of most organizations prevents high density in such networks.

As the size of a network increases, the possibility of fragmentation (individuals' forming subgroups) increases (Berelson & Steiner, 1964; Shaw, 1971). Increases in size make it more difficult for each member of a group or organization to interact with every other member. Because similarity breeds attraction and interaction, subgroups of similar people form. Similarity and increased interaction lead to strong ties among subgroup members, resulting in what network researchers refer to as strong cliques—densely connected subgroups of reciprocated ties within the network (Doreian, 1979).

Given a limit to the number of strong ties a person can maintain, dense connections within a group may decrease the probability of strong connections across groups. There is a rich history of research on group membership and its effects on intergroup conflict, stereotypes, and biases of in-groups and out-groups (Simmel, 1955; Tajfel & Turner, 1985; Coser, 1956; see Pruitt & Rubin, 1985, for review). In general, in-group strength and density may promote positive in-group biases and negative out-group biases. As the size of an organization increases, the fragmentation of the network (into cliques) may also decrease the possibility of common norms and mutual expectations and obligations across groups within the entire organization (Granovetter, 1985). Thus, it may be difficult for large organizations to maintain the social capital of the collective across fragmented cliques.

The problem of the formation of cliques and the trade-off between individual and collective social capital may be simultaneously remedied if leaders pursue structural holes by forming ties with members of other groups. Such a strategy should help provide nonredundant information to the leader and his or her group and constrain the possibility of prejudices between in-groups and out-groups and the homogeneous thinking that can lead to groupthink. At the same time, these bridging links between otherwise disconnected groups may provide the opportunity for establishing common norms, expectations, and obligations. Thus, leaders may be able to share in the collective social capital while also gaining individual social capital.

Knowledge of the Network

Knowledge of the social network might properly be classified as human capital that enables the acquisition of social capital. Krack-hardt (1990) has shown that accurate perceptions of the social network are related to power in an organization. Connecting to central others and connecting those who are not connected require some knowledge of the interaction patterns in organization. Yet Krackhardt's results also show that people are not very good at assessing the political landscape. This may result from a lack of awareness of the benefits of social capital. Leaders need to assess their own position within a network, as well as gain some awareness of the overall patterns of social relationships. Such an assessment would seem easier for those already in central positions as compared to those in peripheral positions. Thus, it is likely that centrality leads to improved assessment of the social network, which itself can lead to greater centrality and more social capital. Social capital and human capital are intertwined, each affecting and being affected by the other.

Conclusion

In discussing the possible benefits of social relationships to leaders in organizations, I have tried to nudge the study of leadership toward a more social, less individualistic approach. Among other benefits, social relationships provide access to the human capital of others. Because leadership involves accomplishing goals through others, social capital is essential to good leadership, just as human capital is.

Putnam (1995) has characterized the decline of social capital in America as synonymous with "bowling alone." He proposes the rebirth of associations, the building of dense networks that can restore the trust, mutual expectations and obligations, and common norms that Coleman (1988) suggests exemplifies social capital. This may be a requirement for transformational leadership. We may be in need of leaders who can envision collective values that transcend the individual preference for bowling alone. Not only can leaders gain social capital by building networks, but they can act as the hub around which others gather to benefit from the social capital of the collective. By connecting to central others, connecting those who are not connected, and gaining knowledge of the network, leaders can provide the synergy for the aggregation of human capital in getting things done. They can build networks of strong multiplex ties that are appropriable for a variety of tasks. And they can embrace the diversity of human capital that is available by linking otherwise disconnected individuals and groups. From the social capital perspective, this is leadership.

References

Bass, B. M. (1990). From transactional to transformational leadership: Learning to share the vision. *Organizational Dynamics, 18*, 19–31.

Bass, B. M. (1996). *A new paradigm of leadership: An inquiry into transformational leadership.* Alexandria, VA: U.S. Army Research Institute for the Behavioral and Social Sciences.

Bennis, W. G., & Nanus, B. (1985). *Leaders: The strategies for taking charge.* New York: HarperCollins.

Berelson, B., & Steiner, G. (1964). *Human behavior: An investigation of scientific findings.* Orlando, FL: Harcourt Brace.

Bourdieu, P. (1977). *Outline of a theory of practice.* New York: Cambridge University Press.

Boxman, E.A.W., De Graaf, P. M., & Flap, H. D. (1991). The impact of social and human capital on the income attainment of Dutch managers. *Social Networks, 13*, 51–73.

Brass, D. J. (1984). Being in the right place: A structural analysis of individual influence in an organization. *Administrative Science Quarterly, 29*, 518–539.

Brass, D. J. (1985). Men's and women's networks: A study of interaction patterns and influence in an organization. *Academy of Management Journal, 28*, 327–343.

Brass, D. J. (1992). Power in organizations: A social network perspective. In G. Moore & J. A. Whitt (Eds.), *Research in politics and society.* Greenwich, CT: JAI Press.

Brass, D. J. (1995a). Creativity: It's all in your social network. In C. M. Ford & D. A. Gioia (Eds.), *Creative action in organizations.* Thousand Oaks, CA: Sage.

Brass, D. J. (1995b). A social network perspective on human resources management. In G. Ferris (Ed.), *Research in personnel and human resources management* (Vol. 13). Greenwich, CT: JAI Press.

Brass, D. J., & Burkhardt, M. E. (1992). Centrality and power in organizations. In N. Nohria & R. Eccles (Eds.), *Networks and organizations: Structure, form, and action.* Boston: Harvard Business School Press.

Brass, D. J., & Burkhardt, M. E. (1993). Potential power and power use: An investigation of structure and behavior. *Academy of Management Journal, 36,* 441–470.

Brass, D. J., Butterfield, K. D., & Skaggs, B. C. (1998). Relationships and unethical behavior: A social network perspective. *Academy of Management Review, 23,* 14–31.

Brass, D. J., & Krackhardt, D. (1998). The social capital of twenty-first-century leaders. In J. G. Hunt & R. L. Phillips (Eds.), *Out-of-the-box leadership: Transforming the twenty-first-century army and other top performing organizations.* Greenwich, CT: JAI Press.

Burt, R. S. (1983). Distinguishing relational contents. In R. S. Burt & M. J. Miner (Eds.), *Applied network analysis.* Thousand Oaks, CA: Sage.

Burt, R. S. (1992). *Structural holes: The social structure of competition.* Cambridge, MA: Harvard University Press.

Burt, R. S. (1997). The contingent value of social capital. *Administrative Science Quarterly, 42,* 339–365.

Burt, R. S., & Knez, M. (1995). Kinds of third-party effects on trust. *Rationality and Society, 7,* 255–292.

Coleman, J. S. (1988). Social capital in the creation of human capital. *American Journal of Sociology, 94,* 95–120.

Coleman, J. S. (1990). *Foundations of social theory.* Cambridge, MA: Harvard University Press.

Coser, L. (1956). *The functions of social conflict.* New York: Free Press.

Doreian, P. (1979). *Mathematics and the study of social relationships.* London: Weidenfeld & Nicolson.

Emerson, R. M. (1962). Power-dependency relations. *American Sociological Review, 27,* 31–41.

Fukuyama, F. (1995). *Trust: Social virtues and the creation of prosperity.* London: Hamish Hamilton.

Gabbay, S. M. (1997). *Social capital in the creation of financial capital.* Champaign, IL: Stipes.

Gargiulo, M., & Benassi, M. (1999). The dark side of social capital. In S. M. Gabbay & R.T.A.J. Leenders (Eds.), *Corporate social capital and liability.* Boston: Kluwer.

Geletkanycz, M. A., & Hambrick, D. C. (1997). The external ties of top executives: Implications for strategic choice and performance. *Administrative Science Quarterly, 42,* 654–681.

Graen, G. B., & Uhl-Bien, M. (1995). Relationship-based approach to leadership: Development of leader-member exchange (LMX) theory over 25 years: Applying a multi-level, multi-domain perspective. *Leadership Quarterly, 6,* 219–247.

Granovetter, M. S. (1973). The strength of weak ties. *American Journal of Sociology, 78,* 1360–1380.

Granovetter, M. S. (1982). The strength of weak ties: A network theory revisited. In P. V. Marsden & N. Lin (Eds.), *Social structure and network analysis*. Thousand Oaks, CA: Sage.

Granovetter, M. S. (1985). Economic action and social structure: The problem of embeddedness. *American Journal of Sociology, 91*, 481–510.

House, R. J., Spangler, W. D., & Woycke, J. (1991). Personality and charisma in the U.S. presidency: A psychological theory of leader effectiveness. *Administrative Science Quarterly, 36*, 364–396.

Ibarra, H. (1992). Homophily and differential returns: Sex differences in network structure and access in an advertising firm. *Administrative Science Quarterly, 37*, 422–447.

Ibarra, H. (1993). Personal networks of women and minorities in management: A conceptual framework. *Academy of Management Review, 18*, 56–87.

Jacobs, J. (1965). *The death and life of great American cities*. New York: Penguin.

Kilduff, M., & Krackhardt, D. (1994). Bringing the individual back in: A structural analysis of the internal market for reputation in organizations. *Academy of Management Journal, 37*, 87–108.

Krackhardt, D. (1990). Assessing the political landscape: Structure, cognition, and power in organizations. *Administrative Science Quarterly, 35*, 342–369.

Krackhardt, D. (1992). The strength of strong ties: The importance of philos. In N. Nohria & R. Eccles (Eds.), *Networks and organizations: Structure, form, and action*. Boston: Harvard Business School Press.

Krackhardt, D., & Brass, D. J. (1994). Intraorganizational networks: The micro side. In S. Wasserman & J. Galaskiewicz (Eds.), *Advances in social network analysis*. Thousand Oaks, CA: Sage.

Krackhardt, D., & Stern, R. N. (1988). Informal networks and organizational crisis: An experimental simulation. *Social Psychology Quarterly, 51*, 123–140.

Kuhnert, K. W., & Lewis, P. (1987). Transactional and transformational leadership: A constructive/developmental analysis. *Academy of Management Review, 12*, 648–657.

Labianca, G., & Brass, D. J. (1997). Exploring the social ledger: The role of negative affective relationships in social networks. In *Proceedings of the Academy of Management Meetings*. Boston: Academy of Management.

Labianca, G., Brass, D. J., & Gray, B. (1998). Social networks and perceptions of intergroup conflict: The impact of negative relationships and third parties. *Academy of Management Journal, 41*, 55–67.

Larwood, L., Falbe, C. M., Kriger, M. P., & Miesing, P. (1995). Structure and meaning of organizational vision. *Academy of Management Journal, 38*, 740–768.

Leavitt, H. J. (1951). Some effects of certain communication patterns on group performance. *Journal of Abnormal and Social Psychology, 46,* 38–50.

Lin, N., Ensel, W. M., & Vaughn, J. C. (1981). Social resources and strength of ties: Structural factors in occupational status attainment. *American Sociological Review, 46,* 393–405.

Loury, G. C. (1977). A dynamic theory of racial income differences. In P. A. Wallace & A. M. La Monde (Eds.), *Women, minorities, and employment discrimination.* San Francisco: New Lexington Press.

Luthans, F., Rosenkrantz, S. A., & Hennessey, H. W. (1985). What do successful managers really do? An observational study of managerial activities. *Journal of Applied Behavioral Science, 21,* 255–270.

Meindl, J. R. (1993). Reinventing leadership: A radical social psychological approach. In J. K. Murnighan (Ed.), *Social psychology in organizations: Advances in theory and practice.* Upper Saddle River, NJ: Prentice Hall.

Mintzberg, H. (1973). *The nature of managerial work.* New York: Harper-Collins.

Pfeffer, J. (1981). *Power in organizations.* Marshfield, MA: Pittman.

Pfeffer, J., & Salancik, G. R. (1978). *The external control of organizations.* New York: HarperCollins.

Pruitt, D., & Rubin, J. Z. (1985). *Social conflict: Escalation, impasse, and resolution.* Reading, MA: Addison-Wesley.

Putnam, R. D. (1995). Bowling alone: America's declining social capital. *Journal of Democracy, 6,* 65–78.

Scott, J. (1991). *Social network analysis: A handbook.* Thousand Oaks, CA: Sage.

Shaw, M. E. (1964). Communication networks. In L. Berkowitz (Ed.), *Advances in experimental social psychology* (Vol. 1). Orlando, FL: Academic Press.

Shaw, M. E. (1971). *Group dynamics: The psychology of small group behavior.* New York: McGraw-Hill.

Simmel, G. (1955). *Conflict and the web of group affiliations.* New York: Free Press.

Skowronski, J. J., & Carlston, D. E. (1989). Negativity and extremity biases in impression formation: A review of explanations. *Psychological Bulletin, 105,* 131–142.

Sparrowe, R. T., & Liden, R. C. (1997). Process and structure in leader-member exchange. *Academy of Management Review, 22,* 522–552.

Tajfel, H., & Turner, J. C. (1985). The social identity theory of intergroup behavior. In S. Worchel & W. G. Austin (Eds.), *Psychology of intergroup relations* (2nd ed.). Chicago: Nelson-Hall.

Taylor, S. E. (1991). Asymmetrical effects of positive and negative events: The mobilization-minimization hypothesis. *Psychological Bulletin, 110,* 67–85.

Tichy, N. M., & Devanna, M. A. (1986). *The transformational leader.* New York: Wiley.

Uzzi, B. (1997). Social structure and competition in interfirm networks: The paradox of embeddedness. *Administrative Science Quarterly, 42,* 35–67.

Wegener, B. (1991). Job mobility and social ties: Social resources, prior jobs, and status attainment. *American Sociological Review, 56,* 60–71.

Westley, F., & Mintzberg, H. (1989). Visionary leadership and strategic management. *Strategic Management Journal, 10,* 17–32.

Yammarino, F. J., & Bass, B. M. (1990). Long-term forecasting of transformational leadership and its effects among naval officers. In K. E. Clark (Ed.), *Measures of leadership.* West Orange, NJ: Leadership Library of America.

Yukl, G. (1994). *Leadership in organizations* (3rd ed.). Upper Saddle River, NJ: Prentice Hall.

CHAPTER 6

The Contest for Corporate Control

Catherine M. Daily
Dan R. Dalton

The distribution of power among chief executive officers (CEOs), top management team (TMT) members, and boards of directors has been the subject of considerable academic inquiry (Daily & Schwenk, 1996; Fredrickson, Hambrick, & Baumrin, 1988; Mizruchi, 1983; Pearce & Zahra, 1991). At issue is the extent to which management, as compared to the board of directors, is the more influential of these two powerful organizational groups. The popular press too is replete with examples of power contests between corporate management and directors. Many of these examples center around key corporate events such as hostile takeovers, mergers and acquisitions, board reform issues (for example, adoption of poison pill provisions, golden parachutes, staggered board provisions), and executive succession. CEO compensation also is a recurring theme.

Discussions of the balance of power between firm executives and boards of directors challenge us to consider the view we hold of organizational leaders. Agency theory, for example, suggests the need for formal separation between firm management and the board of directors (see Eisenhardt, 1989, and Jensen & Meckling, 1976, for overviews of agency theory). This theoretical perspective emanates from the separation of ownership and control in the modern corporation (Berle & Means, 1932). In earlier periods (circa 1870–1920) of U.S. enterprise development, the owners of the business were its managers. Since then, ownership, principally through shareholdings, is diffuse. The contemporary corporation may have hundreds of thousands of owners. By contrast, then, it is extremely unusual for TMT members to hold substantive equity in their firm. These are professional managers, rarely owners.

As a consequence of this separation and a function of managers' firm-specific knowledge and managerial expertise, managers may elect to pursue actions that are arguably more self-serving than they are organizational-serving in focus and outcome (Mizruchi, 1988). The board of directors, most of them independent, objective decision makers, was designed as a means of protecting shareholders from this potential managerial opportunism (Fama & Jensen, 1983; Jensen & Meckling, 1976; Williamson, 1985).

Not all observers, however, embrace this view of managers or perceive the need for protective mechanisms such as the board of directors. Those advocating stewardship theory (see Donaldson, 1990, and Donaldson & Davis, 1991, 1994, for overviews) note that managers are sufficiently self-motivated to serve the interests of shareholders, absent some oversight body. According to this perspective, having control of the corporation centralized in the hands of managers will lead to greater profitability and shareholder returns as managers effectively discharge their duties (Donaldson & Davis, 1994). Consistent with this perspective, a series of studies have demonstrated the positive impact of inside (management) directors (Baysinger, Kosnik, & Turk, 1991; Boyd, 1994; Hill & Snell, 1988; Hoskisson, Johnson, & Moesel, 1994).

We rely on these two theoretical perspectives to examine two prominent areas of potential tension between corporate executives and board members: board composition and board leadership structure. We also discuss an emerging power in corporate control contests: institutional investors. Institutional investors, particularly public pension funds, have been at the forefront of board reform efforts in recent years. Much of institutions' efforts have been devoted to structuring more independent boards through recomposition of the board and formal separation of the CEO and board chairperson positions. As noted by John Biggs, CEO and chair of TIAA-CREF, one of the largest and most powerful institutional investors, "We believe that modern and sound practices of corporate governance will make a difference in the future performance of

companies. Those with able and qualified independent directors . . . will eventually outperform companies that do not have such
boards." Finally, we conclude with discussion of the manner in
which either board or management dominance may affect two of
the more critical corporate leadership processes: CEO succession
and setting CEOs' compensation. We focus on the CEO when discussing succession and compensation because this role represents
the pinnacle of formal leadership in the corporate organization.

Dominance or Balance?

Research has proposed a distinction between balanced and dominant governance configurations (Daily & Schwenk, 1996). At issue
is the extent to which there is an asymmetrical level of influence
between a firm's top executives and board members with regard
to firm processes and outcomes, or whether these two powerful organizational groups act as countervailing forces (Daily & Schwenk,
1996). As Pearce and Zahra (1991, p. 135) noted, many organizational observers would like to see "a healthy balance between CEO
and board powers."

Pearce and Zahra (1991, p. 135) have also noted that a balance
between management and the board will "ensure effective company performance." Ultimately, assessing the bottom-line impact
of any contest for control in the corporation is essential. It may be,
for example, that managerial dominance, board dominance, or a
balanced approach would lead to differential firm performance.
We explore these perspectives by focusing on the two governance
configurations that may provide the most insight into balancing
managerial and shareholder interests: board composition and
board leadership structure.

Board Composition

One means for achieving balance between executives and board
members is through careful attention to the composition of the
board of directors. A central issue with regard to board composition is the extent to which the CEO may effectively dominate the
board. Previous research has demonstrated that certain board configurations may facilitate CEO power at the expense of board

power (Daily & Johnson, 1997). Imbalances of this sort place share-holders at risk of being unduly subject to managerial opportunism. Other board configurations, however, may better facilitate board, as compared to executive, power.

The three most commonly used measures of board composition are inside director proportion, outside director proportion, and affiliated director proportion. Each of these may differentially afford management, specifically the CEO, an ability to influence the board of directors. We also consider a fourth measure of board composition that has recently emerged in the literature: the distinction between independent and interdependent directors (for a comprehensive overview of these board composition categories, see Daily, Johnson, & Dalton, 1999).

Inside Directors

Inside directors are typically defined as members of the firm's management who also serve on the board of directors (Byrd & Hickman, 1992; Gilson, 1990; Goodstein & Boeker, 1991; Hermalin & Weisbach, 1988). Because these board members are also members of firm management, they are considered to constitute the TMT (Krishnan, 1997; Michel & Hambrick, 1992). Under the tenets of agency theory, appointment of inside directors to the board would generally be seen as potentially harmful to shareholders' interests. The primary criticism of inside directors is their general inability or unwillingness to monitor the CEO effectively (see Johnson, Daily, & Ellstrand, 1996). Inside directors, as a function of their direct reporting relationship with the CEO, are placed in the uncomfortable position of having to evaluate their boss (Fleischer, Hazard, & Klipper, 1988; Patton & Baker, 1987; Weisbach, 1988). Importantly, these directors may also be involved in decisions that present them with a direct conflict of interest, such as the adoption of anti-takeover devices. John Smale, General Motors Corp. outside director, has bluntly noted, "Inside directors, for governance purposes, are essentially useless" (Firstenberg & Malkiel, 1994, 30).

Johnson and associates (1996) note, however, that agency theory might support inside directors if they serve to reduce information asymmetry between management and the board. It may, for example, be more difficult for a CEO to withhold critical information from the general board in the presence of inside directors (see Vancil, 1987, for related discussion). In addition, stewardship theory would advocate the appointment of inside directors. In their desire to improve the organization and enhance shareholder wealth, inside directors are able to provide valuable firm-specific perspectives to board deliberations (Baysinger & Hoskisson, 1990).

Lorsch and MacIver (1989) have noted an interesting tension between these diverse perspectives with regard to the appointment of inside directors. Although insiders may provide firm-specific information critical to effective board discussions, this same information may hinder the active involvement of nonmanagement directors. Lorsch and MacIver recount one executive's view of the CEO's power over the board:

> I would say that the CEO has a certain unique power over the board. He's the only guy who knows the operations of the firm in depth. He's an expert on the company and that fact alone puts constraints on directors. For example, they may know he came up in the mill and learned all the workings of the company from the bottom up. The directors, on the other hand, may have just joined the board and they may devote, at most, three days a month to the company. They are coming from a different perspective and definitely feel a sense of inferiority to the CEO, and other inside directors, in terms of knowledge [pp. 81–82].

From the perspective of balancing power in the organization, then, significant proportions of inside directors favor management power as compared to board power. Given the noted reticence of many inside directors to challenge the CEO directly, insider-dominated boards strongly favor the CEO in the contest for corporate control.

Outside Directors

A second measure of board composition is outside director proportion. Outside directors are those nonmanagement members of the board with no personal or professional ties to the firm or its management (Buchholtz & Ribbens, 1994; Johnson, Hoskisson, & Hitt, 1993; Weisbach, 1988). The majority of both academics and practitioners have expressed a preference for outsider-dominated boards (Lorsch & MacIver, 1989; Mizruchi, 1983; Zahra & Pearce, 1989). This preference is largely grounded in agency theory. Outside directors, as a function of their independence from the firm and firm management, are believed to provide the most effective monitoring and in the process best protect shareholder interests (Johnson et al., 1996; Mangel & Singh, 1993; Singh & Harianto, 1989).

Stewardship theory, with its focus on firm management, might suggest little need for outside directors as a means to enhance firm performance. Rather than focus directly on the role of outside directors, however, stewardship theory focuses on inside directors, specifically the CEO (Donaldson & Davis, 1991). Stewardship theory views firm managers as both capable and sufficiently motivated to usher the organization toward high performance.

Reliance on significant proportions of outside directors tips the balance of power in favor of the board, as compared to firm management. While greater proportions of inside directors do not necessarily suggest that the CEO's power base will be weak, these directors do provide a tempering force, which may serve as an effective system of checks and balances on firm management.

Affiliated Directors

Affiliated directors are nonmanagement members of the board with personal and professional ties to the firm or firm management (Daily & Dalton, 1994a). Securities and Exchange Commission Regulation 14A, Item 6(b), sets forth criteria for determining outside directors' status as affiliated or nonaffiliated. Affiliated directors are those (1) employed by the firm or an affiliate within the last five years, (2) with a family relationship to an officer or director by blood or marriage, (3) with an affiliation with a supplier, banker, or creditor of the firm within the last two years, (4) with an affiliation with an investment banker within the past two years or within the coming year, (5) associated with a law firm engaged by the corporation, or (6) with significant stock ownership. As with inside directors, at issue is the extent to which these directors are able to fulfill their director roles effectively (especially the control role) given their relationships to the firm or firm management.

Affiliated directors with significant business ties to the firm (such as legal counsel or an accountant) may be hesitant to challenge executives who were likely instrumental in establishing and maintaining the business relationship (Johnson et al., 1996). A level of scrutiny that is perceived as too close may result in the CEO's severing the business relationship with affiliated directors' firms (Johnson et al., 1996). Where affiliated directors' relationships are of a personal nature, the costs to challenging managers may be even more significant and long lasting. Imagine, for example, a case of the CEO's spouse who serves on the board of directors publicly questioning the CEO's actions. Consistent with agency theory, affiliated directors would not be viewed as desirable members of the board as a function of their potential conflict of interests.

Although not directly addressed in the literature, stewardship theory might reasonably be expanded to nonmanagement directors with inside director interests. To the extent to which affiliated directors bring firm-specific information to board discussions, stewardship theory might support the appointment of affiliated directors. As a function of their dependence on the focal firm for some portion of their firm's business, affiliated directors are likely to have a strong interest in maintaining an effective level of firm performance.

Yet another theoretical perspective clouds the potential linkage between affiliated board members and firm outcomes. While it is true that monitoring and control are a necessary role of the contemporary board, there are other fundamental roles as well. Foremost among these is the resource-dependence perspective. A central premise of resource dependence is that directors may enhance firm performance by providing linkages to critical elements of the firm's environment (Pfeffer, 1972, 1973; Pfeffer & Salancik, 1978; Provan, 1980; Selznik, 1949; Zald, 1967). These boundary-spanning agents provide critical access to information, resources, services, and markets that might otherwise be unavailable to the firm.

There is an interesting disconnect, however, between the control role of directors and that of resource dependence. Consider an example. In the former, affiliated (6[b]) directors are considered a threat to board independence; their personal or professional relationships with the CEO are alleged to compromise their otherwise dispassionate judgment. Alternatively, one might imagine board members who are representatives of investment banking firms or crucial suppliers. Presumably these board members could contribute meaningfully in the resource-dependence domain. It is not clear, then, why a board with a high proportion of such directors would invariably constitute a competitive disadvantage to the firm. In this instance, the presence of directors who might lack some of the independence required of agency theory, thereby skewing the balance of power toward the CEO and firm management, may prove extraordinarily beneficial to firm performance. This would be fully consistent with stewardship theory.

Independent and Interdependent Directors

A fourth board composition distinction has emerged in recent years: independent and interdependent director proportion (Boeker, 1992; Daily & Dalton, 1994b; Wade, O'Reilly, & Chandratat, 1990). This measure may be most directly related to CEO power in relation to that of the board. As compared to the other three measures of board composition (inside, outside, and affiliated), this distinction relies on the timing of directors' appointment to the board of directors. Independent directors are those board members appointed prior to the current CEO's tenure (Wade et al., 1990). Interdependent directors are appointed during the tenure of the incumbent CEO (Boeker, 1992).

While most boards maintain nominating committees, it is widely recognized that CEOs typically have a strong influence over director appointments (Mizruchi, 1983). As a consequence, directors appointed during the tenure of the incumbent CEO may feel some sense of loyalty to the CEO and be less vigilant in their monitoring role. This is true regardless of the nature of the board member with regard to the inside, outside, and affiliated director distinctions. Firstenberg and Malkiel (1994, p. 29) have captured this perspective: "Boards have a natural inclination to support management; management has a live persona that the directors interact with and form relationships with, in contrast to an amorphous body of shareholders. The board's shared experience with management in working through problems further builds an innate loyalty."

Consistent with agency theory, then, interdependent directors are not prescribed. As with prescriptions regarding outside directors, agency theory would suggest the need for boards comprising predominantly or exclusively independent directors. Interdependent directors, although they might have no personal or professional relationship with the firm or firm management, may be unwilling to challenge that individual to whom they owe their board seat: the CEO. Their presence on the board, then, strengthens the CEO's power at the expense of board power.

As with affiliated directors, we have not seen direct discussion of the costs and benefits of independent and interdependent directors in treatments of stewardship theory. We might anticipate that advocates of stewardship theory, however, would not share the concerns about interdependent directors that proponents of agency theory would raise. Similarly, we might expect proponents of stewardship theory to be somewhat indifferent with regard to independent directors. Given the belief that inside (or quasi-inside) directors effectively discharge their managerial and director duties for the ultimate benefit of shareholders, independent directors may be not be viewed as comparatively superior in enhancing shareholder value.

Board Leadership Structure

Another indicator of the balance of power in the corporation is board leadership structure, which addresses whether the CEO jointly serves as board chairperson. Joint service is commonly referred to as CEO duality. We focus on this position due to the emphasis on the CEO. Some organizational observers have suggested that the most powerful position in the modern corporation is that of CEO (Harrison, Torres, & Kukalis, 1988; Hosmer, 1982; Pearce, 1981; Pearce & Robinson, 1987). Norburn (1989, p. 2) has suggested that the CEO is "THE corporate leader." Holding the positions of both the CEO and board chair simultaneously ensures an even greater level of formal, if not informal, power (Harrison et al., 1988; Mizruchi, 1983; Ocasio, 1994). We would note that centralization of power through the dual board leadership structure is the standard, not the exception, in large corporations (Lorsch & MacIver, 1989; Rechner & Dalton, 1991).

Agency and stewardship theories are informative here as well. Under the agency theory perspective, CEO duality is not advocated.

At issue is the potential for managerial domination of the board (Firstenberg & Malkiel, 1994; Herman, 1981; Kesner & Johnson, 1990; Lorsch & MacIver, 1989; Mace, 1971; Rechner & Dalton, 1989). As the formal leader of the oversight body, the board of directors, the combined CEO-chairperson controls the agenda of board meetings, determines the information that directors will receive in advance of board meetings, and leads board discussions (Firstenberg & Malkiel, 1994). Moreover, as consistent with the discussion of inside directors, management members of the board may be unlikely to challenge a CEO, especially when he or she also yields power as chairperson of the board.

According to Rechner and Dalton (1989, p. 141) such concentrated authority under the dual structure "represents a prima facie case of conflict of interest." Finkelstein and D'Aveni (1994, p. 1079) have also observed that duality "promotes CEO entrenchment by reducing board monitoring effectiveness." Consequently, CEO duality may significantly skew the balance of power in the corporation toward management and away from the board, in particular away from board independence.

Contrary to agency theory, stewardship theory would advocate reliance on the dual leadership structure. Anderson and Anthony (1986) have noted the benefits of unity of command with CEO duality (see also Alexander, Fennel, & Halpern, 1993; Donaldson, 1990; Finkelstein & D'Aveni, 1994). One of the direct benefits of unified leadership under the dual board leadership structure is the removal of any internal or external ambiguity regarding firm leadership. Proponents of stewardship theory have suggested that this leads to enhanced firm performance and higher shareholder value. Donaldson and Davis (1991, p. 52), for example, have noted "that fusion of the incumbency of the roles of chair and CEO will enhance effectiveness and produce, as a result, superior returns to shareholders than separation of the roles of chair and CEO."

The Emergence of Institutional Investors

In the past decade, institutional investors have emerged as a significant force in shaping the structure of corporate boards and, therefore, the relationship between the board and corporate executives. Institutional investors' focus has largely been on tempering managerial influence in the boardroom. The impact of institutions is largely a function of their rapidly increasing control over corporate equity. Institutions currently control greater than 50 percent of the equity in large U.S. corporations (Useem, 1993). These ownership stakes are believed to provide strong incentive for institutional investors to take an active interest in firm affairs by addressing the problems in the separation of ownership and control (Useem, 1993; see also Coffee, 1994; Davis & Thompson, 1994).

The level of equity held by institutions has led them to take a more active role in ensuring that corporations are structured effectively. Institutions' stock holdings make it difficult for them simply to sell their shares when they become dissatisfied with the way a firm is governed or with the firm's performance (Coffee, 1991; Davis & Thompson, 1994; Johnson & Millon, 1993). To do so may lead to a catastrophic reduction in the value of their holdings. The increasing levels of institutional ownership and relatively inelastic avenues of disposition, then, have largely led to the dramatic rise in institutional investor activism.

The vast majority of institutions' initiatives focus on corporate governance issues, specifically reapportionment of the board of directors and separation of the CEO and board chairperson positions (Bainbridge, 1993; Biggs, 1995; Black, 1992; Cox, 1993; Rock, 1991; Wahal, 1996). The dominant rationale for institutional investors' focus on corporate board reforms is their belief that all too frequently "directors are in management's hip pocket" (Fromson, 1990, p. 78). In sum, their efforts are aimed at redirecting the balance of control in corporations. The desired outcome of institutional investors' activism is increased firm performance (Baldwin, 1984; De Mott, 1980; Kesner, Victor, & Lamont, 1986; Midgley, 1982; Mintzberg, 1983; Nussbaum & Dobryznski, 1987; Tricker, 1984; Weidenbaum, 1985). For example, institutions believe that board composition has a direct impact on shareholder value—that greater board independence will result in higher firm performance (Fromson, 1990; Kim, 1992; Schellhardt, 1991). Interestingly, Wahal (1996) has found that although institutional investors, particularly activist institutions, have been successful in their efforts to affect the governance of targeted firms, these same firms have not demonstrated performance improvements.

Despite the lack of evidence to demonstrate uniformly performance advantages as a function of institutions' focus on corporate governance reforms, institutional investors appear not to be dissuaded in their efforts. Lublin (1997) predicted that one of the largest and most active of institutional investor funds, California Public Employees' Retirement System (CalPERS), would escalate its focus on board reform by seeking corporate board seats. Not only did CalPERS move forward with this initiative, but several other large institutional investors such as TIAA-CREF followed suit (Schultz & Warren, 1998). This represents a dramatic shift in institutional investors' activities and may compromise their ability to act as independent, outside observers by essentially conferring insider status on these fund representatives (Lublin, 1997, p. A3).

At present, however, institutions have proven to be a strong tempering force on managerial power. An institution's impact is consistent with substitution effects (Rediker & Seth, 1995). In the general domain of governance, the substitution hypothesis addresses the extent to which external and internal governance mechanisms "set boundaries on managerial discretion and align the interests of managers with those of shareholders" (Rediker & Seth, 1995, p. 97). The substitution hypothesis provides a more integrative way to examine governance mechanisms because this perspective accounts for interrelationships among governance mechanisms rather than considering each mechanism in isolation. Institutional investor activism in concert with an independently structured board and the separate board leadership structure may prove to be a powerful combination for tempering managerial control of the corporation.

The Bottom Line

Ultimately the bottom line (that is, firm performance) should dominate discussions of the contest for corporate control. Agency theory and stewardship theory lead to different conclusions regarding the appropriate balance of corporate power among executives and board members. Support can be found in the empirical literature for board structures that facilitate board power and those that allow some measure of control to reside in the management ranks. Consistent with agency theory, studies have found that outside directors lead to greater firm performance (Baysinger & Butler, 1985; Ezzamel & Watson, 1993; Pearce & Zahra, 1992; Rosenstein & Wyatt, 1990; Schellenger, Wood, & Tashakori, 1989). Moreover, performance-based support has been noted for the separate board leadership structure (Rechner & Dalton, 1991).

Alternatively, consistent with stewardship theory, inside directors (Kesner, 1987; Vance, 1964, 1978) and CEO duality (Donaldson & Davis, 1991) have been found to be positively associated with firm performance. Moreover, Daily and Johnson (1997) found that lower firm performance led to decreases in the proportion of independent directors on the board, but that these decreases did not subsequently lead to decreased performance. This finding suggests that performance may create degrees of freedom for the CEO in constituting the board and that CEOs used this discretion to appoint directors. Increases in the proportion of interdependent directors (directors appointed during the tenure of the incumbent CEO) did not, however, compromise firm performance. One conclusion from these findings is that CEOs choose board members who are appropriate for the organization's needs and therefore serve shareholders' needs.

There is also a series of research that does not provide specific guidance with regard to the directional impact of either firm management or the board of directors having the balance of power in the corporation (Berg & Smith, 1978; Chaganti, Mahajan, & Sharma, 1985; Daily & Dalton, 1992, 1993; Kesner et al., 1986; Rechner & Dalton, 1989; Schmidt, 1975; Zahra & Stanton, 1988). A recent meta-analytical review of some 159 studies with 40,120 companies may provide further perspective on this debate (Dalton, Daily, Ellstrand, & Johnson, 1998). This analysis indicates that board composition—whether measured by proportion of inside directors, affiliated directors, or interdependent directors—is unrelated to corporate financial performance. The results are invariant when moderated by firm size. Moreover, these results are invariant when moderated by the nature of performance indicators (that is, accounting as compared to market returns).

A related issue is the extent to which there are differences in the financial performance of firms with CEOs who also serve as board chairperson as compared to firms with separate individuals in those roles. Recent research evidence suggests that the choice of dual versus independent leadership structure is unrelated to firms' financial performance. Studies of announcement effects, for example, conclude that "the market is indifferent to changes in a firm's duality status" (Baliga, Moyer, & Rao, 1996: 41; see also Daily & Dalton, 1997a, 1997b; Worrell, Nemec, & Davidson, 1997). Also, an extensive meta-analysis combining the results of some sixty-nine studies (a total of 12,915 companies) provides no evidence of a systematic relationship between duality and corporate financial performance (Dalton, Daily, Ellstrand, & Johnson, 1998). It is also notable that these results are the same for traditional large corporations and entrepreneurial firms. These results do not differ as a function of particular performance measures: accounting returns (for example, return on equity, return on investment, return on assets) or market returns (a series of measures all based on share value).

The Succession and Compensation Contexts

The contest for corporate control is especially salient in two additional contexts: the selection of a CEO and determining CEO compensation. Both activities are the responsibility of the board of directors but may be subject to management influence. The selection of CEO and setting the CEO's compensation are two opportunities for the board to exercise considerable independence and to appoint and motivate a CEO to behave in a manner consistent with shareholders' interests.

CEO Succession

One of the most critical functions of the board is the replacement—voluntary or involuntary—of the CEO (Lorsch & MacIver, 1989; Vancil, 1987). In fact, there may be few other corporate events that better capture the contest for control in corporations than does CEO succession. As Zald (1965, p. 142) noted, "The process and outcome of succession situations—how the appointment is made and who is appointed to positions of ultimate authority—are vital indices of the underlying political structure."

Some examples illustrate the potential negative fallout of tensions between directors and management in the CEO succession process. A 1996 succession at Trans World Airlines (TWA) provides a graphic illustration of the impact of protracted tension between management and the board on the CEO succession process. As a function of TWA's activist board, which has demonstrated little confidence in any of the company's recent CEOs, the airline has experienced unusually high turnover among its chair, CEO, and top management positions (Carey, 1996). A recent TWA CEO, Jeffrey Erickson, commented that one of the difficulties in dealing with the board was that it "managed more than it monitored" (Carey, 1996, p. B4).

AT&T Corp. also provides an example of the impact of tensions between management and directors. A former AT&T Corp. president, John Walter, resigned as a result of tensions between himself and the board chairperson, Robert Allen (Cauley, 1997; Keller, 1997). Some suggest that Walter's resignation was as much a function of Allen's unwillingness to name an heir apparent for the CEO position as it was specifically about tension between himself and Allen (Keller, 1997). Clearly these tensions had a direct impact on Walter's overall relationship with the board, as evidenced by outside director Walter Elisha's comment that Walter lacked "the intellectual leadership" to serve as CEO of AT&T (Keller, 1997, p. B1; see also Cauley, 1997).

Although CEOs are generally believed to have a significant amount of influence regarding the timing of their departure (Firstenberg & Malkiel, 1994), poor performance may significantly erode a CEO's ability to protect his or her positions. Research has found, for example, that the probability of executive-level turnover greatly increases with poor firm performance (Coughlan & Schmidt, 1985; Daily & Dalton, 1995; Gilson, 1989; Lo Pucki & Whitford, 1993b; Warner, Watts, & Wruck, 1988; Weisbach, 1988). The bankruptcy context further illustrates the tenuous position in which CEOs might find themselves as a function of poor firm performance. As Daily (1994) noted, bankruptcy provides an unambiguous measure of poor firm performance and therefore is the ultimate performance measure. In general terms, officer and director turnover is three times greater in failed firms as compared to those that are financially healthy (Ang & Chua, 1981; Hermalin & Weisbach, 1988; Warner et al., 1988; Weisbach, 1988).

CEOs in particular are subject to greater turnover surrounding a bankruptcy (Daily & Dalton, 1995; see also, Barker & Duhaime, 1997; Gilson, 1989, 1990; Lo Pucki & Whitford, 1993a, 1993b). In a bankruptcy situation, the rate of CEO turnover has been reported to increase at a rate of nine times the normal CEO turnover rate (Lo Pucki & Whitford, 1993b). Lo Pucki and Whitford (1993b) documented a 91 percent average turnover rate for CEOs of bankrupt firms, as compared to an average turnover rate of 10 percent.

There is also some evidence that board composition may have a differential impact on the succession process. Outside directors, as a result of the absence of financial dependence on the firm, may be better suited to replacing CEOs when necessary (Chaganti et al., 1985; Nussbaum & Dobryznski, 1987). Boeker (1992), for example, found an interactive effect with poor firm performance and board composition. The chance of CEO dismissal significantly increased when there were higher proportions of outside directors and poor firm performance (also see Weisbach, 1988).

Board composition has also been found to affect the likelihood of a successor being appointed from within the organization, as compared to outside the firm. Boeker and Goodstein (1993), for example, noted that greater proportions of inside directors were positively associated with an inside succession. Board leadership structure has also been associated with an successor origin. Cannella and Lubatkin (1993), for example, found that an outside CEO succession was less likely under the dual structure.

The extent of CEOs' equity holdings may also have an impact on the succession process. Weisbach (1988), for example, found that higher levels of equity holdings by CEOs reduced the likelihood of their being replaced. Based on these findings, Weisbach concluded that "the amount of power the CEO has within the firm" determines the relationship between performance and CEO turnover (p. 453).

Another factor in the struggle for control of the corporation (that is, appointment as CEO) is the extent to which there are ready candidates to assume the CEO position should the incumbent either leave or be dismissed by the board of directors. A strong determinant of successor origin (inside or outside) is the availability of internal candidates (Finkelstein & Hambrick, 1995). Available internal candidates may encourage a board to remove the incumbent CEO and replace him or her with an inside appointment. As Finkelstein and Hambrick (1995) noted, a viable horse race—a common form of succession—requires multiple viable contestants.

Strong inside successor candidates also serve the function of tempering the potential power of the CEO (Vancil, 1987). Too often CEOs serve as gatekeepers of firm-specific information. Having several internal successor candidates, some or all of whom may serve on the board, provides outside directors with an additional avenue of information. Moreover, these interactions between potential inside successors and the board provide directors with an excellent opportunity to become acquainted with these CEO candidates (Vancil, 1987).

Fama (1980) has also suggested that the presence of outside directors, potential CEO successors, may keep the level of rivalry between firm managers who are vying for the CEO position at a manageable level. This may be especially important when there are inside directors. Inside directors, the most likely internal candidates, tend to be significantly more powerful than other firm executives (Finkelstein, 1988). This increased level of power may enhance the level of rivalry for the top post and result in turnover among those executives identified formally or informally as potential successors (Friedman & Olk, 1995; Friedman & Saul, 1991; Lazear & Rosen, 1981).

Although CEO succession often epitomizes the potential for control contests between management and boards of directors, the succession process need not be contentious. The unexpected loss of Coca-Cola Company's CEO and chairperson, Roberto Goizueta, illustrates a classic case of a smooth succession process. Goizueta and the board of directors had worked closely together to identify and groom a successor well in advance of Goizueta's unexpected illness. As a consequence, when Goizueta passed away, his heir apparent, Douglas Ivester, was quickly approved by the board of directors as the new CEO. This smooth transition is a tribute to both Goizueta and Coca-Cola's board of directors ("Secrets of Succession," 1997).

CEO Compensation

CEO compensation has been the focus of considerable discussion and debate, largely due to the continued upward trajectory of overall CEO compensation. CEOs' compensation packages may prove one of the best barometers of the extent to which the CEO exercises control in the corporation. Although CEOs formally have no voice in the nature and level of their compensation packages

(CEOs of public corporations are not permitted to vote even if they serve on the compensation committee), it is widely recognized that CEOs have numerous avenues for influencing this process.

CEOs may, for example, exercise influence over the nature of their compensation packages. One of the prominent themes in CEO compensation is the balance between contingent and noncontingent pay (Gomez-Mejia, 1994). Executives generally prefer noncontingent pay because it provides a stable stream of income (Tosi & Gomez-Mejia, 1994). Consistent with this, Westphal (1998) found that CEO influence, as captured by persuasion and ingratiation, was positively associated with an increase in compensation but a decrease in contingent compensation. As further demonstration of the impact of the balance of power between directors and management on CEO compensation, Westphal also noted that board independence was associated with smaller increases in CEO compensation and greater portions of contingent CEO compensation.

In another examination, Westphal and Zajac (1995) found that interdependent directors were more demographically similar to CEOs and that this similarity was positively related to overall CEO compensation. Daily and Johnson (1997) noted that powerful CEOs may use their influence to appoint directors of their choice and increase their own compensation. Finkelstein and Boyd (1998) found that managerial discretion was positively related to CEO compensation. Also consistent with the Daily and Johnson (1997) study, they found that this relationship was stronger among highly performing firms, further evidence that the ability to influence organizational processes is, in part, a function of having led "a financially successful corporation" (Daily & Johnson, 1997, p. 113).

Research has also demonstrated the power of institutional investors to temper CEO influence with regard to compensation. Daily, Johnson, Ellstrand, and Dalton (1998) found that institutional investor holdings were positively related to contingent, as compared to noncontingent, CEO pay. Moreover, David, Kochhar, and Levitas (1998) found that pressure-resistant institutional investors' holdings (holdings by institutional investors not subject to managerial influence) reduced CEO compensation more than when pressure-sensitive institutions held firm equity. In fact, pressure-sensitive institutional investor holdings (holdings by institutions subject to potential managerial influence such as banks and insurance companies) were associated with higher CEO compensation. In addition, pressure-resistant holdings were associated with an increase in the proportion of long-term incentives in CEO compensation.

The results of these studies clearly indicate that powerful CEOs may use their influence to structure more attractive compensation packages for themselves. In concert, then, these findings support agency theory predictions. Stewardship theory would not be supported, as affording firm management significant latitude would not necessarily be in the shareholders' best interests.

Conclusion

Firstenberg and Malkiel (1994, p. 27) have noted that the "once archetypal model of the CEO's unchallengeable control of the board of directors and shareholders is fading." This theme—the extent to which management or the board of directors controls the modern corporation—has guided our investigation. We began by introducing two distinct theoretical approaches that are directly applicable to the contest for corporate control: agency theory and stewardship theory. Each provides different prescriptions regarding the appropriate balance of power between firms' executives and boards of directors. For us, adherence to one or the other perspective should be guided by firm performance. It is performance that often serves as the equalizer in contests for corporate control.

To this end, institutional investors have risen as a powerful voice in the governance of the firms in which they invest. Institutions have steadfastly focused on restructuring boards of directors toward more independence in an effort to improve firm performance. We would also note that institutions have not been alone in their demands for greater independence between management and the board. A number of regulatory and oversight bodies, too, have developed guidelines for board independence (Kesner, 1988). The Securities and Exchange Commission, the New York Stock Exchange, the American Stock Exchange, and the National Association of Securities Dealers, for example, have developed guidelines concerning the composition of the more central board committees (for example, audit, compensation, nominating).

It is clear that control of the modern corporation continues to be of practical and academic interest. It is equally clear that there is evidence of alignment of interests between managers and directors that best serve shareholder interests, as well as evidence of conflicts of interest that arguably fail to effectively serve share-holder interests. Zajac and Westphal (1996), for example, recently noted that both executives and directors have demonstrated self-serving, as well as shareholder-serving, tendencies. They found that powerful executives tend to prefer board members with experi-ence on passive boards who do not bring reputations as activist di-rectors. Moreover, they found that passive boards—those not noted for challenging management—also do not want new board mem-bers with activist reputations. However, they also noted that active boards—those noted for challenging management—tend to re-cruit new board members who are equally as likely to be activist in their orientation. These results interest us because they provide ev-idence for both the agency and stewardship perspectives.

Based in part on these challenges in determining the best pre-scriptions regarding the structure and balance of power appropri-ate in the modern corporation, we find corporate governance to be a particularly exciting area of investigation. Part of the attrac-tion is that inquiry in this domain bridges both the academic and practitioner communities. Ben Rosen, chairperson of Compaq Computer Corporation, has noted the centrality and importance of corporate governance, whether from the academic or practi-tioner perspective: "Some consider the topic fit only for academic research papers, but it saved Compaq. My emphatic lesson? Gov-ernance counts. Governance is important. Governance affects shareholder value" (Rosen, 1997, p. 36).

References

Alexander, J. A., Fennel, M. L., & Halpern, M. T. (1993). Leadership in-stability in hospitals: The influence of board-CEO relations and or-ganizational growth and decline. *Administrative Science Quarterly, 38,* 74–99.

Anderson, C. A., & Anthony, R. N. (1986). *The new corporate directors.* New York: Wiley.

Ang, J., & Chua, J. (1981). Corporate bankruptcy and job losses among top-level managers. *Financial Management, 10*(5), 70–74.

Bainbridge, S. M. (1993). Independent directors and the ALI corpo-rate governance project. *George Washington Law Review, 61,* 1034–1083.

Baldwin, F. R. (1984). *Conflicting interests.* San Francisco: New Lexington Press.

Baliga, B. R., Moyer, R. C., & Rao, R. S. (1996). CEO duality and firm performance: What's the fuss? *Strategic Management Journal, 1,* 41–53.

Barker, V. L., & Duhaime, I. M. (1997). Strategic change in turnaround process: Theory and empirical evidence. *Strategic Management Journal, 18,* 13–38.

Baysinger, B. D., & Butler, H. H. (1985). Corporate governance and the board of directors: Performance effects of changes in board composition. *Journal of Law, Economics, and Organization, 1,* 101–124.

Baysinger, B. D., & Hoskisson, R. E. (1990). The composition of boards of directors and strategic control. *Academy of Management Review, 15,* 72–87.

Baysinger, B. D., Kosnik, R. D., & Turk, T. A. (1991). Effects of board and ownership structure on corporate R&D strategy. *Academy of Management Journal, 34,* 205–214.

Berg, S. V., & Smith, S. K. (1978). CEO and board chairman: A quantitative study of dual vs. unitary board leadership. *Directors and Boards, 3,* 34–39.

Berle, A., & Means, G. C. (1932). *The modern corporation and private property.* Old Tappan, NJ: Macmillan.

Biggs, J. (1995, November). Why TIAA-CREF is active in corporate governance. *Participant,* p. 2.

Black, B. S. (1992). Agents watching agents: The promise of institutional investor voice. *UCLA Law Review, 39,* 811–893.

Boeker, W. (1992). Power and managerial dismissal: Scapegoating at the top. *Administrative Science Quarterly, 37,* 400–421.

Boeker, W., & Goodstein, J. (1993). Performance and successor choice: The moderating effects of governance and ownership. *Academy of Management Journal, 36,* 172–186.

Boyd, B. K. (1994). Board control and CEO compensation. *Strategic Management Journal, 16,* 301–312.

Buchholtz, A. K., & Ribbens, B. A. (1994). Role of chief executive officers in takeover resistance: Effects of CO incentives and individual characteristics. *Academy of Management Journal, 37,* 554–579.

Byrd, J. W., & Hickman, K. A. (1992). Do outside directors monitor managers? Evidence from tender offer bids. *Journal of Financial Economics, 32,* 195–221.

Cannella, A. A., & Lubatkin, M. (1993). Succession as a sociopolitical process: Internal impediments to outsider selection. *Academy of Management Journal, 36,* 763–793.

Carey, S. (1996, October 28). TWA insiders say CEO's departure was no surprise. *Wall Street Journal,* p. B4.

Cauley, L. (1997, August 8). Will Seidenberg face static moving up at Bell Atlantic? *Wall Street Journal,* pp. B1, B8.

Chaganti, R. S., Mahajan, V., & Sharma, S. (1985). Corporate board size, composition, and corporate failures in retailing industry. *Journal of Management Studies, 22,* 400–417.

Coffee, J. C., Jr. (1991). Liquidity versus control: The institutional investor as corporate monitor. *Columbia Law Review, 91,* 1277–1368.

Coffee, J. C., Jr. (1994). The SEC and the institutional investor: A half-time report. *Cardozo Law Review, 15,* 837–907.

Coughlan, A. T., & Schmidt, R. M. (1985). Executive compensation, managerial turnover, and firm performance: An empirical investigation. *Journal of Accounting and Economics, 7,* 43–66.

Cox, J. D. (1993). The ALI, institutionalization, and disclosure: The quest for the outside director's spine. *George Washington Law Review, 61,* 1233–1273.

Daily, C. M. (1994). Bankruptcy in strategic studies: Past and promise. *Journal of Management, 20,* 263–295.

Daily, C. M., & Dalton, D. R. (1992). The relationship between governance structure and corporate performance in entrepreneurial firms. *Journal of Business Venturing, 7,* 375–386.

Daily, C. M., & Dalton, D. R. (1993). Board of directors leadership and structure: Control and performance implications. *Entrepreneurship Theory and Practice, 17,* 65–81.

Daily, C. M., & Dalton, D. R. (1994a). Bankruptcy and corporate governance: The impact of board composition and structure. *Academy of Management Journal, 37,* 1603–1617.

Daily, C. M., & Dalton, D. R. (1994b). Corporate governance and the bankrupt firm: An empirical assessment. *Strategic Management Journal, 15,* 643–654.

Daily, C. M., & Dalton, D. R. (1995). CEO and director turnover in failing firms: An illusion of change? *Strategic Management Journal, 16,* 393–400.

Daily, C. M., & Dalton, D. R. (1997a). CEO and board chairperson roles held jointly or separately: Much ado about nothing. *Academy of Management Executive, 11,* 11–20.

Daily, C. M., & Dalton, D. R. (1997b). Separate, but not independent: Board leadership structure in large corporations. *Corporate Governance, 5,* 126–136.

Daily, C. M., & Johnson, J. L. (1997). Sources of CEO power and firm financial performance: A longitudinal assessment. *Journal of Management, 23,* 97–117.

Daily, C. M., Johnson, J. L., & Dalton, D. R. (1999). On the measurements of board composition: Poor consistency and a serious mismatch of theory and operationalization. *Decision Sciences, 30,* 83–106.

Daily, C. M., Johnson, J. L., Ellstrand, A. E., & Dalton, D. R. (1998). Compensation committee composition as a determinant of CEO compensation. *Academy of Management Journal, 41,* 209–220.

Daily, C. M., & Schwenk, C. (1996). Chief executive officers, top management teams, and boards of directors: Congruent or countervailing forces? *Journal of Management, 22,* 185–208.

Dalton, D. R., Daily, C. M., Ellstrand, A. E., & Johnson, J. L. (1998). Meta-analytic reviews of board composition, leadership structure, and financial performance. *Strategic Management Journal, 19,* 269–290.

David, P., Kochhar, R., & Levitas, E. (1998). The effect of institutional investors on the level and mix of CEO compensation. *Academy of Management Journal, 41,* 200–208.

Davis, G. F., & Thompson, T. A. (1994). A social movement perspective on corporate control. *Administrative Science Quarterly, 39,* 141–173.

De Mott, D. A. (1980). *Corporations at the crossroads: Governance and reform.* New York: McGraw-Hill.

Donaldson, L. (1990). The ethereal hand: Organizational economics and management theory. *Academy of Management Review, 15,* 369–381.

Donaldson, L., & Davis, J. H. (1991). Stewardship theory or agency theory: CEO governance and shareholder returns. *Australian Journal of Management, 16,* 49–64.

Donaldson, L., & Davis, J. H. (1994). Boards and company performance: Research challenges the conventional wisdom. *Corporate Governance, 2,* 151–160.

Eisenhardt, K. M. (1989). Agency theory: An assessment and review. *Academy of Management Review, 14,* 57–74.

Ezzamel, M. A., & Watson, R. (1993). Organizational form, ownership structure, and corporate performance: A contextual empirical analysis of U.K. companies. *British Journal of Management, 4,* 161–176.

Fama, E. F. (1980). Agency problems and the theory of the firm. *Journal of Political Economy, 88,* 288–307.

Fama, E. F., & Jensen, M. C. (1983). Separation of ownership and control. *Journal of Law and Economics, 26,* 301–325.

Finkelstein, S. (1988). *Managerial orientations and organizational outcomes: The moderating roles of managerial discretion and power.* Unpublished doctoral dissertation, Columbia University.

Finkelstein, S., & Boyd, B. K. (1998). How much does the CEO matter? The role of managerial discretion in the setting of CEO compensation. *Academy of Management Journal, 41,* 179–199.

Finkelstein, S., & D'Aveni, R. A. (1994). CEO duality as a double-edged sword: How boards of directors balance entrenchment avoidance and unity of command. *Academy of Management Journal, 37,* 1079–1108.

Finkelstein, S., & Hambrick, D. C. (1995). *Strategic leadership: Top executives and their effects on organizations.* St. Paul, MN: West.

Firstenberg, P. B., & Malkiel, B. G. (1994, Fall). The twenty-first century boardroom: Who will be in charge? *Sloan Management Review,* pp. 27–35.

Fleischer, A., Hazard, G. C., & Klipper, M. A. (1988). *Board games: The changing shape of corporate power.* New York: Little, Brown.

Fredrickson, J. W., Hambrick, D. C., & Baumrin, S. (1988). A model of CEO dismissal. *Academy of Management Review, 13,* 255–270.

Friedman, S. D., & Olk, P. (1995). Four ways to choose a CEO: Crown heir, horse race, coup d'état, and comprehensive search. *Human Resource Management, 34,* 141–164.

Friedman, S. D., & Saul, K. (1991). A leader's wake: Organizational member reactions to CEO succession. *Journal of Management, 17,* 619–642.

Fromson, B. D. (1990, July 30). The big owners roar. *Fortune,* pp. 66–78.

Gilson, S. C. (1989). Management turnover and financial distress. *Journal of Financial Economics, 25,* 241–262.

Gilson, S. C. (1990). Bankruptcy, boards, banks, and blockholders. *Journal of Financial Economics, 27,* 355–387.

Gomez-Mejia, L. R. (1994). Executive compensation: A reassessment and a future research agenda. In G. R. Ferris (Ed.), *Research in personnel and human resources management* (Vol. 12). Greenwich, CT: JAI Press.

Goodstein, J., & Boeker, W. (1991). Turbulence at the top: A new perspective on governance structure changes and strategic change. *Academy of Management Journal, 34,* 306–330.

Harrison, J. R., Torres, D. L., & Kukalis, S. (1988). The changing of the guard: Turnover and structural change in the top-management positions. *Administrative Science Quarterly, 33,* 211–232.

Hermalin, B., & Weisbach, M. (1988). The determinants of board composition. *RAND Journal of Economics, 19,* 589–606.

Herman, E. S. (1981). *Corporate control, corporate power.* New York: Cambridge University Press.

Hill, C.W.L., & Snell, S. A. (1988). External control, corporate strategy, and firm performance in research intensive industries. *Strategic Management Journal, 9,* 577–590.

Hoskisson, R. E., Johnson, R. A., & Moesel, D. D. (1994). Corporate divestiture intensity in restructuring firms: Effects of governance, strategy, and performance. *Academy of Management Journal, 37,* 1207–1251.

Hosmer, L. T. (1982). The importance of strategic leadership. *Journal of Business Strategy, 3,* 47–57.

Jensen, M. C., & Meckling, W. H. (1976). Theory of the firm: Managerial behavior, agency costs and ownership structure. *Journal of Financial Economics, 3,* 305–360.

Johnson, J. L., Daily, C. M., & Ellstrand, A. E. (1996). Boards of directors: A review and research agenda. *Journal of Management, 22,* 409–438.

Johnson, R. A., Hoskisson, R. E., & Hitt, M. A. (1993). Board of director involvement in restructuring: The effects of board versus managerial controls and characteristics. *Strategic Management Journal, 14,* 33–50.

Johnson, L., & Millon, D. (1993). Corporate takeovers and corporate law: Who's in control? *George Washington Law Review, 61,* 1177–1211.

Keller, J. J. (1997, July 17). AT&T's Walter quits after boardroom rebuff. *Wall Street Journal,* pp. B1, B9.

Kesner, I. F. (1987). Directors' stock ownership and organizational performance: An investigation of Fortune 500 companies. *Journal of Management, 13,* 499–508.

Kesner, I. F. (1988). Directors' characteristics and committee membership: An investigation of type, occupation, tenure, and gender. *Academy of Management Journal, 31,* 66–84.

Kesner, I. F., & Johnson, R. B. (1990). An investigation of the relationship between board composition and stockholder suits. *Strategic Management Journal, 11,* 327–336.

Kesner, I. F., Victor, B., & Lamont, B. (1986). Board composition and the commission of illegal acts: An investigation of Fortune 500 companies. *Academy of Management Journal, 29,* 789–799.

Kim, J. (1992, October 28). Boards hold management accountable. *USA Today,* pp. B1–B2.

Krishnan, H. A. (1997). Diversification and top management team complementarity: Is performance improved by merging similar or dissimilar teams? *Strategic Management Journal, 18,* 361–374.

Lazear, E., & Rosen, S. (1981). Rank-order tournaments as optimum labor contracts. *Journal of Political Economy, 89,* 841–864.

Lo Pucki, L. M., & Whitford, W. C. (1993a). Patterns in the bankruptcy reorganization of large, publicly held companies. *Cornell Law Review, 78,* 597–618.

Lo Pucki, L. M., & Whitford, W. C. (1993b). Corporate governance in the bankruptcy reorganization of large, publicly held companies. *University of Pennsylvania Law Review, 141,* 669–800.

Lorsch, J. W., & MacIver, E. (1989). *Pawns or potentates: The reality of America's corporate boards.* Boston: Harvard Business School Press.

Lublin, J. S. (1997, December 26). CalPERS considers seeking board seats. *Wall Street Journal,* pp. A3, A4.

Mace, M. L. (1971). *Directors: Myth and reality.* Boston: Harvard Business School Press.

Mangel, R., & Singh, H. (1993). Ownership structure, board relationships and CEO compensation in large U.S. corporations. *Accounting and Business Research, 23,* 339–350.

Michel, J. G., & Hambrick, D. C. (1992). Diversification posture and top management team characteristics. *Academy of Management Journal, 35,* 9–37.

Midgley, K. (1982). *Management accountability and corporate governance.* Old Tappan, NJ: Macmillan.

Mintzberg, H. (1983). *Power in and around organizations.* Upper Saddle River, NJ: Prentice Hall.

Mizruchi, M. S. (1983). Who controls whom? An examination of the relation between management and boards of directors in large American corporations. *Academy of Management Review, 8,* 426–435.

Mizruchi, M. S. (1988). Managerialism: Another reassessment. In M. Schwartz (Ed.), *The structure of power in America: The corporate elite as a ruling class.* New York: Holmes & Meier.

Norburn, D. (1989). The chief executive: A breed apart. *Strategic Management Journal, 10,* 1–15.

Nussbaum, B., & Dobryznski, J. H. (1987, May 18). The battle for corporate control. *Business Week,* pp. 102–109.

Ocasio, W. (1994). Political dynamics and the circulation of power: CEO succession in U.S. industrial corporations, 1960–1990. *Administrative Science Quarterly, 39,* 285–312.

Patton, A., & Baker, J. C. (1987). Why won't directors rock the boat? *Harvard Business Review, 65*(6), 10–13.

Pearce, J. A., III. (1981). An executive-level perspective on the strategic management process. *California Management Review, 24,* 39–48.

Pearce, J. A., III, & Robinson, R. B. (1987). A measure of CEO social power in strategic decision making. *Strategic Management Journal, 8,* 297–304.

Pearce, J. A., III, & Zahra, S. A. (1991). The relative power of CEOs and boards of directors: Associations with corporate performance. *Strategic Management Journal, 12,* 135–153.

Pearce, J. A., III, & Zahra, S. A. (1992). Board composition from a strategic contingency perspective. *Journal of Management Studies, 29,* 411–438.

Pfeffer, J. (1972). Size and composition of corporate boards of directors: The organization and its environment. *Administrative Science Quarterly, 17,* 218–229.

Pfeffer, J. (1973). Size, composition, and function of hospital boards of directors: The organization and its environment. *Administrative Science Quarterly, 18,* 349–364.

Pfeffer, J., & Salancik, G. R. (1978). *The external control of organizations: A resource-dependence perspective.* New York: HarperCollins.

Provan, K. G. (1980). Board power and organizational effectiveness among human service agencies. *Academy of Management Journal, 23,* 221–236.

Rechner, P. L., & Dalton, D. R. (1989). The impact of CEO as board chairperson on corporate performance: Evidence vs. rhetoric. *Academy of Management Executive, 3,* 141–143.

Rechner, P. L., & Dalton, D. R. (1991). CEO duality and organizational performance: A longitudinal analysis. *Strategic Management Journal, 12,* 155–160.

Rediker, K. J., & Seth, A. (1995). Boards of directors and substitution effects of alternative governance mechanisms. *Strategic Management Journal, 16,* 85–99.

Rock, E. B. (1991). The logic and (uncertain) significance of institutional shareholder activism. *Georgetown Law Journal, 79,* 445–506.

Rosen, B. (1997, Fall). Endpaper. *Hermes,* p. 36.

Rosenstein, S., & Wyatt, J. G. (1990). Outside directors, board independence, and shareholder wealth. *Journal of Financial Economics, 26,* 175–191.

Schellenger, M. H., Wood, D., & Tashakori, A. (1989). Board of directors composition, shareholder wealth, and dividend policy. *Journal of Management, 15,* 457–467.

Schellhardt, T. D. (1991, March 20). More directors are recruited from outside. *Wall Street Journal,* p. B1.

Schmidt, R. (1975). Does board composition really make a difference? *Conference Board Record, 12,* 38–41.

Schultz, E. E., & Warren, S. (1998, May 29). Pension system ousts company's board in big victory for institutional investors. *Wall Street Journal,* p. A2.

The secrets of succession. (1997, October 25). *Economist,* p. 73.

Selznik, P. (1949). *TVA and the grass roots: A study in the sociology of formal organizations.* New York: HarperCollins.

Singh, H., & Harianto, F. (1989). Top management tenure, corporate ownership structure and the magnitude of golden parachutes. *Strategic Management Journal, 10* (Summer Special Issue), 143–156.

Tosi, H. L., & Gomez-Mejia, L. R. (1994). CEO compensation monitoring and firm performance. *Academy of Management Journal, 37,* 1002–1016.

Tricker, R. I. (1984). *Corporate governance.* London: Gower.

Useem, M. (1993). *Executive defense: Shareholder power and corporate reorganization.* Cambridge, MA: Harvard University Press.

Vance, S. C. (1964). *Boards of directors: Structures and performance.* Eugene: University of Oregon Press.

Vance, S. C. (1978). Corporate governance: Assessing corporate performance by boardroom attributes. *Journal of Business Research, 6,* 203–220.

Vancil, R. F. (1987). *Passing the baton: Managing the process of CEO succession.* Boston: Harvard Business School Press.

Wade, J., O'Reilly, C. A., & Chandratat, I. (1990). Golden parachutes: CEOs and the exercise of social influence. *Administrative Science Quarterly, 35,* 587–603.

Wahal, S. (1996). Pension fund activism and firm performance. *Journal of Financial and Quantitative Analysis, 31,* 1–23.

Warner, J. B., Watts, R. L., & Wruck, K. H. (1988). Stock-price performance and top-management changes. *Journal of Financial Economics, 20,* 461–492.

Weidenbaum, M. L. (1985, September 23). The best defense against the raiders. *Business Week,* p. 21.

Weisbach, M. S. (1988). Outside directors and CEO turnover. *Journal of Financial Economics, 20,* 431–460.

Westphal, J. D. (1998). Board games: How CEOs adapt to increases in structural board independence from management. *Administrative Science Quarterly, 43,* 511–537.

Westphal, J. D., & Zajac, E. J. (1995). Who shall govern? CEO-board power, demographic similarity, and new director selection. *Administrative Science Quarterly, 40,* 60–83.

Williamson, O. E. (1985). *The economic institutions of capitalism: Firms, markets, relationship contracting.* New York: Free Press.

Worrell, D. L., Nemec, C., & Davidson, W. N. (1997). One hat too many: Key executive plurality and shareholder wealth. *Strategic Management Journal, 18,* 499–507.

Zahra, S. A., & Pearce, J. A., III. (1989). Boards of directors and corporate financial performance: A review and integrative model. *Journal of Management, 15,* 291–334.

Zahra, S. A., & Stanton, W. W. (1988). The implications of board of directors composition for corporate strategy and performance. *International Journal of Management, 5,* 229–236.

Zajac, E. J., & Westphal, J. D. (1996). Director reputation, CEO-board power, and the dynamics of board interlocks. *Administrative Science Quarterly, 41,* 507–529.

Zald, M. N. (1965). Who shall rule? A political analysis of succession in a large welfare organization. *Pacific Sociological Review, 8,* 52–60.

Zald, M. N. (1967). Urban differentiation, characteristics of boards of directors, and organizational effectiveness. *American Journal of Sociology, 73,* 261–272.

Zald, M. N. (1969). The power and functions of boards of directors: A theoretical synthesis. *American Journal of Sociology, 74,* 97–111.

CHAPTER 7

Leadership, Vision, and Organizational Effectiveness

Stephen J. Zaccaro
Deanna J. Banks

A fundamental requirement of organizational leadership is setting the direction for collective effort on behalf of organizational progress. Leaders define and articulate a direction in line with external or environmental contingencies for their subordinate unit. They also create the internal conditions to accomplish the tasks specified by this direction. Direction setting and operational management represent the two fundamental means by which leaders at all organizational levels add value to their organization (Zaccaro, 1996).

Accordingly, these tasks have been an integral part of many leadership definitions and models. For example, Jacobs and Jaques (1990, p. 282) suggested that "leadership is a process of giving purpose [meaningful direction] to collective effort, and causing willing effort to be expended to achieve purpose." Most empirically derived descriptions of managerial work, particularly at the executive level, specify a direction-setting role for leaders, including policymaker (Baehr, 1992; Stogdill, Shartle, Wherry, & Jaynes, 1955), long-range planner (Hemphill, 1959; Tornow & Pinto, 1976), and strategic problem solver or decision maker (Morse & Wagner, 1978; Page & Tornow, 1987). Understanding organizational leadership, then, requires an understanding of this direction-setting role and its centrality to many models of leader effectiveness.

Although leaders at all organizational levels are required to set the directions for action by their constituent units, the nature and content of these directions change qualitatively at different levels. At the top of the organization, leader direction making generally takes the form of developing a broad, long-term, and often ambiguous vision. Top managers translate this vision into more specific organizational strategies and propagate them to units at lower organizational levels. At middle organizational levels, leaders interpret organizational visions into subsystem goals and more short-term strategies. At the lowest levels of organizational leadership, managers convert strategies and objectives that their superiors developed into even more specific short-term goals and tasks for their units (Kelly, 1993; Kotter, 1990). Note that executives are generally not responsible for defining the implications of their vision for day-to-day and monthly activities; that task is the province of their subordinate managers at lower organizational levels. Executives have the responsibility for formulating a vision, linking it to a long-term corresponding strategic plan, articulating these to the organization, and persuading organizational constituents to adopt and implement the plan.

This vertical translation suggests two important distinctions with regard to the direction setting of leaders at different organization levels. First, direction setting proceeds from providing more ambiguous information at higher organizational levels to more concrete objectives at lower levels. Fundamentally, though, direction setting at lower organizational levels occurs within the context of directions set at higher levels. Thus, the top managers' vision and strategies set the stage for direction setting throughout the organization. Second, direction setting reflects a longer time frame at higher organizational levels. Visions and strategies can range up to fifty years or more into the future, while directions at the lowest organizational level can reflect daily or monthly time perspectives (Jacobs & Jaques, 1990, 1991; Zaccaro, 1996).

These points highlight the importance of vision to organizational effectiveness. Indeed, recent studies of organizational leadership have placed the articulation of vision squarely in the center of their conceptual frameworks (Bass, 1985, 1996; Conger & Kanungo, 1987; House, 1977, House & Shamir, 1993; Sashkin, 1988). Despite the centrality of this concept, however, there has been little systematic research to define and articulate its nature. The purpose of this chapter is to describe the nature of executive visions and their influences on organizational effectiveness.

What Are Visions?

Despite the ubiquity of vision concepts in the strategic leadership literature, the nature of this construct remains ambiguous. Our discussion is intended to provide some clarity.

Characteristics of Vision

Strategic management researchers typically have as their central construct the notion of strategy. Often their discussions appear to reflect what others would call vision. What, then, is vision, as opposed to strategy? From the definitions of vision in Table 7.1, we can discern several common characteristics. The first is that visions often provide an idealized representation of what the organization should become. As such, they can be based on the leader's images of what the organization ought to be rather than what it is. For example, the corporate vision of what McDonald's ought to be is "the world's best quick service restaurant experience. Being the best means consistently satisfying customers better than anyone else through outstanding quality, service, cleanliness, and value" (McDonald's Corporate Webpage, 2000).

In contrast, strategies are typically direction statements that emerge from a relatively rational analysis of the organization's resources and capabilities and the dynamics of its operating environment. They essentially represent a judgment or decision of the way the organization in its current form can be best aligned with its changing environment. For example, McDonald's has a set of strategies designed to align the organization with its environment and to accomplish its vision of becoming what the organization ought to be. These include developing its people, fostering innovation, and expanding its global mind-set. Visions, unlike strategies, are not necessarily derived from objective environmental criteria and organizational characteristics. Indeed, they often reject the status quo to propose a very different perspective of how organizations ought to fit with their environments.

Table 7.1. Definitions of Vision.

Source	Definition
Bennis and Nanus (1985, p. 89)	To choose a direction, a leader must first have developed a mental image of a possible and desirable future state of the organization. This image, which we call a vision, may be as vague as a dream or as precise as a goal or mission statement. The critical point is that a vision articulates a view of a realistic, credible, attractive future for the organization, a condition that is better in some important ways than what now exists.
Collins and Porras (1991, p. 33)	At the broadest level, vision consists of two major components: A *Guiding Philosophy* that, in the context of expected future environments, leads to a *Tangible Image*.
Gardner and Avolio (1999, p. 39)	A "vision" can be defined as a mental image the leader conjures up to portray a highly desirable end state for an organization.
House and Shamir (1993, p. 97)	Charismatic leaders are visionary. More specifically such leaders articulate an ideological goal that describes a better future for followers. This goal is ideological in the sense that the leader asserts that it is the moral right of the followers to realize the goal. . . . Since the vision of the leader is ideological, it is stated in terms of values.
Kirkpatrick and Locke (1996, p. 37)	A vision is a general transcendent ideal that represents shared values; it is often ideological in nature and has moral overtones.
Kotter (1990, p. 36)	In the sense that it is used here, vision is not mystical or intangible, but means simply a description of something (an organization, a corporate culture, a business, a technology, an activity) in the future, often the distant future, in terms of the essence of what it should become. Typically, a vision is specific enough to provide real guidance to people, yet vague enough to encourage initiative and to remain relevant under a variety of conditions.

Table 7.1. Definitions of Vision, Cont'd.

Source	Definition
Kouzes and Posner (1987, p. 85)	Vision, first of all . . . is a "see" word. It evokes images and pictures. Visual metaphors are very common when we are talking about the long-range plans of an organization. Second, vision suggests a future orientation—a vision is an image of the future. Third, a vision connotes a standard of excellence, an ideal. It implies a choice of values. Fourth, it also has the quality of uniqueness. Therefore, we define vision as an ideal and unique image of the future.
Nanus (1992, pp. 25–26)	A vision is a mental model of a future state of a process, a group, or an organization. As such, it deals with a world that exists only in the imagination, a world built upon plausible speculation, fabricated from what we hope are reasonable assumptions about the future, and heavily influenced by our own judgments of what is possible and worthwhile. A vision portrays a fictitious world that cannot be observed or verified in advance and that, in fact, may never become reality. It is a world whose very existence requires an act of faith.
Sashkin (1986, p. 59)	Visions vary infinitely in the specifics of their content. Yet, some basic elements must be dealt with by any vision that is to have a substantial impact on an organization. One of these elements is *change*. . . . Another basic element all visions must incorporate is a *goal*. . . . A final element of an effective vision: It centers on *people*, both customers and employees.
Yukl (1994, p. 362)	The vision should convey an intuitive, appealing picture of what the organization can be in the future. The core of the vision is the organization's mission statement. The mission statement is a general picture rather than a detailed blueprint, and it should reflect the major themes and values in the vision. It should be expressed in ideological terms, not just in economic terms to help people develop a sense of purpose about their membership in the organization.

Source: Adapted from Zaccaro, 2001. Copyright © 2001 by the American Psychological Association. Adapted with permission.

This is not to say that visions are out of touch with environmental realities. Instead, they reveal the executive's interpretation of some future environment and his or her preferences about how the organization ought to be aligned with that environment. This suggests another characteristic of vision, as opposed to strategies. Visions typically reflect a longer time span than strategies. For example, Boeing's vision for the year 2016 is to be the "future of flight," which includes having the best design and production systems in the world. Kotter (1990) has suggested that visions have a time frame of three to twenty years, while strategies typically operate on a time frame of one to five years.

Effective visions are not rigid, static, or inflexible (Nanus, 1992). Instead, executives modify how they are translated into strategies and goals in accordance with changing environmental events (although effective executives do not change the value-based core of their visions; Conger & Kanungo, 1987). Thus, models of visionary leadership recognize the importance of environmental forces and characteristics cited by strategic contingency and choice models of executive leadership (Gupta, 1984, 1987, 1988; Hambrick, 1981a, 1981b, 1982, 1989; Hambrick & Mason, 1984).

As statements of preference about what the organization should be, visions reflect the primary value orientation of the visionary. Hambrick and Brandon (1988) suggested that executive values dictate certain patterns of executive behavior (that is, "behavior channeling"). They also asserted, however, that the more common effect of values is to create a screen for executive perceptions of environmental stimuli. Regarding visions, values have a more pervasive role in that they influence what executives prefer as a desired future state for their organization.

A final characteristic of visions is that they become symbols of change that executives use to reorient the collective behavior of organizational members. Both strategies and visions are used to produce organizational change. However, whereas strategies often serve as the basis for structural changes in organizational processes (for example, changes in production methods or the development of particular functional units), visions may be used more often to enact changes in the organizational culture and climate. In essence, visions become the means by which senior leaders and organizational executives inspire and give meaning to the actions of their subordinates (Shamir, House, & Arthur, 1993).

Content of Visions

Some researchers have defined visions as a mental model formed by the leader. Accordingly, Nanus (1992, pp. 25–26) defines vision as "a mental model of a future state of a process, a group, or an organization." Zaccaro, Marks, O'Connor-Boes, and Costanza (1995) argued that such mental models contained several pieces of information. The first is an understanding or interpretation of organizational characteristics in the form they are likely to have at a future point. For example, the U.S. Army's vision referred to as Force XXI was developed from an interpretation of what the army will be like from the present to about 2010; its vision for the period from 2010 to about 2025 is called Army After Next (AAN; Hunt, Dodge, & Phillips, 1999). Both visions were derived from and reflected several anticipated characteristics of the army, including the demographic nature of the soldier recruitment pool, the technological capabilities that would be available to future soldiers, and the kinds of organizational arrangements that would be likely in the future.

Because organizations are open systems embedded within typically dynamic environments (Katz & Kahn, 1978), another component of vision models is an understanding of environmental dynamics and elements as they are likely to appear at a future point in time. Thus, the army's Force XXI and AAN visions reflected judgments and information about what the future battlefield would be like (undoubtedly highly digitized) and what kinds of enemies would likely need to be confronted.

Not all aspects of a vision mental model are about an organization's future, however; visions also link the organization's past and its mission to suggestions about how the organization should evolve in the future. Thus, Force XXI emphasizes how the fundamental mission of the army, as it has always existed, is to be sustained in the significantly changing environment over the next fifteen years.

Also of particular importance in vision models is knowledge about the changing dynamics that govern the transition anticipated by the leader between the current and future state of the organization and its environment. Leaders need to have not only a comprehensive understanding of the organization's current state but also a map of how the elements in this state are likely to change over time.

Perhaps the most important element of a vision mental model is the value orientation already described. These values guide executive action and determine how top leaders evaluate and interpret environmental events. Values provide the passion and persuasiveness that effective leaders convey when articulating to their subordinates the desired image they have of their future organization; hence, values are the basis for the role of vision in facilitating organization-wide leader influence (Senge, 1990). For this reason, visions are important social influence tools.

Senge (1990) noted that effective visions are grounded in positive values that reflect an aspiration for growth and long-term change; ineffectual visions call for maintaining the status quo in the face of environmental changes. He highlighted another key content of visions: the degree to which they are changed oriented (see also Collins & Porras, 1991; Sashkin, 1986, 1988). Status quo visions are not generally effective because they fail to ignite the passions of followers. Regarding this point, Senge (1990) notes:

> Negative visions are limiting for three reasons. First, energy that could build something new is diverted to "preventing" something we don't want to happen. Second, negative visions carry a subtle yet unmistakable message of powerlessness: our people really don't care. They can pull together only when there is sufficient threat. Lastly, negative visions are inevitably short term. The organization is motivated so long as the threat persists. Once it leaves, so does the organization's vision and energy [p. 225].

This suggests that effective vision mental models are those that encode growth values reflecting long-term aspiration and organizational change in concurrence with dynamic environmental factors. Ineffective vision models are those that encode status quo values that reflect a resistance to environmental change and a preference for retaining current organizational characteristics and conditions.

Force XXI illustrates a strong growth-oriented visionary perspective for the U.S. Army. Indeed, General Gordon Sullivan and Secretary of the Army Togo West described Force XXI as "a reconceptualization and redesign of the force at all echelons, from the foxhole to the industrial base, to meet the needs of a volatile and ever changing world" (U.S. Army, 1995, p. 1). This is not a retention of the status quo but rather a statement of change to maintain effectiveness in a dynamic world environment.

The importance of vision mental models is that they provide a broad basis for the leader's selection of problem solutions or a frame of reference. That is, a particular vision will prime several classes of potential problem solutions to the exclusion of others. Also, vision models result in the derivation of congruent strategies, goals, and plans that govern leader actions (Kotter, 1990; Zaccaro, 1996). Nanus (1992, p. 29) notes that visions set standards of excellence, clarify organizational purpose and direction, and serve as a guide for planning and strategy development. Thus, they serve as one of the means by which executives galvanize collective resolve and motivation within their organizations.

Despite the conceptual work, few research studies have empirically investigated the content of organizational visions. In response to this lack, Larwood, Falbe, Kriger, and Miesing (1995) asked 331 top executives to describe their visions and then rate them using a set of descriptors (for example, *action oriented, responsive to competition, long term, changing, directs effort, formalized, risky*). They then factor-analyzed these ratings and uncovered seven factors related to vision content. The first factor, labeled *vision formulation,* referred to whether the vision reflected a long-term, strategic perspective. The second factor, labeled *implementation,* reflected the degree to which the vision was widely understood and communicated throughout the organization. The third factor, defined as *innovative realism,* referred to the innovativeness of the vision and its flexible responsiveness to environmental changes. The remaining factors had fewer items loading on them and were termed *general* (or "difficult to describe"), *detailed, risk-taking,* and *profit-oriented,* respectively.

Thus, the content of visions reported by Larwood and associates reflects the definitions shown in Table 7.1 in that these definitions describe visions as having a long-term focus, being innovative (that is, different from the status quo), and reflecting environmental and organizational dynamics. What is missing from the report, though, is an exploration of value orientation as a key vision content variable.

Zaccaro and associates (1995) investigated the role of values by presenting to army officers a scenario requiring them to construct a vision monograph for the army and asking them to rate the importance of seventy-eight items. These items included a subset of twelve growth-oriented or positive-value statements that were developed from a review of the literature on personal and executive values (Allport, Vernon, & Lindzey, 1960; England, 1975; Hambrick & Brandon, 1988; Rokeach, 1973). This item pool also contained another subset of items reflecting status quo values for the army. Zaccaro and associates asked officers to select the ten most important items that characterized their vision and to complete several problem-solving exercises. The officers ranged in rank from first and second lieutenant to colonel.

Zaccaro and associates (1995) found that colonels reported more growth-oriented (instead of status quo) values as part of their organizational visions than lieutenants did. They also found that lieutenants were more likely than majors and colonels to select no values as part of their vision core (that is, "value-less visions") or select only status quo values as the basis for their vision. Indeed, no colonel reported a valueless vision, and only 4 percent reported a status quo vision. Analyses of responses to the problem-solving exercises indicated that officers with more growth-oriented visions developed higher-quality solutions than officers with status quo visions. These results indicate the importance of values as a component of effective visions.

Sources of Visions

Our reading of the literature on envisioning (that is, "the process by which the CEO and top management create and utilize visions for the future"; Robbins & Duncan, 1988, p. 206) suggests two perspectives on how visions emerge in the psychological space of executives. One is that they evolve from sense-making and consensus-seeking and -making processes. For example, Robbins and Duncan (1988) describe two phases of envisioning. The first is an individual sense-making phase, whereby top executives become aware of a growing problem or misalignment between the organization and its environment and the need for organizational change. The interpretation of a problem as a vision problem, that is, one requiring a vision, triggers the vision creation process. This process consists of top executives' putting forth an image for the company and generating consensus around this image. At this stage, the vision becomes a negotiated reality, "arising from the political activity among members of the top management team" (Robbins & Duncan, 1988, p. 229). Note that the development of vision proceeds from an environmental and organizational analysis and is fairly reactive in character. It also emerges in final form as a reflection of negotiation processes among top managers.

An alternate view suggests that the seeds of a vision reside in the values a top executive brings to the analysis of environmental and organizational contingencies (Kouzes & Posner, 1987). That is, a flickering image of how the organization should be exists in the mind of the executive and is grounded in his or her values. This image takes form as the executive interacts with fellow executives, stakeholders, and constituencies. An environmental and organizational analysis proceeds from this value-based orientation as the executive seeks opportunities to employ visionary images. Thus, this process is at once both reactive and proactive. It is reactive in that the form a visionary image takes follows from the existing and anticipated contingencies and the contributions of key stakeholders. The envisioning process is proactive because executives bring core values concerning desired organizational states to a search for enactment opportunities.

Recent studies of the envisioning process describe these two viewpoints as the single executive as the progenitor of vision versus the top management team yielding a vision from its own negotiation and political processes (Conger & Kanungo, 1998). We suggest, though, that the latter view neglects the role of personal values, and the former does not give sufficient weight to social construction processes. The personal values of chief executives become implicated in how they scan the operating environment, how problems are interpreted, and how potential solutions are derived. However, these values offer only potentialities and vague images. Their actualization into a meaningful and useful visionary statement is a social construction process that captures the commitment and requirements of necessary top managers. The value core of this negotiated reality, though, ultimately reflects the deeply held orientation of the top executive and is not negotiable.

Case studies of visionary leaders often reflect both of these processes. The romantic image of the visionary leader that is so prominent in the popular literature minimizes inappropriately the social constructed reality of organizational visions. Nonetheless, the evidence is strong for the influence of visionary individuals in shaping the meaning of constructed visions. We suggest that this influence resides not in their environmental analysis or negotiation skill but rather in the values they seek to propagate through organizational change.

Vision and Organizational Effectiveness

Do visions promote organizational effectiveness? Surprisingly little research has directly examined this question. In this section we review several conceptual models that link vision to effectiveness and then look at the limited empirical evidence for this link.

Conceptual Models

Conceptual models of organizational leadership suggest that visions influence organizational effectiveness in several ways. First, the content of visions provides a frame of reference for both the leader and followers. As already noted, a vision mental model contains an image of a future changed organization coaligned with a future changed environment. This mental model also contains a logic about "how to get from here to there." Thus, a vision is a sense-making mechanism that leaders use to explain the strategic direction required of the organization. Several theorists have argued that a vision must be "radical" in that it is a clarion call to change the status quo in response to a crisis (Trice & Beyer, 1986; Weber, 1947; House, 1977). Along these lines, Beyer (1999) argues, in describing vision and charismatic leadership, that

> unless a leader's vision is a radical break with the past . . . it should not qualify as charismatic, no matter how attractive to followers. Making a radical vision a distinguishing requirement for charisma or for transformational leadership makes a sensible linkage with the presumption that charismatic and transformational leaders are those who bring about change [p. 315].

Thus, a vision provides a conceptual frame to followers that at once points to a way out of a social or organizational crisis and provides the rational foundation for trusting the maverick visionary. Wofford and Goodwin (1994) also argued that unlike transactional leaders, visionary or transformational leaders retain a work schema that tends to center on a vision and its link to superordinate and subordinate goals. Such schemas, then, provide followers with an action-oriented road map that structures their work activities.

A second way that visions influence organizational effectiveness is by providing a source of impassioned empowerment that motivates followers. This source resides in the value core of the vision. Along this line, House and Shamir (1993) noted that a vision reflects "an ideological goal that describes a better future for followers. This goal is ideological in the sense that the leader asserts that it is the moral right of followers to realize this goal. As Burns (1978) states, such leaders emphasize fundamental values such as beauty, order, honesty, dignity, and human rights" (p. 97). They go on to state that "in fact, articulation of an ideological goal as a vision for a better future, for which followers have a moral claim is the sine quo non of all charismatic visionary theories" (p. 97). The moralistic values of the vision compel the motivation and passion of followers who accept the underlying ideological goal.

A third way that visions influence organizational effectiveness is through the actions of the visionary leader: the articulation and communication of the vision to followers in a manner that galvanizes support for the vision, managing his or her image to build trust and loyalty among followers, showing confidence in and empowering subordinates in order to engage followers in the task, and fostering a collective identity and higher individual self-worth among followers in line with the value core of the vision (House & Shamir, 1993).

These basic notions are part of several visionary leadership models. We review four of the most prominent.

House's Theory of Charismatic Leadership

House's (1977) theory argues that charismatic leaders produce organizational change by articulating a vision for the organization and establishing a strong emotional attachment with followers that leads to their acceptance of this vision. The mediating link in this influence is the link formed between the vision, in particular its value core, and the self-concepts of followers (Shamir et al., 1993).

House defined several leadership behaviors that result in stronger follower identification and loyalty: articulation of an ideological goal; role modeling of attitudes, values, and beliefs engendered by the leader's vision; image management that fosters the implicit trust of organizational members; setting high performance expectations; and communicating confidence in the followers' ability to meet these expectations. The effect of these behaviors is the development of high trust and intense loyalty in subordinates that results in their unqualified acceptance of proposed organizational changes. These behaviors also increase motivation and efficacy on the part of subordinates to meet the strategic and tactical goals engendered by the leader's vision (Eden, 1984, 1990).

Bass's Transformational Leadership Theory

Bass (1985, 1996) argued that effective leadership involves transforming and empowering subordinates so that they are motivated to act beyond their self-interest in the service of a larger community. He contrasted this mode of influence with transactional leadership, where the exchange between the leader and the follower was based less on transcending ideals and more on the ability of the leader to provide for the personal gain of followers. Thus, transformational leaders, as opposed to transactional leaders, seek to activate higher-order growth and self-actualizing needs (Maslow, 1954); they do so by clarifying the importance of organizational tasks and actions beyond the personal perspective of the follower.

Bass's model differs from those describing charismatic leadership. Whereas charismatic leaders institute change by establishing an intense emotional attachment in the follower that leads to an unquestioning trust in the leader's vision, transformational leaders empower subordinates as co-agents of organizational change (Bass, 1985; Westley & Mintzberg, 1989; Yukl & Van Fleet, 1992). For example, Westley and Mintzberg (1989) suggest that

> there are important instances when the "followers" stimulate the leader, as opposed to the other way around. In most cases, however, it would appear that leader and follower participate together in creating the vision. The specific content—the original idea or perception—may come from the leader . . ., but the form which it takes, the special excitement which marks, is co-created [p. 21].

Bass (1985, 1990, 1996; Bass & Avolio, 1993) proposed several behavioral characteristics of transformational leaders similar to those offered by House (1977), including the articulation of a vision, the communication of strong performance expectations, and the use of symbols to manage the meaning of critical information and components of their vision. However, Bass also argued that transforming empowerment required that leaders encourage their subordinates to think autonomously and examine problems from different perspectives. Such leaders provide individual and focused attention to their subordinates, often in the role of mentor or adviser. Bass (1990, p. 216) noted that these qualities, particularly intellectual stimulation, prevent the "habitual followership" and blind obedience engendered by purely charismatic leadership styles.

Bass offered a model of visionary leadership that incorporates and expands on House's charismatic leadership theory by elaborating the role of followers as co-agents of change (see House & Shamir, 1993, for their own integration of these different perspectives). The next leadership model described here extends the place of followers by highlighting their role in legitimizing such leaders.

Conger and Kanungo's Theory of Charismatic Leadership

Conger and Kanungo (1987, 1992; Kanungo & Conger, 1992) suggested that charisma is an attribution by followers to a leader based on his or her display of three specific leader cognitive and behavioral patterns. One is a leader's evaluation of the status quo that determines the need for change and the organization's capacity to effect such change. Another is the articulation of a vision that is discrepant from the status quo. To be successful, the leader's articulation to subordinates needs to be logical, cogent, and persuasive. Accordingly, vision presentation encompasses problems in the current organizational state, the nature of the vision itself, how the vision resolves or improves the problems noted in the status quo, and the strategic plans needed to implement the vision (Kanungo & Conger, 1992). Finally, the attribution of charisma also results from the leader's use of unconventional and innovative behaviors to implement the vision. Conger and Kanungo (1987) argued that because such behaviors are counternormative, they entail considerable personal risk by the leader, in turn leading to greater admiration and perceptions of credibility from followers.

Conger and Kanungo argue that for leaders to emerge in this model, followers need to perceive a crisis confronting the organization that requires significant change. Thus, charismatic leaders need to convince their potential followers of an organizational crisis that requires a response or at least persuade them of the advantages of a new organizational direction.

Sashkin's Visionary Leadership Theory

More than the other models described thus far, Sashkin's (1988; Sashkin & Fulmer, 1988) model focuses on the content of a leader's vision and the process of visioning. He noted that visions deal with change in the environment and what is necessary for organizational adaptation, offer ideal goals that raise the standards for the organization, and place value on a people-oriented focus within the company and its customers. This last quality means that visions provide a picture of new roles for organizational members as well as the centrality of consumers of organizational products.

Sashkin (1988) described several visionary leadership behaviors. One is focusing subordinate attention on the critical points and key issues that comprise the vision. Another is developing two-way communication that provides an open forum for the transmission of a vision and information on how followers receive and respond to the vision. A third behavior is demonstrating consistency and trustworthiness. Such consistency conveys the sincerity and value-based core of the executive's vision. A fourth behavior is conveying respect for the subordinates. Finally, visionary executives take personal risks for the purpose of conveying their commitment to the vision.

Summary: A Model of Leadership, Vision, and Organizational Effectiveness

Based on an integration of these models and other conceptual contributions, Figure 7.1 suggests several ways in which visions influence organizational effectiveness. Vision content and vision articulation establish the context for several leader and follower responses. Vision content variables include ideological goals, value-based core, a rationalizing frame of reference, growth of future-oriented theme, and change orientation. The communication of the vision involves the use of inspirational and persuasive imagery, clear and compelling arguments, challenging language that calls for commitment, and the specification of tasks and goals (that is,

Figure 7.1. Model of Leadership, Vision, and Organizational Effectiveness.

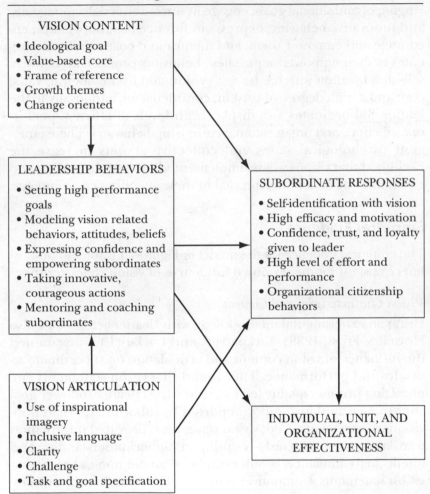

VISION CONTENT
- Ideological goal
- Value-based core
- Frame of reference
- Growth themes
- Change oriented

LEADERSHIP BEHAVIORS
- Setting high performance goals
- Modeling vision related behaviors, attitudes, beliefs
- Expressing confidence and empowering subordinates
- Taking innovative, courageous actions
- Mentoring and coaching subordinates

VISION ARTICULATION
- Use of inspirational imagery
- Inclusive language
- Clarity
- Challenge
- Task and goal specification

SUBORDINATE RESPONSES
- Self-identification with vision
- High efficacy and motivation
- Confidence, trust, and loyalty given to leader
- High level of effort and performance
- Organizational citizenship behaviors

INDIVIDUAL, UNIT, AND ORGANIZATIONAL EFFECTIVENESS

strategic and tactical plans) that derive from the leader's vision. Vision articulation also involves high levels of inclusion language, incorporating phrases that are unifying (using *we* and *our*) rather than divisive (*them* and *they*) (Fiol, Harris, & House, 1999). Finally, leaders who are communicating visions use a "charismatic tone . . . [they] speak with a captivating voice tone, make direct eye contact, show animated facial expressions, and have a dynamic interaction style" (Kirkpatrick & Locke, 1996, p. 38)

Effective visionary leaders model vision-related attitudes, beliefs, values, and behaviors; set high performance expectations and challenging organizational goals; engage in unconventional, courageous, and innovative behavior; express confidence in subordinates; encourage and empower them; and mentor and coach their subordinates in their empowerment. These behaviors produce in followers self-identification with the leader's vision and its ideological/value core and a high degree of trust in, confidence in, and loyalty to the leader. Subordinates also display high levels of efficacy, performance effort, and organizational citizenship behaviors. These emergent psychological states and collective actions increase the likelihood that visions will be implemented successfully and that organizations thrive and remain vital in their operating environments.

Empirical Evidence

The empirical evidence for the model in Figure 7.1 is somewhat scant but consistent for the proposed influences of vision characteristics.

Vision Characteristics and Content

Using an experimental methodology with "leader-actors" (see also Howell & Frost, 1989), Kirkpatrick and Locke (1996) examined the influence of vision content and articulation on subordinate attitudes and performance. They found that vision statements emphasizing product quality led to greater trust, leader-follower goal congruence, and inspiration reported by subordinates than nonvisionary statements. Also, vision statements provided information translating vision into tasks resulting in higher understanding and intellectual stimulation by subordinates than did non-task-clarifying vision statements. Communication style did not influence subordinate attitudes. Both aspects of vision content resulted in stronger subordinate performance, with these effects being mediated by the influence of content on subordinate goals and self-efficacy.

Baum, Locke, and Kirkpatrick (1998) studied the effects of vision attributes, content, and articulation on organizational performance within the architectural woodwork industry. They rated the visions of 127 CEOs on the attributes of brevity, clarity, abstractness, challenge, future orientation, stability, and ability to inspire. Vision content reflected the degree to which the vision specifically emphasized business growth. The outcome variables were three measures of venture growth: sales growth, employment growth, and profit growth. Baum and associates found that both vision attributes and vision content as well as the degree to which vision was communicated to the employees influenced the three measures of organizational growth. They also found that vision communication partially mediated the effects of vision characteristics on performance. This study provides evidence, then, for the importance of vision to organizational effectiveness. It is also useful as one of the few studies, and perhaps the only one, that empirically examines this relationship.

Leadership Behaviors

These two studies focused on how vision content and attributes influence several subordinate and organizational outcomes. Other studies have examined whether visionary leadership behaviors influence subordinate attitudes and behavior. Hater and Bass (1988) examined the association between charisma and intellectual stimulation, respectively, and performance ratings of fifty-four managers by their superiors. Subordinates of each manager provided ratings of his or her display of these two behaviors. The results indicated significant correlations between the visionary leadership behaviors and the performance ratings. Yammarino, Spangler, and Bass (1993) also investigated the effects of displayed transformational leadership on the individual performance of junior naval officers. Subordinates provided ratings of each focal officer's display of charisma, individualized consideration, intellectual stimulation, and inspirational leadership, as well as ratings of their job effectiveness. Yammarino and associates also collected performance ratings from each officer's superior as well as recommendations for early promotion. These ratings were combined into a measure of appraised performance. Yammarino and associates found that transformational leadership behaviors were significantly associated with measures of officer performance from both superiors and subordinates.

Podsakoff, MacKenzie, Moorman, and Fetter (1990) examined the effects of transformational leadership on subordinate attitudes, commitment, and degree of felt empowerment. They asked subordinates in a diversified petrochemical company to provide ratings of their manager on six behaviors: identifying and articulating a vision, providing an appropriate model, fostering the acceptance of group goals, high performance expectations, providing individualized support, and providing intellectual stimulation. Followers also rated their own satisfaction, their trust in their leader, and their organizational citizenship behavior. Podsakoff and associates found that visionary leadership behavior was associated with both greater follower trust and satisfaction and higher amounts of organizational citizenship behavior. These results held even when same source bias was controlled.

Howell and Avolio (1993) investigated the link between visionary or transformational leadership and organizational performance. They acquired measures of transformational and transactional leadership in seventy-eight managers from the top four organizational levels of a single company, as well as measures of the performance of each manager's consolidated unit. These measures were based on the achievement of targeted goals one year after measures of leadership were obtained. The results indicated that "leaders who displayed less management by exception and less contingent reward and more individualized consideration, intellectual stimulation, and charisma positively contributed to the achievement of business-unit goals" (p. 899).

The strength or magnitude of correlations between transformational leadership predictors and outcomes has varied widely across studies (see Bass & Avolio, 1993, for a review). Lowe, Kroeck, and Sivasubramaniam (1995) completed a meta-analysis of these correlations to determine the average magnitude of correlations adjusted for statistical and methodological artifacts. They examined several moderators of these correlations—the organizational level of the leaders (upper or lower), the type of organization (public or private), and the nature of the criterion (subordinate perceptions or organizational measures)—and whether the study has been published. They found that the transformational factors of charismatic influence (raw $r = .62$), individualized consideration (raw $r = .53$), and intellectual stimulation (raw $r = .51$) were all strongly related to outcomes, with charismatic influence demonstrating the strongest association (inspirational motivation was not measured in many of these studies). The range of correlations for each of the transformational leadership factors suggested the presence of moderators. Accordingly, Lowe and associates found that the effects of transformational leadership were stronger in public versus private organizations and when using subordinate perceptions as criteria. The magnitude of the correlations with subordinate perceptions was on average about 40 points higher (mean raw correlation = .71) than the correlations with organizational measures (.30). However, Lowe and associates also noted that the latter correlations were still statistically significant. This study demonstrates both the strength of transformational leadership effects and at least two moderators of these effects.

Implications for the Vision Effectiveness Model

Taken together, these studies support several of the linkages modeled in Figure 7.1. There is limited but consistent support for the influence of vision characteristics and content on follower attitudes, beliefs, and performance, as well as on indexes of organizational performance. Many more studies have demonstrated the influence of visionary leadership behaviors on follower responses and effectiveness. Indeed, Shamir and associates (1993) provide the following summary from thirty-five empirical studies of charismatic leadership:

> Collectively, these findings indicate that leaders who engage in the theoretical charismatic behaviors produce the theoretical effects. In addition, they receive higher performance ratings, have more satisfied and more highly motivated followers, and are viewed as more effective leaders by their superiors and followers than others in positions of leadership. Further, the effect size of charismatic leader behavior on follower satisfaction and performance is consistently higher than prior field study findings concerning other leader behavior, generally, ranging well below .01 probability of error due to chance, with correlations frequently ranging in the neighborhood of .50 or better [pp. 578–579].

Leader Attributes That Contribute to Effective Envisioning

The relationships proposed and found among vision, vision communication, leadership behaviors, follower responses, and organizational effectiveness lead to an important question: What are the personal leader attributes that foster effective envisioning? This is a critical question for industrial and organizational (I/O) psychologists, because the answer would serve as the foundation for leader assessment, selection, training, and development efforts (Zaccaro, 1996). In this next section we describe leader qualities that promote the development of an effective vision, as well as those that enhance the leader's ability to elicit trust, an emotional attachment, and a strong organizational commitment from followers.

Cognitive Abilities

The development of an effective vision requires that top leaders be able to derive an adaptive and appropriate fit between the organization and its environment at some point in time, ranging up to fifty years in the future (Jacobs & Jaques, 1987; Lewis & Jacobs, 1992; Sashkin, 1988). Thus, senior leaders are required to create a logical framework from highly ambiguous and complex data. They also need to understand how their organization structures are to evolve within the context of their emerging vision. Finally, they have to derive the strategies and tactics required to implement their vision. This suggests that several cognitive abilities, such as creativity, reasoning skills, and intelligence, are necessary for effective visionary leadership (Atwater, Penn, & Rucker, 1991; Sashkin, 1988; Tichy & Devanna, 1986a, 1986b). Along this line, Sashkin (1988, 1992) argued that the ambiguity of both the environment and the organization, particularly as they must correspond at a distant point in the future, requires cognitive complexity in the visionary leader. After Jaques (1986), Sashkin (1988) added four cognitive skills, related to the leader's expression, explanation, extension, and expansion of his or her vision.

Recent research on metacognitive skills suggests that they also should contribute to effective envisioning. Perhaps the most common definition of metacognition is one's "knowledge and cognition about cognitive phenomena" (Flavell, 1979, p. 906; see also Brown, 1978; Davidson, Deuser, & Sternberg, 1994; Jausovec, 1994a, 1994b; Osman & Hannafin, 1992). Problem solvers use cognitive abilities and skills such as inductive reasoning, deductive reasoning, divergent thinking, information processing skills, and verbal reasoning to derive effective solutions. Metacognitive skills regulate and monitor the application of these skills in three general ways (Brown, 1978; Davidson et al., 1994; Geiwitz, 1993). First, they facilitate an understanding of the problem itself and its critical parameters. Second, they promote the search for and specification of effective solutions. Finally, these skills are used in monitoring solution implementation, generating feedback regarding such implementation, and adapting solutions to changing conditions.

Davidson and associates (1994) noted that such skills are more critical for unstructured, insight, or creative problems, exactly the kinds of problems represented by visions. Accordingly, they present three metacognitive processes—selective encoding, selective combination, and selective comparison—that facilitate the representation of unfamiliar problems. Taken together, these processes reflect novel uses of existing information to generate new understandings and, hence, previously unknown solution paths. They also represent the kinds of cognitive and metacognitive processes that are most applicable to effective envisioning.

Self-Confidence

High self-confidence is another attribute of effective visionary leaders (Atwater et al., 1991; Bass, 1985; Boal & Bryson, 1988; House, 1977; House & Howell, 1992). It contributes to the envisioning process in several ways. First, high confidence helps leaders develop an innovative vision that breaks with the status quo. Second, it helps them confront the difficult challenges associated with implementing such a vision. Finally, when leaders display a strong sense of confidence, they convey a positive message to their followers about the feasibility and workability of their vision; accordingly, they facilitate the trust necessary for successful vision implementation. Along these lines, House and Howell (1992) suggested that self-efficacy, self-confidence, and an internal locus of control will affect the influence tactics that leaders select. A self-confident leader is more likely to select supportive and rational modes of influence, such as those related to transformational leadership. Low self-confidence leads to more reward-based or coercive modes of leader influence.

Socialized Power Motive

Creating and implementing an innovative vision involves moving followers and, indeed, the entire organization in a new direction. This calls for substantial motivation on the part of visionaries to be willing to influence others. However, history is filled with charismatic leaders who were destructive in their social influence. A major distinction between destructive and constructive charismatics is that the latter are more likely to be operating from high power needs but with a socialized orientation, or what McClelland (1985) terms "activity inhibition." House and Howell (1992) defined this characteristic as "an unconscious motive to use social influence, or to satisfy the power need, in socially desirable ways, for the betterment of the collective rather than for personal self-interest" (p. 95). Sashkin (1988) also noted that socialized power motives lead to the leader's predisposition to empower subordinates. Personalized power will engender the opposite behavior pattern, where all power is retained by the leader. Along these lines, Bass (1990) noted that "*intrapreneurs* (individuals who behave innovatively in large complex organizations) are task-oriented personnel who use power whenever they can to ensure that their ideas, inventions, and innovations are accepted in their organization (Pinchot, 1985). Such intrapreneurs regard power as being instrumental for the accomplishment of tasks and as something they share with others, rather than as a basis for personal aggrandizement" (p. 129).

House and his colleagues argued that dominance needs were critical aspects of charismatic leadership. For example, House, Woycke, and Foder (1988) found higher power needs in six charismatic presidents (Jefferson, Jackson, Lincoln, Theodore and Franklin Roosevelt, and Kennedy) than in six presidents judged low in charisma (Tyler, Pierce, Buchanan, Arthur, Harding, and Coolidge). House and Howell (1992) argued that the distinction between personalized and socialized power was necessary in separating "good" charismatic leaders from those whose actions resulted in whole-scale harm and destruction within their constituent organizations (such as Hitler and Stalin). In the latter case, need for power was decoupled from the desire to wield it for the sake of others rather than for personal gain (Conger, 1990; Kets de Vries, & Miller, 1985).

Openness and Adaptability

Openness and a strong sense of curiosity promote a leader's exploration and learning of new areas and domains (Barrick & Mount, 1991; Keller, 1986; McCrae & Costa, 1987). This quality facilitates the creative problem solving necessary for envisioning, because it encourages leaders to attend to discrepant information and activate multiple and more diverse cognitive representations (Mumford, Costanza, Threlfall, Baughman, & Reiter-Palmon, 1993).

Leaders who are high in openness explore new and uncharted areas. The uncertainty that accompanies such exploration signals a high possibility of subsequent failure. Thus, personality characteristics related to adaptability and risk taking become important for visionary leadership because they promote boldness in confronting new ideas. Leaders low in adaptability (or, alternatively, exhibiting a defensive rigidity and anxiety) perform poorly as visionaries because their dispositions interfere with the effective application of cognitive resources (Mumford, Baughman, Threlfall, Costanza, & Uhlman, 1993; Mumford, Costanza, et al., 1993). They are also more threatened by instability and therefore less motivated in such situations.

A related attribute for effective envisioning is risk propensity. Recall that Conger and Kanungo (1987, 1992) contended that the attribution of charisma derives from the leader's articulating an unconventional vision. Further, this attribution occurs when the leader takes personal risks in the service of this vision. Tichy and Devanna's model of transformational leadership (1986a, 1986b) made a similar point: that visionary leaders are intellectually and emotionally courageous. They understand when it is possible to confront a painful reality and when the risk is too strong to pursue. Also, they are able to resist conformity, and they risk saying things to their subordinates that are unpalatable. Thus, a strong propensity for risk taking appears to be a critical aspect of the personality of successful visionary leaders.

Social Intelligence

Visionary leaders often need to implement solutions in social environments that are dynamic, complex, and ambiguous. Often subordinates are initially hostile to the fundamental changes in the status quo engendered by a vision. Zaccaro (1999; Zaccaro, Gilbert, Thor, & Mumford, 1991) defined several competency sets related to social intelligence that also apply to effective envisioning. One set, labeled relational competencies, facilitates complex interactions with organizational subordinates, peers, and superiors. These competencies include behavioral flexibility, negotiation skills, conflict management, persuasion and social influence skills, and skills related to empathy and coaching.

Zaccaro (1999) defined the second set of competencies as social reasoning skills. These skills promote effective perception, judgment, and diagnosis of social demands, needs, and requirements. They also foster situational responsiveness, effective management of social diversity, and social persuasiveness. Conger and Kanungo (1987) argued that to be effective, charismatic leaders need to be sensitive to and acutely aware of environmental contingencies and realities. They also noted that such leaders are "sensitive to both the abilities and emotional needs of followers, and they understand the resources and constraints of the physical and social environments in which they operate" (p. 643). Zaccaro defined these as social perceptiveness skills and argued that they reflect competencies in two fundamental processes. The first is an ability to identify social cues that are relevant to organizational problem solving (that is, social awareness skill). Socially intelligent behavior obviously cannot proceed if leaders are unable even to perceive important social contingencies. The second social perception skill reflects an ability to interpret or infer the meaning of important social information accurately (this is social acumen skill). Both skills, together with interactional competencies, contribute to the effective development and implementation of vision.

The Performance Imperatives of Visionary Leadership

This book defines organizational leadership as occurring within a context often characterized by the influence of several performance imperatives. The acts of envisioning involve responses to and consideration of several of these imperatives. We have already noted the cognitive demands implicit in the envisioning process. Although the statement of an effective vision itself may be brief, clear, and unambiguous, the frame of reference on which it is based is likely to be quite complex, reflecting a variety of cause-and-effect relationships. Effective visions are thoughtful in their inception and their implementation. Thus, they represent a high form of responsiveness to the cognitive imperatives of executive leadership.

Social imperatives arise from the need for visionaries to be aware of different social constituencies in both the development and implementation of vision. The quality of a vision is defined by how well it will align the organization with the trends and expectations in a changing environment. Executive leaders developing a strategic direction for the organization as a whole need to respond to many stakeholders, performance expectations, and environmental trends. For these reasons, their information networks or their social capital (see Chapter Five, this volume) need to be widespread and diverse. Also, the implementation within an organization of a vision that necessarily argues against the status quo will call forth its own social imperatives that executives will need to address.

Personal imperatives are reflected in the visioning process in two ways. First, the values of the executive that form the core of his or her vision are intensely personal. They cause the executive to own the vision or be identified with it more closely than would be the case with a strategy. Also, an executive's vision is fundamentally a career choice. Its successful implementation can garner great recognition for the visionary; its failure can lead to an ignoble dismissal or retirement.

The opportunity to implement a vision comes only with the accrual of sufficient power. Thus, executives must engage in the activities that result in power acquisition, and do so early in the envisioning process. Accordingly, they need to build coalitions and form intra- and interorganizational alliances that would be useful at various phases of vision implementation. They also need to understand the process of sharing power that promotes effective empowerment. Thus, visionaries simultaneously need to accrue and retain the power to push and enforce a vision, while being prepared to share it with appropriate subordinates. This balance is achieved by the visionary's acquiring different forms of power, only some of which are released. Forms of reward power are distributed in transformational leadership while leaders retain referent power. Different aspects of expert and legitimate power may be alternatively shared or retained in transformational leadership depending on situational contingencies. The political imperatives of visionary leadership concern the careful balancing of these power issues.

The remaining leader performance imperatives have more ancillary but no less important influences on envisioning. Technology imperatives often drive the imaginative scope of a particular vision. New forms of technology often broaden the horizons of what is possible. One sees such scope in today's Internet environment, where new forms of business emerge at an escalating rate. Financial imperatives provide the criteria for vision effectiveness, but they also exert undue pressures on the envisioning process. There is often a tug of war in an executive's strategic decision making between short-term and long-term considerations. Visions inherently reside in the long term and often require the expenditures of funds that may not result in immediate gain. Indeed the risk is considerable that no gain will ever be realized. Many visions have been dashed on the rocks of financial reality. Finally, envisioning processes influence staffing imperatives. Indeed, executives who are concerned about staffing their top management teams will likely select candidates who hold values similar to those reflected in their vision's being implemented. Indeed, value congruence may override other important selection criteria.

These arguments point to the assertion that the development and implementation of vision are best understood from a contextual perspective. Indeed, an enduring argument in the charismatic leadership literature is that such leaders cannot emerge or be effective unless an organizational crisis exists (Beyer, 1999; Conger & Kanungo, 1987, 1992; Trice & Beyer, 1986; Weber, 1947). Such a crisis signals the need for a fundamental change in the status quo and enhances the likelihood that organizational members will attend to the alternative perspective (or vision) offered by a charismatic leader. As noted, several of the imperatives will derive from this context.

Implications for Industrial and Organizational Psychologists

The role of vision and the envisioning process in organizational effectiveness has several significant implications for research and practice in I/O psychology. First, the importance of vision, visioning skills, and visionary leadership behaviors suggests the need for high-quality assessment instruments that measure these qualities. Prominent among current instruments is the Multi-Factor Leadership Questionnaire (MLQ; Bass, 1985, 1996; Bass & Avolio, 1993; Hater & Bass, 1988; Waldman, Bass, & Einstein, 1987). The MLQ contains the major dimensions of transformational leadership, as well as items assessing transactional leadership and nonleadership. The transformational leadership factors include charisma, effectively subsuming the work of House (1977) and Conger and Kanungo (1987, 1992). This factor reflects the vision-setting role of leaders (for example, the leader "transmits a sense of joint mission and ownership"; Bass & Avolio, 1983, p. 56). The factor "inspirational motivation" also contains vision-setting behaviors (for example, the leader "presents an optimistic and attainable view of the future"; Bass & Avolio, 1983, p. 56). Podsakoff and associates (1990) offered a similar assessment instrument (for example, the leader "paints an interesting picture of the future for our group," "inspires others with his/her plans for the future"; p. 118). Also, Conger and Kanungo (1994) developed an instrument that measured vision articulation ("has vision, often brings up ideas about possibilities for the future"; p. 448), environmental sensitivity ("readily recognizes new environmental opportunities"), favorable physical and social conditions that may facilitate achievement or organizational objectives, as well as other dimensions of charismatic leadership.

These measures appear to be applicable to assessment of vision articulation and implementation behaviors. They do not assess the characteristics of vision, nor do they measure an executive's ability to develop vision. Thoms and Blasko (1999) offer an assessment instrument that is intended to measure "the ability of an individual to create a positive and vivid vision of an organization's future" (p. 106). However, this scale is currently too newly developed to assess its psychometric quality fully (Thoms & Blasko, 1999, do provide preliminary validation evidence). There are no well-tested instruments for measuring the content and quality of visions, although Larword and her colleagues provide the foundation for such assessments (Larwood et al., 1995; Larwood, Kriger, & Falbe, 1993). Thus, one implication for research in I/O psychology is the development and validation of instruments that assess multiple dimensions of vision and the envisioning process.

Another research question is the role of vision in staffing and executive selection processes. Typically, I/O psychologists have emphasized the match between applicant attributes and job requirements as the primary basis of selection systems. Nonetheless, the match between applicant values and the leader's vision may become equally as important. Executives will likely select their top management team according to the congruence they see between their own vision and the values displayed by potential applicants. For example, Frank Shrontz, the former CEO and chairman of Boeing, developed the vision behind the Boeing 777 project and reflected this vision in his subsequent staffing of the project (Zaccaro & Marks, 1999). He envisioned a manufacturing process that was customer friendly, technologically advanced, functionally interdisciplinary, and more efficient in terms of product delivery. These goals became the basis for a new way of operating that Shrontz urged for his company. However, they were also readily apparent in the values of the executives he hired to implement this project. Two in particular were Philip Condit, who at various times during the developmental phase of the 777 jet was general manager of the Boeing 777 Division, executive vice president of the Boeing Commercial Airplane Group, and president of the Boeing Corporation, and Alan Mulally, who was vice president of engineering for the 777 Division and, after Condit moved up, general manager for the division. Both men were viewed by their colleagues and employees as people oriented with an ability to integrate different functional perspectives, key qualities, and values that were important to the vision that Shrontz espoused. An important question for research on executive selection is how much emphasis is placed on the congruence of values and vision versus other selection criteria and what the validity is of selection tools and processes designed to assess such congruence.

We would also direct the attention of I/O psychologists to the development and training of skills related to the visioning process. How best might these attributes be developed? We suspect that several types of developmental interventions would facilitate growth in these skills, such as specially designed course work that includes skill-based training and feedback-intensive programs (Avolio & Bass, 1991; Avolio & Gibbons, 1988; Quinn, Faerman, Thompson, & McGrath, 1990), developmental job assignments (see Chapter

Eleven; see also McCauley, Ruderman, Ohlott, & Morrow, 1994), and mentoring and coaching (McCauley & Douglas, 1998). Most of these efforts have focused on skills necessary for implementing vision, such as transformational leadership and subordinate empowerment. There are few leader development programs that specifically target skills related to vision construction and that have been extensively or empirically evaluated. Such programs would likely need to focus on the development of conceptual, planning, and complex problem-solving skills. We suspect that such development could not be short term and perhaps would integrate multiple methods and types of interventions (for example, course work, self-development, experience-based training, and mentoring) (Hunt, 1991; Mumford, Marks, Zaccaro, Connelly, & Reiter-Palmon, 2000). Future practice and research on executive leadership development are likely to focus more broadly and deeply on the most feasible means of developing envisioning skills

Conclusion

This chapter has focused on the role of vision in executive leadership and organizational effectiveness. We examined the nature of vision and its attributes; described several models of visionary leadership and the personal attributes that contribute to such leadership; and concluded with some implications for research and practice in I/O psychology.

This book reflects a contextualized perspective of organizational leadership that emphasizes executive responses to several performance imperatives. Often visions and envisioning processes become the mechanisms through which such responses occur. Accordingly, we contend that modeling the nature, content, and process of vision will contribute significantly to understanding the fundamental dynamics of effective executive leadership.

References
Allport, G. W., Vernon, P. E., & Lindzey, G. (1960). *A study of values.* Boston: Houghton Mifflin.
Atwater, L. E., Penn, R., & Rucker, L. (1991). Personal qualities of charismatic leaders. *Leadership and Organizational Development Journal, 12,* 7–10.

Avolio, B. J., & Bass, B. M. (1991). Charisma and beyond. In J. G. Hunt, B. R. Baliga, H. P. Dachler, & C. A. Schriesheim (Eds.), *Emerging leadership vistas*. Lexington, MA: Heath.

Avolio, B. J., & Gibbons, T. C. (1988). Developing transformational leaders: A lifespan approach. In J. A. Conger & R. N. Kanungo (Eds.), *Charismatic leadership: The elusive factor in organizational effectiveness*. San Francisco: Jossey-Bass.

Baehr, M. E. (1992). *Predicting success in higher-level positions: A guide to the system for testing and evaluation of potential*. Westport, CT: Quorum Books.

Barrick, M. R., & Mount, M. K. (1991). The big five personality dimensions and job performance: A meta-analysis. *Personnel Psychology, 44,* 1–26.

Bass, B. M. (1985). *Leadership and performance beyond expectations*. New York: Free Press.

Bass, B. M. (1988). The inspirational process of leadership: *Journal of Management Development, 7*(5), 21–31.

Bass, B. M. (1990). *Bass and Stogdill's handbook of leadership: Theory, research, and managerial applications* (3rd ed.). New York: Free Press.

Bass, B. M. (1996). *A new paradigm of leadership: An inquiry into transformational leadership*. Alexandria, VA: U.S. Army Research Institute for the Behavioral and Social Sciences.

Bass, B. M., & Avolio, B. J. (1993). Transformational leadership: A response to critiques. In M. M. Chemers & R. Ayman (Eds.), *Leadership theory and research*. Orlando, FL: Academic Press.

Baum, J. R., Locke, E. A., & Kirkpatrick, S. A. (1998). A longitudinal study of the relation of vision and vision communication to venture growth in entrepreneurial firms. *Journal of Applied Psychology, 83,* 43–54.

Bennis, W. G., & Nanus, B. (1985). *Leaders: The strategies for taking charge*. New York: HarperCollins.

Beyer, J. M. (1999). Taming and promoting charisma to change organizations. *Leadership Quarterly, 10,* 307–330.

Boal, K. B., & Bryson, J. M. (1988). Charismatic leadership: A phenomenological and structural approach. In J. G. Hunt, B. R. Baliga, H. P. Dachler, & C. A. Schriesheim (Eds.), *Emerging leadership vistas*. Lexington, MA: Heath.

Brown, A. L. (1978). Knowing when, where, and how to remember: The problem of metacognition. In R. Glaser (Ed.), *Advances in instructional psychology*. New York: Halsted Press.

Burns, J. M. (1978). *Leadership*. New York: HarperCollins.

Collins, J. C., & Porras, J. I. (1991). Organizational vision and visionary organizations. *California Management Review, 34,* 30–82.

Conger, J. A. (1990). The dark side of leadership. *Organizational Dynamics, 19*(2), 44–55.

Conger, J. A., & Kanungo, R. N. (1987). Toward a behavioral theory of charismatic leadership in organizational settings. *Academy of Management Review, 12,* 637–647.

Conger, J. A., & Kanungo, R. N. (1992). Perceived behavioural attributes of charismatic leadership. *Canadian Journal of Behavioural Science, 24*(1), 86–102.

Conger, J. A., & Kanungo, R. N. (1994). Charismatic leadership in organizations. *Journal of Organizational Behavior, 15,* 439–452.

Conger, J. A., & Kanungo, R. N. (1998). *Charismatic leadership in organizations.* Thousand Oaks, CA: Sage.

Davidson, J. E., Deuser, R., & Sternberg, R. J. (1994). The role of metacognition in problem solving. In J. Metcalf & A. P. Shimamura (Eds.), *Metacognition: Knowing about knowing.* Cambridge, MA: MIT Press.

Eden, D. (1984). Self-fulfilling prophecy as a management tool: Harnessing Pygmalion. *Academy of Management Review, 12,* 76–90.

Eden, D. (1990). *Pygmalion in management: Productivity as a self-fulfilling prophecy.* San Francisco: New Lexington Press.

England, G. W. (1975). *The manager and his values: An international perspective.* New York: Ballinger.

Fiol, C. M., Harris, D., & House, R. J. (1999). Charismatic leadership: Strategies for effecting social change. *Leadership Quarterly, 10,* 449–482.

Flavell, J. H. (1979). Metacognition and cognitive monitoring: A new area of cognitive-developmental inquiry. *American Psychologist, 34,* 906–911.

Geiwitz, J. (1993). *A conceptual model of metacognitive skills.* Alexandria, VA: U.S. Army Research Institute for the Behavioral and Social Sciences.

Gupta, A. K. (1984). Contingency linkages between strategy and general managerial characteristics: A conceptual examination. *Academy of Management Journal, 9,* 399–412.

Gupta, A. K. (1987). SBU strategies, corporate-SBU relations, and SBU effectiveness in strategy implementation. *Academy of Management Journal, 30,* 477–500.

Gupta, A. K. (1988). Contingency perspectives on strategic leadership: Current knowledge and future research directions. In D. C. Hambrick (Ed.), *The executive effect: Concepts and methods for studying top managers.* Greenwich, CT: JAI Press.

Hambrick, D. C. (1981a). Environment, strategy, and power within top management teams. *Administrative Science Quarterly, 26,* 253–275.

Hambrick, D. C. (1981b). Specialization of environmental scanning activities among upper-level executives. *Journal of Management Studies, 18,* 299–320.

Hambrick, D. C. (1982). Environmental scanning and organizational strategy. *Strategic Management Journal, 3,* 159–174.

Hambrick, D. C. (1989). Guest editor's introduction: Putting top managers back in the strategy picture. *Strategic Management Journal, 10,* 5–15.

Hambrick, D. C., & Brandon, G. (1988). Executive values. In D. C. Hambrick (Ed.), *The executive effect: Concepts and methods for studying top managers.* Greenwich, CT: JAI Press.

Hambrick, D. C., & Mason, P. A. (1984). Upper echelons: The organization as a reflection of top managers. *Academy of Management Review, 9,* 193–206.

Hater, J. J., & Bass, B. M. (1988). Supervisors' evaluations and subordinates' perceptions of transformational leadership. *Journal of Applied Psychology, 73,* 695–702.

Hemphill, J. K. (1959). Job descriptions for executives. *Harvard Business Review, 37,* 55–67.

House, R. J. (1977). A 1976 theory of charismatic leadership. In J. G. Hunt & L. L. Larson (Eds.), *Leadership: The cutting edge.* Carbondale: Southern Illinois University Press.

House, R. J., & Howell, J. M. (1992). Personality and charismatic leadership. *Leadership Quarterly, 3,* 81–108.

House, R. J., & Shamir, B. (1993). Toward an integration of transformational, charismatic, and visionary theories. In M. M. Chemers & R. Ayman (Eds.), *Leadership theory and research: Perspectives and directions.* Orlando, FL: Academic Press.

House, R. J., Woycke, J., & Foder, E. M. (1988). Charismatic and non-charismatic leaders: Differences in behavior and effectiveness. In J. A. Conger & R. N. Kanungo (Eds.), *Charismatic leadership: The elusive factor in organizational effectiveness.* San Francisco: Jossey-Bass.

Howell, J. M., & Avolio, B. J. (1993). Transformational leadership, transactional leadership, locus of control, and support for innovation: Key predictors of business unit performance. *Journal of Applied Psychology, 78,* 891–902.

Howell, J. M., & Frost, P. J. (1989). A laboratory study of charismatic leadership. *Organizational Behavior and Human Decision Processes, 43,* 243–269.

Hunt, J. G. (1991). *Leadership: A new synthesis.* Thousand Oaks, CA: Sage.

Hunt, J. G., Dodge, G. E., & Phillips, R. L. (1999). Out-of-the-box leadership for the twenty-first century: An introduction. In J. G. Hunt, G. E. Dodge, & L. Wong (Eds.), *Out-of-the-box leadership: Transforming the twenty-first-century army and other top-performing organizations.* Greenwich, CT: JAI Press.

Jacobs, T. O., & Jaques, E. (1987). Leadership in complex systems. In J. Zeidner (Ed.), *Human productivity enhancement: Vol. 2. Organizations, personnel, and decision making.* New York: Praeger.

Jacobs, T. O., & Jaques, E. (1990). Military executive leadership. In K. E. Clark & M. B. Clark (Eds.), *Measures of leadership.* Greensboro, NC: Center for Creative Leadership.

Jacobs, T. O., & Jaques, E. (1991). Executive leadership. In R. Gal & A. D. Manglesdorff (Eds.), *Handbook of military psychology.* New York: Wiley.

Jaques, E. (1986). The development of intellectual capability: A discussion of stratified systems theory. *Journal of Applied Behavioral Science, 22,* 361–384.

Jausovec, N. (1994a). *Flexible thinking: An explanation for individual differences in ability.* Cresskill, NJ: Hampton Press.

Jausovec, N. (1994b). Metacognition in creative problem solving. In M. A. Runco (Ed.), *Problem finding, problem solving, and creativity.* Norwood, NJ: Ablex.

Kanungo, R. N., & Conger, J. A. (1992). Charisma: Exploring new dimensions of leadership behavior. *Psychology and Developing Societies, 4,* 21–38.

Katz, D., & Kahn, R. L. (1978). *The social psychology of organizations* (2nd ed.). New York: Wiley.

Keller, R. T. (1986). Predictors of the performance of project groups in R&D organizations. *Academy of Management Journal, 29,* 715–726.

Kelly, J. (1993). *Facts against fictions of executive behavior: A critical analysis of what managers do.* Westport, CT: Quorum Books

Kets de Vries, M.F.R., & Miller, D. (1985). Narcissism and leadership: An object relations perspective. *Human Relations, 38,* 583–601.

Kirkpatrick, S. A., & Locke, E. A. (1996). Direct and indirect effects of three core charismatic leadership components on performance and attitudes. *Journal of Applied Psychology, 81,* 36–51.

Kotter, J. P. (1990). *A force for change: How leadership differs from management.* New York: Free Press.

Kouzes, J. M., & Posner, B. Z. (1987). *The leadership challenge: How to get extraordinary things done in organizations.* San Francisco: Jossey-Bass.

Larwood, L., Falbe, C. M., Kriger, M. P., & Miesing, P. (1995). Structure and meaning of organizational vision. *Academy of Management Journal, 38,* 740–769.

Larwood, L., Kriger, M. P., & Miesing, P. (1993). Organizational vision: An investigation of the vision construct-in-use of AACSB business school deans. *Group and Organization Management, 18,* 214–236.

Lewis, P., & Jacobs, T. O. (1992). Individual differences in strategic leadership capacity: A constructive/development view. In R. L. Phillips

& J. G. Hunt (Eds.), *Strategic leadership: A multiorganizational perspective*. Westport, CT: Quorum Books.

Lowe, K. B., Kroeck, K. G., & Sivasubramaniam. (1995). *Effectiveness correlates of transformational and transactional leadership: A meta-analytic review*. Paper presented at the tenth annual meeting of the Society for Industrial and Organizational Psychology, Orlando, FL.

Maslow, A. (1954). *Motivation and personality*. New York: HarperCollins.

McCauley, C. D., & Douglas, C. A. (1998). Developmental relationships. In C. D. McCauley, R. S. Moxley, & E. Van Velsor (Eds.), *The Center for Creative Leadership handbook of leadership development*. San Francisco: Jossey-Bass.

McCauley, C. D., Ruderman, M. N., Ohlott, P. J., & Morrow, J. E. (1994). Assessing the developmental components of managerial jobs. *Journal of Applied Psychology, 79*, 544–560.

McClelland, D. C. (1985). *Human motivation*. Glenview, IL: Scott, Foresman.

McCrae, R. R., & Costa, P. T. (1987). Adding *Liebe* and *Arbeit:* The full five-factor model and well-being. *Personality and Social Psychology Bulletin, 17*, 227–232.

McDonald's Corporate Webpage. (2000, November). Website: http://www.mcdonalds.com/corporate/investor/about/vision/index.html.

Morse, J. J., & Wagner, F. R. (1978). Measuring the process of managerial effectiveness. *Academy of Management Journal, 21,* 23–35.

Mumford, M. D., Baughman, W. A., Threlfall, K. V., Costanza, D. P., & Uhlman, C. E. (1993). Personality, adaptability, and performance: Performance on well-defined and ill-defined problem-solving tasks. *Human Performance, 6*, 245–285.

Mumford, M. D., Costanza, D. P., Threlfall, K. V., Baughman, W. A., & Reiter-Palmon, R. (1993). Personality variables and problem construction activities: An exploratory investigation. *Creativity Research Journal, 6*, 365–389.

Mumford, M. D., Marks, M. A., Zaccaro, S. J., Connelly, M. S., & Reiter-Palmon, R. (2000). Development of leadership skills: Experience, timing, and growth. *Leadership Quarterly, 11*, 87–114.

Nanus, B. (1992). *Visionary leadership: Creating a compelling sense of direction for your organization*. San Francisco: Jossey-Bass.

Osman, M. E., & Hannafin, M. J. (1992). Metacognition research and theory: Analysis and implications for instructional design. *Educational Technology Research and Development, 40*, 83–99.

Page, R. C., & Tornow, W. W. (1987). *Managerial job analysis: Are we further along?* Paper presented at the annual meeting of the Society for Industrial and Organizational Psychology, Atlanta.

Pinchot, J., III (1985). *Intrapreneuring*. New York: HarperCollins.

Podsakoff, P. M., MacKenzie, S. B., Moorman, R. H., & Fetter, R. (1990).

Transformational leader behaviors and their effects on followers' trust in leader, satisfaction, and organizational citizenship behaviors. *Leadership Quarterly, 1,* 107–142.

Quinn, R. E., Faerman, S. R., Thompson, M. P., & McGrath, M. R. (1990). *Becoming a master manager.* New York: Wiley.

Robbins, S. R., & Duncan, R. B. (1988). The role of the CEO and top management in the creation and implementation of strategic vision. In D. C. Hambrick (Ed.), *The executive effect: Concepts and methods for studying top managers.* Greenwich, CT: JAI Press.

Rokeach, M. (1973). *The nature of human values.* Old Tappan, NJ: Macmillan.

Sashkin, M. (1986). True vision in leadership. *Training and Development Journal, 40,* 58–61.

Sashkin, M. (1988). The visionary leader. In J. A. Conger & R. N. Kanungo (Eds.), *Charismatic leadership: The elusive factor in organizational effectiveness.* San Francisco: Jossey-Bass.

Sashkin, M. (1992). Strategic leadership competencies. In R. L. Phillips & J. G. Hunt (Eds.), *Strategic leadership: A multiorganizational perspective.* Westport, CT: Quorum Books.

Sashkin, M., & Fulmer, R. M. (1988). Toward an organizational leadership theory. In J. G. Hunt, B. R. Baliga, H. P. Dachler, & C. A., Schriesheim (Eds.), *Emerging leadership vistas.* San Francisco: New Lexington Press.

Senge, P. M. (1990). *The fifth discipline: The art and practice of the learning organization.* New York: Doubleday.

Shamir, B., House, R. J., & Arthur, M. (1993). The motivational effects of charismatic leadership: A self-concept based theory. *Organization Science, 4,* 577–594.

Stogdill, R. M., Shartle, C. L., Wherry, R. J., & Jaynes, W. E. (1955). A factorial study of administrative behavior. *Personnel Psychology, 8,* 165–180.

Thoms & Blasko (1999). Preliminary validation of a visioning ability scale. *Psychological Reports, 85,* 105–113.

Tichy, N., & Devanna, M. A. (1986a). The transformational leader. *Training and Development Journal, 40,* 27–32.

Tichy, N., & Devanna, M. A. (1986b). *Transformational leadership.* New York: Wiley.

Tornow, W. W., & Pinto, P. R. (1976). The development of a managerial job taxonomy: A system for describing, classifying, and evaluating executive positions. *Journal of Applied Psychology, 61,* 410–418.

Trice, H. M., & Beyer, J. M. (1986). Charisma and its routinization in two social movement organizations. In B. M. Staw & L. L. Cummings (Eds.), *Research in organizational behavior.* Greenwich, CT: JAI Press.

U.S. Army. (1995). *Force XXI: Meeting the 21st century challenge.* Washington, D.C.: Headquarters, Department of the Army.

Waldman, D. A., Bass, B. M., & Einstein, W. E. (1987). Executive succession and organizational outcomes in turbulent environments: An organizational learning approach. *Organization Science, 3,* 72–91.

Weber, M. (1947). *The theory of social and economic organization* (T. Parsons, Trans.). New York: Free Press.

Westley, F., & Mintzberg, H. (1989). Visionary leadership and strategic management. *Strategic Management Journal, 10,* 17–32.

Wofford, J. C., & Goodwin, V. L. (1994). A cognitive interpretation of transactional and transformational leadership theories. *Leadership Quarterly, 5,* 161–168.

Yammarino, F. J., Spangler, W. D., & Bass, B. M. (1993). Transformational leadership and performance: A longitudinal investigation. *Leadership Quarterly, 4,* 81–102.

Yukl, G. A., & Van Fleet, D. D. (1992). Theory and research on leadership in organizations. In M. D. Dunnette & L. M. Hough (Eds.), *Handbook of industrial and organizational psychology* (Vol. 3). Palo Alto, CA: Consulting Psychologists Press.

Zaccaro, S. J. (1996). *Models and theories of executive leadership: A conceptual/empirical review and integration.* Alexandria, VA: U.S. Army Research Institute for the Behavioral and Social Sciences.

Zaccaro, S. J. (1999). Social complexity and the competencies required for effective military leadership. In J. G. Hunt, G. E. Dodge, & L. Wong (Eds.), *Out-of-the-box leadership: Transforming the twenty-first-century army and other top-performing organizations.* Greenwich, CT: JAI Press.

Zaccaro, S. J., Gilbert, J. A., Thor, K. K., & Mumford, M. D. (1991). Leadership and social intelligence: Linking social perceptiveness and behavioral flexibility to leader effectiveness. *Leadership Quarterly, 2,* 317–331.

Zaccaro, S. J., & Marks, M. A. (1999). The roles of leaders in high-performance teams. In E. Sundstrom (Ed.), *The ecology of work group effectiveness: Design guidelines for organizations, facilities, and information systems for teams.* San Francisco: Jossey-Bass.

Zaccaro, S. J., Marks, M. A., O'Connor-Boes, J., & Costanza, D. P. (1995). *The nature and assessment of leader mental models.* Bethesda, MD: Management Research Institute.

CHAPTER 8

The Chief Executive Officer and Top Management Team Interface

Richard J. Klimoski
K. Lee Kiechel Koles

While it may be understandable that the popular press treats senior organizational leadership as a solitary and even heroic phenomenon, it is surprising how current models and theories in organizational studies also assume this perspective. As a result, the nature of effective senior leadership is often tied to an individual's personal qualities and actions (House & Podsakoff, 1994). Even when there is recognition that CEO work is frequently collective work (Finkelstein & Hambrick, 1996), the emphasis is shifted to the nature of the top management team, focusing specifically on its dynamics. In our view, there is inadequate treatment of what we call the interface between the senior manager and his or her team. Such a treatment must address how the senior leader is responsible for, interacts with, and is affected by the top management team.

The Team at the Top

Only recently has the literature recognized that the senior executive or CEO usually operates in close collaboration with others. Concepts such as the dominant coalition (Cyert & March, 1963), upper echelons (Hambrick & Mason, 1984), senior working group, executive office, and senior leadership group (Katzenbach, 1998) all convey the idea that CEO work is collective work. A number of alternative titles are used to describe the highest-level executive team—for example:

- Dominant coalition
- Executive committee
- Executive office
- Policy committee
- Senior leadership group
- Senior working group
- Top management group
- Top management team
- Upper echelon

Throughout this chapter we refer to this collective entity as the top management team (TMT).

Note that we are focusing on the most senior organizational leader. Although we refer in this chapter to this individual as the CEO, the leader at this level of management is sometimes referred to as a chief operating officer (COO), a group general manager, or the manager of an autonomous division. Thus, it should be clear that we are dealing with a level of power and authority that is greater than a plant manager or a general manager of a strategic business unit (Kotter, 1982).

This chapter also focuses attention on the activities and interactions of TMT members themselves. Unfortunately, there is little consensus among researchers regarding which organizational members constitute the TMT. Wiersma and Bantel (1992) stated that this group includes "the very highest level of management": the chair, CEO, president, and COO, as well as the next-highest tier. These researchers point out, however, that arbitrary use of position titles to define TMT membership can lead to the inclusion of between two and five levels of management. Other literature defines TMT members as the group of top executives with overall responsibility for the organization (Mintzberg, 1979) or those who report directly to the CEO, excluding administrative support staff (Sutcliffe, 1994). Still others argue that TMT members include all officers above the level of vice president (Michel & Hambrick, 1992) or all corporate officers who are also board members (Finkelstein & Hambrick, 1990).

The CEO as Organizational Leader

Is the CEO really important? Charan and Colvin (2000) stated it plainly: "Two or more wrong CEOs in succession can destroy a company. . . .The fact is inescapable: These choices of single human beings exert enormous influence over entire enterprises. In the aggregate, they determine the prosperity of the nation" (p. 226).

We sometimes hear an opposing view: that what really matters is corporate culture and strategy. Both are crucial, obviously, but they are secondary to the choice of CEO. The right culture provides an organization with a formidable competitive advantage, but it is the company's CEO who drives and energizes the culture—or does not. The same is true of strategy. If an organization hires the "wrong" CEO, who propagates an inferior strategy, it is unlikely that TMT action will make things copacetic. Decisions most crucial to the company's future proceed from the choice of the CEO (Charan & Colvin, 2000). Indeed, research reveals that executive leadership explained between 20 and 40 percent of the variance in organizational effectiveness (Day & Lord, 1988). Barrick, Day, and Lord (1991) found that the positive organizational impact of a high-performing executive was at least 15 percent greater than that of an average-performing executive. This difference could translate into at least $25 million in a Fortune 500 company.

Little research has been devoted to examining the distinct role and impact of the CEO on the TMT (Hambrick, 1994). In fact, there has been an inclination for the TMT literature simply to include the CEO as a member of the group, averaging in his or her characteristics in establishing such things as overall TMT characteristics (Jackson, 1992). This tendency is not consistent with the degree of importance placed on the CEO in organizations in practice. After all, it is the CEO who is generally held accountable for the performance of an entire firm (Ireland & Hitt, 1999). CEOs of profitable organizations are publicly lauded and often rewarded with increased levels of compensation. Conversely, CEOs whose companies are faltering must face the likelihood of being replaced by a new CEO who presumably will be better equipped to lead an organization toward success. Thus, it is critical to examine the means by which the CEO leads the TMT and uses it to establish the CEO's true potential impact on overall organizational effectiveness.

To be fair, there are perspectives that recognize CEOs as existing in a category different from his or her nominal direct reports. Zaccaro (1996) addressed the specific characteristics of executives at the highest organizational level and stressed the notion of flexibility. He suggested that executive leadership is composed of three dimensions of flexibility:

Social and behavioral flexibility, which is grounded in social reasoning skills that enable the CEO to behave appropriately across diverse social situations

Flexible integrative complexity, which refers to the leader's ability to develop a repertoire of responses necessary in complex social domains

Flexibly oriented disposition, which means displaying adaptiveness instead of rigidity in dynamic social situations

Zaccaro stressed the importance of a leader's being strong in all three flexibility dimensions. Effective executive leadership is not likely to emerge from just one or two of these qualities.

What else do we know about the qualities of TMT leaders? Literature suggests that effective CEOs possess superior wisdom, intellect, and discipline (Katzenbach, 1998). Levinson and Rosenthal's 1984 study of organizational executives concluded that company CEOs shared a number of common traits. They were found to be persuasive and skilled interpersonally, and they were often characterized by a restless dissatisfaction with the organization's performance. In addition, CEOs generally instilled a climate for risk taking, had good conceptual skills, and were able to make sense of dynamic, often turbulent working environments. That is, they possessed a greater intellectual capacity.

Overall, the CEO is required to take on multiple roles as leader of the TMT, among them figurehead, liaison, disseminator, spokesperson, disturbance handler, resource allocator, and negotiator (Mintzberg, 1973). These roles may vary depending on the degree of interface between the team and the leader (Katzenbach, 1998). That is, CEOs may play more directive leadership roles if their knowledge of the activity being addressed exceeds that of the team. Also, CEOs will engage in more facilitative roles as levels of TMT member knowledge equal or exceed their own.

Nature of CEO Work

In examining the nature of how CEO work is different from the work of leaders at other levels of an organization, Zaccaro (1996) stated that executive-level leaders must first manage team and organizational boundaries, as well as set the appropriate direction for processes prior to carrying out actions and implementing ideas. Specifically, the CEO must scan and analyze the environment, evaluate the organization's capabilities and requirements, and form a strategy or vision that will enable the organization to adapt within a dynamic environment. Once the CEO has practiced these activities, he or she can engage the TMT in operational management. That is, the CEO must guide the TMT in implementing the formulated vision or strategy, changing organizational structure and policy to fit with that vision, and appropriately altering the organizational climate and culture. Zaccaro explains that these executive responsibilities can be linked directly to organizational effectiveness and adaptation to the environment.

Environmental issues constitute a primary CEO concern. Specifically, the leader must partake in environmental scanning to ensure awareness of societal, technological, and economic developments. Attention to environmental factors has grown in importance since institutional shareholders more frequently compare investment opportunities worldwide. Companies and their executives are now judged less against their domestic neighbors and more against the best firms and executives worldwide (Useem, 1998). CEOs must therefore be cognizant of the issues affecting the surrounding industrial climate.

CEOs spend considerable effort dealing with and preparing for global competition. As a result of recent technological advances, operation in international markets is no longer reserved solely for large, multibusiness corporations. Small organizations too have become active players in global markets (Hitt, Keats, & De Marie, 1998). As a result, CEOs must identify the global leadership approaches that will bring about above-average returns in order for their organization to perform effectively (Zahra & O'Neill, 1998). Never before has it been so critical for executives to be in touch with the competition (Ireland & Hitt, 1999).

Much of a CEO's work concerns managing strategy. Strategic leadership is defined as the ability to anticipate change, envision the future, maintain flexibility, and work with others to initiate changes to create a viable future for an organization (Ireland & Hitt, 1999). Today's dynamic global economy has made it critical for CEOs to engage in these strategic leadership behaviors. An effective CEO provides strategic directives, encourages learning that translates into intellectual capital, and verifies mechanisms that transfer intellectual capital within the organization (Ireland & Hitt, 1999).

In addition, the CEO must manage people. To do this, he or she must play the roles of disciplinarian, value enforcer, strategic educator, political diffuser, executive skill builder, and decision maker (Katzenbach, 1998). While facilitating team discussions, the CEO must allow or encourage conflicting points of view, yet be able to intercede and lead the team to an integrative resolution, making the best of all viewpoints. A CEO who is willing to step in and break up counterproductive pecking-order behaviors will greatly enhance the team potential of the group. In addition, the CEO must ensure the continual, systematic enhancement of knowledge of the TMT. A continued emphasis on employee training and development is likely to improve organizational performance (Ireland & Hitt, 1999).

The CEO is responsible for managing resources, which includes acquiring capital and sustaining the supply of raw materials. These resources, as well as knowledge surrounding them, tend to come from outside constituents (Katz & Kahn, 1978). It is up to the CEO to cull the information from outside the TMT and organization so that resources may be used in an optimally beneficial manner (Drucker, 1997).

CEOs must have the capacity to manage change in their companies. Today, renewed attention is being focused on organizational downsizing and cost reductions (Ireland & Hitt, 1999). As a result, companies are developing dynamic capabilities that can be used as platforms from which to offer new products, goods, and services to remain competitive. This ability to adapt to novel situations while harvesting creativity and knowledge among employees is a critical part of CEO work (Zahra, 1999).

Thus, we can see that there are many ways in which the nature of CEO work is different from that of leaders at other levels. Specifically, CEO work comprises the following areas:

- Boundary management
- Attention to environmental factors
- Preparing for global competition
- Strategy management
- Relationship management
- Resource management
- Change management

The Nature of Teams at the Top

Teams are human collectives made up of two or more individuals who interact on a regular and continuing basis in support of accomplishing one or more common goals. Most organizational team work is task work, aimed at performing task-relevant functions. Some teams do not have formal leadership, but most have status and influence hierarchies (Kozlowski et al., 1999; Argote & McGrath, 1993).

It can be argued that the TMT is created and exists for many of the same reasons that teams are relied on in organizations. Specifically, team theory asserts that certain tasks and decisions demand attentional, cognitive, and energy resources that exceed the capacity of any one individual (Hackman, 1987). Clearly, as our brief treatment of the numerous functions and demands placed on the CEO shows, CEO work should indeed be collective work.

Critical Features of Teams

As in the case of work teams in general, the functioning and effectiveness of the TMT is related to the institution and articulation of several critical features: team size, team composition, team structure, team processes, team culture, team power, and team staffing (Kozlowski et al., 1999; Cohen & Bailey, 1997).

Team Size

Theories and models of work design are in their infancy, so it is not surprising that there are few firm answers to the question of appropriate team size. This said, certain issues and principles nevertheless seem to be useful in guiding such decisions. Traditional management writing has always focused on the appropriate span of control as a balance of the work to be done, the management systems used to ensure collaboration, communication and control, and the skills of the manager. This should be relevant to TMT size as well. The number of team members represents both resources and liabilities when it comes to effective functioning. Optimal team size involves considerations that are managerial as much as task related.

There is little consensus in the literature regarding the typical size of the TMT. Research cites executive teams with as few as two (Wiersma & Bantel, 1992) and as many as nineteen members (West & Anderson, 1996). The mean size, however, is typically clustered between three and a half and six members (Finkelstein, 1992; Finkelstein & Hambrick, 1990; Michel & Hambrick, 1992; Simons, Pelled, & Smith, 1999; Smith, Ford, & Kozlowski, 1997; Wiersma & Bantel, 1992).

But team size seems to be established in relation to other considerations. These include the distribution of knowledge (Hambrick, 1994), the speed with which decisions must be made, and the challenge of performing or implementing the will of the group after decisions are made. Occasionally team size is constrained by technology, legal charter, or agreements or by macro-organizational structure considerations (Zahra & O'Neill, 1998). Specifically, the external environment affects the size and configuration of the TMT. This may occur through purposeful attempts to align the nature of the group with the dominant requirements of the environment (Hambrick, 1987) or through more evolutionary, emergent processes of covariation (Hambrick, 1994).

Team Composition

The issue of composition relates to the kinds of individuals who are and should be on the team. A major consideration derived from team theory relates to team task demands. As a generalization, the task or issues addressed should determine the knowledge, skills, abilities, and other attributes (style, interest, motivation) that team members should have (Klimoski & Jones, 1995). It is important to note that in arriving at the appropriate composition, both the level of the attributes and their distribution (variability) among group members need to be determined. For example, it is common to prefer all team members to exhibit high levels of integrity and teamwork skills, but one should ensure members have varied backgrounds or areas of specialization. Moreover, some tasks require the exemplary performance of only one individual, while others demand this of all team members (McGrath, 1984).

In most work organizations, the issue of appropriate team composition will also involve considerations of legitimacy, contacts, power, and influence (Klimoski & Zukin, 1998). This is rooted in the nature of teams as open systems. Thus, for teams to do their work, they need to have resources (such as information) that are largely derived from others in the organization. Similarly, acceptance or implementation is problematic for most decision-making teams. In fact, other parties must carry out the decisions that the team has made. This often requires high levels of commitment and sustained effort. Having credible, connected, and influential individuals on the team becomes a staffing consideration.

By virtue of their place in the organization, the makeup of TMTs has great symbolic importance, both internally and externally (Hambrick, 1994). TMTs may influence the decisions of their constituents by their mere surface characteristics. So TMTs are typically composed of individuals who have demonstrated significant and sustained accomplishments during their careers, are relatively aggressive and achievement oriented, and expect a considerable degree of autonomy and discretion regarding the conduct of their affairs (Hambrick, 1994; Kotter, 1982). A recent survey by Egon Zehnder International, an executive search firm, revealed technological knowledge to be an important TMT member asset. Specifically, 70 percent of new chief information officers (CIOs), the individuals largely responsible for organizing corporate computer systems, are TMT members. This percentage has increased sharply; a decade ago, only 10 percent of CIOs were TMT members. It is important to note, however, that the environment in which the team is embedded also affects its attributes. Research indicates that member age, tenure, education, and homogeneity differ depending on the organization's industry (Harris, 1979; Norburn, 1986).

When it comes to the composition of the top management team, there appears to be a great deal of variability. The ages of TMT members vary widely depending on the firm. The TMT composition of today's Internet start-up companies, in particular, tend to include more youthful members than the typical TMT of the past. The organizational tenure of TMT members also varies considerably, ranging anywhere between five and thirty-eight years (Wiersma & Bantel, 1992). Thus, it is difficult to pinpoint a "right" or "wrong" composition for TMTs. Interestingly, though, some research indicates that TMTs possessing certain member characteristics are more inclined to breach corporate ethics standards. For example, TMTs whose members are young, have a greater amount of management education (for example, a greater percentage of those who hold the M.B.A.), or are very similar to each other show a greater propensity to engage in illegal activity (Daboub, Rasheed, Priem, & Gray, 1996).

It is clear that there is no specific prototype of TMT members. With this in mind, we should be cautious in assuming that there is one "type" of executive group that leads organizations. The TMT literature, unfortunately, is equivocal regarding the various types of TMTs that may exist. Much of the literature describes TMTs as being composed of CEOs and direct reports who are responsible for lines of business and corporate functioning. This is more of a multidivisional approach to conceptualizing teams. Other research allows the inclusion of general managers (Conger & Kottner, 1982), whose direct reports have primarily functional responsibilities. Both of these perceptions of TMT structure vary considerably, particularly in terms of power and counter-power issues. Katzenbach (1998) is one of the few researchers who has attempted to distinguish between different types of TMTs, noting that the configuration changes depending on the issues at hand. Although we expand on Katzenbach's work, to do justice to trying to model the full range of different TMT scenarios in a single chapter is not possible. Thus, for our purposes, we will take on the multidivisional view of TMT composition.

Team Structure

Team structure usually implies more than one dimension. One is work flow, or how the work to be completed is divided up and shared among team members. Another reflects communications patterns. As important as these are, it is often the structure of interpersonal power and influence that is most relevant to team success. Although these structural considerations are involved in the design or creation of teams, they are also what might be called emergent properties of the teams. Thus, no matter what the designer had in mind, individual and interpersonal forces will have an effect on the actual nature of work flow, communication, and influence. In most organizational contexts, the team manager is in an excellent position to control or contribute to team structure. Thus, he or she may make decisions that extend beyond team size and composition issues, including specifications of team and individual work obligations.

It is difficult to gain a clear picture relative to the structure of the typical TMT. Rather than provide a specific template, the literature states that TMT structure is dictated by factors existing both within and outside the team. For example, there is evidence regarding the impact of member roles and relationships on TMT structure (Finkelstein & Hambrick, 1996). Central to this concept is the degree of interdependency among team members. That is, the structural makeup of the team is dependent on the extent to which resource sharing and coordination within the TMT affect firm performance. TMT configuration may also be affected by the structure of the organization. In highly centralized organizations, lower-level members are not typically involved in important decision making and may be unaware of the impact of environmental information (Fredrickson, 1986). Thus, important and relevant information may not reach TMTs accurately, if at all.

The CEO may establish policies and practices that can increase or decrease behavioral integration of the team (Hambrick, 1994). In situations low in integration, the TMT functions more like a single-leader working group, with the CEO dictating group functions (Katzenbach, 1998). A TMT may act in this capacity if it is difficult to identify either a clear group purpose or a set of high-value, collective work products that encompass the entire group. The CEO alone may also be responsible for creating this working group atmosphere. If the CEO is unwilling to shift the top leadership roles among various group members, the TMT structure will remain so that functioning is dependent on CEO demands. Team members will be reluctant to lead without the CEO's taking a step back from the work process. This will also be true if the CEO has not demonstrated a history of allowing others to function in leadership positions. Thus, the CEO's traditional methods of interacting with other executives will be ingrained in the minds of TMT members, thereby affecting the manner in which they act as a group.

Just as the CEO may break down what Katzenbach (1998) refers to as the traditional team structure, he or she can also facilitate team interactions. In this capacity, the CEO encourages other executives to lead team efforts whenever more of a team mode is appropriate. The literature indicates that fully interactive teams may be especially necessary if situational needs are clear and there is a compelling purpose of action (Katzenbach, 1998). For example, the CEO will need considerable help and cooperation from TMT members when the industry is undergoing significant changes, if competitors are modifying strategies and structures, or if growth prospects are becoming more difficult to identify and realize. Including the entire executive group in these situations will help ensure the strength of the organization's strategic positioning.

The importance of collective work products and a CEO's task know-how relative to the rest of the group also affects the approach to team design (structure). As the importance of collective work products increases relative to individual work products, it becomes more important for the CEO to function in more of a supportive role. This way, the actual leadership of the group shifts to the appropriate member or members, based on the task at hand. Similarly, as the actual task know-how of the various members of the team exceeds the know-how of the designated group leader, it becomes more important for that leader to shift the group into a "real team" approach, in which members work interdependently as members of a collective without significant influences from outsiders (Katzenbach, 1998).

Clearly there is not one specific model for TMT composition or structure. As would be expected, the makeup and functioning of the TMT becomes increasingly complex when companies undergo mergers. Figure 8.1 depicts the probable TMT that will form once the America Online and Time Warner merger is finalized. Note the anticipated overlapping and sharing of roles: there are eleven chief executives.

Team Process

Processes are activities or actions that unfold over time and are directed toward some outcome or conclusion. In the context of work teams, dimensions of structure can be reconceptualized as processes.

Figure 8.1. Managing After the Merger.

STEPHEN M. CASE
Job: Chairman of the board
Old Company: America Online

KENNETH J. NOVACK	GERALD M. LEVIN	RICHARD J. BRESSLER
Vice chairman	Chief executive	Head of investments
America Online	*Time Warner*	*Time Warner*

TED TURNER
Vice chairman
Time Warner

WILLIAM J. RADUCHEL
Chief technology officer
America Online

GEORGE VRADENBURG
Global and strategic policy
America Online

J. MICHAEL KELLY	KENNETH B. LERER
Chief financial officer	Communications and
America Online	investor relations
	America Online

ROBERT W. PITTMAN	RICHARD D. PARSONS
Co-chief operating officer	Co-chief operating officer
America Online	*Time Warner*

REPORTING TO MR. PITTMAN	REPORTING TO MR. PARSONS
Chief Executives	Chief Executives
BARRY SCHULER	BARRY M. MEYER
America Online	Warner Brothers
America Online	*Time Warner*
JOSEPH J. COLLINS	ROBERT K. SHAYE
Time Warner Cable	New Line Cinema
Time Warner	*Time Warner*
DON LOGAN	ROGER AMES
Time Inc. (magazines)	Warner Music Group
Time Warner	*Time Warner*
JEFFREY L. BEWKES	LAURENCE J. KIRSHBAUM
Home Box Office	Time Warner
Time Warner	Trade Publishing (books)
TERENCE F. McGUIRK	*Time Warner*
Turner Broadcasting	Executive President
System	PAUL T. CAPPUCCIO
Time Warner	General counsel
JAMIE KELLNER	*America Online*
WB television network	Senior Vice President
Time Warner	ANDREW J. KASLOW
President	Human resources
DAVID M. COLBURN	*Time Warner*
Business development	
America Online	

Source: Adapted from Hansell, 2000. Reprinted with the permission of *The New York Times.*

This is consistent with the dual notion of structure as both configurations and patterns of activities (Dow, 1988). Thus, key team processes that have to be managed for effective team performance include task and work flow, communications and influence, and interpersonal relations (McGrath, 1984). Hackman (1987) refers to the goals of process management as involving the modulation of team member effort around individual and team tasks, including the application of member knowledge. It also calls for the development or selection of performance strategies.

We view teams in work organizations as embedded social systems; they are part of and are influenced by the larger organizational context. This implies still another set of what are called boundary role processes that must be managed (Ancona & Caldwell, 1992; Klimoski & Zukin, 1998). In particular, all teams must be concerned with their capacity to manage intrusions and distractions (that is, buffering), with relating to others who are not part of the team (known as boundary spanning), and with maintaining a sense of integrity or social identity with the team among its members (bringing up the boundaries).

Boundary management would not be problematic if team members did all their work while in the presence of other team members. Similarly, issues of commitment and loyalty would not be great if an individual belonged to only one team. But organizational realities are such that these conditions rarely obtain. Most team members experience what is called partial inclusion, meaning that they often work separately and are rewarded for subtask performance. Moreover, members typically belong to more than one organizational social unit. Indeed, social identity and boundary issues are likely to become even more important to address as information technology makes geographical dispersion and asynchronous interaction and vicarious participation in teams feasible (Townsend, De Marie, & Hendrickson, 1998). Such arrangements provide very few opportunities for team members and leaders to use traditional mechanisms for building and maintaining cohesion or social unity.

Team management systems include established protocols for information acquisition and distribution, especially with regard for operational feedback to team members about performance and accomplishments (Kozlowski, 1998). This details the kind of reports that are generated, by whom and for whom. It also implies programs for compensation or the allocation of sanctions. Here, any number of practices might be adopted as these would emphasize the attainment of short- or long-term goals and focus on individual or team-level accomplishments. Hackman (1987) stresses as a management prerogative the design of systems set up for training or for otherwise enhancing the skill or knowledge base of team members.

The leader sets the stage for the size, compositional, and structural aspects of team life. However, he or she is far more potent as a controller of social processes. More specifically, current thinking about leadership in team settings highlights both interpersonal (dyadic) and team-level dynamics. Indeed, much teamwork in organizations is done as individuals or in subgroups. In either event, the relationship that the leader develops and maintains regarding each team member as an individual is important for ensuring work effort and performance. Thus, patterns of communication and the flow of work at this level become key processes to manage. Ethical and principled leadership, that is, relationships based on mutual respect and the development of trust with each member, is important.

In this regard, the use and distribution of power and influence between the leader and among team members will be associated with the effective management of team processes. While the level of autonomy granted by the leader may be associated with team member maturity, there is ample evidence that the leader is in a key position to create conditions for subordinates' feelings of empowerment (Avolio, 1998).

To a team leader, team process management implies activities as mundane as controlling the frequency of meetings, their agenda, the use of outsiders as sources of information, and, more profound, the way that meetings are conducted. Meeting management skills and preferences will have a strong impact on the extent that team members come to share a common ground, contribute distributed information in an appropriate way, sustain effort, stay focused on team task goals, coordinate their contributions, come to feel that the group is powerful, and, after the conclusion of the meeting, stay committed to implementing the team's decisions (Klimoski & Mohammad, 1994; Littlepage, Robinson, & Reddington, 1997; Nutt, 1989).

But here too the leader modulates the extent to which he or she assumes total responsibility for team process management. In this regard, it is a design choice, as team members individually or collectively are usually capable of such activities. Indeed, the functional perspective of team leadership requires only that the leader ensures that such processes are in place and managed well and not that the leader performs them directly (Fleishman & Zaccaro, 1992). In fact, this is where team member participation can be encouraged, usually to mutual advantage (West & Anderson, 1996).

The team leader is also responsible for the development of individual team members. Depending on circumstances, the time available, and the values and needs of the leader, attention to individual subordinates and their development needs can be considerable. There is ample evidence to suggest that leaders do differentiate among their direct reports when it comes to relationship building and management (Liden, Wayne, & Stilwell, 1993). In fact, it appears that power sharing and subordinate discretion are both tools that a manager uses and a manifestation of mutual influence. But whether personalized attention is always a conscious phenomenon or in response to either the subordinate's or the leader's needs is not always apparent. The point here is that the quality of relationships is clearly under the potential control of the leader.

Whether relating to an individual team member or to the team as a whole, there is ample evidence that the personal style and qualities of the leader make a difference in terms of how team processes are carried out. Differences include the leader's own work habits and effectiveness and the kind of reputation he or she enjoys (Yukl, 1994). Some of the effect is due to social imitation and learning as the team members adopt the leader as a model (Weiss, 1990). Much of it derives from the expectations that the leader communicates. The leader's words and deeds imply rewards or sanctions for what is considered appropriate behavior in the workplace (Graen & Scandura, 1987).

Information regarding the management of TMT processes by the CEO focuses primarily on upper-echelon task work and boundary management. TMT task work is different from that of teams in other levels of an organization. Specifically, TMT tasks possess multiple elements of complexity. For example, many of the responsibilities of TMTs have no bounded time frame; the work at this level lacks a clear beginning and end. TMTs engage in ongoing, day-in, day-out administrative actions that collectively shape the organization's form and greatly affect the types of problems and alternatives that are even brought to its attention (Hambrick, 1994). In addition, TMT task work is generally fraught with ambiguity (Katz & Kahn, 1978), in part because the TMT must operate at the boundary of the organization and its environment (Mintzerg, 1973; Zaccaro, 1996). Among other things, the group, along with the CEO, must monitor and interpret external events and trends, deal with external constituents, and formulate, communicate, and monitor the organization's responses to the environment (Hambrick, 1994).

Many TMT tasks center on the process of strategic renewal, an iterative process associated with promoting, accommodating, and using new knowledge and innovative behavior to bring about change in an organization's core competencies or product market domain (Doz, 1996). This involves aligning the organization's strategy with changing environmental circumstances. Thus, much TMT task work concerns deciding on the resources necessary to achieve a given strategy and approving and directing these resources to reinforce the strategic position (Floyd & Lane, 2000).

Boundary management processes are of particular importance in TMTs. Not only must TMT members be able to identify, understand, and address the complex demands of their stakeholders, but they must do this under serious time pressures, as technology has made it possible for different stakeholders to follow almost every move a company makes (Zahra, 1999). The CEO, in particular, is responsible for acting as a liaison between the TMT and the board of directors (Conyon & Peck, 1998). He or she is also held accountable for guiding the firm in ways that best serve outside constituents, and thus must be aware of stakeholder values and needs (Ireland & Hitt, 1999).

To acquire and communicate environmental information, TMT members must consistently scan their environment and monitor firm performance (Sutcliffe, 1994). The more intense and frequent the scanning is, the more that environmental changes, threats, and opportunities will be recognized. In addition, TMTs need to gather real-time information regarding the organization's ability to fulfill the goals and the requirements of stakeholders. Members must gather internal information and be in tune with the status of current performance targets and measures.

The TMT literature focuses on two main social processes: social integration and consensus (Finkelstein & Hambrick, 1996). Social integration refers to the attraction to the group, satisfaction with other group members, and the social interaction among the group members (O'Reilly, Chatman, & Caldwell, 1991). In order for a TMT to make strategic decisions and carry out action plans, members must be able to communicate ideas and concerns with each other efficiently and effectively.

Consensus refers to the agreement of all parties to a group decision (Dess & Origer, 1987). The need for speed to consensus will vary, and it is often the CEO who determines the extent to which TMT members are involved in resolving issues. For instance, Scott McNealy, head of Sun Microsystems, acknowledges that business leaders must often make quick decisions without consulting other top constituents. "I hate to overdo the sports analogies, but hockey players don't have a huddle," he said. "It requires a lot of spontaneity. Management in the Internet age—it's certainly not like management in any other industry" (Furchgott, 2000). Although it may be difficult for teams to reach consensus at all times, it is important to have the buy-in of top executives when it comes to carrying out organizational initiatives.

Team Culture

The construct of culture, traditionally used to describe societies, is helpful in characterizing the nature of organizational life (Deal & Kennedy, 1982; Denison, 1996). It also can be applied to work teams. In this context, team culture refers to the nature of the values and assumptions that are shared among team members. These can relate to the meaning of work, morality, and interpersonal justice. Culture is usually affected by the personal qualities of team members—their needs, values, and beliefs. It can also be shaped by leaders and affected by the work to be done. Culture is often reflected in the rules, standards, and protocols that team members follow. Moreover, it usually has a profound effect on the quality of team life, affecting such diverse matters as team processes and members' work satisfaction and commitment to the team.

Although there is no standard way of characterizing culture, three dimensions are especially relevant. One is the extent to which emphasis is placed on productivity or performance. Units or teams high on this dimension tend to stress personal styles, procedures, and incentives that keep up competitive pressures on its members. High achievement is expected and rewarded (Sheridan, 1992). Such environments tend to emphasize aggressiveness, individualism, status, and personal power.

A second dimension might be characterized as relationship emphasis. Here, the quality of interactions and the level of supportiveness of the work unit or team are of paramount importance. Staff members' well-being and feelings of trust are important as well. The individuals in this context tend to favor teamwork and value collective effort; power sharing is the norm (Sheridan, 1992, O'Reilly, Chatman, & Caldwell, 1991).

The third dimension relates to support for innovation (West & Anderson, 1996). Although there is evidence that environments that support innovation have many of the same qualities of high-relationship cultures, the reverse is not true. Thus, achieving innovation outcomes may require more than a supportive, team-oriented, high-trust environment. One also needs a specific emphasis on innovation and the clarity and commitment to innovation to go with it (West & Anderson, 1996).

Beyond the people involved, the culture of the TMT is probably also affected by the company's recent history (Ireland & Hitt, 1999), industry norms and practices (Gordon, 1991), the strategic context of the firm (Joyce & Slocum, 1990), and even the stage of the organization's life cycle (Romanelli, 1989). The literature's characterization of the TMT culture tends to focus on qualitative evidence. The general perception is that TMT culture is rooted in history, held collectively, and reflects what the firm has learned across time through its responses to the continuous challenges of survival and growth. TMT culture provides the context within which strategies are formulated and implemented (Ireland & Hitt, 1999). The TMT is in the unique position of being able to have an impact on symbols, heroes, rituals, and practices. It essentially acts as a reflection of and force toward the culture of the corporation. Research reveals that CEOs who shape organizational culture in strategically relevant ways will become a valued source of competitive advantage (Hitt, Keats, & De Marie, 1998; Ireland & Hitt, 1999).

Team Power

The power that a team possesses can manifest itself though its composition (Tushman & Romanelli, 1983) and processes (Finkelstein & Hambrick, 1996). Power dynamics are particularly prevalent in TMTs due to the unstructured and ambiguous nature of upper-echelon activities (Finkelstein & Hambrick, 1996). The literature describes four power realities of the TMT based on its composition: structural power, ownership power, expert power, and prestige power.

Because of where it lies in the organizational hierarchy, TMT members possess structural power (Brass, 1984; Hambrick, 1981; Tushman & Romanelli, 1983). The CEO has structural power over the other members of dominant coalitions because of his or her formal organizational position. In addition, TMT members have ownership power due to their close ties with the CEO and their ability to act on behalf of company shareholders (Finkelstein, 1992). The ability to decide on TMT compensation is part of a CEO's ownership power.

Expert power refers to influence based on extensive knowledge of a given topic. TMT members typically possess expertise regarding different facets of organizational life and may therefore have significant influence on corporate strategies. Because of their knowledge, they may be called on to diffuse uncertainties arising from dealing with organizational competitors, suppliers, or the government (Finkelstein, 1992). In addition, the combined expert power of TMT members enables organizations to deal with environmental contingencies and contribute to corporate success (Hambrick, 1981; Tushman & Romanelli, 1983).

Finally, the status or reputation of managers reflects prestige power. An individual's standing in the managerial elite sends out powerful messages to other top managers about their personal importance (Finkelstein, 1992). Managerial prestige promotes power by suggesting that an individual is highly qualified for the position and has influential colleagues.

Power can also be understood as a process. The circulation of control model demonstrates that the power of executives is subject to challenge, political struggle, and contestation (Jackall, 1988). Power is a process that applies to the recurrent struggles among individuals, intraorganizational groups, and interorganizational groups for command and control of formal authority. Ocasio (1994) explained that the circulation of power is guided by two interrelated mechanisms: obsolescence and contestation. Obsolescence refers to the TMT's fixed notion of schemas, ideologies, and conceptions of control, despite a firm's changing economic, political, and cultural environments. The literature distinguishes between two types of obsolescence: technical and political. Technical obsolescence involves the inability of executives to provide satisfactory solutions to strategic organizational contingencies. Political obsolescence refers to executives' continued reliance on their original sources of power, without deriving new bases of social and cultural capital to sustain their power as the firm's political environment changes. CEOs should ensure that neither type of obsolescence occurs within their TMTs, as it is sure to limit innovation.

Contestation refers to the emergent and recurrent struggles for position and control among contending individuals, groups, and identities within organizations (White, 1992). Conceptions of control serve to institutionalize the power of TMTs, as the goals and orientation of the governing group become infused with values espoused by the organization (Ocasio & Kim, 1999). Essentially the power of the dominant group becomes culturally embedded within the organization's dominant conception of control (Fligstein, 1987, 1990). As members of the corporate elite, those composing the TMT will protect and enforce these values by implementing programs and selecting executives consistent with dominant ideologies (Ocasio & Kim, 1999). Again, CEOs must be wary of contestation yet understand that the homogeneity of values and ideologies may inhibit organizational progress and the expansion of ideas.

Team Staffing

Staffing refers to the recruitment, assessment, selection, and socialization of new organizational members (Heneman, Heneman, & Judge, 1997). There are analogous requirements at the team level (Klimoski & Jones, 1995). Team size, task demands, and composition considerations play an important role in team staffing.

The recruitment and integration of new team members will have a profound impact on team processes and team culture as well.

Writers tend to distinguish between the staffing of an entire team at one time and the addition or replacement of a new member. Both are intrinsic to organizational team life, and both involve special considerations (Klimoski & Zukin, 1998).

Start-ups represent a unique opportunity to approach the design of the team and the selection of its members in a systematic manner. As such, much of the wisdom for theory and practice might be brought to bear, subject to constraints of time and resources. The work to be done by the newly formed team can be analyzed relative to its set of individual member and team-level worker requirements. Candidates can be considered not only relative to their assignments but also with due attention to how they would fit together and complement one another. Indeed, team members may be identified based on their social skills and social networks, with resulting benefits. Also important, team members may have substantial impact on their closest collaborators.

A start-up has other implications relative to team process and culture. In effect, the recruitment, socialization, and integration of new members are contemporaneous with team development. There are coevolution of team structure, instantiation of team processes, and growth of team culture. Issues of individual and team task definition and of work roles must be resolved. Moreover, as team members learn to adapt to one another, they must also adapt and deal with their external environment.

The replacement of a team member presents other challenges. Here, the newcomer might be selected relative to his or her capacity to fit into existing team features (task roles, processes, and culture). Indeed, it is not uncommon for current team members in addition to the manager to have an active role in screening applicants for their suitability and compatibility (Kotter, 1982). Alternatively, the newcomer may be identified and selected based on some perceived need for change or the transformation of the team. In either event, the adjustment of the newcomer and to the newcomer will be strongly affected by the conditions under which the team position became open (for example, through resignation, death, promotion, or termination).

Under most scenarios, the team manager will have a central role in recruiting and selecting team members. Thus, the leader owns much of the staffing burden. Although there will be a great deal of variability in the number of openings that he or she can fill, the size of the team is arbitrary, so the leader is usually in a position to add individuals in order to shape the team.

In staffing at the senior level, the leader has particular discretion regarding the qualities of the new people promoted or hired. Thus, issues of loyalty and complementarity can be addressed. Moreover, both practical and political considerations may enter into the staffing decision as both friends (as a reward) and potential rivals (as a preemptive strategy) may be added.

The literature indicates that the staffing of the TMT may be facilitated by head hunters, assessment centers, employee interviews, personality testing, and informal information (such as recommendations of other TMT members). More often than not, however, the responsibility for selecting TMT members resides with the CEO, thereby making him or her an extremely powerful figure in the eyes of the organization (Kotter, 1982). Nevertheless, it would be naive to assume that the CEO makes staffing decisions without the influence of outside constituents. He or she may have to consider the perspectives of other stakeholders, such as the board of directors, venture capitalists, other top managers, and important outside organizations. When Michael Jordan took over the leadership of the Washington, D.C.-based Wizards basketball team, his decision to fire the head coach was affected by the attitudes of some influential players. Generally the more powerful and dominant the CEO is, the more influence he or she will have on the TMT member selection process.

The amount of time it takes to staff a TMT varies. For instance, the head of the Smithsonian Institute, Lawrence Small, restaffed his TMT just three months after his arrival, a reorganization that the *Washington Post* ("Smithsonian Chief's Team Is Set," 2000) commended as being "quick." Other CEOs may spend well over a year building a new TMT.

The staffing of the TMT may differ depending on the way it was formed. It may be that the CEO forms the TMT as part of a start-up organization. Today, however, many CEOs are forced to backfill the TMT because members have moved to other companies. In other cases, a CEO inherits a TMT and must change or prune the team. Research reveals that CEOs selected from outside the firm tend to replace more members of the TMT in the first two years than did those promoted from within (Baumrin, 1990; Helmich & Brown, 1972; Gabarro, 1987). Ted Waitt, the founder of Gateway, a personal computer–producing organization, had to restructure his entire TMT in order to maintain his company's competitive edge. He hired new executives for ten of the fourteen executive positions and many more for lower positions (Colvin, 2000).

Team Effectiveness

The effectiveness of a team has been referred to quite frequently in the literature, but without much specification. Most theories of team effectiveness take a multidimensional perspective. For example, Hackman (1987) stresses three factors. One is that the members of the team feel that their own needs are being met as a result of the team experience. This is often operationalized in terms of team member satisfaction. A second criterion relates to the extent to which the capability of the team to work together in the future is strengthened as a result of the team experience. Here, we might think of team learning (Smith et al., 1997) and of the team as having greater adaptability (Kozlowski, 1998). Hackman also argues that effectiveness should be judged in terms of the team's work products and the extent to which they are acceptable by those who receive or review them. We can think of such matters as customer satisfaction or of stakeholder satisfaction generally.

TMT effectiveness has been primarily operationalized by outcomes including return on equity, assets or investment (O'Reilly & Flatt, 1989; Michel & Hambrick, 1992; Smith et al., 1994), growth (among new firms) (Eisenhardt & Schoonhoven, 1990), interdependence of diversification posture (Michel & Hambrick, 1992), corporate strategic change (Wiersma & Bantel, 1992), profitability (Glick, Miller, & Huber, 1993), and sales growth (Smith et al., 1994). Effectiveness has additionally been expressed through the innovativeness of TMT ideas (Bantel & Jackson, 1989; O'Reilly & Flatt, 1989), the cohesion of TMT members (Glick, Miller, & Huber, 1993), and adaptive organizational change (O'Reilly, Snyder, & Boothe, 1993). These outcome measures are often subject to the limitations of accounting-based measures, such as variations in inventory valuation, depreciation schedules, and historical costs (Michel & Hambrick, 1992).

In addition to viewing team effectiveness in terms of outcomes, several writers believe that it can be reflected in team processes (Finkelstein & Hambrick, 1996). Thus, an effective TMT would reflect excellent communication, collaboration, and cooperation among its members. It would have established means of handling internal conflict and threats from the outside. In addition, members of effective TMTs would evidence high levels of trust and mutual influence.

We have already touched on the importance of key processes for the TMT, but there is additional insight to be gained from empirical research of the process-to-outcome linkage. For example, research has been found to link social integration to organizational innovation (O'Reilly & Flatt, 1989) and sales growth (Smith et al., 1994), constructive conflict with growth (Eisenhardt & Schoonhoven, 1990), creativity with diversity of beliefs (Glick et al., 1993), and cooperation with adaptive organization change (O'Reilly et al., 1993).

TMT outcomes also differ depending on whether CEOs establish clear boundaries of the team and its work. When boundaries were made clear, team performance was generally good. Difficulties emerged when there was chronic uncertainty regarding which issues should be addressed by the team and which should be handled by an outside executive (Eisenstat & Cohen, 1989). Research indicated that team members could accept whatever boundaries the CEO established, as long as they were made clear.

Another important process involves the shaping of TMT initiatives. Katzenbach (1998) stated that the CEO must identify critical team opportunities and ensure that they are addressed by the TMT. The CEO must structure team interactions so that member efforts are concentrated on those key themes. This helps TMT members energize collaborations and hone in on the group activities that should take priority. Better team performance outcomes are believed to result from this process.

Kouzes and Posner (1995) stress that leaders foster trust in decision-making groups. They explain that team members who are unable to trust others will either attempt to make decisions by themselves or will be overly involved in the work and decisions of others, attitudes that will lead to distrust among team members. Research found more trusting group members to be more open regarding their perspectives, more knowledgeable regarding the group's basic problems and goals, more willing to search for alternative courses of action, and more motivated to implement decisions (Kouzes & Posner, 1995).

Along with promoting trust, the CEO must encourage the sharing of TMT information and resources. Specifically, the leader should make certain that all team members participate in the decision-making process (Kouzes & Posner, 1995). This helps foster a more open forum for competing viewpoints to be aired and discussed. This open forum will lead to more effective decisions and team performance.

Similar to this view, leaders should stress collaboration over competition to promote performance. Trying to do well and trying to beat others are two different things. One is about achievement and the other about subordination. Thus, an effective CEO should foster collaboration among TMT members. Cooperative team interactions have been found to lead to friendliness, cohesion, and high morale (Kouzes & Posner, 1995).

Team Leadership

There is some evidence that effective team leadership is inspirational leadership. Downtown (1973) stated that leaders are inspirational to the extent that they motivate followers to accept and comply with their initiatives. Although inspirational leadership has occasionally been considered a specific leadership style (Bass, 1990), the leadership literature most often refers to it as a broader theoretical domain that encompass a variety of leadership approaches, one being transformational leadership (Yukl, 1994).

Avolio and Bass (1999) state that transformational leaders gain follower commitment by finding commonalities among follower motives when shaping a vision. They appeal to followers by offering a chance to be elevated to a higher moral level (Burns, 1978). Thus, the vision the transformational leader promotes appeals to higher values rather than baser emotions such as fear or hatred (Yukl, 1994). In addition, the transformational leader stresses the importance of long-term strategy in making the vision a reality.

Team development in the context of a vision for the future of the team (and for the organization) is important. Thus, the CEO must serve as a transformational leader within the TMT. The leader has the option to involve the team in the development of a vision statement. This participation itself has a profound impact on building alignment and cohesion among individuals. But even when a vision statement is brought to the team as a fait accompli, when it is introduced and woven into team development efforts effectively, the leader's vision will have both guidance and motivational consequences.

Vision is defined as the shared aspired future state that identifies team or organizational values, aligns priorities for goals and objectives, and sets the guidelines by which these goals and objectives will be pursued (Robbins & Duncan, 1988). Strategic visions are complex, novel images that contain an element of strategy. They are also embedded within the external strategic contexts of issues and organization, and the internal personal context of the life experiences of the leaders themselves (Westley & Mintzberg, 1988). (Chapter Seven in this book explores vision in further detail.)

As leader of the TMT and overall organization, the CEO must make articulating a vision a priority. A survey of 1,450 executives from twelve global corporations found the ability to "articulate a tangible vision, values, and strategy" to be the most critical competency needed for organizational progress (Ireland & Hitt, 1999, p. 48). Thus, the CEO must be able to identify the organization's values and beliefs, as well as the goals that should be pursued. He or she must set organizational priorities, indicating to organizational members which goals and values are important to achieve. Finally, the CEO must determine how priorities will be accomplished (Robbins & Duncan, 1988).

The CEO alone cannot create and communicate an organizational vision. For example, in their study of CEOs, Levinson and Rosenthal (1984) concluded that visions emerged from interactions between the CEO and TMT. Specifically, the CEO and TMT members compared perceptions of the organization's current state and then conceived a strategic plan that addressed these perceptions. TMT members must be empowered to design and execute strategies and course of action to accomplish the organization's purpose and goals (Ireland & Hitt, 1999).

Aside from creating vision, there are other ways a CEO may affect the TMT. Stewart and Manz (1995) suggested that team leadership be examined along two dimensions: leader involvement and leader power orientation. Leader involvement ranges from active to passive. An active leader is highly visible by team members and very much involved in team activities. A more passive leader is likely not involved in the daily activities of the team, nor is his or her influence felt directly by team members. We describe leader power orientation as ranging from autocratic to democratic, with autocratic leaders seeking sole possession of authority and democratic leaders sharing authority, power, and control with members of the team. Leadership behaviors and team member reactions to those behaviors can vary dramatically depending on where an individual lies on both of these dimensions, thereby affecting team outcomes. For instance, an active, democratic individual is said to promote power-building leadership. Here, the leader provides guidance and encouragement while delegating team activities and reinforcing effective behaviors. Stewart and Manz suggest that team members respond to this type of leadership by engaging in teamwork activities and building and learning relevant skills. As a result, teams are more likely to become self-managed.

As team leader, it is up to the CEO to address and actively work through problems that arise. Avoiding TMT problematics will only serve to fragment the team (Eisenstat & Cohen, 1989). For example, Greve (1995) revealed that strategy abandonment in the face of uncertainty can be contagious. Given this situation, the CEO must ensure that TMT members remain unified when faced with difficulties and trying to remedy a problem. All team members must be included in this process; if the CEO unilaterally makes decisions affecting the TMT, competition between members will intensify, further increasing group fragmentation.

The CEO must also neutralize the contestation that exists within the team. The natural pecking order of organizational positions often inhibits teams from reaching their potential; the essential skill mix and leadership shifts required to make the TMT perform effectively suffer (Katzenbach, 1998). It is up to the CEO to break apart the existing team hierarchy so that members feel free to exchange ideas and information.

In addition, the behavior of the CEO affects the trust that exists among TMT members. Eisenstat and Cohen (1989) explain that the degree to which the CEO implicitly or explicitly encouraged team members to compete for his or her attention and favor shifted the basis of trust within the team. Specifically, trust and learning within the team were found to deteriorate when the CEO conducted team-relevant business with members outside the group. Conversely, CEOs who dealt explicitly with difficult topics as a group boosted the ability of the team to learn from its own experiences.

In order to promote trust, Kouzes and Posner (1995) recommend that leaders ensure that team members are not working in isolation. For instance, regular team meetings should be held to develop a better sense of community. Leaders should also see that team members have the opportunity to express their personal opinions regarding team issues and decisions. Finally, the leader should make his or her own trust in the team readily apparent by disclosing information regarding his or her own personal beliefs, listening attentively to team members, and not speaking negatively of other team members.

Finally, the CEO must make TMT members aware that the skills that have made them successful executives may inhibit team learning (Hesselbein, Goldsmith, & Beckhard, 1996). For instance, being a forceful, articulate advocate for a particular organizational division may actually impede progress of the TMT. CEOs must encourage team members to inquire into their own thinking and expose the areas where their thinking is weak. In addition, the CEO must encourage team members to develop the capability to think strategically together.

Special Challenges of the CEO as Team Leader

CEOs face challenges that are unique to other organizational leaders. One involves creating conditions that enable TMT members to spend time together and focus specifically on issues that require their collective expertise. Nadler and Heilpern (1998) explain that "the internal and external forces tearing at the fabric of the executive team can be enormous. They are constantly at work, eroding the time, energy, and commitment of each member of the collective entity" (p. 29). The TMT is different from teams at other levels in that its members may not depend directly on each other when completing tasks. That is, less task interdependence exists in the TMT because each member is generally responsible for running his or her own operation (Nadler & Heilpern, 1998). Thus, it is up to the CEO to mold the TMT into an interdependent, cohesive unit. The CEO must communicate to team members that the marginal value of their working together exceeds the marginal cost of taking them away from their primary jobs.

The CEO is largely responsible for retaining the key players that compose a TMT. This can be quite a challenge considering the great number of organizations that have recently formed as a result of technological advancements. Consequently, there are many alternative business opportunities for the high-level executives who reside on the TMT. For instance, Eugene Lockhart, president of AT&T's core consumer unit, stepped down from his position after only one year on the job. He was lured away by the opportunity to join a start-up operation that would provide him with significant corporate equity stakes (Schiesel, 2000). Prior to that, AT&T had lost another division head who left to become president of an Internet shopping service.

There is no easy way to prevent top executives from being seduced by other job prospects. When a qualified candidate emerges, the bidding is on to see which company can offer high pay, extensive responsibility, and unusual perks. Executives may receive as many as ten calls per week from executive recruiters (Schafer & Joyce, 2000). As a result, CEOs are hard pressed to find ways to retain their top employees. Philip Seifert, chief executive of a Virginia-based start-up company that is seeking a top-level executive, joked about the situation, "You're wondering what the next thing is going to be . . . paying for people's mortgages?" (p. 18).

Noer (1996) suggested that CEOs increase retention rates by empowering TMT members and holding them accountable for the work and strategies produced by the team. He also noted that clear goals and shared leadership serve to promote team loyalty. Finkelstein and Hambrick (1996) stated that CEOs may promote TMT loyalty through tasks that require the true interdependence and cooperation of members.

Another challenge of the CEO is understanding how to deal with change. Nadler and Spencer (1998) state that successful adaptive change is "simply impossible" without the active and committed involvement of the CEO. Change requires the aggressive exercise of power—something that the CEO possesses above all other organizational constituents. This is not to deny the importance of other stakeholders; their involvement and support may also be critical for effective change. It is the CEO, however, who is most closely linked to these other constituents. He or she is faced with the challenge of motivating them to grow, adapt, and change. Specifically, the CEO must enable constituents to envision a change, energize others to achieve challenging goals associated with meeting the demands of change, and enable others to achieve these goals by providing them with confidence, authority, and necessary resources (Nadler & Tushman, 1989).

It is the CEO who has the ultimate responsibility of developing an integrated change agenda, noting the specific role the TMT will play in collectively implementing and managing that agenda. Nadler and Spencer (1998) suggest components critical to aiding a CEO when dealing with change. First, the CEO must recognize when change must take place. That is, he or she must possess the ability to understand the environment and recognize at an early stage the massing of forces likely to create disequilibrium and require adaptation and change. Second, the CEO must be able to employ the appropriate strategic choices to position the organization as a strong competitor in a dynamic and changing industry. Finally, the CEO must possess the ability to design changes creatively and implement them to enable the organization to function successfully in a new environment. Exhibit 8.1 offers a glimpse of the agenda items that William H. Donaldson tackled during his first sixty days of being appointed CEO of Aetna, the nation's biggest health insurer.

The CEO must be in touch with technological changes and advancements. Because technology now touches every corner of almost every company's business, CIOs have become more likely to be advanced to the position of CEO (Siwolop, 2000). For example, Michael D. Capellas, former CIO of Compaq Computer, and Edward M. Rafter III, former CIO of Prudential Property and Casualty Insurance, were both promoted to CEO of their companies. CIOs are also being recruited by outside organizations. Sharon D. Garrett, former CIO of Walt Disney, and William W. Wilson III, former CIO of Marsh, an insurance brokerage, are now CEOs of Zyan Communications and ClientSoft, respectively.

Exhibit 8.1 The To-Do List of Aetna's New CEO.

Stop heavy losses at Prudential Health Care
STATUS: Still problematical. Higher premiums and cost-cutting seem to be taking hold. Clearer early results expected next month.

Placate angry doctors and hospitals
STATUS: Talks set with medical societies on improving managed care practices.

Fend off investors calling for a sell-off of Aetna businesses
STATUS: Analysts say the clamor will grow unless financial results and Aetna's stock price improve later this year.

Split Aetna into health and wealth companies
STATUS: Internal groups examine tax, legal, and governance aspects. Consultants report soon on health business. Headhunters seek new health chief.

Cut $150 million from payroll, advertising, and travel costs
STATUS: Well along.

Sell lackluster overseas units
STATUS: Negotiations under way with 30 partners in 17 countries.

Source: Adapted from Freudenheim, 2000.

The CEO is also challenged with maintaining a healthy working relationship with the organization's board of directors. It is the CEO's responsibility to help shape a board that is truly engaged and involved in the direction of the organization. In addition, the CEO should ensure that board members are actively involved in strategic process decisions. Thus, they must thoroughly understand the strategic issues facing the organization and be updated by continuing-education efforts.

The CEO-board relationship is particularly important because the board monitors and assesses CEO performance. Thus, the CEO should strive to establish a trusting and sharing relationship with this unit, particularly when it comes to gleaning feedback regarding his or her decisions and actions. This process may become more challenging as CEO tenure and confidence increase; he or she may grow less inclined to seek the board's assessment of performance, although this might be the time when honest feedback is most needed (Nadler & Spencer, 1998). A formal performance appraisal system should be implemented to ensure that the CEO fully understands the board's views and concerns. This feedback process will help provide the CEO the opportunity to modify his or her own performance and work strategies.

Perhaps the greatest challenge for the CEO is the need to lead while under immense pressure from stakeholders within and outside the organization. An article in the business section of the *Economist* ("Thank You and Goodbye," 1999) said it well: "Nobody is more powerful than a chief executive, right up until the end. Then suddenly, at the end, he has no power at all." An examination of thirteen hundred occasions between 1980 and 1996 when chief executives of Fortune 500 firms left their jobs revealed that the boss had been fired in a third of the cases. For a similar level of performance, a CEO appointed after 1985 is three times as likely to be fired as one appointed before that date ("Thank You and Goodbye," 1999).

Why the increase in CEO firings? Some experts state that directors realize that failure to release a poorly performing executive is bad for their own reputation. In addition, institutional investors have become more willing to challenge managers rather than simply sell their stock if it is doing poorly ("Thank You and Goodbye," 1999). For example, the Campbell Soup Company was undergoing struggles due to the falling sales of condensed soup, which account for half of its profits. The president and CEO, Dale F. Morrison, established several product launches and advertising and strategic changes to remedy the problem, but was unable to keep the company stock from plummeting. As a result, he stepped down from his position after less than three years on the job (Hays, 2000). A similar fate was met by Richard L. Huber, former CEO of Aetna, Inc. Huber resigned after shareholders, upset with the company's poor performance, pressed the board to make changes.

The special challenges for a CEO as team leader can be summarized:

- Fostering cohesion
- Retaining TMT leaders
- Understanding and reacting to change
- Fostering a healthy relationship with the board of directors
- Responding to stakeholder pressures

The TMT as a Platform for Meeting the CEO's Personal Needs

The TMT is largely a creation of the CEO. As such, we believe that its nature and dynamics must serve the needs of the CEO as much as the needs of the firm. Thus, it may be a very special case for modeling. In this section, we speculate just what this means, entertaining the notions of performance strategies, protection, leveraging influence, and legacy.

Performance Strategy

The popular press more so than our textbooks insinuates that the typical CEO is usually looking out for his or her best long-term interests. Thus, the CEO is characterized as having a relatively short time horizon when it comes to making an impact or to making the move to a different firm. In setting up and managing the TMT, the CEO may acknowledge the past and expect to spend a fair amount of time dealing with current pressures and performance demands, but he or she is keenly aware of the next move.

This consideration is most likely to be revealed in the desire to make an impact on the firm and its performance in the relatively near future. When it comes to the TMT, we would imagine that such a short-term perspective would show up in staffing decisions that imply susceptibility to conformity pressures. Thus, team members would be brought on board in part because of their loyalty and tractability, given that fast decisions are needed. But the CEO also needs individuals who are capable of carrying out initiatives that are likely to show up in terms of results that the market would easily recognize (such as a favorable change in market share or a major acquisition). This implies some adequate level of competence among those recruited to be on the TMT. In this regard, one may expect that the composition of the TMT may be shaped to favor the strategic direction to be pursued. Thus, if new technology is to be on the critical path to success, individuals with this background may be recruited.

A short-term perspective may also be exhibited in team policies and practices. Compensation for the CEO and the members of the TMT may be negotiated to favor immediate results. Similarly, one may see only a limited number of agenda items being entertained at TMT meetings.

Protection

The TMT is essentially a vehicle for protecting the interests of the CEO. In this regard, we can expect the message to be the same for a person who has any kind of horizon, be it short term or for the long haul.

As we see it, the manifestation of the protection motif in TMT staffing and management will depend on the kind of vulnerabilities felt by the CEO as well as the nature of the personal and corporate threats or opportunities that he or she is likely to encounter.

Clearly, few individuals, CEOs included, are omniscient or omnipotent. In this regard, the staffing of the TMT represents an opportunity for the CEO to create a proprietary resource to draw on as needed. We predict that the talent implied by such staffing decisions would tend to complement the strengths of the CEO. Similarly, the members of the TMT may also be selected for their power and influence, both within and outside the firm. If a historical perspective is important for CEO effectiveness, he or she could include as team members individuals who have been with the firm a significant period of time. Finally, individuals may be placed on the TMT because of their capacity to create difficulties for the CEO. This implies that the CEO may be advantaged having a potential adversary in plain view rather than elsewhere within the firm and in some position to undermine the CEO's authority. Indeed, it may also make sense to bring into the TMT outsiders who share this distinction. In this regard, Kotter (1982), Pfeffer and Salancik (1978), and others remark on the potential use of cooptation as a mechanism for controlling dependencies. Here, potential adversaries are brought into or are made part of an initiative in order to garner their support.

The kind of talent being amassed in the TMT may also be related to the strategic direction favored by the CEO. Thus, rather than being complementary, the competencies may actually overlap those of the CEO but serve to add depth and integrity to the strategic effort being put forth.

Leveraging Influence

The essence of leadership is influence. Most writers on leadership conceive of power as some mixture of potential influence derived from both the position and personal qualities of the incumbent. Many of these same writers also note that the CEO is often not as powerful as one may think.

The staffing and skillful use of the TMT is a major way that a CEO can extend his or her influence. In the first place, there is the issue of time available to exert personal power. The fact is that the CEO must almost always operate through intermediaries in order to get things accomplished. In this regard, it makes sense for those on the TMT to be expected to serve as agents of influence. Thus, in staffing, one would expect to find the (confident) CEO recruiting as direct reports men and women with substantial personal qualities. This, with the proviso of loyalty, would let the CEO leverage his or her influence.

Under certain circumstances, the CEO may be able to anticipate that given that a strategic initiative is to be undertaken, greater influence will be required with regard to certain influences (say, R&D or sales) relative to certain markets or in certain geographical locations. Here too, the prescient CEO may be able to recruit and embrace specific individuals who, because of their specialty or personal following, can serve to augment the CEO's power and ensure that the leader's directives will be followed.

The most efficient means of leveraging influence may be through delegation or empowerment. Here, the CEO seeks to recruit TMT members who share the former's values and vision and have the technical skills and the personal qualities (including trustworthiness and integrity) to act on the CEO's behalf. Moreover, the results of delegation may be quite favorable to the extent that the CEO seriously considers the need to create a shared common ground among TMT members, provide needed information and resources, and promote a TMT culture with a risk-taking orientation.

Legacy

The case of the opportunist notwithstanding, it is likely that many CEOs seek to leave a legacy when they move on or retire from their position. For some, this may mean creating an organization that is substantially stronger and more competitive than when the title of CEO was assumed.

"Stronger" may imply a corporate vision that is widely shared and implemented (such as to be a more customer-focused organization). It may also imply better management processes, including information and control systems or personnel practices that are appropriate for meeting environmental pressures (as in retaining key personnel). In all these examples, the CEO is unlikely to accomplish his or her agenda alone and relies on the TMT to play a major role.

In some ways, legacy building may be the equivalent of team building. That is, one of the best things a CEO can do for an organization is to ensure that the TMT in place at the time of retirement or resignation is strong and fully capable of continuing the vigorous and effective work at the top. This implies that in addition to recruiting good people and developing the TMT and its microculture, the CEO sets up systems for retention of key people and the propagation of important traditions and practices. Like all other systems, the TMT would have the propensity to wind down (entropy). Mechanisms must be put in place to supply the guidance and the energy needed for continuity. Of course, one of the most obvious ways to ensure a legacy is to have a plan for succession.

The evidence on management succession is not reassuring in that the outgoing executive is as likely to fail as to succeed in plans to elevate a chosen protégé to the title. But even while acknowledging this, we would argue that this will continue to be a common practice, and when done well, the outcomes can be positive for the firm and the outgoing CEO.

There is ample evidence that executives serve as mentors (Finkelstein & Hambrick, 1996). Typically this role is a result of an informal understanding and is based on mutual respect and needs. In this regard, the protégé may or may not be considered and groomed to replace the CEO. The mentoring is done with more general goals in mind.

Finkelstein and Hambrick (1996) explain that the CEO may exit from office through death, illness, mandatory retirement, early retirement for personal reasons, accepting a position in another company, or dismissal. The most common reason is mandatory retirement; death and illness account for under 5 percent of exits (Vancil, 1987). Early retirement has not been singled out for study, but it should be. In terms of dismissals, most accounts suggest a range of 10 to 20 percent (Herman, 1981; James & Soref, 1981; Vancil, 1987; Boeker, 1992).

One aspect of legacy relates to CEO succession. Several questions within this issue must be answered. First, who should select the new CEO? The succession process may be incumbent driven, board driven, or a combination of the two. Choosing a CEO is generally the most important decision a board makes, and directors cannot blame anyone but themselves if the decision is a bad one. Naming a committee of the board to facilitate the work is fine. It should comprise no more than five members, and its duties should include evaluating the company's TMT and its leadership development. Of course, involving the incumbent CEO is important and good, but he or she should not chair the committee (Charan & Colvin, 2000). Research reveals that companies that leave the bulk of succession decisions to the incumbent CEO tend to wind up with the worst succession outcomes. This implies that if the CEO seeks to influence his or her successor, the outcome may not be favorable to the organization. It seems that CEOs are often blind to the faults of internal candidates whom they have brought along and built up (Charan & Colvin, 2000). Incumbents lack objectivity about the new talents most needed and the abilities that a variety of candidates may possess (Levinson, 1974). In addition, CEOs often select incumbents with styles similar to their own. This may or may not be beneficial to an organization. For example, a former Apple employee noted that interim CEO Steve Jobs handpicked individuals who act in the same way he does. The former employee explained, "That only perpetuates the style and reinforces bad behavior. My point is that Jobs's leaving might not solve any problems, since he systematically replaced many of the decent human beings who were in management positions with barbarians of his ilk" (Finkelstein & Hambrick, 1996, p. xxx).

Two succession strategies cited in the TMT literature are the so-called relay race and the horse race. In the relay race, an heir apparent is selected well before the incumbent's departure and is elevated to a number two position in the organizational hierarchy (Vancil, 1987). This strategy may be ineffective if the designated individual is perceived as merely a "crowned prince" who has yet to be tested in a chief executive position. Experience shows that many successful COOs do not work as CEOs (Charan & Colvin, 2000).

Other companies may set up a horse race in which internal candidates for the CEO position are put into similar posts eighteen to twenty-four months before a successor must be named. This is not only demoralizing to those excluded from the race, but may also miss the best candidate as the job's requirements evolve.

Research reveals that the most successful companies do not make a choice until a few months before the succession, and they exclude no one from the running (Charan & Colvin, 2000). Specifically, the board and the CEO should work constantly to identify the company's future leadership. This means they must continually invest time articulating the skills that the company's future leader must possess. Approached in this way, choosing the next CEO is a process that is never launched and never completed. It is always ongoing.

For example, Jack Welsh, CEO of GE, has spent more than twenty years fostering the company's social operating system to aid in building talent among employees. Welsh's system involves a series of ten strategic meetings that are held every year. These meetings range in scope from large gatherings of over five hundred executives, to smaller, more intimate discussions with only key organizational players. This enables Welsh to diagnose and review current talent, provide coaching regarding business acumen, and strategize the company's future. In addition, he extends his social operating system to the board, where there is informal discussion of top talent. At the time this chapter went to press, Welsh identified his successor (Jeffrey Immelt, head of GE's medical systems division since 1997), fully fourteen months before he plans to step down. Welsh also made it clear that Immelt's relatively young age (44) was a factor in his proposal to the GE Board. "It's just a better game with a longer run. You can't give people these jobs for less than ten years" (Swoboda, 2000).

Implications for Future Research

When we began writing this chapter, we were somewhat aware of the state of knowledge regarding the TMT-CEO interface that existed in our field. As it turned out, however, we had been more optimistic than we had a right to be. It is not that we had no past research to discuss and integrate; the reference list at the end of this chapter attests to this. It was the lack of available detail that we found unsettling. To put it simply, the material that we had to rely on for this chapter was far less sophisticated than we needed to be able to model the phenomena of interest.

But to lament the situation is not very helpful. Thus, in the spirit of trying both to motivate and guide research in the future, we offer the following suggestions.

Need for Descriptive Information

The field should build theories and models that are well grounded by knowledge of the impact of the CEO on the TMT in work organizations. Based on our review of the TMT and CEO literature, however, it appears that this will be difficult to do. We found far less descriptive information about TMTs and the leadership of TMTs than is needed to be able to design well-grounded theories. Moreover, we are hard pressed to advise those designing experimental studies in this topic area regarding the appropriate variables, conditions, and manipulations that should be examined. This is because there is a dearth of knowledge information concerning such basic information as the size and composition of TMTs, the average tenure of a team member, or the frequency with which the CEO is able to configure the senior leadership group completely. True, we did find this type of information in case studies as well as anecdotes in the popular press. We also gained some descriptive insights from the empirical studies in the area. However, these we obtained mostly from the "methods sections" of technical articles. Such data were not often the focus of the research itself.

We are calling for more studies that address the description of the TMT in all its forms and permutations. We need to have a better grasp of the distribution of most of the aspects of the TMT that we have covered in this chapter. In short, we need data suitable for establishing parameter estimates.

Types of TMTs

At the outset, we acknowledged that there are various ways researchers and writers have conceptualized the TMT. This is also manifested in the many terms or synonyms that we found for the TMT. Most problematic, however, is that we do not have an agreed-on operational definition with which to work. For example, the prototype we chose for this chapter is the senior group reporting to the senior manager of a multidivisional firm. We trust that this choice is not too controversial. Yet in viewing the TMT as made up of (mostly) division presidents and vice presidents, one does buy into many assumptions regarding such things as member expertise, ambitions, network contacts, and power. This prototype also implies the potential for operational measures of performance and data that would be available to a CEO and possibly become the basis for accountabilities and compensation. A different set of assumptions would unfold if the TMT were operationalized at a level where managers responsible for functional performance reported to the CEO.

We are not implying that the findings and inferences we have summarized in this chapter are not generalizable across TMT types. They could indeed be. Clearly more work on a typology of TMTs is needed (Kotter, 1982). At a minimum, the literature should come to some form of consensus as to what variations of TMT structure are acceptable and can be subsumed under the term.

TMT Leadership

We have identified a curious lack of systematic research on how the CEO goes about leading, managing, or otherwise using the members of the TMT to his or her personal advantage (that is, accomplishing a personal agenda) or to the service of organizational strategy. While Nadler and Spencer (1998) and Katzenbach (1998) attempt to illustrate this, they do not provide the needed theories, models, or empirical support that would be required of writers making recommendations (for example, in the leadership of production teams). We need to model such things as the extent to which TMT members are in fact led as a team, how they are involved in strategic issues, how labor is divided, and how the CEO confronts leadership problematics (Does it motivate them? Align them with a vision? Control their ambition? Retain them?). As implied in this chapter, much of the dynamics at this rarified level of the corporation revolves around issues of power; we suspect that much of the leadership of TMTs has to do with attaining, retaining, and wielding power.

Thus, a variation of this question is the role of the TMT in agenda setting. When and where do the members of the TMT effectively control the direction of the firm? Similarly, although we do have some insights regarding CEO-board dynamics, how, when, and why do TMT members interact with board members? When are they implicated in board structures or committees?

Staffing of the TMT

To be sure, research on team staffing generally is in its infancy (Klimoski and Zukin, 1998). However, we believe it would be fruitful for future work to emphasize the special issues of staffing (and refilling) positions on the TMT. In particular, how would a model of effective team staffing be developed? What criteria should be used for validating such a model? What is the role of outsiders (such as search firms and key constituencies) in the identification and selection of TMT members? How much is it the personal prerogative of the CEO?

One focus of research on TMT staffing should be on the qualities needed for effective performance as a top-level team member. Certainly studies of teams at lower levels (Guzzo & Salas, 1995) have uncovered the potential for selecting key attributes that are functional for a wide variety of operational teams (such as teamwork skills). Would we expect to find similar results for TMTs? There is also a need to consider the effects of existing team members and the preferred composition of the TMT when recruiting and replacing members. What theories of composition will aid in efficient and effective staffing?

Compensation and the TMT

The volume of writing and research on executive compensation is enormous (Finkelstein & Hambrick, 1996). Much of it relates to the effects (both intended and unintended) of policy and practices on the distribution of direct and deferred income for the CEO (Beatty & Zajac, 1994) and on the consequences for firm performance (Raviv, 1985; Chapter Nine of this volume). Moreover, while some studies have placed compensation in the context of social relationships, such as CEO-board interaction, there is little reference to how executive compensation plays out at the TMT. How are TMT members' compensation packages designed? Who (or what) controls such designs? To what extent are CEO and TMT member compensation linked, and how does this affect TMT dynamics? Similarly, what are the implications of individual- versus group-based compensation plans for TMT member interaction, cooperation, conflict, and ultimately effectiveness? There may be some insight regarding these topics from literature concerning group pay plans for lower-level personnel. It is yet to be seen, however, whether these theories and models are valid for the TMT.

Organizational Leadership and the TMT

The premise for this chapter is that the work of the senior organizational leader, for better or for worse, is embedded in a social context. We have chosen to refer to this collective as the top management team. But the nature and processes of this group at the top are not given, nor are they something that is thrust on the CEO. In part, at least, these will be an outgrowth of the CEO's needs, goals, and skills. The good news (for the leader) is that he or she will have a strong impact on TMT dynamics. This is one part of what we call the TMT-CEO interface.

We suspect that the members of TMT, individually and especially collectively, represent a powerful force. The fate of the firm and of the CEO will be strongly influenced by this special partnership. Therein lies the need to organize, summarize, and critically examine the existing theory and research on the CEO-TMT interface in any book on senior organizational leadership.

References

Ancona, D. G., & Caldwell, D. F. (1989). Beyond tasks and maintenance: Defining external functions in groups. *Group and Organization Studies, 13,* 468–494.

Argote, L., & McGrath, J. E. (1993). Group processes in organizations: Continuity and change. In C. L. Cooper & I. T. Robertson (Eds.), *International review of industrial and organizational psychology.* New York: Wiley.

Avolio, B. J. (1998). Examining a full-range leadership development system. In G. Griffin (Ed.), *Management theory and practice.* Old Tappan, NJ: Macmillan.

Avolio, B. J., & Bass, B. M. (1999). Individual consideration viewed at multiple levels of analysis: A multi-level framework for examining the diffusion of transformational leadership. In F. Dansereau & F. J. Yammerino (Eds.), *Leadership: The multiple-level approaches: Classical and new wave.* Greenwich, CT: JAI Press.

Bantel, K. A., & Jackson, S. E. (1989). Top management and innovations in banking: Does the composition of the top team make a difference? *Strategic Management Journal, 10* (Special Issue), 107–124.

Barrick, M. R., Day, D. V., Lord, R. G., & Alexander, R. A. (1991). Assessing the utility of executive leadership. *Leadership Quarterly, 2,* 9–22.

Bass, B. M. (1990). *Bass and Stogdill's handbook of leadership: Theory, research, and managerial applications* (3rd ed.). New York: Free Press.

Baumrin, S. W. (1990). *New CEOs at the helm in large firms: The relationship of the succession context to subsequent organizational change and performance.* Unpublished doctoral dissertation, Columbia University.

Beatty, R. P., & Zajac, E. J. (1994). Managerial incentives, monitoring, and risk-bearing: A study of executive compensation, ownership, and board structure in initial public offerings. *Administrative Science Quarterly, 39,* 313–335.

Boeker, W. (1992). Power and managerial dismissal: Scapegoating at the top. *Administrative Science Quarterly, 27,* 538–547.

Brass, D. J. (1984). Being in the right place: A structural analysis of individual influence in an organization. *Administrative Science Quarterly, 29,* 518–539.

Burns, J. M. (1978). *Leadership.* New York: HarperCollins.

Charan, R., & Colvin, G. (2000, April). The right fit. *Fortune,* pp. 226–238.

Cohen, S. G., & Bailey, D. E. (1997). What makes teams work: Group effectiveness research from the shop floor to the executive suite. *Journal of Management, 23,* 239–290.

Colvin, G. (2000, February 7). The truth can hurt—get used to it.

Conger, J. A., & Kotter, J. P. (1982). General managers. In J. W. Lorsch (Ed.), *Handbook of organizational behavior.* New York: Free Press.

Conyon, M. J., & Peck, S. I. (1998). Board control, remuneration committees, and top management compensation. *Academy of Management Journal, 41,* 146–157.

Cyert, R. M., & March, J. G. (1963). *A behavioral theory of the firm.* Upper Saddle River, NJ: Prentice Hall.

Daboub, A. J., Rasheed, A.M.A., Priem, R. L., & Gray, D. A. (1996). Top management team characteristics and corporate illegal activity. *Academy of Management Review, 20,* 138–170.

Day, D. V., & Lord, R. G. (1988). Executive leadership and organizational performance: Suggestions for a new theory and methodology. *Journal of Management, 14,* 453–464.

Deal, T. E., & Kennedy, A. A. (1982). *Corporate cultures: The rules and rituals of organizational life.* Reading, MA: Addison-Wesley.

Denison, D. R. (1996). What is the difference between organizational culture and organizational climate? A native's point of view on a decade of paradigm wars. *Academy of Management Review, 21,* 619–654.

Dess, G. G., & Origer, N. K. (1987). Environment, structure, and consensus in strategy formulation: A conceptual integration. *Strategic Management Journal, 12,* 313–330.

Doesn't work well with others. (2000, January). *Inc.,* p. 95.

Dow, G. E. (1988). Configurational and coactivational views of organizational structure. *Academy of Management Review, 13,* 53–64.

Downtown, J. V. (1973). *Rebel leadership: Commitment and charisma in the revolutionary process.* New York: Free Press.

Doz, Y. L. (1996). The evolution of cooperation in strategic alliances: Initial conditions or learning processes. *Strategic Management Journal, 17,* 55–84.

Drucker, P. F. (1997). The future that has already happened. *Harvard Business Review, 75,* 20–24.

Eisenhardt, K. M., & Schoonhoven, C. B. (1990). Organizational growth: Linking founding team, strategy, environment, and growth among U.S. semiconductor ventures, 1978–1988. *Administrative Science Quarterly, 35,* 504–529.

Eisenstat, R. A., & Cohen, S. G. (1989). Summary: Top management groups. In J. R. Hackman (Ed.), *Groups that work (and those that don't): Creating conditions for effective teamwork.* San Francisco: Jossey-Bass.

Finkelstein, S. (1992). Power in top management teams: Dimensions, measurement, and validation. *Academy of Management Journal, 35,* 505–538.

Finkelstein, S., & Hambrick, D. C. (1990). Top-management-team tenure and organizational outcomes: The moderating role of managerial discretion. *Administrative Science Quarterly, 35,* 484–503.

Finkelstein, S., & Hambrick, D. C. (1996). *Strategic leadership: Top executives and their effects on organizations.* St. Paul, MN: West.

Fleishman, E. A., & Zaccaro, S. J. (1992). Toward a taxonomy of team performance functions. In R. W. Swezy & E. Salas (Eds.), *Teams: Their training and performance.* Norwood, NJ: Ablex.

Fligstein, N. (1987). The intraorganizational power struggle: Rise of finance personnel to top leadership in large corporations, 1919–1979. *American Sociological Review, 52,* 44–58.

Fligstein, N. (1990). *The transformation of corporate control.* Cambridge, MA: Harvard University Press.

Floyd, S. W., & Lane, P. J. (2000). Strategizing throughout the organization: Managing role conflict in strategic renewal. *Academy of Management Review, 25,* 154–177.

Fredrickson, J. W. (1986). The strategic decision process and organizational structure. *Academy of Management Review, 11,* 280–297.

Freudenheim, M. (2000, April 27). Aetna's new chief wants to be consumer-friendly. *New York Times,* p. C6.

Furchgott, R. (2000, March). *Worth,* p. 87.

Gabarro, J. J. (1987). *The dynamics of taking charge.* Boston: Harvard Business School Press.

Glick, W. H., Miller, C. C., & Huber, G. P. (1993). Upper-level diversity in organizations: Demographic, structural, and cognitive influences on organizational effectiveness. In G. P. Huber & W. H. Glick (Eds.), *Organizational change and redesign: Ideas and insights for improving performance.* New York: Oxford University Pres.

Gordon, G. G. (1991). Industry determinants of organizational culture. *Academy of Management Review, 16,* 396–415.

Graen, G. B., & Scandura, T. A. (1987). Toward a psychology of dyadic organizing. *Research in Organizational Behavior, 9,* 175–208.

Greve, H. R. (1995). Jumping ship: The diffusion of strategy abandonment. *Administrative Science Quarterly, 40,* 444–473.

Guzzo, R. A., & Salas, E. (Eds.). (1995). *Team effectiveness and decision making in organizations.* San Francisco: Jossey-Bass.

Hackman, J. R. (1987). The design of work teams. In J. W. Lorsch (Ed.), *Handbook of organizational behavior.* Upper Saddle River, NJ: Prentice Hall.

Hambrick, D. C. (1981). Environment, strategy, and power within top management teams. *Administrative Science Quarterly, 18,* 279–290.

Hambrick, D. C. (1987). Top management teams: Key to strategic success. *California Management Review, 30,* 88–108.

Hambrick, D. C. (1994). Top management groups: A conceptual integration and reconsideration of the "team" label. In B. M. Staw & L. L. Cummings (Eds.), *Research in organizational behavior.* Greenwich, CT: JAI Press.

Hambrick, D. C., & Mason, P. (1984). Upper echelons: The organization as a reflection of its top managers. *Academy of Management Review, 9,* 193–206.

Hansell, S. (2000, May 5). Time Warner and AOL offer a blueprint. *New York Times,* p. C1.

Harris, R. G. (1979). *The potential effects of deregulation upon corporate structure, merger behavior, and organizational relations in the rail freight industry.* Draft report. Washington, D.C.: Public Interest Economics Center.

Hays, C. L. (2000, March 23). Campbell Soup chief resigns as long-term slump persists. *New York Times.*

Helmich, D. L., & Brown, W. B. (1972). Successor type and organizational change in the corporate enterprise. *Administrative Science Quarterly, 17,* 371–378.

Heneman, H. H., Heneman, R. L., & Judge, T. A. (1997). *Staffing organizations.* Burr Ridge, IL: Irwin.

Herman, E. S. (1981). *Corporate control, corporate power.* New York: Cambridge University Press.

Hesselbein, F., Goldsmith, M., & Beckhard, R. (Eds.). (1996). *The leader of the future: New vision, strategies, and practices for the next era.* San Francisco: Jossey-Bass.

Hitt, M. A., Keats, B. W., & De Marie, S. M. (1998). Navigating in the new competitive landscape: Building strategic flexibility and competitive advantage in the twenty-first century. *Academy of Management Executive, 12,* 22–42.

House, R. J., & Podsakoff, P. M. (1994). Leadership effectiveness: Past perspectives and future directions for research. In J. Greenberg (Ed.), *Organizational behavior: The state of the science.* Mahwah, NJ: Erlbaum.

Ireland, R. D., & Hitt, M. A. (1999). Achieving and maintaining strategic competitiveness in the twenty-first century: The role of strategic leadership. *Academy of Management Executive, 13,* 43–57.

Jackall, R. (1988). *Moral mazes: The world of corporate managers.* New York: Oxford University Press.

Jackson, S. E. (1992). Consequences of group composition for the interpersonal dynamics of strategic issue processing. *Advances in Strategic Management, 8,* 345–382.

James, D. R., & Soref, M. (1981). Profit constraints in managerial autonomy: Managerial theory and the unmaking of the corporate president. *American Sociological Review, 46,* 1–18.

Joyce, W. F., & Slocum, J. W. (1990). Strategic context and organizational climate. In B. Schneider (Ed.), *Organizational climate and culture.* San Francisco: Jossey Bass.

Katz, D., & Kahn, R. L. (1978). *The social psychology of organizations* (2nd ed.). New York: Wiley.

Katzenbach, J. R. (1998). *Teams at the top.* Boston: Harvard Business School Press.

Klimoski, R. J., & Jones, R. G. (1995). Staffing for effective group decision making: Key issues in matching people and teams. In R. A. Guzzo & E. Salas (Eds.), *Team effectiveness and decision making in organizations.* San Francisco: Jossey-Bass.

Klimoski, R. J., & Mohammad, S. (1994). Team mental models: Construct or metaphor? *Journal of Management, 20,* 403–437.

Klimoski, R. J., & Zukin, L. (1998). Selection and staffing for team effectiveness. In E. Sundstrom et al. (Eds.), *Supporting work team effectiveness: Best management practices for fostering high performance.* San Francisco: Jossey-Bass.

Kotter, J. P. (1982). *The general managers.* New York: Free Press.

Kouzes, J. M., & Posner, B. Z. (1995). *The leadership challenge: How to keep getting extraordinary things done in organizations* (Rev. ed.). San Francisco: Jossey-Bass.

Kozlowski, S.W.J. (1998). Training and developing adaptive teams: Theory, principles, and research. In J. A. Cannon-Bowers & E. Salas (Eds.) *Making decisions under stress: Implications for individual and team training.* Washington, D.C.: American Psychological Association.

Kozlowski, S.W.J., Toney, R. J., Mullins, M. E., Weissein, D. A., Brown, K. G., & Bell, B. S. (1999). In E. Salas (Ed.), *Human/technology interaction in complex systems* (Vol. 10). Greenwich, CT: JAI Press.

Levinson, B. (1974). Don't choose your own successor. *Harvard Business Review, 52,* 53–62.

Levinson, H., & Rosenthal, S. (1984). *CEO: Corporate leadership in action.* New York: Basic Books.

Liden, R., Wayne, S., & Stillwell, D. (1993). A longitudinal study of the early development of leader-member exchanges. *Journal of Applied Psychology, 78,* 662–674.

Littlepage, G., Robinson, W., & Reddington, K. (1997). Effects of task experience and group experience on group performance, member ability, and recognition of expertise. *Organizational Behavior and Human Decision Processes, 69,* 133–147.

McGrath, J. E. (1984). *Groups: Interaction and performance.* Upper Saddle River, NJ: Prentice Hall.

Michel, J. G., & Hambrick, D. C. (1992). Diversification posture and top management team characteristics. *Academy of Management Journal, 35,* 9–37.

Mintzberg, H. (1973). *The nature of managerial work.* New York: Harper-Collins.

Mintzberg, H. (1979). *The structuring of organizations.* Upper Saddle River, NJ: Prentice Hall.

Nadler, D. A., & Heilpern, J. D. (1998). The CEO and the executive team: Managing the unique dynamics and the special demands. In D. A. Nadler & J. A. Spencer (Eds.), *Executive teams.* San Francisco: Jossey-Bass.

Nadler, D. A., & Spencer, J. A. (Eds.). (1998). *Executive teams.* San Francisco: Jossey-Bass.

Nadler, D. A., & Tushman, M. L. (1989). Leadership for organizational change. In A. M. Mohrman, S. A. Mohrman, G. E. Ledford Jr., T. G. Cummings, & E. E. Lawler III (Eds.), *Large-scale organizational change.* San Francisco: Jossey-Bass.

Noer, D. M. (1996). A recipe for glue. In F. Hesselbein, M. Goldsmith, & R. Beckhard (Eds.), *The leader of the future: New visions, strategies, and practices for the next era.* San Francisco: Jossey-Bass.

Norburn, D. (1986). GOGOS, YOYOS, and DODOS: Company directors and industry performance. *Strategic Management Journal, 7,* 110–117.

Nutt, P. C. (1989). *Making tough decisions: Tactics for improving managerial decision making.* San Francisco: Jossey-Bass.

Ocasio, W. (1994). Political dynamics and the circulation of power: CEO succession in U.S. industrial corporations, 1960–1990. *Administrative Science Quarterly, 39,* 285–314.

Ocasio, W., & Kim, H. (1999). The circulation of corporate control: Selection of functional backgrounds of new CEOs in large U.S. manufacturing firms, 1981–1992. *Administrative Science Quarterly, 44,* 532–562.

O'Reilly, C. A., Chatman, J. A., & Caldwell, D. (1991). People and organizational culture: A profile comparison approach to assessing person-organizational fit. *Academy of Management Journal, 3,* 487–516.

O'Reilly, C. A., & Flatt, S. (1989). *Executive team demography, organizational innovation, and firm performance.* Working paper, University of California, Berkeley.

O'Reilly, C. A., Snyder, R. C., & Boothe, J. N. (1993). Executive team demography and organizational change. In G. P. Hunter & W. H. Glick (Eds.), *Organizational change and redesign: Ideas and insights for improving performance.* New York: Oxford University Pres.

Pfeffer, J., & Salancik, G. (1978). *The external context of organizations: A resource dependence perspective.* New York: HarperCollins.

Raviv, A. (1985). Management compensation and the managerial labor markets: An overview. *Journal of Accounting and Economics, 7,* 239–245.

Romanelli, E. (1989). Environments and strategies of organizational start-up: Effects on early survival. *Administrative Science Quarterly, 34,* 369–387.

Robbins, S. R., & Duncan, R. B. (1988). The role of the CEO and top management in the creation and implementation of strategic vision. In D. C. Hambrick (Ed.), *The executive effect: Concepts and methods for studying top managers.* Greenwich, CT: JAI Press.

Schafer, S., & Joyce, A. (2000, May 1). Managers making their move. *Washington Post,* pp. 17–18.

Schiesel, S. (2000, February 14). Head of a core AT&T unit to leave after one year on job. *New York Times,* p. C2.

Sheridan, J. E. (1992). Organizational culture and employee retention. *Academy of Management Journal, 35,* 1036–1056.

Simons, T., Pelled, L. H., & Smith, K. A. (1999). Making use of difference: Diversity, debate, and decision comprehensiveness in top management teams. *Academy of Management Journal, 42,* 662–673.

Siwolop, S. (2000, May 10). Breaking out of the back room. *New York Times,* p. C6.

Smith, E. M., Ford, J. K., & Kozlowski, S.W.J. (1997). Building adaptive expertise: Implications for training design strategies. In M. A. Quinones & A. Ehrenstein (Eds.), *Training for a rapidly changing workplace: Applications of psychological research.* Washington, D.C.: American Psychological Association.

Smith, K. G., Smith, K. A., Olian, J. D., Sims, H. P., O'Bannon, D. P., & Scully, J. A. (1994). Top management team demography and process: The role of social integration and communication. *Administrative Science Quarterly, 39,* 412–438.

Smithsonian chief's team is set. (2000, May 2). *Washington Post,* p. C6.

Stewart, G. L., & Manz, C. C. (1995). Leadership for self-managing work teams: A typology and integrative model. *Human Relations, 48,* 747–770.

Sutcliffe, K. M. (1994). What executives notice: Accurate perceptions in top management teams. *Academy of Management Journal, 5,* 1360–1378.

Swoboda, F. (2000, November 28). GE Picks Welch's successor. *Washington Post,* p. E1.

Thank you and goodbye. (1999, October 30). *Economist,* p. 67.

Townsend, A. M., De Marie, S. M., & Hendrickson, A. R. (1998). Virtual teams: Technology and the workplace of the future. *Academy of Management Executive, 12,* 17–29.

Tushman, M. L., & Romanelli, E. (1983). Uncertainty, social location, and difference in decision making. *Management Science, 28,* 12–23.

Useem, M. (1998). Corporate leadership in a globalizing equity market. *Academy of Management Executive, 12,* 43–59.

Vancil, R. F. (1987). *Passing the baton.* Boston: Harvard Business School Press.

Weiss, H. M. (1990). Learning theory and industrial and organizational psychology. In M. D. Dunnette & L. M. Hough (Eds.), *Handbook of industrial and organizational psychology* (Vol. 1, 2nd ed.). Palo Alto, CA: Consulting Psychologists Press.

West, M. A., & Anderson, N. R. (1996). Innovation in top management teams. *Journal of Applied Psychology, 81,* 680–693.

Westley, F. R., & Mintzberg, H. (1988). Profiles of strategic vision: Levesque and Iacocca. In J. A. Conger & R. N. Kanungo (Eds.), *Charismatic leadership: The elusive factor in organizational effectiveness.* San Francisco: Jossey-Bass.

White, H. C. (1992). *Identity and control: A structural theory of action.* Princeton, NJ: Princeton University Press.

Wiersma, M. F., & Bantel, K. (1992). Top management team demography and corporate strategic change. *Academy of Management Journal, 35,* 91–121.

Yukl, G. (1994). *Leadership in organizations* (3rd ed.). Upper Saddle River, NJ: Prentice Hall.

Zaccaro, S. J. (1996). *Models and theories of executive leadership: A conceptual/empirical review and integration.* Alexandria, VA: U.S. Army Research Institute for the Behavioral and Social Sciences.

Zahra, S. A. (1999). The changing rules of global competitiveness in the twenty-first century. *Academy of Management Executive, 13,* 36–42.

Zahra, S. A., & O'Neill, H. M. (1998). Charting the landscape of global competition: Reflections on emerging organizational challenges and their implications for senior executives. *Academy of Management Executive, 12,* 13–21.

CHAPTER 9

Executive Characteristics, Compensation Systems, and Firm Performance

Review and Integrative Framework

Yan Zhang
Nandini Rajagopalan
Deepak K. Datta

Much of the literature on the impact that executives have on firm performance has focused on two sets of antecedent factors: executives' demographic characteristics and executive compensation systems. In this chapter we review and synthesize the theoretical and empirical literatures associated with these two streams. Based on this review, we then present an integrative framework that identifies the central role of social and cognitive processes and their influence on executives' strategic choices and firm performance.

Executive Demographic Characteristics, Strategic Choices, and Firm Performance

The considerable literature on the relationships of executives' demographic characteristics, strategic choices, and firm performance has been based primarily on three theoretical perspectives: upper echelons, contingency theory, and managerial discretion. The upper-echelons perspective (Hambrick & Mason, 1984) posits that executive demographic attributes such as age, functional background, firm, and industry tenure are proxies for their experiences and, hence, their underlying cognitions and skills. Consequently, demographic characteristics of senior executives have been viewed as representing powerful explanations for variations in their strategic choices. The upper-echelons perspective also argues that the composition of top executive groups (especially demographic heterogeneity within groups) has important implications for strategic decision processes and, hence, strategies that are developed and enacted. This perspective suggests that heterogeneity among key executives may contribute to the generation of a greater number of strategic alternatives, higher quality of strategic decisions, and, consequently, superior firm performance.

The literature on executive characteristics grounded in contingency theory has emphasized the contingency effects of environmental and organizational factors on the relationships between executive demographics and firm performance. Contingency theorists (Gupta, 1988) argue that the appropriateness of senior leaders' strategic choices depends on the extent to which these choices are consistent with the contingencies posed by the firm's organizational and environmental contexts. Hence, the fit between leaders' demographic attributes and contextual conditions results in superior firm performance. The third perspective, managerial discretion (Hambrick & Finkelstein, 1987), seeks to incorporate elements of both the upper-echelons and the contingency theories but relates demographic characteristics and the firm's operating context to variations in the latitude of action available to senior leaders. In this model, senior leaders' strategic choices reflect variations in the extent and type of latitude that leaders enjoy in different operating contexts. Constraints on managerial latitude stem from both individual characteristics of leaders, as well as organizational and environmental factors.

The empirical relationships of executive demographic characteristics, strategic choices, and firm performance most commonly examined in prior research are summarized in Figure 9.1. We review the empirical literature associated with the various links identified in this framework.

**Figure 9.1. Executive Demographics
and Firm Performance.**

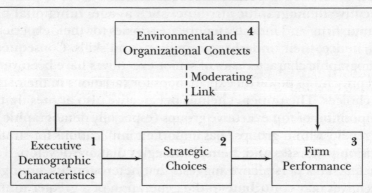

Executive Demographic Characteristics and Performance (Link 1–3)

Studies linking executive characteristics to firm performance can be broadly classified into two categories: those that focus on the CEO and those that examine the top management team (TMT). Research belonging to this stream is typically grounded in the upper-echelons perspective and the assumption that observable demographic characteristics reflect executives' underlying cognitive orientations and knowledge base (Hambrick & Mason, 1984). As such, demographic characteristics have been viewed as valid predictors of strategic choices and, consequently, firm performance (Finkelstein & Hambrick, 1996). Furthermore, studies belonging to this link have typically adopted a strategic contingency perspective of executive leadership (Gupta, 1984, 1988), wherein the relevance and value of specific executive characteristics are viewed as being contingent on the firm's organizational and environmental context.

The empirical research on this link, at the individual level, has been dominated by studies that have explored the relationships between CEO origin (insider versus outsider) and performance. Results have been mixed. While studies by Reinganum (1985), Lubatkin, Chung, Rogers, and Owers (1986), and Warner, Watts, and Wruck (1988) report positive performance effects associated with the selection of outside CEOs (those with limited firm-specific experience), Worrell and Davidson (1987), Furtado and Rozeff (1987), and Zajac (1990) found the selection of CEOs with significant firm experience to be associated with better performance. In addition, relatively weak evidence exists on the performance implications of matching executives to key contextual contingencies. In the most recent examination of the normative predictions of contingency theory, Rajagopalan and Datta (1996) and Datta and Rajagopalan (1998) found limited support for their argument that firms that match their CEOs to environmental context outperform firms that do not. In addition, Guthrie and Datta (1998) found that the selection of outsider CEOs is positively associated with postsuccession firm performance in firms characterized by less diversification.

At the TMT level, the effect of TMT heterogeneity (operationalized along various demographic traits) on firm performance has received the most research attention. However, findings again have been equivocal. Murray (1989) examined the relationship between TMT heterogeneity and firm performance and found relatively weak evidence to support the theoretical proposition that such heterogeneity is negatively associated with short-term performance. Similarly, Michel and Hambrick (1992) examined the effect on firm performance of the interaction of TMT tenure heterogeneity, TMT dominant functional heterogeneity, and the firm's diversification posture and found no significant results.

Recent studies of TMT heterogeneity have incorporated a more contingent perspective in examining the TMT-performance relationship. A frequently examined contingency factor is the firm's operating environment, variously operationalized in terms of the level of managerial discretion, rate of change and velocity, and the degree of uncertainty. Finkelstein and Hambrick (1990), for example, observed that the TMT's average organizational tenure was positively associated with the extent to which firm performance adhered to industry average in industries with high managerial discretion but not in low-discretion industries. In addition, some studies have addressed the issue of whether firms with heterogeneous TMTs perform better than those with homogeneous teams in high-velocity industries and turbulent environments, under the assumption that heterogeneity leads to constructive debate and conflict. Consistent with this argument, Eisenhardt and Schoonhoven (1990) found a positive relationship between heterogeneity in industry experiences and firm performance in high-velocity environments. Similarly, Hambrick, Cho, and Chen (1996) found a positive association between TMT heterogeneity and firm performance in the airline industry between 1979 and 1986, a period characterized by environmental turbulence. However, Smith et al. (1994) found mixed results on the performance consequences of TMT heterogeneity in tenure, education, and functional backgrounds in a sample of sixty-seven firms from high-velocity industries.

Overall, findings suggest that there are no universally consistent relationships between TMT heterogeneity and performance. As posited by some scholars (Finkelstein & Hambrick, 1996; Hambrick et al., 1996; Hambrick & Mason, 1984), TMT heterogeneity can be a double-edged sword when it comes to firm performance. While TMT heterogeneity may enhance creative thinking and result in the use of expanded information sources (with potentially positive performance effects), it may also serve to decrease communication and social integration, with a negative impact on performance. However, the effects of TMT heterogeneity on the intellectual and social interaction processes within the team have seldom been examined The study by Smith and others (1994) is probably the only exception. As a result, it is unclear whether inconsistent findings stem from contextual heterogeneity across studies or underspecified theoretical models.

While TMT heterogeneity has attracted the most research attention, TMT size has also been related to firm performance. In a study of forty-seven firms in the computer and natural gas distribution industries, Haleblian and Finkelstein (1993) examined the moderating effects of environmental turbulence on the relationship between TMT size and firm performance. Larger TMTs performed better in turbulent environments, presumably because of their superior information processing capability. Similarly, in a sample of ninety-two U.S. technology-based new ventures between 1978 and 1985, Eisenhardt and Schoonhoven (1990) found that the size of the founding TMT was positively related to firm sales growth. In contrast, Smith and others (1994) found that TMT size did not directly influence either firm return on investment or sales growth in their sample of fifty-three high-technology firms.

Executive Demographic Characteristics and Strategic Choices (Link 1–2)

Studies belonging to this link have focused on the relationships between executive characteristics and firms' strategic choices. Grounded in the strategic choice paradigm (Child, 1972), which postulates that key managers exercise considerable control over an organization's future direction, studies here have linked variations in executives' experience and knowledge base to the choice of firm strategy. Consistent with theory, Smith and White (1987) found systematic relationships between new CEOs' functional backgrounds and firms' diversification strategies. Similarly, studies by Chaganti and Sambharya (1987) and Govindarajan (1989) indicate significant relationships between top managers' functional backgrounds and firms' competitive strategies. In addition, studies by Miller, Kets de Vries, and Toulouse (1982) and Miller and Toulouse (1986) suggest that a CEO's personality is linked to his or her strategy-making behavior. They found that firms led by confident and aggressive CEOs pursued risky and innovative strategies, and those led by CEOs given to feelings of "helplessness" tended to adopt more conservative strategies. Finally, in a recent study, Datta, Rajagopalan, and Zhang (1999) found that demographic characteristics of newly selected CEOs predicted the direction and magnitude of postsuccession strategic change. Interestingly, their study also found the relationship between CEO characteristics and strategic change to be contingent on industry conditions: CEOs had greater influence on firm strategy in high-discretion than in low-discretion industries. In sum, reasonably consistent findings across studies within this stream offer descriptive validity to the proposition that systematic relationships exist between individual executive characteristics and firm strategies.

At the TMT level, prior studies have examined the effects of TMT traits and trait heterogeneity on firm strategy. (Studies that examine traits focus on the average levels of demographic attributes such as tenure, age, and education. Studies that examine heterogeneity focus on the distribution of a trait within the team.) The empirical literature has associated longer TMT tenure with greater commitment to status quo, lower levels of risk taking, and restricted information processing. Specifically, TMT tenure has been found to be positively associated with strategic persistence and strategic conformity (Finkelstein and Hambrick, 1990), the extent of interdependence in diversification posture (Michel and Hambrick, 1992), and executives' commitment to the status quo (Hambrick, Geletkanycz, & Fredrickson, 1993). However, the effects of TMT tenure on firm strategy are also moderated by managerial discretion; Finkelstein and Hambrick (1990) and Hambrick and others (1993) found that the positive relationship between TMT tenure and commitment to strategic conformity and status quo held in high-discretion but not in low-discretion industries.

Other TMT traits examined include average age, educational level, and functional background. Wiersema and Bantel (1992) found that the firms with TMTs characterized by lower average age, higher educational level, and higher academic training in the sciences were most likely to experience strategic change. However, contrary to expectations, TMT team tenure was found to be positively related to corporate strategic change. In another study involving Midwest banks, Bantel and Jackson (1989) found little evidence of a significant association between TMTs' average education level, age, tenure, and organizational innovation.

In contrast to the significant findings on TMT traits, studies generally indicate that TMT heterogeneity has limited influence on firm strategy. In Bantel and Jackson's 1989 study of innovation among banks, only one of the eight hypotheses linking TMT heterogeneity and organizational innovation was supported. Similarly, Wiersema and Bantel (1992) found little evidence of an association between TMT heterogeneity and corporate strategic change. Among the four measures of TMT heterogeneity, only heterogeneity in educational specialization was positively related to the direction of corporate strategic change. In addition, Michel and Hambrick (1992) found no support for the hypothesized relationships between TMT heterogeneity and firm diversification posture.

The above nonfindings raise an interesting question: Why have studies found significant results for TMT traits but not for TMT heterogeneity? Two possible explanations emerge. First, there are significant differences in how TMT traits and heterogeneity affect strategy. TMT traits serve as a proxy for executives' cognitive orientation or preference sets (Finkelstein, 1988), which may be more directly related to their specific strategic choices. In contrast, TMT heterogeneity or homogeneity is more likely to affect the social interaction and integration within the TMT (Knight et al., 1999; Smith et al., 1994) rather than the specific content of strategic choices. This explanation is partially supported by Knight et al. (1999), who found that TMT heterogeneity in functional background and education was negatively associated with strategic consensus (defined as the degree of overlap in individual mental models). Second, when researchers use TMT heterogeneity as a proxy for their cognitive ability (Bantel & Jackson, 1989; Wiersema & Bantel, 1992), they are assuming that heterogeneity will increase the quality of the strategic decision-making process. This may not be necessarily true. As Finkelstein and Hambrick (1996) argued, a substantial gap often exists between the quality of decision making and the content of strategic decision. If that is indeed the case, TMT heterogeneity may not be a good predictor of strategic choices.

Demographic Characteristics, Strategic Choices, and Performance (Link 1–2–3)

Surprisingly, only a limited set of studies has simultaneously addressed the relationships of executive characteristics, strategic choices, and firm performance. In research that examined the fit between the CEO's functional background and the firm strategy, Reed and Reed (1989) observed that fit resulted in better postimplementation performance. Other studies (Thomas, Litschert, & Ramaswamy, 1991; Gupta & Govindarajan, 1984; Govindarajan, 1989) have found that the alignment between firm strategy and executive characteristics (in terms of age, tenure, educational level, and functional background) contributes to superior performance. Studies by Gupta and Govindarajan (1984) and Govindarajan (1989) indicate that superior performance is achieved when new managers are matched to the strategic needs of their organizations. In their recent study, Datta and others (1999) found that firms achieved better postsuccession performance if newly selected CEOs' characteristics were consistent with the requirement of the firm's postsuccession strategy. Finally, studies by Tushman and his colleagues (Tushman & Rosenkopf, 1996; Virany, Tushman, & Romanelli, 1992) indicate that improvement in firm performance in the postsuccession phase is greater when CEO change is accompanied by changes in the executive team and firm strategy. Further, Tushman and Rosenkopf (1996) found that a combination of CEO change and executive team change resulted in superior performance only in a turbulent environment.

In spite of the fact that relationships between TMT composition, strategic choices, and performance are undoubtedly important, research simultaneously addressing all three factors is sparse. A notable exception is the study by Michel and Hambrick (1992). They predicted that a fit between TMT social cohesion (high TMT average tenure, homogeneity in tenure, and homogeneity in functional background) and firm diversification posture would contribute to superior performance. However, study findings failed to provide support for their theoretical proposition.

In summary, although the normative view that the match between executive characteristics and firm strategy results in better performance has received moderate support at the individual executive level, it has not been the case at the TMT level. However, the evidence is at best indirect. Most empirical studies within this stream that have examined the "fit" hypothesis have been cross-sectional (rather than longitudinal), making it difficult to separate cause from effect meaningfully. For example, it is plausible that instead of executives' driving strategic choices, the reverse occurs, with current strategies' influencing the selection of certain types of executives. The underlying theoretical model gets even more tenuous when we examine the TMT (rather than the individual executive), with the effects of intra-team interactions coming into play. In other words, although a simple model linking executive characteristics, strategic choices, and performance may hold at the individual leadership level, it is much less likely to be valid at the TMT level. At the TMT level, research needs to incorporate issues related to power structure (Finkelstein, 1992) and the TMT interaction process (Eisenhardt & Bourgeois, 1988), factors that have been generally ignored in empirical executive characteristics performance literature.

Demographics and Firm Performance: Theoretical and Methodological Extensions

The review of the empirical literature on the relationships between executive demographics and firm performance identifies several gaps and inconsistencies, which in turn suggest several theoretical and methodological extensions.

Better Model Specification

The demographic approach that has dominated prior research is primarily based on the "congruence" assumption: that observable managerial characteristics are valid proxies for underlying managerial competencies and cognitive orientations (Hambrick & Mason, 1984). However, as Lawrence (1997) pointed out, this assumption may not necessarily be valid because the relationship between demographic variables and the underlying subjective concepts allows for multiple interpretations. Specifically, the upper-echelon perspective falls within what Lawrence calls the indicator model, in which the demographic variable (such as age) is viewed as an indicator of an underlying subjective concept (for example, ability to change), which is related to the outcome variable (for example, change in strategy). On the other hand, Pfeffer's theory of organizational demography (1983) represents what Lawrence termed the intervening model. Here the subjective concept intervenes between the demographic and outcome variables, and the demographic variable is not directly related to the outcome. The differences between the indicator and intervening theoretical specifications are important in that they may help explain some of the inconsistencies in prior empirical findings. For example, in the indicator model, TMT heterogeneity is viewed as a proxy for diversity in cognitive sources. Consequently, heterogeneous TMTs are expected to initiate strategic changes and organizational innovation, contributing to superior firm performance. In contrast, studies that have invoked the intervening model argue that TMT heterogeneity increases interpersonal conflict and decreases communication and social integration. In this case, heterogeneity will result in TMTs' being less able to implement strategic change and innovation effectively, resulting in inferior performance. It is therefore important that future studies examine both the cognitive resources of top managers as proxied by their demographic traits and heterogeneity (the indicator model) and the effects of such demographic characteristics on intervening social processes (the intervening model).

Causal Relationships Between Demography and Behavioral Constructs

In demography-based research, scholars have typically associated a single demographic variable with multiple underlying behavioral attributes. For example, TMT tenure is treated as a proxy for the team's commitment to status quo, information diversity, and attitudes toward risk and change (Finkelstein & Hambrick, 1990). These multiple representations create critical problems of correspondence between the operational measure and the underlying subjective concept. A related problem is that organizational demographers also tend to link various demographic variables to the same underlying variable of interest. For example, lower levels of age, organizational tenure, team tenure, and higher educational level have all been linked to creative decision making and attitudes toward risk and change (Wiersema & Bantel, 1992). Similarly, TMT heterogeneity along different dimensions is viewed as having the same effect on both strategy and firm performance (Bantel & Jackson, 1989; Hambrick et al., 1996; Wiersema & Bantel, 1992). However, the findings of recent empirical research (Knight et al., 1999) suggest that heterogeneity along various demographic dimensions may differ in both the extent and direction of their effects.

We suggest that future research on executive characteristics distinguish among demographic variables. It is particularly important that researchers carefully define the underlying causal linkages from demography, to individual and team behaviors, to organizational outcomes. A recent example of this approach is the typology of demographic variables provided in Pelled (1997) that categorizes such variables based on their levels of visibility and job relatedness. In this typology, diversity in age, race, and gender is characterized as high visibility and low job relatedness, while diversity in group tenure is categorized as high visibility and high job relatedness. On the other hand, diversity in organizational tenure, education, and functional background is viewed as being low visibility and high job relatedness. Pelled proposes that group conflict (affective conflict versus substantive conflict) mediates the relationship between demographic diversity and group outcomes in terms of both turnover and cognitive task performance. Pelled argues that substantive conflict is the perception among group members that there are disagreements about task-related issues such as goals, procedures, and actions. Affective conflict is the perception among group members that there are interpersonal clashes characterized by emotions such as anger and fear. Furthermore, Pelled suggests that the more job-related a particular type of diversity is, the stronger its relationship with substantive conflict will be; the more visible a particular type of diversity is, and the stronger its relationship with affective conflict will be. In a sample of forty-five teams, Pelled, Eisenhardt, and Xin (1999) found empirical support for their hypothesis that group conflict would be differentially related to various measures of team heterogeneity. Although this study did not focus on executives, there is much we can learn from their research approach on the importance of carefully distinguishing between demographic characteristics and related behavioral effects.

We also suggest that researchers develop a more careful classification of demographic characteristics according to the underlying attributes they proxy, whether emotional or cognitive. If a variable proxies for a cognitive attribute, it can be further classified into the degree versus type of cognitive attributes. For example, educational level can be viewed as a proxy for the "degree" of cognitive resources, and educational specialization represents a proxy for the "type" of cognitive resources. Based on this classification, we argue that all demographic variables and heterogeneity therein are not equally relevant to the content of strategic choices. Demographic traits that proxy for cognitive attributes are more likely to be translated to strategic choices than those indicating emotional attributes. In particular, researchers need to distinguish carefully between demographic traits that serve as a proxy for cognitive level (such as average education level or functional background) and the heterogeneity in such traits that serve as a proxy for cognitive type (such as heterogeneity in educational specialization and functional background).

Incorporating the Effects of Power Distribution and TMT Interactions

The effect of TMT characteristics on strategic choices and firm performance is not as direct or symmetric as prior research suggests. Given that a TMT consists of several managers with different characteristics, it raises an interesting question: Whose characteristics will be translated into specific strategic outcomes? It obviously depends on who has the power to translate individual preferences into firm-level strategic choices (Finkelstein, 1992). Executive leadership research implies certain assumptions about power distribution that may not be valid (Finkelstein & Hambrick, 1996). For example, studies focusing on CEOs make the implicit assumption that power is concentrated in the hands of the CEO. In fact, CEOs in most cases share power with others (Hambrick & Mason, 1984). On the other hand, TMT studies assume equal power distribution within a TMT, suggesting that each executive has an equal influence on strategic choices. This assumption is also questionable because the power distribution within a TMT is typically unbalanced (Finkelstein, 1992). It is therefore important that researchers incorporate measures of differential power distribution within the TMT in their future studies.

Theories of the strategic decision process present another opportunity to improve understanding of TMTs' impact on organizations. Strategic decision process may both moderate and mediate the relationships between executive characteristics and organizational consequences (Rajagopalan, Rasheed, & Datta, 1993). First, the influence of executive characteristics may vary depending on the stage of the strategic decision process. As Finkelstein and Hambrick (1996) suggested, TMT heterogeneity may be positively related to the quality of strategy formation but negatively associated with the quality of strategy implementation. Second, strategic decision processes may intervene between executive characteristics and organizational outcomes. Recent empirical evidence suggests that process variables, such as interpersonal conflict, agreement seeking, social integration, and communication (Knight et al., 1999; Smith et al., 1994), may play a critical intervening role in these relationships. Other promising process variables include decision speed (Eisenhardt, 1989), strategic decision comprehensiveness (Fredrickson & Mitchell, 1984), and politics (Eisenhardt & Bourgeois, 1988). Unfortunately, little research has examined the relationships between TMT demography, strategic decision processes, and organizational outcomes, making it a particularly promising area for future research.

Executive Compensation Systems, Strategic Choices, and Firm Performance

In addressing the relationships of executive compensation systems, strategy, and firm performance, much of the literature has invoked the agency and contingency theory perspectives. Within the agency framework, compensation systems serve to address the two central problems in agency literature: managerial motivation and control (Jensen & Meckling, 1976) and managerial risk bearing (Holmstrom, 1979; Shavell, 1979). From the viewpoint of the firm's principal, problems of managerial motivation and control arise when managerial behaviors cannot be a priori specified by the principal and can therefore deviate from what would be optimal for the principal (Jensen & Murphy, 1990). Compensation systems can then be used to align managers' self-interests with the interests of the principal, achieving the purpose of managerial motivation and control. From the viewpoint of the manager, however, the alignment of managerial interests and the principal's interests also shifts risk from the principal to managers. Given that managers in general are more risk averse than principals, compensation systems that encourage risk-taking behavior will better align managerial actions to principals' interests. In sum, agency theory proposes that executive compensation systems affect executives' strategic choices and firm performance through influencing managerial motivation and control and managerial risk bearing.

The contingency perspective, on the other hand, argues that the performance benefits of executive compensation systems are contingent on key firm strategic contingencies such as the extent and type of diversification, product and market strategy, technology emphasis, and stage in the product life cycle. The rationale is that a firm's strategic contingencies have direct implications for the type and extent of managerial discretion available to executives within the firm (Rajagopalan, 1997). Variations in managerial discretion manifest themselves in variations in the availability of options, the extent to which managerial behaviors can be programmed, the degree of ambiguity in cause-and-effect relationships and the extent of outcome uncertainty (Rajagopalan & Finkelstein, 1992). Variations in these factors in turn have implications for the problems of managerial motivation and control and managerial risk bearing. Miles and Snow (1978) define Prospectors as firms that aggressively seek growth opportunities through product and market development and innovation. In contrast, Defenders are firms that adopt and protect narrow and stable product market domains. Prospectors are externally oriented and innovative; Defenders are internally oriented and efficient. Relative to the Defender strategy, the

Prospector strategy offers executives considerable discretion by providing a wide array of options, less behavior programmability, ambiguous cause-and-effect relationship, and uncertain outcomes. Thus, Prospector firms will benefit from executive compensation systems that align managerial interests with that of the principal and do not shift too much risk to managers. In summary, the contingency view suggests that it is the fit between firm strategy and executive compensation systems that results in superior performance (Rajagopalan, 1997).

The relationships between executive compensation systems, strategic choices, and firm performance can be depicted in the form of the theoretical framework of Figure 9.2. In the following section we review the empirical literature related to the various links in this framework.

Executive Compensation Systems and Firm Performance (Link 5–7)

Most studies on executive compensation have focused on the direct relationship between executive compensation systems and firm performance (Gomez-Mejia, 1994; Pavlik & Belkaoui, 1991). The first set of studies focusing on this link examines whether there are systematic relationships between the level and amount of executive pay (fixed and contingent) and firm performance. Overall,

Figure 9.2. Executive Compensation Systems and Firm Performance.

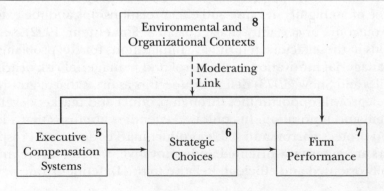

findings suggest that the pay level–firm performance linkage is rather weak, with the percentage of variation in executive pay attributed to firm performance seldom exceeding 15 percent, and most often falling under 10 percent (Gomez-Mejia, 1994). In addition, studies on the pay level–performance linkage have yielded contradictory findings. Although several studies have found a positive relationship between executive pay and firm performance (Deckop, 1988; Lambert & Larcker, 1987; Masson, 1971; Murphy, 1986), others have found no evidence (Kerr & Bettis, 1987; Jensen & Murphy, 1990; Leonard, 1990). Still others have found mixed relationships depending on the performance measures used (Abowd, 1990; Antle & Smith, 1986). These equivocal findings can be partly attributed to the difficulties associated with estimating the value of deferred and stock-based incentive payments. Although complex mathematical approaches have been used to value incentive payments, they require uncertain estimations on future interest rates and opportunity costs, leading to widely divergent estimates of the cash value of these plans (Gomez-Mejia, 1994).

The second set of studies within this stream has examined the pay-performance relationship in terms of the incentive properties of various compensation plans rather than the amounts actually awarded under such plans. These studies have yielded more consistent results. Tehranian and Waegelein (1985) and Waegelein (1988), for example, found that the adoption of short-term bonus plans led to favorable stock market reactions and, hence, increases in shareholder returns. Larcker (1983) and Brickley, Bhagat, and Lease (1985) found similar effects in the context of long-term performance plans, and Long (1988) reported positive performance effects in the case of stock option plans as well. The more consistent pattern of results provided by these studies (when compared to studies that have used compensation level and amounts) suggests that the links between the *types* of incentives and firm performance may be less tenuous than the relationships between the *amount* of rewards and performance.

Moreover, contextual factors tend to moderate the association between executive compensation and firm performance (Finkelstein & Hambrick, 1996). Performance-contingent compensation has been negatively associated with greater firm performance variability. In addition, the pay-performance association also depends on managerial power within firms. Hill and Phan (1991), for example, found that CEOs' pay-performance association decreased with longer CEO tenure. With longer time to build influence, CEOs are in a position to align their compensation packages to their own preference. Similarly, Clarke, Conyon, and Peck (1998) found that executive compensation and firm performance are more closely aligned in firms that have outsider-dominated boards and remuneration committees.

The compensation-performance relationship is also moderated by the firm's ownership structure, with compensation being more sensitive to performance in owner-controlled firms than in manager-controlled firms (Gomez-Mejia, Tosi, & Hinkin, 1987; Hambrick & Finkelstein, 1995; Lambert, Larcker, & Weigelt, 1993). In addition, firm strategy also affects the executive compensation-performance relationship. For instance, Bushman, Indjejikian, and Smith (1995) found that the association between the compensation of business unit managers and the aggregate company performance was moderated by the company's diversification strategy. The association was stronger with greater intrafirm interdependencies and weaker with higher levels of geographical and product line diversification.

Although most prior studies have focused on the level and mix of individual pay packages in examining firm performance, several researchers have also identified the important role of pay dispersion within the top management team. Pay dispersion within the TMT has important consequences for how it functions as a group. While tournament theory (Lazear & Rosen, 1981; Lazear, 1989) suggests that pay differentials might act as incentives prompting superior performance, social comparison theory suggests otherwise. According to the latter, negative consequences of unequal pay can be significant, especially when the degree of group interaction is high. If the TMT is characterized by high levels of interactions, pay dispersion can result in undesired turnover and inferior performance (Finkelstein & Hambrick, 1996). In other words, tournament theory and social comparison theory offer different predictions on the effects of pay dispersion and inequality on firm performance. Main, O'Reilly, and Wade (1993) found no significant relationships between pay inequality, TMT interdependence, and firm performance, suggesting that the positive incentive effects of pay dispersion may be neutralized by the negative social effects of pay inequality.

Executive Compensation Systems and Strategic Choices (Link 5–6)

Studies belonging to this link have examined the relationships between executive compensation systems and firm strategy. Most are grounded in agency theory. Indeed, a primary goal of normative agency theory is to specify optimal incentive contracts that yield desired outcomes. As such, empirical work here has sought to examine the assumption that long-term incentive compensation systems are aligned with outcomes that are consistent with shareholders' interests, such as greater risk acceptance and longer time horizons. In one such study, Larcker (1983) found that the adoption of compensation plans based on long-term performance was associated with increases in capital expenditures. Given that such expenditures tend to entail greater risk and a longer payoff period, they are likely to be consistent with shareholders' interests. Similarly, Lambert and Larcker (1984) found that the adoption of stock option plans is positively related to variability in equity returns, suggesting that managers in such firms exhibit a greater propensity for risky investments that may be in line with shareholders' long-term interests. Studies have also examined the association between executive compensation and R&D expenditures (which involve risk and have a longer payoff period, but benefit shareholders in long term). Rappaport (1978) found a positive relationship between long-term contingent pay and R&D expenditures. Similarly, Waegelein (1983) and Hoskisson, Hitt, and Hill (1993) reported negative relationships between short-term bonus plan adoption, division financial incentives, and R&D expenditure. Moreover, Govindarajan and Gupta (1985) observed that bonuses based on long-term, nonfinancial performance promoted the adoption of strategies aimed at growing or building the business unit, whereas short-term, financial incentives promoted less growth-oriented strategies among business units.

In general, these studies offer descriptive validity to the proposition that there are systematic relationships between executive compensation systems and firm corporate and business strategies. However, none of these studies has examined the performance implications of the fit between compensation systems and strategic choice. As such, not much is known about whether certain compensation system-strategic choice combinations are more beneficial than others from the standpoint of firm performance.

Executive Compensation Systems, Strategic Choices, and Firm Performance (Link 5–6–7)

Not many studies have examined executive compensation systems, strategic choices, and firm performance simultaneously. Exceptions include studies by Gomez-Mejia and his colleagues. In one such study of a sample of 105 firms, Balkin and Gomez-Mejia (1987) found the effectiveness of incentive pay systems to be contingent on firm size, stage in the product life cycle, and technology emphasis. Using a larger, multi-industry sample of 212 firms, Balkin and Gomez-Mejia (1990) found that "mechanistic" compensation systems, which emphasized formalized rules and procedures, job-related pay, and centralized pay practices, contributed to effectiveness in related diversified firms and business units at the maintenance stage. In contrast, "organic" compensation systems that emphasized flexible pay packages, individualized compensation patterns, and decentralized practice were more effective in nondiversified firms and business units in the growth stage. In a subsequent study, Gomez-Mejia (1992) also found that mechanistic compensation systems improved financial performance among dominant and related product firms, whereas flexible compensation systems were more effective in the case of single-product firms.

In another study, Rajagopalan (1997) used pooled cross-sectional, time-series data within the electric utility industry to examine the performance implications of fit between executive compensation and strategic orientation. Using Miles and Snow's typology of business strategy (1978), her study found support for the proposition that the match between executive compensation systems and strategic orientation leads to superior firm performance. Specifically, annual bonus plans that offered cash incentives and were based on accounting measures of performance led to better performance among firms with Defender strategic orientations, whereas stock-based incentive plans based on market measures of performance led to better performance among firms with Prospector strategic orientations.

Compensation and Firm Performance: Theoretical and Methodological Extensions

The review of the empirical literature on the relationships between executive compensation systems and firm performance identifies several gaps and inconsistencies, which in turn suggest several theoretical and methodological extensions.

Individual Differences as Moderators

Our review indicates that in general, studies on executive compensation systems tend to look for universal linkages between compensation and strategic choices and firm performance. However, such linkages may be moderated by individual differences. Recall that executive compensation systems affect strategic choices and firm performance partially because compensation systems are related to managerial risk-taking behaviors (Rajagopalan, 1997). There is ample reason to believe that individuals not only perceive risk differently but also differ in risk-taking propensity. Therefore, different executives are likely to react differently to the same compensation system. For example, in a sample of high-technology firms, Gomez-Mejia and Balkin (1989) found that individuals with a low risk propensity and a low tolerance for ambiguity did not react well to a pay mix that emphasized variable compensation. As suggested by Gomez-Mejia (1994), the upper-echelons perspective (Hambrick & Mason, 1984) can be used to address how the characteristics of individual executives and top management teams moderate the relationship between compensation systems and strategic choices and firm performance. In fact, this represents one possible way to integrate the studies on executive demographic characteristics and executive compensation systems.

Executive Compensation as Economic Motivation Versus Social Norm

Studies on executive compensation systems have been dominated by economic arguments: that compensation systems affect executives' motivation and risk-taking propensity, which in turn affects strategic choices and firm performance (Rajagopalan, 1997). However, given the complexities surrounding the motivations and behaviors of top executives, it is not clear that incentive compensation will necessarily motivate greater managerial effort. Some researchers (Donaldson & Lorsch, 1983) even argue that top managers are not motivated purely by financial incentives (as agency theorists would suggest). In fact, expectancy theory suggests that top managerial incentives may have only limited motivational impact because of the uncertainties of executive leadership that serve to weaken the perceived effects of managerial efforts on firm outcomes (Hambrick & Finkelstein, 1987). Moreover, executive compensation may be a function of social expectations (O'Reilly, Main, & Crystal, 1988), where executives are compensated not just based on performance but also on social norms regarding acceptable pay levels.

Unit of Analysis: Individual Versus TMT

Most prior studies on executive compensation have focused on the level and mix of individual pay and their impact on strategic choices and firm performance. The unit of analysis most commonly adopted is the individual executive (for example, the CEO), and the underlying assumption is that only the CEO matters. However, as Hambrick and Mason (1984) pointed out, we need more studies that use the TMT as the unit of analysis and examine the effects of pay dispersion and pay differentials within the TMT. The need to move from the individual to the team in compensation research can be justified on several bases. First, the TMT aligns well with Cyert and March's concept of the dominant coalition (1963). In most cases, the CEO shares the task and power with other members within the coalition. Thus, taking the TMT as the unit of analysis would increase the explanatory power and predictive validity of executive compensation studies. Second, the study of the TMT has the added advantage of allowing inquiry into distribution characteristics of executive pay, such as dispersion and inequality. Tournament theory and social comparison theory provide sound theoretical explanations on how pay dispersion and inequality may affect organizational outcomes such as executive turnover and firm performance. However, with few exceptions (Lazear & Rosen, 1981; Lazear, 1989; Main, O'Reilly, & Wade, 1993), very little research attention has examined the organizational consequences of variations in the level and dispersion of TMT pay, making this a particularly promising area for future research.

Overall, it is evident that in the empirical research on how top executives affect firm performance, prior studies have focused on one of the two important sets of antecedents: demographic characteristics or compensation systems. As such, we organized our review along the two streams. However, our discussion in the preceding section suggests that there are obvious benefits, from both a theoretical and methodological standpoint, to integrating these two streams.

An Integrative Research Framework and Conclusions

There are several compelling reasons for simultaneously studying the role of demographic characteristics and compensation systems on organizational performance. First, both affect organizational outcomes, such as strategic choices and firm performance, although the causal mechanisms are somewhat different. Demographic characteristics are used as proxies for executives' cognitive attributes and knowledge base and hence are expected to affect strategic choices and firm performance. Underlying this research stream is the predisposition argument: that executives select strategic choices from those available to them based on their existing cognitive orientation and skills set. In comparison, the underlying argument linking executive compensation systems and organizational outcomes is one of motivation: that executives are motivated to make certain strategic choices in order to gain the rewards offered by the compensation system. However, the question of how executives affect firm performance can be better explained by combining the predisposition and motivation arguments. In this combined perspective, executives make strategic choices that are often consistent with their preexisting cognitive orientations, but such choices can also be shaped by the organization's compensation system that rewards certain managerial behaviors and not others. In sum, we contend that both demographic characteristics and compensation systems need to be examined simultaneously because they capture different aspects of executive orientations and behaviors. Examining one without the other may result in incomplete model specification and hence, inconsistent or even contradictory findings.

Consistent with this unified perspective we propose the integrative framework of Figure 9.3. In agreement with prior literature, we acknowledge the direct effects of executive demography and compensation systems on firm strategy; however, based on our review of the contradictions within these streams, we identify the crucial intervening role of social and cognitive processes in these relationships. We propose that executive predisposition and motivation are likely first to affect social and cognitive processes, which in turn influence the content of strategic choices and firm performance.

Links 1–6 and 2–6 in Figure 9.3 examine the direct effects of executive characteristics and compensation systems on firm performance. For research that focuses on the individual level of analysis, link 1–6 addresses the performance impact of individual demographic characteristics such as age, educational level, and

Figure 9.3. Integrative Theoretical Framework.

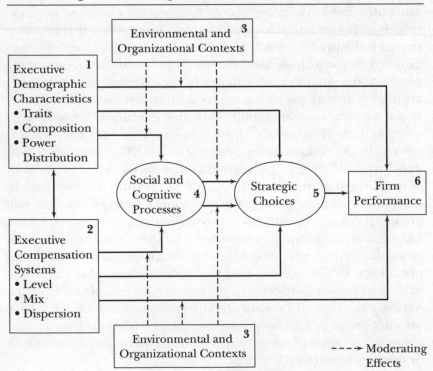

functional background. For studies examining the TMT, we suggest that this link include levels of demographic traits within the team (such as average educational level), distribution of these traits (for example, educational-level heterogeneity) within the team, and distribution of power within the TMT. Similarly, link 2–6 addresses the performance consequences of individual pay levels and incentive mix when we examine the CEO. However, when researchers are interested in the TMT, they need to include not only team pay levels but also the distribution of pay within the team (through measures of pay differentials and dispersion).

Links 1–5–6 and 2–5–6 in Figure 9.3 capture the critical role of strategic choices in explaining firm performance. From a theoretical perspective, there is little reason to believe that executive characteristics and compensation systems affect firm performance directly. Upper-echelons theory, managerial discretion, strategic contingency, and agency theory all highlight the critical role of executive behaviors as manifested in firm-level strategic choices. However, prior empirical research that has invoked one or more of these theories has also typically ignored the crucial intervening role of strategic choices. In fact, the contradictory and inconsistent findings of studies that have focused on the direct effects of executives on firm performance might be largely attributed to the incomplete causal model used in these studies. This suggests that future studies need to pay greater attention to the interrelationships between executive characteristics/compensation and strategic choices in explaining variations in firm performance.

Figure 9.3 also highlights the central role of executives' social and cognitive processes, as identified by links 1–4–5 and 2–4–5. Incorporating process variables in the framework helps address a key unanswered question in past research: How do the structural and compositional attributes of top management teams affect their social and cognitive interactions? There is sufficient reason to believe that such interactions have important effects on the content and quality of strategic decisions (Finkelstein & Hambrick, 1996). However, prior research has rarely examined such interactions within top management teams—exceptions being studies by Knight and others (1999) and Smith and others (1994). Because of few empirical studies on interactions within the TMT and due to the relatively underdeveloped theories of the strategic process (Rajagopalan et al., 1993), it is difficult to identify the theoretical domain of social and cognitive processes. In the spirit of motivating more research within this domain, we identify selected social and cognitive processes within the TMT pertinent to the various links in our framework. First, the traits of individual executives and the TMT may affect their cognitive processes such as knowledge bases, cognitive orientation, propensity for risk taking, and change (link 1–4). Second, TMT heterogeneity may affect cognitive processes such as the diversity of knowledge bases within the team and social processes such as task conflict, interpersonal conflict, and strategic dissent and consensus (link 1–4). Third, the level and mix of individual executive compensation and the level of TMT compensation may affect managerial motivations and propensity for risk taking (link 2–4). Finally, the dispersion and inequality of compensation within the TMT may affect the likelihood of cooperative versus competitive behaviors (link 2–4).

We believe that much of the impact that executive demographic characteristics and compensation systems have on strategic choices is through the intervening effects of these social and cognitive processes. By testing the intervening effects model where demographic and compensation factors affect strategic choices through their effects on social and cognitive processes, researchers will be able to identify both the direct and indirect effects of such factors. In addition, consistent with prior empirical literature, Figure 9.3 retains the moderating effects of contextual factors (see the various moderating effects identified through dotted links). Empirical evidence to date within both streams offers significant support for a contextual perspective according to which the performance effects of executives are likely to depend on key environmental and organizational factors (Gupta, 1988). Consistent with the arguments of strategic contingency theory, very little empirical evidence supports the universal effects of either demographic or compensation characteristics on both firm strategy and firm performance. However, our ability to identify the specific causal mechanisms through which the context influences executive choices (and performance) is constrained by two tendencies in prior empirical work. First, studies tend to focus on different contextual factors (for instance, managerial discretion theorists focus on the level of industry discretion, environmental contingency theorists focus on uncertainty and velocity, firm contingencies examined include size and prior performance, and so on). Hence, it is difficult to generalize from one study to another and build cumulative findings. Although we do not advocate focusing on one type of contingency to the exclusion of others, we do urge researchers to examine variables used in prior research more carefully so that we can move toward a more parsimonious set of contextual contingencies. Second, most prior research has paid little attention to the underlying causal mechanisms through which contextual factors influence executive decisions. In other words, we know that the context matters but do not quite understand the underlying reason.

Conclusion

Our review indicates that over the past couple of decades, several empirical studies have examined the role of executive demographic characteristics and compensation systems in explaining variations in firm performance. However, there is still much that we do not know about underlying relationships. Based on the gaps we identified in the empirical literature, we have developed an integrative framework that we hope will be useful in guiding future research. In particular, we believe that such research needs to examine executive characteristics and compensation systems simultaneously, incorporate the intervening roles of the TMT's social and cognitive processes and strategic choices, and identify and test a parsimonious set of environmental and organizational contextual factors as moderators. Research that incorporates these suggestions should contribute to an improved understanding of the complex set of issues surrounding the question of how top managers affect firm performance.

References

Abowd, J. M. (1990). Does performance-based managerial compensation affect corporate performance? *Industrial and Labor Relations Review, 43,* 52–73.

Antle, R., & Smith, A. (1986). An empirical investigation into the relative performance of corporate executives. *Journal of Finance, 18,* 593–616.

Balkin, D. B., & Gomez-Mejia, L. R. (1987). Toward a contingency theory of compensation strategy. *Strategic Management Journal, 8,* 169–182.

Balkin, D. B., & Gomez-Mejia, L. R. (1990). Matching compensation and organizational strategies. *Strategic Management Journal, 1,* 153–169.

Bantel, K., & Jackson, S. (1989). Top management team and innovations in banking: Does the composition of the top team make a difference? *Strategic Management Journal, 10,* 107–124.

Brickley, J. A., Bhagat, S., & Lease, R. C. (1985). The impact of long-range managerial compensation plans on shareholder wealth. *Journal of Accounting and Economics, 7,* 115–129.

Bushman, R. M., Indjejikian, R. J., & Smith, A. (1995). Aggregate performance measures in business unit manager compensation: The role of intrafirm interdependencies. *Journal of Accounting Research, 3*(Suppl.), 101–128.

Chaganti, R., & Sambharya, R. (1987). Strategic orientation and characteristics of upper management. *Strategic Management Journal, 8,* 393–401.

Child, J. (1972). Organizational structure, environment and performance: The role of strategic choice. *Sociology, 6,* 1–22.

Clarke, R. N., Conyon, M. J., & Peck, S. I. (1998). Corporate governance and directors' remuneration: Views from the top. *Business Strategy Review, 9,* 21–30.

Cyert, R. M., & March, J. G. (1963). *A behavioral theory of the firm.* Upper Saddle River, NJ: Prentice Hall.

Datta, D. K., & Rajagopalan, N. (1998). Industry structure and CEO characteristics: An empirical study of succession events. *Strategic Management Journal, 19,* 833–852.

Datta, D. K., Rajagopalan, N., & Zhang, Y. (1999). *CEO succession: Empirical relationships between CEO dynamism, strategic change and industry characteristics.* Working paper.

Deckop, J. (1988). Determinants of chief executive officer compensation. *Industrial and Labor Relations Review, 41,* 215–226.

Donaldson, G., & Lorsch, J. W. (1983). *Decision making at the top.* New York: Basic Books.

Eisenhardt, K. M. (1989). Making fast strategic decisions in high-velocity environments. *Academy of Management Journal, 32,* 534–576.

Eisenhardt, K. M., & Bourgeois, L. J. (1988). Politics of strategic decision making in high-velocity environments: Toward a midrange theory. *Academy of Management Journal, 31,* 373–370.

Eisenhardt, K. M., & Schoonhoven, C. B. (1990). Organizational growth: Linking foundation team, strategy, environment, and growth among U.S. semiconductor ventures, 1978–1988. *Administrative Science Quarterly, 35,* 504–529.

Finkelstein, S. (1988). *Managerial orientations and organizational outcomes: The moderating roles of managerial direction and power.* Unpublished Ph.D. dissertation, Columbia University.

Finkelstein, S. (1992). Power in top management team: Dimensions, measurement, and validation. *Academy of Management Journal, 35,* 505–538.

Finkelstein, S., & Hambrick, D. C. (1990). Top-management-team tenure and organizational outcome: The moderating role of managerial discretion. *Administrative Science Quarterly, 35,* 484–503.

Finkelstein, S., & Hambrick, D. C. (1996). *Strategic leadership: Top executives and their effects on organizations.* St. Paul, MN: West.

Fredrickson, J., & Mitchell, T. (1984). Strategic decision process: Comprehensiveness and performance in an industry with an unstable environment. *Academy of Management Journal, 27,* 399–423.

Furtado, E.P.H., & Rozeff, M. S. (1987). The wealth effects of company initiated management changes. *Journal of Financial Economics, 18,* 147–160.

Gomez-Mejia, L. R. (1992). Structure and process of diversification, compensation strategy, and firm performance. *Strategic Management Journal,* 13, 381–397.

Gomez-Mejia, L. R. (1994). Executive compensation: A reassessment and a future research agenda. In G. R. Ferris (Ed.), *Research in personnel and human resources management* (Vol. 12). Greenwich, CT: JAI Press.

Gomez-Mejia, L. R., Tosi, H., & Hinkin, T. (1987). Managerial control, performance, and executive compensation. *Academy of Management Journal, 30,* 51–70.

Govindarajan, V. (1989). Implementing competitive strategies at the business unit level: Implications of matching managers to strategies. *Strategic Management Journal, 10,* 251–270.

Govindarajan, V., & Gupta, A. K. (1985). Linking control systems to business unit strategy: impact on performance. *Accounting, Organizations and Society, 10,* 51–66.

Gupta, A. K. (1984). Contingency linkages between strategy and general manager characteristics: A conceptual examination. *Academy of Management Review, 9,* 399–412.

Gupta, A. K. (1988). Contingency perspectives on strategic leadership: Current knowledge and future research directions. In D. C. Hambrick (Ed.), *The executive effect: Concepts and methods for studying top managers.* Greenwich, CT: JAI Press.

Gupta, A. K., & Govindarajan, V. (1984). Business unit strategy, managerial characteristics, and business unit effectiveness at strategy implementation. *Academy of Management Journal, 27,* 25–41.

Guthrie, J. P., & Datta, D. K. (1998). Corporate strategy, executive selection, and firm performance. *Human Resource Management Journal, 37,* 101–115.

Hambrick, D. C., Cho, T. S., & Chen, M. J. (1996). The influence of top management heterogeneity on firms' competitive moves. *Administrative Science Quarterly, 41,* 659–684.

Hambrick, D. C., & Finkelstein, S. (1987). Managerial discretion: A bridge between polar views on organizations. In L. L. Cummings & B. M. Staw (Eds.), *Research in organizational behavior* (Vol. 9). Greenwich, CT: JAI Press.

Hambrick, D. C., & Finkelstein, S. (1995). The effect of ownership structure on conditions at the top: The case of CEO pay raise. *Strategic Management Journal, 16,* 175–194.

Hambrick, D. C., Geletkanycz, M. A., & Fredrickson, J. W. (1993). Top executive commitment to the status quo: Some tests of its determinants. *Strategic Management Journal, 14,* 401–418.

Hambrick D. C., & Mason, P. (1984). Upper echelon: The organization as a reflection of its top managers. *Academy of Management Review, 9,* 193–206.

Hill, C.W.L., & Phan, P. (1991). CEO tenure as a determinant of CEO pay. *Academy of Management Journal, 34,* 707–717.

Holmstrom, B. (1979). Moral hazard and observability. *Bell Journal of Economics, 10,* 74–91.

Hoskisson, R. E., Hitt, M. A., & Hill, C.W.L. (1993). Managerial incentives and investment in R&D in large multiproduct firms. *Organization Science, 4,* 325–341.

Jensen, M., & Meckling, W. (1976). Theory of the firm: Managerial behavior, agency costs, and ownership structure. *Journal of Financial Economics, 3,* 305–360.

Jensen, M., & Murphy, K. J. (1990). Performance pay and top management incentives. *Journal of Political Economy, 98,* 225–264.

Kerr, J. L., & Bettis, R. A. (1987). Boards of directors, top management compensation, and shareholder returns. *Academy of Management Journal, 30,* 645–664.

Knight, D., Pearce, C., Smith, K., Olian, J., Sims, H., Smith, K., & Flood, P. (1999). Top management team diversity, group process, and strategic consensus. *Strategic Management Journal, 20,* 445–465.

Lambert, R. A., & Larcker, D. F. (1984). *Stock options and managerial incentives.* Working paper, Northwestern University, J. L. Kellogg Graduate School of Management.

Lambert, R. A., & Larcker, D. F. (1987). An analysis of the use of accounting and market measures of performance in executive compensation contracts. *Journal of Accounting Research, 25,* 85–125.

Lambert, R. A., Larcker, D. F., & Weigelt, K. (1993). The structure of organizational incentives. *Administrative Science Quarterly, 38,* 438–461.

Larcker, D. F. (1983). The association between performance plan adoption and corporate capital investment. *Journal of Accounting and Economics, 5*(3), 3–30.

Lawrence, B. S. (1997). The black box of organizational demography. *Organization Science, 8,* 1–22.

Lazear, E. P. (1989). Pay inequality and industrial politics. *Journal of Political Economy, 97,* 561–580.

Lazear, E. P., & Rosen, S. (1981). Rank-order tournaments as optimum labor contracts. *Journal of Political Economy, 89,* 841–864.

Leonard, J. S. (1990). Executive pay and firm performance. *Industrial and Labor Relations Review, 43,* 13S–29S.

Lubatkin, M., Chung, K., Rogers, R., & Owers, J. (1986). Stockholder reactions to CEO changes in large corporations. *Academy of Management Journal, 32,* 47–68.

Main, B. G., O'Reilly, C. A., & Wade, J. (1993). Top executive pay: Tournament or teamwork? *Journal of Labor Economics, 11,* 606–628.

Masson, R. T. (1971). Executive motivations, earnings, and consequent equity performance. *Journal of Political Economy, 79,* 1278.

Michel, J. G., & Hambrick, D. C. (1992). Diversification posture and top management team characteristics. *Academy of Management Journal, 35,* 9–37.

Miles, R. E., & Snow. C. C. (1978). *Organizational strategy, structure, and process.* New York: McGraw-Hill.

Miller, D., Kets de Vries, M.F.R., & Toulouse, J. M. (1982). Top executive locus of control and its relationship to strategy-making, structure, and environment. *Academy of Management Journal, 25,* 237–253.

Miller, D., & Toulouse, J. M. (1986). Chief executive personality and corporate strategy and structure in small firms. *Management Science, 32,* 1389–1409.

Murphy, K. J. (1986). Incentives, learning, and compensation: A theoretical and empirical investigation of managerial labor contracts. *Rand Journal of Economics, 17,* 59–76.

Murray, A. I. (1989). Top management group heterogeneity and firm performance. *Strategic Management Journal, 10,* 125–141.

O'Reilly, C. A., Main, B. G., & Crystal, G. S. (1988). CEO compensation as tournament and social comparison: A tale of theories. *Administrative Science Quarterly, 33,* 257–274.

Pavlik, E. L., & Belkaoui, A. (1991). *Determinants of executive compensation: Corporate ownership, performance, size, and diversification.* Westport, CT: Quorum Books.

Pelled, L. H. (1997). Demographic diversity, conflict, and work group outcomes: An intervening process theory. *Organization Science, 7,* 615–631.

Pelled, L. H., Eisenhardt, K. M., & Xin, K. R. (1999). Exploring the black box: An analysis of work group diversity, conflict, and performance. *Administrative Science Quarterly, 44,* 1–28.

Pfeffer, J. (1983). Organizational demography. In L. L. Cummings & B. M. Staw (Eds.), *Research in organizational behavior* (Vol. 5). Greenwich, CT: JAI Press.

Rajagopalan, N. (1997). Strategic orientations, incentive plan adoptions, and firm performance: Evidence from electric utility firms. *Strategic Management Journal, 18,* 761–785.

Rajagopalan, N., & Datta, D. K. (1996). CEO characteristics: Does industry matter? *Academy of Management Journal, 39,* 197–215.

Rajagopalan, N., & Finkelstein, S. (1992). Effects of strategic orientation and environmental change on senior management reward systems. *Strategic Management Journal, 13* (Special Issue), 127–142.

Rajagopalan, N., Rasheed, A., & Datta, D. K. (1993). Strategic decision processes: Critical review and future directions. *Journal of Management, 19,* 349–384.

Rappaport, A. (1978). Executive incentives versus corporate growth. *Harvard Business Review, 56*(4), 81–88.

Reed, R., & Reed, M. (1989). CEO experience and diversification strategy fit. *Journal of Management Studies, 26,* 251–270.

Reinganum, M. (1985). The effect of executive succession on stockholder wealth. *Administrative Science Quarterly, 30,* 46–60.

Shavell, S. (1979). Risk sharing and incentives in the principal and agent relationship. *Bell Journal of Economics, 10,* 55–73.

Smith, K. G., Smith, K. A., Olian, J. D., Sin, H. P., O'Bannon, D. P., & Scully, J. A. (1994). Top management team demography and process: The role of social integration and communication. *Administrative Science Quarterly, 39,* 412–438.

Smith, M., & White, M. C. (1987). Strategy, CEO specialization, and succession. *Administrative Science Quarterly, 32,* 263–280.

Tehranian, H., & Waegelein, J. F. (1985). Market reaction to short-term executive compensation plan adoption. *Journal of Accounting and Economics, 7,* 131–144.

Thomas, A., Litschert, R. J., & Ramaswamy, K. (1991). The performance impact of strategy-manager coalignment: An empirical examination. *Strategic Management Journal, 12,* 509–522.

Tushman, M. L., & Rosenkopf, L. (1996). Executive succession, strategic reorientation, and performance growth: A longitudinal study in the U.S. cement industry. *Management Science, 42,* 939–953.

Virany, B., Tushman, M. L., & Romanelli, E. (1992). Executive succession and organization outcomes in turbulent environments: An organization learning approach. *Organization Science, 3,* 72–91.

Waegelein, J. F. (1983). *The impact of executive compensation on managerial decisions: An empirical investigation.* Working paper, School of Management, Boston College.

Waegelein, J. F. (1988). The association between the adoption of short-term bonus plans and corporate expenditures. *Journal of Accounting and Public Policy, 7,* 43–63.

Warner, J. B., Watts, R. L., & Wruck, K. H. (1988). Stock prices and top management changes. *Journal of Financial Economics, 20,* 461–492.

Wiersema, M., & Bantel, K. (1992). Top management team demography and corporate strategic change. *Academy of Management Journal, 35,* 91–121.

Worrell, D. L., & Davidson, W. N., III. (1987). The effect of CEO succession on stockholder wealth in large firms following the death of the predecessor. *Journal of Management, 13,* 509–515.

Zajac, E. J. (1990). CEO selection, succession, compensation, and firm performance: A theoretical integration and empirical evidence. *Strategic Management Journal, 11,* 217–230.

PART 2

Identifying and Developing Effective Leaders

CHAPTER 10

Identifying, Assessing, and Selecting Senior Leaders

Ann Howard

Although personnel selection has long been a hallmark of industrial/organizational (I/O) psychologists, selection of senior leaders has largely proceeded without these professionals. It is not that they have tried and failed; it is more that they have been ignored because they were not expected to add value. Their selection models were dismissed as too general, too backward looking, too intrusive for senior leaders. They created programs for the masses; executives are elite and unique.

When top executives are selected, the assessors are typically untrained amateurs—boards of directors and other executives. Their tools—interviews and reference checks—inhabit the low end of the validity continuum. They operate in secret, although the outcome of their work is publicly dismal; 30 to 50 percent of CEOs meet their Waterloo.

This chapter explores how I/O psychology can make a more meaningful contribution to senior leader selection. Improvement of this process would clearly benefit both organizations that buckle under failed leadership and executives who unnecessarily suffer humiliating defeats.

The Growing Importance of Effective Senior Leadership

Senior leader succession—always an eye-catching transfer of power—is growing even more consequential. One marker is executive pay, which has soared since the mid-1980s. Today's chief executive makes more in one day than a typical American worker earns in a year. A parallel rise in companies' stock market performance has somewhat muted public criticism of this executive largess, but both upward trends track the swelling importance of effective senior leadership (Leonhardt, 2000).

Leadership in the New Economy

By now many of the organizational implications of information technology, global competition, and a knowledge-based economy have become clear. Work is rapidly changing and increasingly complex, which makes long-range planning foolhardy and control impossible. Organizations struggle to become more flexible, streamlined, and innovative lest they lose their competitive edge. At the same time, the bar for satisfactory organizational performance keeps moving up. All of these challenges percolate in a brew of turbulence, uncertainty, and stress (Csoka, 1998; Howard, 1995).

The new economy pleads for superior leadership talent and places it under a spotlight. Global competition, the capital markets, and the news media make a senior executive's performance a high-profile affair (Fernandez-Araoz, 1999). Companies use the competency and vision of their executives to attract large sums of venture capital (Barner, 2000). Nearly all (95 percent) of financial and industry analysts surveyed by Burston-Marsteller, a global public relations firm, would buy stock based on a CEO's reputation (Poe & Courter, 2000).

It takes cunning leaders to guide delayered, disaggregated organizations through wrenching change and uncertainty (Chambers, Foulon, Handfield-Nones, Hankin, & Michaels, 1998). Complex global markets require not only strong leadership, but also sophisticated skills like cultural fluency, international sensitivity, and technological literacy. The senior leader's job is a lot tougher than it used to be.

Executive Failures

It should be no surprise that many senior leaders are not up to the task. In one study of nearly four hundred of the Fortune 1000 companies, 47 percent of executives and managers rated their company's overall leadership capacity as fair or poor; only 8 percent rated it excellent (Csoka, 1998).

This lack of confidence increasingly begets action. The long-running bull market has raised shareholder expectations for high stock prices. And when shareholders bark, boards of directors bite. CEOs are resigning, retiring, or getting fired at a record pace; in late 1999 they exited at an average of three per business day (Jones, 2000).

The costs of these failures are stunning. Although Mattel Inc.'s shares fell 55 percent during the tenure of CEO Jill Barad, she left with $50 million in severance pay ("Severance Package," 2000). After fourteen months as president of Walt Disney Co., Michael Ovitz walked away with an estimated $90 million severance package, and only nine months after becoming AT&T president, John Walter went with $26 million. Turnover of a senior executive within four years typically costs $1 million to $10 million. These costs do not include decreased productivity, lost opportunities, or the insider knowledge that leaves with departing employees (Andersson, 1999).

Coming Shortage of Leaders

The routine failure of executives is just one factor escalating the demand for effective senior leaders. Over the next fifteen years, executive positions will expand by about one-third, assuming an economic growth rate of 2 percent. On top of that, one-fifth of current top managers expect to vacate their posts in the next five years for retirement or other reasons.

Unfortunately, supply is moving in the opposite direction from demand. The traditional executive talent pool of those thirty-five to forty-four years old will fall 15 percent between 2000 and 2015. And not all of them will be up to the challenge of leadership. Although business schools have been churning out high numbers of business analysts since the 1980s, they have a more questionable record in producing leaders (Crainer & Dearlove, 1999; Howard, 1986).

Old economy organizations, accustomed to ample managerial talent pining for a larger office, now find themselves coming up short. Armies of middle managers were swept away in recent waves of downsizing, and the remaining cadres have recast themselves as job market mercenaries. Ten years ago, a high performer changed employers once or twice during a career; today the average executive is expected to work in five companies, and within a decade it could be seven (Chambers et al., 1998). Small and midsize companies, especially start-ups, are intensifying job mobility by poaching on large firms with lucrative offers for talented managers.

"Companies are about to be engaged in a war for senior executive talent that will remain a defining characteristic of their competitive landscape for decades to come. Yet most are ill-prepared, and even the best are vulnerable. . . . Executive talent has been the most undermanaged corporate asset for the past two decades" (Chambers et al., 1998, pp. 46, 48).

What Should Organizations Look For?

An organization's quest for effective senior leaders is doomed unless it clearly identifies what it needs. This clarification should begin with an understanding of how leaders' roles are evolving.

Work Roles: Changes over Time

Two types of leadership positions prevailed at the turn of the twentieth century. At the lower level were foremen, who had unchecked power to hire, order about, punish, and fire the production workers they supervised. There were few personnel departments to moderate the foremen's tyrannical drive system, and except for the railroad industry, middle management was relatively undeveloped (Eilbert, 1959; Jacoby, 1985). Senior leaders were primarily entrepreneurs intent on developing their businesses. Often aggressive and ruthless, they kept tight control over their companies' financial aspects (Livesay, 1979; Newcomer, 1955).

By midcentury, corporations were more firmly established with less concentrated financial control. Strong unions, extensive government regulations, and changed public opinion constricted the power of organizations and their leaders (Newcomer, 1955). Most managers across the corporate hierarchy were now career professionals. The chief executive performed a "management" job of coordinating the firm's activities and approving decisions that flowed up from subordinates—but did less initiating action and risk taking (Gordon, 1945).

The static, bureaucratic model of midcentury management began to churn during the 1970s and 1980s. Managers' work, rather than being formal and structured, encompassed brief, varying, and discontinuous activities (Mintzberg, 1975). Scholars embarked on distinguishing the (somewhat maligned) manager from the (somewhat glorified) leader (Bennis & Nanus, 1985; Zaleznik, 1977). Managers performed administrative functions, such as planning, organizing, and implementing activities and procedures; leaders identified shifts in the environment, developed a vision and strategy for the organization, and pulled it in new directions through inspirational, transformational techniques.

Managerial work roles have continued to shift in the direction of leading and working with people, and leadership competencies have proliferated. Empowering leadership goes well beyond delegation to taking on roles like visionary, change agent, inspirer, trust enhancing model, coach, team builder, supporter, champion, facilitator, and partner (Howard & Wellins, 1994).

Older competencies are not gone, just overshadowed as new skills and qualities emerge. Because managers now perform in a broadened arena of customers, suppliers, consultants, distributors, and other collaborators—often global in reach—they must network, build partnerships, and develop global acumen. The need for horizontal influence in matrix management structures requires managers to assume navigator and mobilizer roles. Leaders charged with implementing reorganizations and downsizing call on personal qualities like resourcefulness, high commitment, and trustworthiness. To cope with changing and complex work, leaders need competencies like continuous learning, openness to change, adaptability, and resilience.

Work Roles: Lower-Level Versus Senior Leaders

As positions move higher in the organizational hierarchy, there is a corresponding increase in the scope and scale of responsibility.

That is, higher-level positions embrace more units (scope) and have greater complexity, diversity, and ambiguity (scale).

Leadership competencies at all organizational levels tend to cluster within the same overarching domains. These include leading others, interacting effectively with others, decision-making and administrative skills, personal characteristics, technical or professional knowledge and skills, and motivational fit. Within these domains, competencies vary in content, scope, and scale by management level, even if they retain the same label. All managers are decision makers, for example, but lower-level supervisors make decisions about carrying out functional work, while middle- or higher-level leaders are concerned with operational decisions for a functional division. Senior leaders' decisions are far more strategic and cover an entire business or a relatively independent business unit. Jacobs and McGee in Chapter Two in this book describe more finely graduated differences by hierarchical level.

Interactive skills vary by level in a parallel way. For instance, lower-level leaders need to build relationships with people outside their work team where interdependent structures and processes affect work accomplishment. The leader's role expands to building partnerships when transactions are needed between teams or major areas in the organization. At still higher levels, leaders must build strategic alliances and networks across business sectors or between the organization and external groups.

Senior Leader Competencies

Table 10.1 illustrates how some representative senior leader competencies map onto the leadership imperatives defined for this book.

Some writers argue that interpersonal competencies predominate in determining executive success and failure. They note that top managers have failed because of their inability to work in teams, political insensitivity, avoidance of conflict, abrasiveness, or cracks in integrity, such as not treating people fairly. Organizations are becoming more attuned to leaders' character, including integrity, honesty, an internalized sense of right and wrong, and the willpower to act on one's principles even though it might be costly, risky, or unpleasant (Sperry, 1999). Proponents claim that emotional intelligence (self-awareness, self-regulation, motivation,

**Table 10.1. Leadership Imperatives
and Representative Competencies.**

Imperative	Issues	Representative Competencies
Cognitive	Complex information processing Organizational sense making	Strategic decision making Establishing strategic direction Global business acumen
Social	Coordinating multiple units Implementing organization change Developing large networks	Change leadership Visionary leadership Building organization relationship Communication
Personal	Managing career and reputation Reflecting personal values	Executive disposition Valuing diversity Building trust
Political	Building coalitions Persuading Resolving conflicts	Building business partnerships Sales ability, persuasiveness Managing conflict
Technological	Using technology in systems Considering technology in strategies	Technical and professional knowledge Information monitoring
Financial	Strategic and short-term gains	Financial acumen Marketing and entrepreneurial insight
Staffing	Building future leaders	Attracting and developing talent

empathy, and social skills) carries considerably more weight in excellent performance than intellect and expertise (Goleman, 1998).

Yet research has demonstrated that there are many ways that executives and managers derail. Among the most prominent are difficulty in molding a staff, difficulty in making strategic transitions, lack of follow-through, poor treatment of others, overdependency, and disagreements with higher management about how the business should be run or about strategy (Lombardo & Mc-Cauley, 1988). When researchers compared the rated importance of existing and future competencies, the biggest gaps were in global understanding, visionary leadership, marketing and entrepreneurial insight, strategic decision making, aligning performance for success, empowering leadership, and innovation (Bernthal, Rioux, & Wellins, 1999). Both of these studies suggest that all major domains of executive competencies are critical.

Methods for Developing Competency Models

When developing competency models, analysts use two approaches: job driven and strategy driven.

Job-Driven Competency Modeling

Job-driven competency modeling, or traditional job analysis, specifies tasks, duties, and responsibilities of particular jobs. It assumes that people, jobs, and the match between them are stable over time. Even where job analyses are oriented toward the future, their underlying assumption is that change is predictable.

Job-driven competency modeling can be differentiated into behavioral and clinical methods. The behavioral approach defines competencies as job-relevant behavior, motivation, or knowledge and skills. Analysts ask incumbents about what they do and have superiors describe critical incidents showing good and poor job performance. Job experts confirm the initial analysis by rating and ranking the competencies and indicating the percentage of the job they cover (Byham & Moyer, 1996).

The clinical approach defines competencies as underlying personal characteristics of superior performers. Each characteristic incorporates motivation, which is not treated separately. Top performers undergo behavioral event interviews, where they are asked to give examples or critical incidents that exemplify the keys to their success (Spencer & Spencer, 1993). The clinical approach compares superior to competent performance and seeks deeper personal constructs; the behavioral approach focuses on observable behaviors and captures the entire performance range (Byham & Moyer, 1996).

Strategy-Driven Competency Modeling

Professionals use organizational strategy to supplement job information in the strategy-driven approach to competency modeling. Business analysts proposed this approach after observing that goals rather than procedures drive performance as environmental uncertainty increases. Broad role definitions rather than narrow job descriptions can better capture the more changeable strategic requirements of the company (Gerstein & Reisman, 1983). Strategic competency modeling and staffing began in the early 1980s and mostly focused on higher management levels. For example, organizations tailored requirements for a general manager to where the business was in its life cycle (for example, growing or mature). The search for a better fit between strategy and staffing was later extended below the general manager level (Snow & Snell, 1992).

Organizations use the strategy-driven approach when they identify core competencies that apply across a band of jobs or even the entire organization (Byham & Moyer, 1996). They combine the core competencies with specific job competencies to determine the requirements for a selection decision. Companies often base their core competencies on the firm's cultural values. These value-based competencies have strong motivating power and can provide direction and continuity over extended periods of time. However, organizations often neglect to define behaviors correlated with the values, rendering the competencies limp and imprecise (Briscoe & Hall, 1999).

Regardless of how they were developed, competencies that lack conceptual and definitional clarity can create more confusion than guidance. Strategy-driven and values-based competency models are particularly susceptible to a failure of methodological rigor. Analysts often generate them from convenience samples and neglect to obtain expert confirmation or quantitative data. Moreover, they frequently do not connect these competencies to actual work or provide a basis on which to establish content validity.

A role-based approach to competency modeling provides more breadth than job-driven analyses without necessarily sacrificing rigor. Organizational experts identify roles that incumbents in a target job or job family must carry out to support the organization's strategy, values, and desired business results. Examples of roles include entrepreneur, project manager, turnaround specialist, and policy advocate. Each role links to competencies that specify how to enact that role effectively. Competencies needed for a policy advocate role, for instance, might include a global perspective, strategic thinking, communication skills, business acumen, and executive presence. The organizational expert reviews, augments, and then confirms the linked competencies as in traditional job analysis. Roles thus provide an organizing structure for well-grounded competencies. Role-based competency modeling provides greater adaptability, clearer business understanding, and more direct links to organizational strategy than the traditional job-driven approach.

Where Do Organizations Look for Senior Leaders?

After organizations define the type of senior leaders they need, their next task is to determine where best to search for candidates.

Sourcing: Changes over Time

In 1900, two of five CEOs were the first president or board chairman of their companies. When they needed other organizational managers or a successor, they typically turned first to their relatives and next to friends. If forced to rely on strangers, an entrepreneur sought to find people he could trust—most often people like him. Mentor-protégé relationships, such as that between Andrew Carnegie and Charles Schwab, proliferated as the scale of business enterprises expanded (Livesay, 1979).

By 1950, founders made up only one in twenty-five top executives. To fill the management ranks, companies looked among the year's college graduates for talented young men to begin their professional careers at the bottom of the organization (Newcomer, 1955). The new college recruits, though supplementing a much larger group of up-from-the-ranks supervisors, became the primary pool for future middle- and higher-level leaders (Howard & Bray, 1988). The source of higher-level managers was nearly always internal, and the eligible candidates nearly always white males.

Companies recruited external candidates in a long, slow process of visiting college campuses, advertising in newspapers, and sifting through referrals from employment agencies and personal contacts. With the arrival of the computer age, human resource staff saved time by screening résumés with keyword searches. As the Internet became popular, companies used job boards and Web sites to advertise open positions, which candidates applied for by sending their résumés electronically.

Today's emerging technology and tight labor market have incited a stampede to electronic recruiting. Most of the jobs advertised on the Web are professional and managerial. The top ten Internet job search sites attracted 17.4 million users in March 2000, up from 8.9 million a year earlier (McClain, 2000). More than fifty-two hundred entities operate Web sites that charge a fee per posting or job advertisement. Their projected annual growth is 25 percent (Interbusiness Network, 2000).

Job boards were a notable improvement over newspaper classified ads in terms of timeliness, reach, and cost. But both employers and job seekers are already growing dissatisfied with them. Job boards like CareerMosaic and Monster.com are picked over and require companies to take fast action to beat the competition. Moreover, job boards do not surface passive candidates—those who are employed and not actively seeking a job change (Boehle, 2000).

Search firms and high-growth companies unearth passive candidates on the Internet using competitive intelligence techniques. They sift through directories, databases, archives, and public Web servers and use meta-search engines to scan for hidden résumés. In the tactic called flip searching, users invade private areas of an employer's Web site and reach links to employee home pages, staff directories, biographies, contact information, and organization charts. Recruiters also lurk in Internet chat rooms, newsgroups, and forums to identify participants with substantive expertise and apparent job dissatisfaction (Barner, 2000; Boehle, 2000).

Many large companies with massive hiring needs find it cost prohibitive to outsource the recruiting function. Over one-third of companies with more than ten thousand employees surveyed by Recruiters Network dedicate at least one human resource staff member solely to Internet recruiting (Boehle, 2000). Corporations also use their own Web sites to lure candidates into employment. In 1999, nearly half (48 percent) of companies' Web sites contained recruitment information, up from 22 percent in 1998 (Interbusiness Network, 2000).

Web screening programs accomplish additional staffing tasks online, which benefits both candidates and employing organizations. To attract talent, the Web site can air a realistic job or organization preview and establish the organization's brand image. It can collect answers from candidates about basic qualifying requirements, experience and accomplishments, or motivations and then match these against the requirements of target jobs. The program can provide customized feedback along the way to encourage the best candidates to continue. After rating and ranking candidates, the site can schedule the best ones for personal follow-up by the company. Web screens reduce staffing costs, but more important in a competitive marketplace, they quickly converge on the most qualified candidates and hustle them off the market.

Sourcing: Lower-Level Versus Senior Leaders

Companies fill most leadership vacancies with internal candidates. According to a recent study, companies more often look internally for front-line management (78 percent) than midlevel management (70 percent) or upper management (63 percent) (Bernthal et al., 1999). Nevertheless, they primarily reserve formal succession plans for higher-level managers. Eighty percent of organizations in another study used their formal succession plans for the top three positions and 85 percent for the multidepartment or multifunction level. Only 53 percent used them at the department, function, or project manager level and only 16 percent for first-level supervisors or team leaders (Rioux & Bernthal, 1999).

Sourcing of external candidates varies sharply by management level. Companies broadcast lower-level job openings widely to generate a large number of applicants. Today that means that candidate and company are likely to meet on the Web. Searching for executives is more strategic, and the organization is likely to lure passive candidates from competitors (Snow & Snell, 1992). The majority (64 percent) of seventy-four hundred recently surveyed executives found their positions by networking. Only 4 percent found jobs using the Internet, 12 percent through search firms, and 11 percent from classified advertising (McClain, 2000).

Should Organizations Look Inside or Outside for Executives?

A pressing question for organizations, especially during changing times, is whether to look internally for a promotable candidate or search outside. Studies consistently show that firms are more likely to recruit a top executive from the outside in an emergency—when the company is either performing poorly or growing rapidly (Datta & Guthrie, 1994; Lauterbach, Vu, & Weisberg, 1999; Puffer & Weintrop, 1995). Outsider successions are also more frequent in firms with greater structural authority at the top, as when the roles of CEO and chair of the board are combined—a sign, perhaps, that external successors seek more power when they change firms. Larger companies are more likely to have internal CEO successions, presumably because they can develop management talent inside the firm (Lauterbach et al., 1999).

Internal successions have a number of advantages. Organizations that promote from within generate loyalty and boost morale. They ensure continuity and capitalize on insiders' knowledge of the firm and established social networks. They also save money; starting compensation is typically less for an insider than an outsider, pursuing outside candidates takes time and effort, and executive search firms are costly.

External successors, on the other hand, bring to the company different sets of skills, unique experiences, fresh ideas, and new perspectives. Outsiders are not bound to the firm's policies, traditions, and practices. They can be more objective when evaluating people and scrutinizing projects. These advantages explain why firms turn to external successors when they are in trouble and need drastic changes. Young and fast-growing organizations also benefit from outsiders' knowledge of new technologies and markets.

Organizations can benefit from recruiting senior leaders from both internal and external sources, varying the ratio according to the firm's circumstances. General Electric, which is known for its successful internal management development, routinely fills up to one-quarter of its senior openings with outsiders to calibrate its existing talent and raise the bar (Chambers et al., 1998). Some evidence even suggests that pools comprising both internal and external candidates for the same position are more successful than pools filled by one source alone (Sessa, Kaiser, Taylor, & Campbell, 1998).

External Executive Recruiting

Companies often call on executive search firms to recruit external managers. These firms' search techniques have evolved over four generations. Search consultants initially relied on personal contacts within exclusive networks (the old boys' network). They later supplemented these methods with published secondary sources and circulation lists of select companies and alumni. Most modern search firms use third-generation research. They cross-check sources in various published and online directories, telephone existing contacts, and make cold calls (Schoyen & Rasmussen, 1999). Some recruiters also engage in notorious trade practices like black market purchases and sales of employee directories. Another tactic is rusing: the recruiter calls a company pretending to be someone else in order to glean information about employees (Boehle, 2000). Fourth-generation executive search techniques are strongly technology driven and include Web searching processes. With electronic tools, recruiters can search faster and cover a broader market.

Electronic recruiting is pitting traditional search firms against upstart Web-based companies, which are extending their reach to executives at the six-figure income level. Some job boards have hired executive recruiters to help them expand this business, and major search firms have launched their own Internet ventures. Executive search firms and Internet career sites could eventually merge to form one-stop hiring agencies offering integrated services—from job analysis through recruiting, screening, assessment, and matching candidates to organizational positions (Barner, 2000). Such agencies would make deep inroads into areas where I/O psychologists have staked a claim.

Internal human resource departments also use the Internet to recruit executives. For example, Motorola recently advertised on the Web for over thirty executive positions at the director level and above (Barner, 2000). Companies are tempted to bypass executive search firms because of their cost; recruiters typically get one-third of a placed executive's first-year cash compensation, plus expenses associated with the search (Colvin & Sellers, 2000; Schoyen & Rasmussen, 1999).

In their hunger for executives, Internet start-up companies are particularly aggressive recruiters. Once venture capitalists hire their CEO, they expect that person to continue the hunt just as fiercely. The CEOs have rewarded good leads handsomely, with Palm Pilots, cash, and even cars (Leonhardt, 2000). The war for talent has also increased the value of executives' compensation packages as well as their complexity and personalization (Colvin & Sellers, 2000).

Internal Executive Recruiting

Internal executive recruiting is often linked to succession planning programs. Companies traditionally instituted formal succession plans in order to target necessary training and development, increase opportunities for high-potential workers, and increase the talent pool of promotable employees (Rothwell, 1994). The fast-paced new economy has created even more potent incentives. Managers surveyed by Development Dimensions International (DDI) cited improving business results, expansion and growth, and new skill requirements to satisfy business demands as the primary challenges driving the need for a good succession management system (Rioux & Bernthal, 1999).

Despite these pressures, the number of succession planning systems has apparently not grown over the past fifteen years (Bernthal et al., 1999). Only 61 percent of companies surveyed by DDI had a formal succession plan in place (Rioux & Bernthal, 1999). However, among those that did have a formal plan, 75 percent had been using it for five or fewer years, which suggests that succession management practices are changing.

Traditional replacement planning depended on a stable organizational structure, fixed jobs, and progressive vertical movement, conditions that are rapidly disappearing with the accelerated pace of change. Today detailed replacement charts are overly rigid and long-term stair-step career plans unrealistic. Only at the very top of the organization is there real payoff for defining specific people as backups. Proposed as an alternative are talent or acceleration pools that assume a fluid organizational structure, expect jobs to change, and use both horizontal and vertical movements as development opportunities (Byham, Smith, & Paese, in press).

A modern succession management system encompasses the following basic steps (Buckner & Savenski, 1994; Byham, 1999):

1. Determine the organization's needs, including its projected leadership shortage and important executive competencies.
2. Identify high-potential individuals for possible inclusion in a succession pool.
3. Assess candidates to identify strengths and skill gaps, and determine which individuals to include in the pool.
4. Tailor a development program for each individual that includes training, job rotation, special assignments, and other experiences.
5. Select and place people into senior jobs based on matching their performance, experience, and assessed potential against a specific job opening.
6. Continuously monitor the system.

The success of the system depends on how these steps are executed. Progressive succession management programs have the following characteristics (Axel, 1994; Beeson, 2000; Buckner & Savenski, 1994; Eastman, 1995; National Academy of Public Administration, 1992; Rioux & Bernthal, 1999):

- *Simplicity.* Excessive paperwork and procedures were the downfall of past succession planning activities. New systems avoid lengthy, paper-intensive reviews.
- *Executive ownership.* The CEO and senior management show visible support for and commitment to the system, including dedicating a significant portion of their time to it and holding executives accountable for it.
- *Partnerships.* Line managers and human resource staff are partners in the process.
- *Objective criteria.* Companies devote time to defining the values and behaviors required for leaders' success and establish meaningful, objective criteria for evaluating leadership skills and capabilities.
- *Rigorous assessment.* Organizations use formal assessment methods, such as an assessment center, to identify succession candidates and curb the role of subjective and anecdotal evaluations.
- *Focused development.* Scarce developmental resources are reserved for individuals possessing the greatest career potential.

The organization creates, with the employee's participation, a planned sequence of stretch assignments, mentoring, and other activities to build new skills and abilities.

* *Open communications.* Succession planning's traditional aura of secrecy is now seen as an impediment to keeping high-potential candidates motivated and loyal. Employees are fully informed of succession procedures and available development opportunities. Some companies also incorporate frequent conversations about career potential.

* *Linkages.* Succession planning is tightly linked to strategic staffing and other human resource systems, such as training, diversity programs, and reward and recognition systems.

* *Success measurements.* Organizations measure the effectiveness of the succession planning system with data like the percentage of candidates in the pool who are selected for key positions and retained by the company and the kinds of business results that selected candidates achieve. Qualitative information about the high-potential candidate, as from attitude surveys and exit interviews, can augment the quantitative measures.

Assessing Potential Senior Leaders

Once organizations find candidates for senior leadership positions, they need to size them up—to determine their strengths and development needs. I/O psychologists have traditionally worked most comfortably in this phase of the selection process, although usually with candidates for lower-level positions.

Assessment: Changes over Time

It wasn't until after World War II that companies routinely used psychological tests to select managers, by then considered professionals. Personality and aptitude testing became widespread, but both eventually drew public criticism. Some writers assailed personality inventories in the mid-1950s for creating organizations of "yes men" (Whyte, 1956). Because validity evidence was scant, I/O psychologists neglected these tests until their resurgence in the late twentieth century.

Aptitude tests met with pervasive criticism in the 1970s on the grounds that they discriminated against groups protected by the Civil Rights Act of 1964. As a result, psychologists put increased emphasis on validation and job relatedness and searched for substitute measures of thinking and reasoning. Aptitude testing was, however, a good fit to selection systems in the old economy. The highest scorers were the best performers on structured jobs, and mechanical scoring methods eliminated subjectivity.

Aptitude-testing approaches are less satisfactory in the more fluid and dynamic new economy. Organizations want to select people who are compatible with each other, meet strategy requirements, and fit into the organizational culture. Such selection decisions engender deliberation and negotiation among managers. As organizations moved toward strategic staffing, they veered away from paper-and-pencil tests and toward assessment centers, where managers can observe interpersonal dynamics and have an opportunity to debate which candidate to select (Snow & Snell, 1993).

AT&T initiated the first management assessment center in mid-century, but only a few other large firms adopted it until the 1970s, when consulting companies began to market simulation materials and assessment techniques. In these early implementations, trained corporate managers administered the centers and served as assessors. Today organizations increasingly outsource the assessment center to consulting firms, which employ professional assessors. This practice increases both objectivity and reliability as assessors hone their skills through experience and come to a common understanding of standards. On the other hand, assessors unacquainted with the host organization lack a sense of job relevance. Modern assessment centers are also more likely to comprise "day-in-the-life" or integrated sets of simulations. This more realistic type of design can mimic an executive's hectic day of moving quickly from one task to another.

Companies are now turning to computerized and Web-based technologies to streamline the assessment process. Here testing is a more natural fit; the computer can quickly and accurately score right and wrong answers. Computerization is less useful for many assessment center simulations, which need an actual assessor to judge the nuances of human behavior. Some organizations try to compromise with video-based job scenarios or situational challenges; the video freezes at designated places and asks participants what they would do next. Where potential answers are in a multiple-choice format, this approach is more akin to testing (eliciting a structured, hypothetical response) than simulation (requiring a live behavioral response).

Even where scoring requires human intervention, technology can streamline assessment by automating many peripheral procedures. For example, candidates can electronically provide biographical information, do simulation prework, get an orientation to the assessment program, receive assessment reports, and track their progress in the selection funnel.

Assessment: Lower-Level Versus Senior Leaders

Managerial selection methods, including the assessment center, have historically concentrated on those in lower and middle management. Michigan Bell established the first operational assessment center in 1958 to evaluate rank-and-file candidates for first-line supervisor positions. Three years later Southern Bell adopted an assessment center to evaluate the executive potential of upper-middle managers, but other corporations seldom followed this practice.

This is not to say that assessment at lower levels is unrelated to later success as an executive. Assessors' original predictions in the AT&T Management Progress Study correlated highly with managerial advancement twenty years later. However, assessors' evaluations of the same participants eight years after their first assessment showed stronger relationships with advancement because of the additional managerial experience and development they had accrued in the interim (Howard & Bray, 1988). In the interest of both fairness and accuracy, a better practice is to assess senior-level candidates close in time to their potential appointment with measures designed to elicit behavior required at the target level.

Executive-level candidates infrequently undergo tests and simulations, despite these methods' demonstrated validity. In 1990, fewer than 5 percent of assessment center users applied the method to select the CEO (Bentson, Gaugler, & Pohley, 1990), although that proportion appears to be growing (Dobrzynski, 1996; Silzer & Slider, 1994). Table 10.2 shows the kinds of data that com-

Table 10.2. Data Sources Used to Evaluate Succession Candidates.

Source	Not at All (Percentage)	Somewhat (Percentage)	Very Much (Percentage)
Recommendations	3	34	63
Performance reviews	5	37	58
Interviews	21	44	35
Analysis of work samples or outputs	28	47	25
360-degree assessments	33	47	20
Personality or psychological testing and assessment	61	27	12
Simulations or role plays (including the assessment center method)	76	19	5
Paper-and-pencil testing (for example, intelligence)	76	17	7

Source: Rioux & Bernthal, 1999. Used with permission.

panies used to evaluate succession pool candidates, most of whom were being considered for senior positions. One-quarter of the respondents made some use of tests and simulations, but the remaining three-quarters ignored them (Rioux & Bernthal, 1999). The most popular techniques were those most lacking in rigor: recommendations and performance reviews.

Some psychologists have argued that traditional selection methods do not apply to positions at the top of the organization. De Vries (1993) dismissed assessment centers as too cumbersome, expensive, and intrusive for executive selection, although the high cost of executive failure today suggest that the benefits of sound selection should far outweigh the cost. Executive selection calls for an in-depth comparison of a few candidates, not evaluation of the masses. The CEO in particular has a one-of-a-kind job. Companies should assess potential CEO successors, it is claimed, by evaluating the fit between the candidate and the company's culture, history, future prospects, and other senior executives. Organizations can assume that candidates have sufficient skill and experience; it is how executives employ this skill and experience that makes the difference (RHR International, 1991).

Yet the complex new demands on executives and their high rate of failure suggest that companies that assume candidates' skills and experience are always up to the job are mistaken. Nonetheless, CEOs can have the vanity of the gods, even when they cannot deliver the goods. Companies are consequently more likely to accept formal assessment if it is placed further down in the senior leadership hierarchy than the CEO.

Techniques for Assessing Executives

Rigorous assessment, deemed essential to succession management programs, requires multiple measures and methods to capture the range and complexity of senior leader positions. These techniques can extract and exploit evidence pertaining to the past, present, and future. Biographical data, performance evaluations, references, and behavior-based interviews summarize past behavior, assuming it will forecast future behavior. Cognitive tests and personality inventories represent existing capacity and inclination; their contribution rests more in identifying what underlies an individual's approach to tasks or assignments. Situational interviews and simulations make projections about the future—that is, how the person is likely to approach a new situation. Future measures are essential when a new position will differ significantly from one tackled in the past.

Biographical Data

Biographical information serves as an important early screen for knowledge and experiences that prepare the person for a particular position. Unfortunately, the prevalence of résumé inflation, reported by more than one-quarter of executives and human resource specialists surveyed by the Ward Howell executive search firm, diminishes the value of biodata. Most survey respondents (62 percent) cited misrepresentation of academic credentials, and more than 40 percent found falsification in compensation history and previous position responsibilities (Schoyen & Rasmussen, 1999).

Internal candidates' biographical data should be considerably more accurate, at least for experiences in the current organization.

Performance Evaluations

Traditional performance appraisals, particularly when tied to salary increases, are often bloated. Even when appraisals do not overrate performance, they are weak tools for comparing candidates if standards are not precisely defined and raters not specifically trained.

The multiperspective, multirater, or 360-degree feedback approach gathers information from colleagues, supervisors, direct reports, and sometimes customers and suppliers. Because ratings by others are usually compared to self-ratings, individuals can gain considerable insight and motivation to develop and change. But multirater methods are not particularly useful for selection. They can easily devolve into popularity contests, deliver damaging and blunt messages, and be corrupted by people who solicit biased ratings to take unfair advantage of the system. Multirater methods also show low levels of interrater agreement and are subject to considerable halo because raters are usually poorly trained, if at all (Howard, Byham, & Hauenstein, 1994).

A live 360-degree assessment can introduce more rigor. This way, an executive coach or other trained, objective evaluator collects performance information by interviewing a broad range of observers. For example, General Electric uses an accomplishment analysis as a concentrated way to gather performance data for its management development system. A consultant interviews the manager for several hours, meets with the manager's boss for several more hours, and interviews former associates and subordinates. The consultant summarizes the individual's achievements and development plans and makes them part of the manager's file (Friedman & Le Vino, 1984).

References

All too often references, especially those provided by external candidates, have limited value. Former or current bosses and colleagues usually praise generously and criticize sparingly. After all, their personal interest lies in protecting their relationship with the candidate, not in helping an organization make a good hiring decision. Respondents' fears of legal repercussions also bury any inclinations to provide specific reference information. Only 19 percent of over eight hundred executives surveyed by the Society of Human Resource Management would reveal to reference seekers why a candidate left their company, and only 13 percent would describe the candidate's work habits (Fernandez-Araoz, 1999).

When filling key positions, companies often rely on executive search firms' interviewing skills to conduct reference checks. These interviews can be extensive, at least in quantity. When Campbell Soup chose a successor for its CEO in 1996, for example, the search firm conducted twenty-eight reference checks on the two outside finalists (Byrne, Reingold, & Melcher, 1997). Executive-level reference checks can include an online news search to see whether the person has been mentioned in the media and in what light (Schoyen & Rasmussen, 1999).

Interviews

Most hiring procedures include an interview. Like résumés, interviews can yield an inflated picture of candidates, who seek to put their best selves forward. The most productive interviews use prepared questions designed to reveal the candidate's competencies.

Behavior-based interviewers evaluate past experiences by asking candidates to describe critical incidents or behavioral examples that illustrate specific competencies of interest. Where contenders have little or no experience to draw on relative to a competency, behavioral interviewing is much less fruitful. Situational interviewers present applicants with hypothetical situations and ask them to describe how they would react. This approach can illuminate candidates' understanding of the important issues, although not their actual behavior.

Cognitive Tests

Cognitive ability tests are well established as strong predictors of success on most jobs, and they are more predictive for complex jobs than simpler ones. They measure an individual's ability to process information and solve problems, although they do not indicate how an executive will approach complex managerial situations. Tests of tacit knowledge have some potential for getting at more practical decision making. Ability tests pose a problem for feedback and development planning because they offer no avenue for improving a low score.

Personality Measures

Personality traits often correlate modestly with job performance, but inventories do not predict criteria in the straightforward fashion of a cognitive test. Results vary by type of job, current situation, type of criterion being predicted, and other factors. Perhaps the best predictions arise from assembling compound personality variables that maximally predict predetermined criteria (Hough & Schneider, 1996).

Projective tests, such as ambiguous pictures or incomplete sentences blanks, can also be useful for understanding executives' motivation. However, scoring these measures requires expert psychological judgment, which is expensive and time-consuming.

Personality measures can provide insights into what lies behind a candidate's observed behavior and help guide his or her development. Organizations should include measures that identify not only positive traits like sociability and ambition, but also potential derailment factors such as arrogance, volatility, or perfectionism. An old saw in the executive search business is that an executive is hired on experience and fired on personality (Fernandez-Araoz, 1999). Candidates given personality-related feedback can learn to leverage their positive qualities and avoid behaviors that erupt from their derailing characteristics (Byham et al., in press).

Simulations

Simulations recreate situations that executives are likely to encounter and provide opportunities for them to exhibit behavior related to specific competencies. Assessors observe and interpret the success of the candidate's pattern of behavior. Designers can customize simulations to reflect the complexities and nuances of various executive challenges.

Executive-level simulations include strategic planning and decision-making exercises, role plays, visioning exercises, marketing challenges, in-basket exercises, media interviews, business games, and group discussions. Candidates can face a myriad of social and political challenges, such as unionization threats, arm twisting by government officials, and sexual harassment lawsuits. Strategic exercises might include in-depth analyses or discussions around business ventures or turnarounds.

Computer-based exercises, still relatively undeveloped, can enrich simulations of complex problem solving and administrative tasks. Designers can include masses of variables and bits of information that raise the complexity of an exercise. Software can track assessees' movements and strategies, such as their willingness to take risks, readiness to explore and experiment, and use of aids and information (Laib, 1993). Computers can also administer in-basket exercises, including voice mail and e-mail exchanges, although scoring requires human judgment.

Role plays by videoconference should become more common as broadband Internet connections proliferate. Computer technology is not yet advanced enough for automated role plays, which would require better voice recognition systems, high-powered interpretive protocols, and extensive branching and storage capabilities (Howard, 1997).

Simulations have many benefits for assessment, including face validity, candidate acceptance, and an inherent plasticity, which lets designers mold them to diverse situations and competencies (Howard, 1997). In addition, they are less susceptible to cross-cultural bias than paper-and-pencil tests are.

Applying Assessment Methods: Who Assesses and How

Each major group of professionals involved in assessing leaders has its own favorite set of assessment tools.

Executive Search Firms

Executive search firms usually meet with clients to develop a position specification, identify and prescreen potential prospects, interview and screen candidates in person, and check references (Schoyen & Rasmussen, 1999). Skilled search consultants form a bond of trust with the candidate, which is one reason they shun impersonal selection techniques that might distance them from prospects. Search firms build a communications bridge between the candidate and the organizational client to prevent misunderstandings and buffer delicate negotiations on topics like compensation. Sometimes they also educate the corporate client on how to interview, conduct effective reference checks, and overcome candidate inertia (Dieckmann & Associates, 1993).

Executive search firms use a holistic, situation-based approach—in contrast to the typical I/O psychologist's analytic, person-based approach—which better positions them to match a candidate to the job and organization (Tragash, 1992). To evaluate a candidate's fit to an organization's culture, search firms take a personal, somewhat clinical approach using a less structured interview (Clark, 1992).

Psychologists have criticized search firms because of the limits of their evaluation methods and their lack of psychological assessment skills (Levinson, 1994). Critics fault search consultants for being more in the presentation business than the executive selection business; their prime objective is approval by the key decision maker rather than a good fit to the organization. Moreover, the validity of executive search placements is inadequately documented in the public literature (De Vries, 1993).

Individual Assessment

Many organizations employ individual psychological consultants, often from a clinical psychology background, for assistance in executive coaching and selection. A psychologist's assessment of an executive might consist solely of interviews (RHR International, 1991) or include a combination of interviews and psychological instruments.

More than three-fourths of a sample of Society of Industrial and Organizational Psychology (SIOP) members engaged in individual assessments used personal history forms, ability tests, personality inventories, and interviews (Ryan & Sackett, 1987). This group was somewhat more likely to use simulations for managerial selection than a sample of non-I/O psychologists who did not belong to SIOP. Across samples, only a small percentage (28.8 percent) used simulations, primarily role plays and group problem-solving exercises (Ryan & Sackett, 1992).

The survey researchers faulted individual assessment practitioners using some of the same criticisms directed at executive search consultants. The individual assessors generally did not incorporate the more sophisticated selection tools or validate the procedures they used. Nor did they typically follow up on the individuals they assessed. Many also conducted inadequate job analyses (Ryan & Sackett, 1987, 1992).

Assessment Centers

Assessment center methodology requires measurement of competencies established by an acceptable job analysis technique, multiple methods of measurement, and the consensus of multiple assessors. Although simulations are essential to and characteristic of this methodology, assessment centers may also incorporate any of the other measures, such as aptitude tests, personality inventories, projective tests, and interviews.

Assessment centers have a number of advantages. Evidence of their ability to predict performance and potential is well documented in the professional research literature, including several meta-analyses. Observers and assessees usually consider the method fair and job relevant. Because it focuses on behaviors and competencies, an assessment center helps clarify to assessees and others what effective performance should look like. Moreover, assessors' feedback reports provide specific, compelling information that motivates and guides development and change.

Researchers have questioned assessment centers' ability to zero in on competencies, given the repeated finding of strong exercise effects. That is, dimensions within an exercise are more highly intercorrelated than are measures of the same dimension across exercises. Practitioners can partially remedy this problem with sound assessor training grounded in behavioral examples and with exercises that target only a few well-measured dimensions.

Practitioners establish the job relatedness of assessment centers through content validity procedures. Given the many innovations in assessment center design, however, they assume a risk if they neglect criterion-related validation. Modifications of competencies and exercises can potentially undermine predictor-criterion relationships, however well established in the past.

Making the Selection Decision

A proper assessment can provide strong job-related information about a candidate's competencies, but the selection decision ultimately requires human judgment. One or more decision makers must weigh all the information about a candidate against all the presumed characteristics and demands of the particular position.

Selection Decisions: Changes over Time

At the turn of the twentieth century, both the head of the firm and the foreman had full power to make their own selection decisions.

Personnel departments gradually assumed many of the responsibilities for selecting lower- and middle-level leaders. The human resource department became a primary authority in the 1970s, when organizations faced the threat of equal opportunity lawsuits and audits. Some organizations established de facto quotas for minority candidates, which human resource staff enforced until reverse discrimination lawsuits began to redress excesses. Line managers reestablished their hiring decision prerogatives in the late twentieth century with the human resource department as a strategic partner.

The war for talent has disrupted the timetable of many selection decisions. An emerging tactical weapon is just-in-time hiring or presearch, whereby organizations acquire scarce executives on a continual basis. The new employees spend their time in extensive training programs or on temporary project teams until a permanent job opens (Barner, 2000). This practice of warehousing talent can become an issue with capable candidates eager to move their careers forward. Employers also prequalify candidates. That is, they screen and preapprove potential new employees so that they can snatch them when an opening materializes (Barner, 2000).

Selection Decisions: Lower-Level Versus Senior Leaders

Human resource personnel often guide lower- and middle-level line management through the selection process because they understand selection tools and how to use them. Human resource staff might help line managers define the competencies they are looking for and then suggest instruments to measure those competencies. Hiring managers will want to interview candidates to judge their compatibility, and human resource staff can generate structured interview guides that point them toward gathering competency-related behavioral examples. Human resource and line managers might jointly integrate the data about candidates, but the line manager makes the final decision.

The board of directors is legally responsible for senior officer selection and evaluation in public corporations. In practice, the CEO generally manages the selection process and comes to the board for advice and ratification (Hollenbeck, 1994). But boards of directors have become more assertive about succession management as organizations have floundered in the new global economy.

In one of the first cases garnering public attention, the board of General Motors revolted in 1992, forcing the demotion of the president and chairman. The board's action telegraphed that the company's officers were not moving fast enough to vanquish humiliating erosion in market share and financial losses. The GM directors set an example for boards of other poorly performing companies to take the initiative (Treece, 1992).

The Selection Decision Process

Organizations preparing to fill a particular open position (as opposed to stocking a succession pool) should begin by specifying what it requires. The specification should include clarification of the position itself, the expectations of the various constituencies with which the executive must deal, the skills needed to work successfully within the organizational culture, and the extent to which the incumbent must be an agent of change (Andersson, 1999).

The organization must also determine who will make the selection decision. Some research indicates that teams make better decisions than individuals. In fact, group decision making and information sharing is the basic philosophy of the assessment center integration session. A group of decision makers provides a broader range of information, corrects for individual biases, and broadens buy-in for the ultimate choice. To make the process work, team members must be candid, listen attentively to others' information, and set aside any individual political agendas (Sessa & Taylor, 1999).

Candidates' source—internal or external—predetermines the type of information used to decide their fate. Consequently, comparing candidates from different sources is difficult and probably unfair. Information gathered on external candidates is likely to tip toward the positive side because of search firms' use of résumés, interviews, and references, all of which the candidate can partially control. Information on internal candidates tends to be more balanced, with pluses and minuses from performance appraisals and succession plans as well as informal data from meetings, personal interactions, and formal presentations. Thus, when internal and external candidates are competing for the same position, the external candidates are likely to appear more favorable.

A selection decision does not ensure that a candidate is hired, particularly when talent is scarce. The organization must sell the candidate on the position, which can be a competitive challenge. The company needs to understand the candidate's primary motives and fears and heed them in its offer, without making promises that it cannot deliver (Fernandez-Araoz, 1999).

To land a desired candidate, the organization needs to change its mind-set from selective buyer to persuasive seller. This can be a surprisingly daunting task. The organization must root out arrogance and presumptiveness. It must also cut through bureaucratic red tape and make an offer quickly before a competitors sweeps the candidate off the market.

Selecting the CEO

Selection of a CEO has been so shrouded in secrecy that it has conjured up images of the election of a pope. There is now a move underfoot to make the process more transparent. Since the new economy has sharply magnified the impact of a succession, business reporters, Wall Street analysts, and institutional investors with stakes in the firm's success are scrutinizing new appointments (Lorsch & Khurana, 1999).

Ironically, as important as CEO selection is, the decision makers are novices. The CEO determines his or her successor only once, and directors are unlikely to have expertise in personnel selection methods. However, this does not imply that those responsible make decisions quickly or without a great deal of thought (Hollenbeck, 1994).

The much-publicized selection in 1999 of a new CEO of Hewlett-Packard (HP) exemplifies both a thorough, deliberate strategy and a more visible procedure. The conservative HP was trying to catch up to its explosive industry. After an exhaustive job specification process, the board identified four prime attributes for its CEO: ability to conceptualize and communicate sweeping strategies, the operations savvy to deliver on quarterly financial goals, the power to bring a sense of urgency to the organization, and the skill to drive a vision for the company. Board members interviewed three hundred people from inside and outside the company before narrowing the field to four. They ultimately chose Carly Fiorina, who met their criteria but had no experience in the computer industry. Time will tell whether their decision-making process produced the desired results (Lear, 1999).

Diversity Issues

Despite much talk that women and minority groups are breaking the glass ceiling, they are still grossly underrepresented in the executive suite. Because of their numbers, women have received the most attention. Women hold only 11 percent of senior executive positions in the Fortune 500 (Sellers, 1999), despite the fact the men and women for the most part do not differ in measured managerial abilities (Howard, 1986; Powell, 1988). Still, there are signs of recent progress. When Carly Fiorina took over the top job at HP, she became the first female CEO of one of America's twenty largest corporations. Two of the three largest U.S. banks now have female finance chiefs (Sellers, 1999).

The talent shortage has opened the door to women's advancement, and it has arrived at a time when many women have acquired enough management expertise to take charge. Whereas the CEO of a major company used to bring thirty years of experience, today twenty years is often thought to be enough. And most of the women in *Fortune*'s "50 most powerful women" of 1999 were in their mid-forties (Sellers, 1999).

Yet men and women do not necessarily get the same quality of experience in their careers. One study at the Center for Creative Leadership found notable gender differences in lessons learned and career events that could teach those lessons (Van Velsor & Hughes, 1990). For example, 40 percent of the men had a turnaround experience compared to only 6 percent of the women. In a later study, men exceeded women in several task-related development activities (higher stakes, managing business diversity, handling external pressure), although they did not differ on six other activities and scored lower than women on influencing without authority (Ohlott, Ruderman, & McCauley, 1994). Women more often experienced one obstacle: lack of personal support.

An emerging diversity issue is the need for more global representation among top executives. As companies expand worldwide, so does their search for leaders, facilitated by the Internet. Cultural fairness will be essential in future assessment and selection procedures.

Effectiveness of Senior Leader Selection

As noted in the introduction to this chapter, selection of top organizational leaders has a dismal success rate. Although the increasing complexity and pressure of the senior leader's role is one contributing factor, the weak selection methods often used at the top are also partly to blame. The challenge is to introduce more rigorous selection tools in a process that is fraught with high stress, cutthroat competition, erratic changes, and often outsized egos.

Current Practices: Lower-Level Versus Senior Leaders

A summary of current practices for identifying, assessing, and selecting leaders at three general levels of management appears in Table 10.3. The last row portrays the thrust of the staffing approach at each level.

Particularly in a sellers' market, organizations must devote intensive human attention to the enticement, negotiation, personalization, and persuasion needed to land senior-level leaders. Executive search firms play this role for outside candidates. When internal executives undergo formal assessment as part of a succession management system, assessors also give them the kid glove treatment: observing them in well-appointed private offices and conference rooms, writing individualized and detailed feedback reports, and providing personalized coaching and hand-holding during the postassessment development stage. These practices help make assessment more palatable to self-important executives.

Table 10.3 suggests that traditional I/O psychology procedures (standard job analysis, structured measurements) still generally fit lower-level leaders, who have simpler roles requiring straightforward competencies. Yet this comfort zone is narrowing as lower-level positions become more fluid and role based. At the same time that work flexibility is moving down the corporate ladder, professional assessment is moving up the corporate ladder through succession management programs. Both trends call for more flexible I/O procedures.

Staffing practices increasingly will call on high technology to save time, costs, and effort. Yet high-tech assessment creates a dilemma because it lends itself so readily to highly structured procedures. Computers need hard and fast rules: yes or no, on or off. Yet the more that psychologists respond to the mechanistic tug of the software engineer, the greater the likelihood is that they will miss the fluid job, the flexible organization, and the idiosyncratic

Table 10.3. Current Practices for Identifying, Assessing, and Selecting Leaders, by Level.

		Lower Level	Midlevel	Senior Level
Work role	Competency model	Job driven	Mixed	Strategy driven
	Competencies	Limited, simple	Moderate range	Complex, varied
	Leadership focus	Functional	Operational	Strategic
	Organization fit	General	Midrange	Specific
	Position uniqueness	Low	Moderate	High
Sourcing	External candidates	College campus, Web	Web, executive search	Executive search
	Internal candidates	Front-line workers, individual contributors	Lower-level leaders	Succession pools
Assessment	Length of process	Immediate	Moderate	Long term
	Precision of tools	High	High	Low external, mixed internal
Selection	Decision maker	Line management with human resource leadership	Line management with human resource partnership	Board of directors, CEO, executive teams
	Overall staffing approach	High tech, structured, fast	Mixed	High touch, flexible, strategic, slow

roles of leaders. Assessment center practitioners face this dilemma in microcosm. The more mechanistic the rules are for scoring simulation behavior, the higher is the interrater reliability, but the greater the risk is that assessors will "leave behavior on the table" and totally miss the mark. The challenge is to keep assessment holistic without losing calibration.

Improving Executive Selection

This chapter began by observing that I/O psychology has been largely left out of senior leader selection. But the clamorous leadership arena is changing the rules of the game. As organizations increasingly call for help to build succession management systems, they open the door to the executive suite. I/O psychologists have a choice between marching in place or embracing the full range of leadership staffing.

Moving beyond traditional models and ways of thinking will help I/O psychologists to add value to executive selection. Instead of merely criticizing executive search firms and clinically trained consultants, they should reflect on what they could learn from them. I/O psychologists could find synergy in combining the best ideas and techniques of consultants with their own deep knowledge of sophisticated assessment methods and scientific bent toward understanding and sharing what methods work and how.

One place to start is with job analysis methodology. I/O psychologists could incorporate into senior leaders' competency models the organizational analyses deemed so important in advance of selecting the CEO. An executive should fit not just the tasks, responsibilities, and roles of a position but also its organizational context: the organization's culture, life cycle stage, technology, feedback cycle, and degree of risk associated with decisions (Beatty, Schneier, & McEvoy, 1987). Other context factors include overall business strategies and priorities, organizational structure, leadership competencies existing elsewhere in the organization, the type of individuals in key positions, and human resource policies (Silzer & Jeanneret, 1998). In other words, I/O psychologists should pursue a deeper understanding of the kinds of sticky and subtle situations that might confront an incumbent.

They also might improve on the interviews and reference checks that executive search firms find so valuable. If they expand their understanding of requirements through better organizational analyses, they should be able to expand their interviewing skills and live 360-degree data-gathering techniques correspondingly. The challenge is not how to evict these tools from the repertoire but how to make them more rigorous.

Improving less precise tools should not override finding acceptable ways to incorporate more precise tools into the selection process. Standard assessment center exercises are quite useful for diagnosing strengths and development needs for an extended range of executive competencies, which makes them ideal for succession management programs. However, high-level leaders might well have mastered many of these competencies. Assessment center methodology might be more useful for top executives if it is aimed at areas where their capabilities are unknown or are likely to fall short. For example, assessment centers could home in on the fault line between executives who think and plan strategically and those who fixate on operational problems and processes.

I/O psychologists also need to explain the assessment center repertoire by creating complex exercises that mirror senior leaders' increasingly difficult challenges. Consider the fact that companies are more likely to turn to external successors in an emergency. An assessment center could simulate a host of organizational crises and evaluate candidates' strategic and interpersonal approaches to resolving them. Such simulations might be more palatable to senior-level candidates than standard exercises enabling assessors to observe both internal and external candidates on the same crisis-ridden playing field.

The integration of candidate data offers another opportunity for improvement. Assessors need to think beyond scores, ratings, and linear correlations and envision how configurations of results foretell behavior in the sticky and subtle situations identified by organizational analyses. For example, instead of just concentrating on how a person will motivate direct reports, the assessor should strive to forecast, say, how the person will function in a start-up situation with inexperienced direct reports and a demanding, micromanaging immediate manager.

Finally, we need to consider how to sharpen organizational decision makers' skills and insights about sophisticated selection methods. Training them on interviewing techniques, as some search firms do, is one possibility. More important, we could encourage strategic partnerships between psychologists as objective third parties and senior management teams as decision makers in full-blown candidate data integration sessions.

Gaining acceptance as senior management's strategic partner is perhaps the most challenging obstacle for I/O psychologists. Like employing organizations switching their role from buyer to seller, I/O psychologists must change their mind-set from detached scientist to handholding, savvy supporter. Unless they learn to speak the language of business and listen with the third ear of clinicians, they will miss the opportunity to apply their technical expertise to senior leader selection.

Where Research Is Needed

The simple answer to where research is needed about senior leader selection is, "Everywhere." Particularly for CEOs, the secrecy with which selection has been conducted and the lack of scientifically trained participants in the process has relegated executive selection to a largely unexamined art (Hollenbeck, 1994).

Just as we need multiple methods to assess executives' capabilities, we need multiple approaches to evaluate and understand the selection system. Here are some possibilities:

Perform and share position analyses. How unique are executive positions? What kinds of situations do senior leaders commonly encounter, and how do these vary by industry? It is hard to accept the common dismissal that the uniqueness of each executive position precludes scientific study. Surely there are some commonalities that will permit systematic accumulation of knowledge.

Conduct organizational analyses. Given the emphasis in executive selection on fit to organizational culture, what are the most important factors to consider? What are the critical ways in which senior leaders match their cultures and clash with their cultures? I/O psychologists need to develop a taxonomy of organization fit and explore the real-world implications of types of misfit.

Collect case studies. As executive selection becomes more transparent, it should be possible to gather public information on successions and their outcome. As we gain credibility in executive circles, we might even be able to gather systematic data from participants in the process. For example, it would be useful to learn what criteria were used for selection, what data were overlooked, and what factors were ultimately the most critical for success or avoiding failure.

Study failure. We usually try to forecast success; given the poor track record of top executives, we should study failure instead. The information gathered is likely to be more meaningful, quantifiable, and useful in the long run. For example, instead of testing the importance of competencies, we might test the proposition that how executives employ their competencies makes the difference.

Conduct longitudinal studies and cohort analyses. I/O psychologists involved in succession management have the opportunity to gather considerable information on aspiring senior leaders. They should conduct systematic research to evaluate how their predictions play out. Researchers should be prepared to follow waves of leaders from one organization to the next, particularly where succession management programs begin early in the career.

Integrate assessment and development data. Where assessment has been used to frame development, we need to investigate who learned the right and wrong lessons and how development transpired or missed the mark. Learning what characteristics are most easily developed can guide future succession management and selection programs.

Expand the criteria of success. One stumbling block in research on executive selection is defining success. Particularly for the CEO, it is difficult to discern what should be attributed to behaviors and actions of the person and what resulted from uncontrollable events in the marketplace. Multifaceted, creative approaches to defining success will aid research.

I/O psychologists can ill afford to disregard the challenge of identifying, assessing, and selecting senior leaders. If boards of directors and senior officers continue to make one-of-a-kind decisions behind closed doors, the selection of senior leaders will forever remain an unexamined art. I/O psychology should at least try to make it a soft science.

References

Andersson, D. (1999, July). Avoid executive failure traps. *Executive Excellence,* p. 5.

Axel, H. (1994). *HR executive review: Succession planning.* New York: Conference Board.

Barner, R. (2000, May-June). Talent wars in the executive suite: Six trends shaping recruitment. *Futurist,* pp. 35–41.

Beatty, R. W., Schneier, C. E., & McEvoy, G. M. (1987). Executive development and management succession. In K. M. Rowland & G. R. Ferris (Eds.), *Research in personnel and human resources management* (Vol. 5). Greenwich, CT: JAI Press.

Beeson, J. (2000, February). Succession planning. Leading-edge practices: What the best companies are doing. *Across the Board,* pp. 38–41.

Bennis, W. G., & Nanus, B. (1985). *Leaders: The strategies for taking charge.* New York: HarperCollins.

Bentson, C., Gaugler, B., & Pohley, K. (1990, March). *Assessment center survey: Preliminary results.* Paper presented at the Eighteenth International Congress on the Assessment Center Method, Orange, CA.

Bernthal, P. R., Rioux, S. M., & Wellins, R. S. (1999). *The leadership forecast: A benchmarking study.* Pittsburgh: Development Dimensions International.

Boehle, S. (2000, May). Online recruiting gets sneaky. *Training,* pp. 66–74.

Briscoe, J. P., & Hall, D. T. (1999). Grooming and picking leaders using competency frameworks: Do they work? An alternative approach and new guidelines for practice. *Organizational Dynamics, 28*(2), 37–52.

Buckner, M., & Savenski, L. (1994). Succession planning. In W. R. Tracey (Ed.), *Human resources management and development handbook.* New York: AMACOM.

Byham, W. C. (1999, February). Grooming next-millennium leaders. *HR Magazine,* pp. 46–50.

Byham, W. C., & Moyer, R. P. (1996). *Using competencies to build a successful organization.* Pittsburgh: Development Dimensions International.

Byham, W. C., Smith, A., & Paese, M. (in press). *Grow your own leaders.* Pittsburgh: Development Dimensions International.

Byrne, J. A., Reingold, J., & Melcher, R. A. (1997, August 11). Wanted: A few good CEOs. *Business Week,* pp. 64–70.

Chambers, E. G., Foulon, M., Handfield-Nones, H., Hankin, S. M., & Michaels, E.G.I. (1998). The war for talent. *McKinsey Quarterly, 3,* 44–57.

Clark, T. (1992). Management selection by executive recruitment consultancies: A survey and explanation cf selection methods. *Journal of Managerial Psychology, 7,* 3–10.

Colvin, G., & Sellers, P. (2000, May 29). How many heads can a headhunter hunt? *Fortune,* pp. 118–128.

Crainer, S., & Dearlove, D. (1999, July-August). Death of executive talent. *Management Review,* pp. 17–23.

Csoka, L. S. (1998). *Bridging the leadership gap.* New York: Conference Board.

Datta, D. K., & Guthrie, J. P. (1994). Executive succession: Organizational antecedents of CEO characteristics. *Strategic Management Journal, 15,* 569–577.

De Vries, D. L. (1993). *Executive selection: A look at what we know and what we need to know.* Greensboro, NC: Center for Creative Leadership.

Dieckmann & Associates. (1993). *Quality-driven executive search.* Chicago: Author.

Dobrzynski, J. H. (1996, September 2). Executive tests now plumb new depths of the job seeker. *New York Times,* pp. 1, 38.

Eastman, L. J. (1995). *Succession planning: An annotated bibliography and summary of commonly reported organizational practices.* Greensboro, NC: Center for Creative Leadership.

Eilbert, H. (1959). The development of personnel management in the United States. *Business History Review, 33,* 345–364.

Fernandez-Araoz, C. (1999, July-August). Hiring without firing. *Harvard Business Review,* pp. 109–120.

Friedman, S. D., & Le Vino, T. P. (1984). Strategic appraisal and development at General Electric Company. In C. J. Fombrun, N. M. Tichy, & M. A. Devanna (Eds.), *Strategic human resource management.* New York: Wiley.

Gerstein, M., & Reisman, H. (1983). Strategic selection: Matching executives to business conditions. *Sloan Management Review, 24,* 33–49.

Goleman, D. (1998). *Working with emotional intelligence.* New York: Bantam.

Gordon, R. A. (1945). *Business leadership in the large corporation.* Washington, DC: Brookings Institution.

Hollenbeck, G. P. (1994). *CEO selection: A street-smart review.* Greensboro, NC: Center for Creative Leadership.

Hough, L. M., & Schneider, R. J. (1996). Personality traits, taxonomies, and applications in organizations. In K. R. Murphy (Ed.), *Individual differences and behavior in organizations.* San Francisco: Jossey-Bass.

Howard, A. (1986). College experiences and managerial performance. [Monograph]. *Journal of Applied Psychology, 71,* 530–552.

Howard, A. (Ed.). (1995). *The changing nature of work.* San Francisco: Jossey-Bass.

Howard, A. (1997). A reassessment of assessment centers: Challenges for the 21st century. *Journal of Social Behavior and Personality, 12*(5), 13–52.

Howard, A., & Bray, D. W. (1988). *Managerial lives in transition: Advancing age and changing times.* New York: Guilford Press.

Howard, A., Byham, W. C., & Hauenstein, P. (1994). *Multirater assessment and feedback: Applications, implementation, and implications.* [Monograph]. Pittsburgh: Development Dimensions International.

Howard, A., & Wellins, R. S. (1994). *High-involvement leadership: Changing roles for changing times.* Pittsburgh: Development Dimensions International.

Interbusiness Network. (2000). *2000 Electronic recruiting index: Performance and the emergence of the middle market.* Available: http://www.interbiznet.com.

Jacoby, S. M. (1985). *Employing bureaucracy: Managers, unions, and the transformation of work in American industry, 1900–1945.* New York: Columbia University Press.

Jones, D. (2000, February 29). Overwhelmed CEOs leaving in droves. *USA Today,* pp. 1–2.

Laib, K. (1993, April). *Use of computer-based exercises in assessment.* Paper presented at the Twenty-First International Congress on the Assessment Center Method, Atlanta.

Lauterbach, B., Vu, J., & Weisberg, J. (1999). Internal vs. external successions and their effect on firm performance. *Human Relations, 52,* 1485–1504.

Lear, R. W. (1999, November). Succession reflection. *Chief Executive Magazine,* p. 14.

Leonhardt, D. (2000, April 2). In the options age, rising pay (and risk). *New York Times,* pp. 1, 12, 14.

Levinson, H. (1994). Beyond the selection failures. *Consulting Psychology Journal: Practice and Research, 46,* 3–8.

Livesay, H. C. (1979). *American made: Men who shaped the American economy.* New York: Little, Brown.

Lombardo, M. M., & McCauley, C. D. (1988). *The dynamics of management derailment.* Greensboro, NC: Center for Creative Leadership.

Lorsch, J. W., & Khurana, R. (1999, May-June). Changing leaders: The board's role in CEO succession. *Harvard Business Review,* pp. 96–105.

McClain, D. L. (2000, May 7). For job hunters, networking beats the Net. *New York Times,* p. G1.

Mintzberg, H. (1975). The manager's job: Folklore and fact. *Harvard Business Review, 53,* 49–61.

National Academy of Public Administration. (1992). *Paths to leadership: Executive succession planning in the federal government.* Washington, DC: Author.

Newcomer, M. (1955). *The big business executive: The factors that made him, 1900–1950.* New York: Columbia University Press.

Ohlott, P. J., Ruderman, M. N., & McCauley, C. D. (1994). Gender differences in managers' developmental job experiences. *Academy of Management Journal, 37,* 46–47.

Poe, R., & Courter, C. L. (2000, May). Fast forward. *Across the Board,* p. 5.

Powell, G. N. (1988). *Women and men in management.* Thousand Oaks, CA: Sage.

Puffer, S. M., & Weintrop, J. B. (1995). CEO and board leadership: The influence of organizational performance, board composition, and retirement on CEO successor origin. *Leadership Quarterly, 6,* 49–68.

RHR International. (1991). The psychological assessment of executives: An interview-based approach. In C. P. Hansen & K. A. Conrad (Eds.), *A handbook of psychological assessment in business.* New York: Quorum.

Rioux, S. M., & Bernthal, P. (1999). *Succession management practices survey report* (Vol. 2). Pittsburgh: Development Dimensions International.

Rothwell, W. J. (1994). *Effective succession planning: Ensuring leadership continuity and building talent from within.* New York: AMACOM.

Ryan, A. M., & Sackett, P. R. (1987). A survey of individual assessment practices by I/O psychologists. *Personnel Psychology, 40,* 455–488.

Ryan, A. M., & Sackett, P. R. (1992). Relationships between graduate training, professional affiliation, and individual psychological assessment practices for personnel decisions. *Personnel Psychology, 45,* 363–387.

Schoyen, C., & Rasmussen, N. (1999). *Secrets of the executive search experts.* New York: AMACOM.

Sellers, P. (1999, October 25). These women rule. *Fortune,* pp. 94–124.

Sessa, V. I., Kaiser, R., Taylor, J. K., & Campbell, R. J. (1998). *Executive selection: A research report on what works and what doesn't.* Greensboro, NC: Center for Creative Leadership.

Sessa, V. I., & Taylor, J. K. (1999, May-June). Choosing leaders: A team approach for executive selection. *Leadership in Action,* pp. 1–6.

Severance package for Mattel chief is called excessive. (2000, May 13). *New York Times,* p. C3.

Silzer, R. F., & Jeanneret, R. (1998). Anticipating the future: Assessment strategies for tomorrow. In R. Jeanneret & R. F. Silzer (Eds.), *Individual psychological assessment.* San Francisco: Jossey-Bass.

Silzer, R. F., & Slider, R. L. (1994, April). *Assessing change, changing assessment: Current and future assessment practices.* Paper presented at the Twenty-Second International Congress on the Assessment Center Method, San Francisco.

Snow, C. C., & Snell, S. A. (1992). Staffing as strategy. In N. Schmitt & W. C. Borman (Eds.), *Personnel selection in organizations.* San Francisco: Jossey-Bass.

Spencer, L. M., & Spencer, S. M. (1993). *Competence at work.* New York: Wiley.

Sperry, L. (1999). The 1999 Harry Levinson Lecture: Leadership dynamics. Character assessment in the executive selection process. *Consulting Psychology Journal: Practice and Research, 51,* 211–217.

Tragash, H. J. (1992). *A question of selection models or selection practices.* Paper presented at the Executive Selection Conference, Center for Creative Leadership, Greensboro, NC.

Treece, J. B. (1992, April 20). The board revolt. *Business Week,* pp. 30–36.

Van Velsor, E., & Hughes, M. W. (1990). *Gender differences in the development of managers: How women managers learn from experience.* Greensboro, NC: Center for Creative Leadership.

Whyte, W. H., Jr. (1956). *The organization man.* New York: Simon & Schuster.

Zaleznik, A. (1977). Managers and leaders: Are they different? *Harvard Business Review, 55*(5), 67–80.

CHAPTER 11

Leader Training and Development

Cynthia D. McCauley

Individuals who perform well in the face of the demands of executive jobs have developed this capacity over time. They could not have stepped into an executive job twenty years (or even ten years) earlier in their careers and been successful. Thus, training and development to achieve successful executive leadership in an organization need to be viewed as a continuous process throughout the future executive's career.

The Leadership Development Process

The process of leadership development has three major components: developmental experiences, the ability to learn, and the organizational context that supports development (Van Velsor, McCauley, & Moxley, 1998). These components are depicted in Figure 11.1.

Developmental experiences provide managers with the opportunity to learn. These opportunities can be formal educational programs and training events, but the majority of these experiences occur on the job through job assignments, relationships with others, and hardships.

The individual brings the ability to learn to the leadership development process. This ability is not a unitary construct, easy to articulate and assess, but rather a complex mixture of motivational factors, personal orientation, and skills. Note in Figure 11.1 that

Figure 11.1. The Process of Leadership Development.

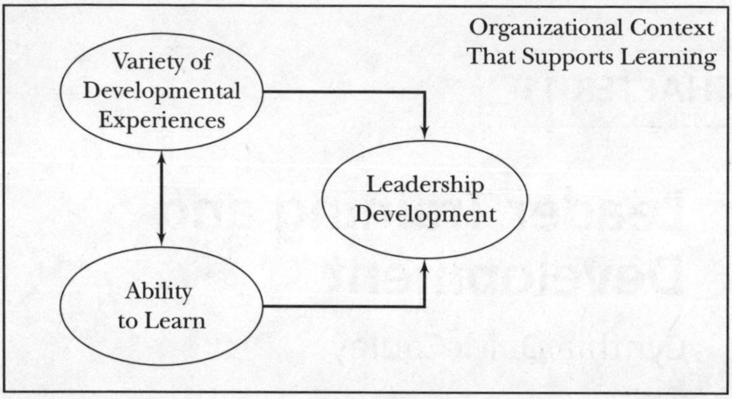

Source: Adapted from Van Velsor, McCauley, & Moxley, 1998. Reprinted by permission of Jossey-Bass, Inc., a subsidiary of John Wiley & Sons, Inc.

developmental experiences and ability to learn have an impact on each other. Developmental experiences can enhance a person's ability to learn, and those with high ability to learn seek out a variety of developmental experiences. Thus, although the model conceptually distinguishes developmental experiences and the learner, they are in fact closely interconnected (Van Velsor et al., 1998).

The final component of the model is the organizational context. All aspects of an organizational system can be examined to see the degree to which the system supports leadership development. Are leadership development outcomes linked to business goals? Do people get rewarded for development? For coaching others? Are jobs analyzed in terms of their developmental opportunities? Are formal feedback and development systems in place? Do succession planning systems take into account a manager's developmental needs? And the culture itself can inhibit or enhance development. How are mistakes viewed? Is learning peripheral or central? Is continuous improvement an expectation?

The model of leadership development in Figure 11.1 suggests three strategies for executive leadership development in organizations: provide a variety of developmental experiences, ensure a high level of ability to learn, and design the context so that it supports development.

Developmental Experiences

When looking back at key developmental experiences in their careers, executives point out experiences that occurred at different times throughout their careers and identify different kinds of experiences as developmental (McCall, Lombardo, & Morrison, 1988; Morrison, White, & Van Velsor, 1992; Wick & Leon, 1993). The range of performance imperatives is astounding—from financial to social to political. The variety and complexity of capacities needed to deal with these imperatives is high. For example, the study of executive development by McCall and others (1988) found that executives reported learning in over thirty specific areas, each one contributing in some way to their success as executives (see Table 11.1). To hone so many capacities to such an expert level requires time—time to learn and relearn across an entire career. And to develop such a well-rounded set of capacities requires learning from a variety of experiences.

One executive asked to think back over his career and identify key developmental experiences, that is, experiences that had a lasting change on him as a manager, began by describing his first supervisory position:

> Early in my career at [Company A], I was promoted to supervisor of cost and general accounting. At the time, I was twenty-three years old and suddenly faced with managing forty-five hourly union employees ranging in age from thirty to sixty-five. In addition, the manager I replaced had been in the position for over ten years. I had to learn not only how to be a supervisor but had to prove myself to these people who were more experienced than me and who had the luxury up until this point of working for a pretty experienced manager. I learned how to gain people's confidence and respect through working with them and having them teach me.

He went on to describe two important midcareer experiences:

> After eleven years in a variety of management positions, I was transferred to a new site to serve as production manager for a wonderful individual. He was and is a plant manager who received respect and loyalty from his subordinates. He delegated responsibility and authority, continually pushed the people and the plant to higher

Table 11.1. Capacities Executives Developed from Key Career Experiences.

Setting and Implementing Agendas
- Technical and professional skills
- Business knowledge
- Strategic thinking
- Taking responsibility
- Building and using structure and control systems
- Innovative problem-solving methods

Handling Relationships
- Handling political situations
- Getting people to implement solutions
- Understanding of executives and how to work with them
- Negotiation strategies
- Influencing without authority
- Understanding other people's perspectives
- Dealing with conflict
- Directing and motivating subordinates
- Developing other people
- Confronting subordinate performance problems
- Managing former bosses and peers

Basic Values
- Shared responsibility for work
- Sensitivity to the human side of management
- Basic management values

Executive Temperament
- Being tough when necessary
- Self-confidence
- Coping with situations beyond your control
- Persevering through adversity
- Coping with ambiguous situations
- Use of power

Personal Awareness
- The balance between work and personal life
- Knowing what really excites you about work
- Personal limits and blind spots
- Taking charge of your career
- Recognizing and seizing opportunities

Source: Adapted from McCall et al., 1988. Reprinted and adapted with the permission of The Free Press, a Division of Simon & Schuster, Inc. Copyright © 1988 by Lexington Books.

performance levels, and was always ready to accept change and new challenges. I certainly learned a lot from watching him in action, but he also gave me the opportunity to try new ideas of mine, and the success gave me confidence in my own ability.

I was selected to attend a nine-week program for executives at the state university. There I was exposed to a multifaceted group of people gathered from all types of industries worldwide. It was a tremendous learning experience through combined group participation and course study. Although accounting was my educational background, I learned a great deal more about financial management. And it was the first time I learned the importance of developing a network of fellow executives outside of my company.

The final event he described was more recent:

I was assigned international responsibility for eleven countries in the Far East. I had to deal with past negative problems in this region and reestablish the company as a viable entity. Additionally, I had responsibility for negotiating and developing new international distributors. This required heavy travel and constant meetings with foreign business groups and government officials. Of course, I learned about the cultural and business differences of each country and how to deal with them. I developed organizational and communications skills necessary in the international marketplace. On a personal level, I think it forced me to be more patient and flexible.

As this example illustrates, some developmental experiences are formal interventions specifically focused on learning and development, and others are a natural part of a person's career—jobs, relationships, hardships—that stimulate learning. Whether formal or naturally occurring, experiences are most likely to be developmental when they provide individuals with assessment, challenge, and support (Van Velsor et al., 1998).

An experience provides assessment when it is rich in information about how a person is doing. Are current leader behaviors effective? What are the person's strengths and weaknesses as a leader? What impact is he or she having on others or on the organization? Where should the person focus to improve? Assessment data help leaders better understand what works and what does not in various leadership situations and where they need to learn and grow. Assessment information can also motivate developmental effort; a recognized gap between current effectiveness as a leader and an ideal level of effectiveness can stimulate efforts to close the gap by working to improve one's effectiveness.

An experience provides challenge when it takes people out of their comfort zone—when current ways of thinking and acting are not adequate to deal successfully with the tasks encountered in the experience. Challenging experiences require that people develop new capacities if they are going to be successful. Some challenges are due to a lack of experience; they require the person to broaden and acquire new skills and perspectives. Other challenges require changing old habits—either the situation has changed and old responses are no longer adequate, or old responses were never that effective in the first place.

An experience provides support when people believe they can learn and grow from it and that their efforts to learn and grow are valued. Development is not easy. If people do not receive confirming messages and others do not allow and encourage them to change, then the challenge posed by the developmental experience may overwhelm them rather than opening them up to learning. Support is also needed to help people handle the struggle and pain of developing and to maintain a positive view of themselves as capable of learning.

Developmental experiences are sources of assessment, challenge, and support. Some may more readily provide one of these elements. For example, formal feedback interventions provide a great deal of assessment information, and job assignments can be a particularly good source of challenge. But the most developmental forms of any of the experiences we examine next will provide all three elements.

Development as Part of Work Experiences

Much of the learning and development that executives undergo during their careers happens as a result of their on-the-job experiences: from the assignments they take on, the people they work with, and the hardships they encounter. Of the key developmental experiences that successful executives described in the study by McCall and others (1988), 56 percent were job assignments, 8 percent were relationships with bosses or role models in the workplace, and 17 percent were hardship experiences. Similarly, Wick and Leon (1993) found 57 percent of the developmental experiences that managers reported were job assignments, and 17 percent were on-the-job relationships.

Job Assignments

The roles, responsibilities, and tasks that managers encounter in their jobs are a major stimulus for ongoing learning and development. In job assignments, managers have the opportunity to learn by doing. They work on problems and dilemmas, have to take action, and can see the consequences of their actions. These are situations in which the outcomes matter, and managers are thus motivated to do well. But all job assignment are not developmentally equal; executives report some kinds of jobs as having more impact on their learning than others (McCall et al., 1988; McCauley, Ruderman, Ohlott, & Morrow, 1994). Developmental jobs are those that stretch managers beyond current capacities or challenge them to think and act in new ways.

Looking across a number of studies that use a variety of methodologies, McCauley and Brutus (1998) noted three broad characteristics most often associated with developmental jobs:

- Transitions that put the manager in new situations with unfamiliar responsibilities. This type of experience is most frequently the outcome of a job move (for instance, a promotion or a move to a new business, function, organization, or location), but can come from expanded responsibilities with the same job or the redefinition of a job due to reorganization or changes in the external environment. New and unfamiliar situations provide an opportunity to learn because they disrupt routines, call for new skills and behaviors, and yield surprises that cause the manager to reexamine assumptions.
- Tasks or projects that require the manager to bring about change or build relationships. Managers are involved in creating change when they are fixing problems or are starting a new initiative. They work with others in various ways: leading subordinates; influencing bosses; collaborating or competing with peers; and negotiating with, persuading, and serving people

outside the organization. Creating change and building relationships is the primary work of leaders; thus, developing leadership expertise requires doing the work of leaders. To do this work, they must take action—a necessary component of the on-the-job learning process. The more complex and uncertain the change efforts are, the more difficult and diverse the working relationships are, and the bigger the learning challenges of the job.

• High-responsibility, high-latitude jobs. In these types of jobs, managers have responsibility for discrete areas of the business, have profit-and-loss responsibility, or make decisions that can have a major impact on the organization. They generally are also given a high degree of latitude in their initiatives and discretion in decision making. High-responsibility, high-latitude jobs offer developmental opportunities because managers in them come face-to-face with complex systems and competing organizational priorities. To succeed in these jobs, managers must develop a better understanding of the interrelatedness of systems and how to balance priorities and make trade-offs. These jobs are also potent because the consequences of actions taken in them often matter a great deal, encouraging managers to explore issues deeply and be more cognizant of actions and their intended consequences. Managers in these jobs usually have some freedom to experiment; they are less constrained by set routines and procedures and can thus test their understanding of a situation by taking actions and seeing the consequences.

Developmental Relationships

Relationships in the workplace play a key role in the development of executives. Some of these relationships are long term and developmentally focused, with people often referred to as mentors (Carden, 1990; Kram, 1985; Levinson, 1978). A mentoring relationship is typically defined as "an intense relationship, lasting eight-to-ten years, in which a senior person oversees the career and psychosocial development of a junior person" (Douglas, 1997, p. 76). Mentors provide two distinct functions for their protégés (Kram, 1985; Noe, 1988): a psychosocial function (acceptance, encouragement, coaching, and counseling) and a career facilitation function (sponsorship, protection, challenging assignments, and visibility).

But relationships do not have to be long term or intense to be developmental. Supervisors, coworkers, human resource professionals, and role models observed at a distance have all been cited as important sources of learning and development during managerial careers (Kram & Isabella, 1985; Little, 1991; McCall et al., 1988; Morrison et al., 1987; Reuber & Fischer, 1993; Zemke, 1985). These individuals can play various roles in the leadership development process (McCauley & Young, 1993; McCauley & Douglas, 1998). Some roles provide assessment information. For example, other people are an important source of ongoing feedback as a person works to learn and improve. They are also needed as feedback interpreters (assisting in integrating and making sense of feedback from others) and sounding boards (providing feedback on strategies before they are implemented). Other roles provide challenge, stretching managers beyond their current skills and abilities. Role models, for example, often challenge managers to emulate new or more complex skills and behaviors. Or bosses often challenge a subordinate to act in new ways or approach a problem from a different perspective. But perhaps some of the most important roles that others play in leadership development are roles that lend support during the struggles of learning and change: counselors who provide emotional support, cheerleaders who encourage and express confidence in the learner, those who reinforce and reward learning, and cohorts who can empathize and console.

Hardships

Executives report learning from hardships—adverse situations (McCall et al., 1988; Morrison et al., 1987): career setbacks (for example, being demoted, fired, or passed over for a promotion), business mistakes and failures, dead-end jobs, personal traumas on and off the job, and being responsible for downsizing.

Hardship experiences are different from the expected challenges encountered in job assignments. In a developmental assignment, managers face challenges such as taking on unfamiliar responsibilities or making highly visible decisions. The outcomes of their actions and decisions in these situations could be positive or negative. And there is a sense of having some control over those outcomes. Facing these challenges can certainly be stressful, but it is the kind of stress Lazarus and Folkman (1984) refer to as anticipatory: it is about future functioning. People can plan for it and work through some of the difficulties in advance. In a hardship experience, damage to the manager has already occurred, and he or she no longer has control over the outcome.

Executives report a sense of failure and aloneness during hardship experiences (McCall et al., 1988). They feel that something they did or failed to do caused things to go wrong. There is also a sense of loss: a loss of credibility, loss of control, loss of self-efficacy, loss of former identity (Moxley, 1998). This sense of failure and loss provokes a turning inward and close self-examination. From hardships, executives report learning about their limits and blind spots, about being sensitive and compassionate toward others, about coping with situations beyond one's control, about life and career balance, and about being flexible and adaptable (Moxley, 1998). Many of these lessons are learned after the hardship as managers are dealing with the aftermath, making sense of the situation, and gaining some perspective on the experience.

Formal Developmental Experiences

Organizations often supplement the leadership development that happens through naturally occurring experiences by structuring additional learning experiences for their managers. Formal developmental experiences focus managers specifically on a learning and development agenda. There is value in stepping out of the day-to-day work and having time to be exposed to new knowledge, examine issues more deeply, reflect, share with fellow managers, listen to feedback, and practice new skills in a safe environment. Planned interventions into the development process generally take the form of structured feedback experiences (such as 360-degree feedback and developmental assessment centers), programs that bring managers together for a formal learning experience (such as training programs, personal growth programs, and action learning programs), or the intentional matching of managers with someone charged with enhancing their learning and development (through formal mentoring programs and executive coaching). A 1999 Conference Board survey asked senior human resource executives in U.S. and European corporations whether their organizations use each of these leadership development interventions for top executives and for other managers. The results of the survey are shown in Table 11.2.

Table 11.2. Percentage of Companies Using Various Leadership Development Interventions.

Intervention	U.S. Companies		European Companies	
	Top Executives	Other Managers	Top Executives	Other Managers
360-degree feedback	79%	81%	53%	58%
Assessment centers	20	20	25	42
Training	72	89	72	81
Action learning	22	45	8	36
Formal mentoring	13	38	17	25
Executive coaching	76	42	61	31

Formal Feedback

Formal feedback is often thought of as a starting point in a leadership development initiative. By receiving formal feedback, people get a clearer sense of their strengths and weaknesses and can identify areas to focus on in their developmental efforts. Certainly there is informal feedback available to managers in the workplace. Coworkers and customers provide praise when a job is well done. They may share insights about what is not working so well or suggestions about how to do a particular task differently. Bosses often let subordinates know when something has been done especially well or when it has not met standards. Managers can see how others react to their ideas and actions.

Formal feedback is needed for development for a number of reasons (Chappelow, 1998). One is that in their day-to-day work, managers are most often focused on what they need to accomplish, what problems need solving, what demands are being made of them. Pieces of feedback may be floating around them all the time as they carry out this work, but they have no time to focus much on it. A second reason is that others may be reluctant to give negative feedback: they feel awkward in this situation and do not want to make the individual feel bad or create conflict in the relationship. Finally, informal feedback is usually not very comprehensive, so managers do not get an in-depth picture of their strengths and weaknesses. To overcome these limitations, formal feedback processes are often sought out or created. Boss-subordinate performance appraisals are a widely used formal feedback process, but more comprehensive and multiple-perspective processes are available and are especially appropriate in the context of leadership development.

Multisource, or 360-degree, feedback is an increasingly popular method of formal feedback (Tornow & London, 1998; Lepsinger & Lucia, 1997). In the typical 360-degree feedback process, a manager is rated by his or her boss, peers, and subordinates on a number of competencies. The data are summarized and provided to the manager, who is encouraged to set developmental goals and action plans based on the information. Ratings by particular individuals are anonymous (ratings from the boss are sometimes the exception), and the results are confidential, shared only with the manager for his or her use in development. Research exploring the impact of 360-degree feedback on leader performance has begun to show support for a positive relationship between feedback and performance improvement (Atwater, Roush, & Fischthal, 1995; Smither et al., 1995).

Developmental assessment centers are another formal feedback method. Although originally designed as a selection tool, assessment centers have been used increasingly for management development (Goodge, 1991; Munchus & McArthur, 1991). Assessment centers assess a broad range of management competencies through multiple methods, for example, in-basket exercises, simulations, ability tests, leaderless group discussions, writing exercises, and presentations, sometimes administered over two to three days. Information gained from observing the process or evaluating outputs of the exercises is summarized and integrated to provide overall assessment on a number of dimensions. Data from these centers are considered to be fairly objective, based on evaluations of trained observers and evaluators who usually do not have a history of working with the manager. As with 360-degree feedback, the data are given to the manager and used as a basis for development planning.

The most in-depth feedback is likely to be obtained from a feedback-intensive development program (Conger, 1992; Guthrie & Kelly-Radford, 1998). These programs usually last from three to five days and combine 360-degree feedback and assessment center exercises with other forms of assessment—all within a classroom context that provides models and frameworks for thinking about effective leadership. Feedback-intensive programs make use of psychological inventories, so participants develop a better understanding of their underlying predispositions toward certain types of behaviors and reactions in the workplace, and they use fellow participants in the program to provide in-the-moment feedback. For example, after completing a group exercise, the group reviews a videotape of the exercise, stopping the tape at points where a group member wants to point out a behavior by another group member that had a particularly positive or negative effect. These programs conclude with the setting of developmental goals and action plans. Follow-up activities (such as a feedback instrument to assess behavioral change or ongoing meetings with a group of fellow participants) may be part of the program design. Feedback-intensive programs have been shown to increase self-awareness, broaden and transform managers' perspectives, lead to successful goal attainment, and change leadership behavior (Guthrie & Kelly-Radford, 1998).

Training Programs

Conger (1992) identified four basic types of leadership development programs. One type is the feedback-intensive program described in the previous section. Conceptual programs and skill-building programs, two other types, fall within what are traditionally thought of as training programs: programs that teach the knowledge and skills that leaders and managers need.

Conceptual approaches to leader training focus on a cognitive understanding of what is involved in the task of leadership and what it takes to be an effective leader. These programs tend to be more theory driven and are traditionally offered by universities. Lectures, case studies, and discussion are the predominant pedagogical tools, although many programs that are primarily conceptual may also use experiential exercises and feedback instruments. Conger (1992) reports that conceptual programs are a natural first step for those with little leadership experience; they can help people gain awareness of what leadership is and create enthusiasm for the idea of leading. Conceptual approaches are also a primary way for managers to learn the business knowledge they need in areas such as finance, operations, marketing, and strategic planning.

Skill building is the most commonly employed approach to management training (Conger, 1992). Programs can range from short workshops focusing on a narrow set of skills to comprehensive programs that cover a wide range of skills and last for as long as a year (Yukl, 1998). Skill-building programs generally consist of modules, each focusing on a specific skill (such as giving feedback, creating a vision statement, or negotiating with external parties). Within a module, participants are given information and strategies for executing the skill, observe the skill in action, and practice the skill themselves. Numerous techniques may be employed: lectures, demonstrations, role modeling, videotapes, role playing, group exercises, and simulations. Training programs are most likely to contribute to lasting change and development when the content of the training is directly relevant to the participant's job, is needed at that time, and can be immediately used in the work setting (McDonald-Mann, 1998).

Personal Growth Programs

The fourth type of leadership development program that Conger (1992) identified was the personal growth program, "based, generally, on the assumption that leaders are individuals who are deeply in touch with their personal dreams and talents and who will act to fulfill them" (p. 45). Therefore, the premise of these programs is that managers need to get in touch with their personal dreams and talents and develop a commitment to making those dreams a reality in order to fulfill their potential as leaders. Programs with this orientation usually take one of two forms: (1) outdoor adventure programs where groups of participants experience increasingly challenging physical activities, many of which require trust and cooperation among group members, and (2) workshops where participants engage in a number of psychological exercises that allow for deep exploration of their personal values and drives. The outdoor programs focus more on developing self-confidence, overcoming fears, and taking risks, while the workshops put more emphasis on self-understanding and tapping into inner resources.

Action Learning

Action learning programs have gained popularity as a method of management development. These programs originated in the United Kingdom and Europe, stimulated by Revans's ideas of integrating management education and practical work on business problems (1980). In a typical action learning program, groups of managers from the same company are brought together for a series of workshops and field experiences linked by a common focus on a business issue in the organization (Dotlich & Noel, 1998; Froiland, 1994; Henderson, 1993; Marsick, 1990). The group has an executive sponsor who "owns" the business issue and is asking the group for analysis and recommendations for action. There is generally a data-gathering phase in which information is sought both inside and outside the organization; then the group analyzes the data together, develops a set of recommendations, and formally presents the recommendations to the executive sponsor. While working on the business issue, the group is also meeting for more formal educational experiences; these might be designed to educate the group on particular business topics, develop skills for working as a team, bring in experts for stimulating new ideas, learn to use tools that will aid them in their analysis of the business issue, or take time out to reflect on their progress and what they are learning.

Dixon (1994) describes an action learning program at Northern Telecom. Twenty-four managers from across the company spend about one-third of their time over a seven-month period in the program. The class is divided into four teams of six people from different functional areas. Each team works on a problem identified by a senior-level executive (for example, how to do low-cost production in digital switching or how to manage human resources on a global basis). Teams are formed during a six-day classroom experience at the beginning of the program. During this time, participants work on team building and also receive individual 360-degree feedback. Over the next few months, teams go all over the world to collect data. At midcourse, all teams get back together for four days to review their progress and take part in a seminar on cross-cultural issues. They have several more months to complete their project work before getting together for two days, when they present their recommendations to the chairman and vice presidents of the company. The executive group makes a go–no go decision about each team's proposal.

The power of action learning programs comes from their pulling together and integrating various learning methodologies in service of a business problem. Classroom training strategies are used, but the content of these classroom sessions is immediately relevant for work on the business problem. Participants go out and seek information for solving a real problem. They work with a group of peers whom they learn from as they work together. And coaching and time for reflection are often built into the process.

Formal Mentoring and Coaching

Organizations have tried to capitalize better on the learning potential of relationships by creating formal developmental relationships in which people are intentionally matched for the primary purpose of learning and development. Two of the most popular strategies are formal mentoring programs and executive coaching.

Formal mentoring initiatives typically involve matching an experienced manager with a junior manager; the experienced manager is expected to provide help, advice, and sponsorship to the junior manager (Douglas, 1997). Mentoring programs have identifiable phases: identification and matching of participants, orientation and training, negotiation of the parameters of the relationship, cultivation of the relationship, concluding the relationship, and evaluation of outcomes (Gray, 1988; Murray & Owen, 1991; Newby & Heide, 1992). These programs are most frequently initiated to help ease the transition of new managers into the organization, facilitate the development of women and minority managers (who lack access to informal mentoring relationships), or provide challenge and support to high-potential managers on the fast track. Although formal mentoring programs have drawn some criticism (commonly limited availability and unintended impact on peers and supervisors), a wealth of practical experience and some research-based evaluations have yielded knowledge on how to design these experiences for the best developmental impact (Douglas, 1997).

Executive coaching is used to help senior managers with their developmental needs. The senior managers are generally paired with external consultants who specialize in executive coaching, although some companies have internal consultants who can serve in this role. One-on-one coaching by external consultants is often used at this level in the organization so that executives can get candid feedback, focus some extra developmental effort on a targeted need, and do so in a flexible way that will fit within their typically chaotic schedules. Witherspoon and White (1997) identified four types of coaching that differ in focus and intensity:

- Coaching for skills, which focuses on improving a particular skill or set of skills needed in a current task or project
- Coaching for performance, which focuses more broadly on improving performance in the current job
- Coaching for development, which focuses on preparing an individual for future, broader job responsibilities
- Coaching for an executive's agenda, which focuses on current organizational issues or changes the executive is dealing with and how to deal with those issues productively

Executive coaching has grown faster than any other area of consulting. Most executives rate coaching experiences positively and report specific, value-added outcomes from their coaching relationships (Hall, Otazo, & Hollenbeck, 1999).

Integrating Multiple Formal Strategies

The different types of formal developmental experiences serve somewhat different purposes. Formal feedback provides comprehensive assessment information and serves as the basis for creating development goals and plans. Training is for exposure to new knowledge and for skill practice and improvement. Personal growth programs are designed to motivate and energize participants and increase their confidence in their ability to lead. Action learning programs also expose participants to new knowledge about the business, but also allow participants the opportunity to practice problem definition, data analysis and interpretation, team problem solving, and presenting to top executives. Formal developmental relationships can serve a wide range of purposes, from special coaching on a particular skill to broad career advice and support. As developmental experiences, each has its strengths and weaknesses.

To maximize the power of specific training and development experiences, organizations integrate them into a broader program of executive development for a targeted set of high-potential managers. For example, a national nonprofit organization, concerned about whether it had the bench strength to fill top leadership positions, designed and implemented a two-year leadership development initiative for twenty middle-level managers who were identified as having high potential for moving into executive roles. The overall intervention integrated multiple developmental experiences.

The program was launched with a week-long, feedback-intensive program. Participants received feedback from multiple sources: their boss, peers, and subordinates in the workplace; trained observers of assessment exercises; peers in the program; and psychological tests. They were also exposed to models, concepts, and research findings about effective leadership.

The group experienced a number of educational events during the two-year period. For example, they attended a workshop on strategic planning and chose among several self-study courses on topics relevant to the history and philosophy of the nonprofit organization. Groups of participants were sent on special assignments to provide services to communities in a particular part of the world. These assignments provided the opportunity to practice leadership skills and gain insights about the service challenges that nonprofit organizations face.

The participants were assigned to two formal relationships. First, each was matched with a senior executive whom they visited, shadowed during his or her work, and discussed the challenges of executive positions. This relationship was created to help the participants get a better understanding of what an executive leadership position entails. The second relationship was one that the participants established with a recognized leader in their community but outside their organization. The goal was to be exposed to new and different perspectives of effective leadership and to establish a relationship with someone who could coach the participant in his or her efforts to achieve developmental goals.

Providing a Variety of Developmental Experiences

To prepare managers for executive-level positions, organizations need to provide them with a variety of developmental experiences, for two important reasons.

The first is that different experiences tend to be best at developing different capacities. For example, managers learn a great deal about setting and implementing agendas and about handling relationships from challenging job assignments. Important value lessons often come from relationships with others. Humility and awareness of personal limits are strongly associated with hardships. Feedback-intensive programs are best at providing in-depth self-awareness. Technical and business knowledge are often mastered in training programs. Serving on a cross-functional task force or an action learning team exposes participants to perspectives from those who work in other parts of the organization.

Even within a category of experiences, there is variety. Starting a new operation teaches different lessons from those learned in a turnaround assignment or a staff job. What is learned from a long-time mentor is different from what can be learned from an assigned coach who has expertise in a particular area in which one is trying to improve or from a colleague who serves as a sounding board and confidante.

Second, changing one's behavior, learning new skills, or developing a new perspective is hard work; one experience is usually not enough for mastery. For example, the manager who wants to be more effective at influencing peers needs to plan a series of experiences, all of them directed at improving this competency. She may start with a training program, get coaching from her boss, get formal feedback from her peers, serve on a task force where she can try out her skills, and eventually take an assignment where she has to influence groups across the company without having direct authority over them.

As an organization thinks about providing the variety of experiences its up-and-coming executives need, one important tool is a matrix that begins to articulate the kinds of experiences that provide the opportunity to develop key executive capacities. An example that uses some of the executive capacities noted in Table 11.1 appears in Table 11.3. Such a matrix can be used in developmental planning to look at gaps in a manager's developmental experiences or at the types of experiences needed to develop a specific executive capacity. It can also highlight to the organization the kinds of experiences it needs to offer to its developing leaders.

Table 11.3. Example Experiences for Developing Selected Executive Capacities.

Capacity	Job Assignments	Relationships	Formal Programs
Strategic thinking	Responsible for design and introduction of new system in the organization Temporary assignment in the planning function	Work as the assistant to an executive	Workshop on strategic thinking
Understanding others' perspectives	Serve as company liaison to a government agency Be a "loaned executive" for a nonprofit organization	Work for a boss who is highly effective at coalition building	Program that exposes manager to executives in other companies
Dealing with conflict	Resolve customer complaints Jointly work on a project with a difficult colleague	Serve as a mentor in the company's program to mentor at-risk middle school students	Formal feedback on preferences for dealing with conflict
Persevering through adversity	Turn around a unit in trouble	Have an assigned coach to use for advice and sounding board during turnaround assignment	Participate in an outdoor adventure personal growth program
Recognizing and seizing opportunities	Work in a new start-up unit Reorganize a system in response to customer demands	Have a highly entrepreneurial colleague as a peer coach	Attend briefings on emerging trends in the industry

Organizations also need ways of thinking about how to sequence developmental experiences. Some capacities may need to be demonstrated or developed earlier in an executive's career than others. For example, Bonoma and Lawler (1989) suggest that functional expertise, the ability to work with and motivate others, a commitment to high performance, and creativity need to be developed early in a manager's career if he or she is going to move to top levels in an organization. These are the screens for junior managers to be considered as having high potential to move to the next level. Experiences in middle management ranks need to build the future executive's capabilities in additional areas: sensitivity to others, the wisdom to make decisions in both familiar and unfamiliar situations, confidence in one's own judgment, and good instincts. Bonoma and Lawler suggest a sequence and assignment paths for developing each of these capacities, including the kind of supervision needed. Dalton (1998) provides similar assignment path suggestions for developing the capacities for effectiveness in global leadership roles. Organizations need to model these sequencing approaches, although they will adapt them to their own competency models and types of experiences available in their organizations.

Ability to Learn

Having the opportunity to learn through access to a variety of developmental experiences is only one part of the leadership development equation. Managers need to make the most of these experiences. Simply going through an experience does not guarantee that learning will occur.

Researchers have begun to look at the characteristics of managers who are particularly good learners (Bunker & Webb, 1992; Dechant, 1990; Marsick & Watkins, 1990; Noer, 1996; McCall, 1994; Perkins, 1994; Spreitzer, McCall, & Mahoney, 1997). The settings and frameworks used in the various studies are quite diverse, but several themes do emerge in descriptions of managers who are particularly adept at learning (McCauley & Brutus, 1998):

- Learning orientation. Learning is a central concept in these managers' approach to their work. They see life as a series of ongoing learning experiences. They accept responsibility for learning and seek experiences that will enhance their personal development.

- Proactive stance toward problems and opportunities. These managers tackle problems head-on; they are biased toward action. They also have a sense of adventure; they like to experience new things, try out new ideas, and meet new people. When they find themselves in a new situation or identify a learning deficit in themselves, they take initiative and are self-directed in their efforts to satisfy their learning needs.
- Critical reflection. These managers bring their assumptions, premises, criteria, and schemata into consciousness and vigorously critique them (Marsick & Watkins, 1990). They pay attention to surprising results and try to understand them. They explore how things work, why things are the way they are, and what makes people tick. They see patterns and connections between seemingly unconnected variables. They ask probing questions and look at questions from different angles. They seek out feedback, comparison points, benchmarks, and role models. They try to understand their own strengths and weaknesses and diagnose the gaps between their current skills and what is needed in a situation.
- Openness. Managers who appear to learn the most from their experiences are not dogmatic or autocratic. They are open to other points of view, to feedback and criticism from others, and to shifting their strategies midstream. They more readily give up ideas or behaviors that prove to be less effective. Their rules-of-thumb for managing emphasize being open to information from the environment. They are sensitive to cultural differences and change behavior in response to these differences.

Van Velsor and Guthrie (1998) have examined how intelligence and personality factors may influence the ease with which managers can take on the various learning behaviors described above. First, there is the issue of intelligence, a factor that is commonly associated with ability to learn. But what most Americans think of as intelligence (a combination of linguistic, logical-mathematical, and spatial intelligences as defined by Gardner, 1993) may not be the kind of intelligence most important for learning from the kinds of developmental experiences managers encounter in their careers. Argyris (1991) even argues that managers who are very "smart" in this way often do not learn because they are unable to recognize the need for personal change or new behaviors. Certainly the type of intelligence assessed most commonly in IQ tests is important for dealing with the complex business information executives must handle, but Van Velsor and Guthrie suggest that two types of personal intelligence are key for learning to be a more effective leader. Gardner (1993) describes interpersonal intelligence as the ability to understand other people and intrapersonal intelligence as the ability to form an accurate model of oneself and to be able to use that model to operate effectively in everyday life.

Several personality dimensions may also play an important role in the ability to learn. Those who are above average on openness to experience (McCrae & Costa, 1990) may more naturally learn from developmental experiences. People with this orientation have a sense of adventure and enjoy trying out new ideas, having novel experiences, and meeting new people. Those who are above average on conscientiousness may also pursue learning more vigorously— taking responsibility for learning, working hard to change as the result of feedback, and persisting in the face of challenge and difficult learning goals. A strong internal locus of control—a belief that outcomes are a direct result of one's own effort—might also predispose managers to be more learning oriented. They may feel that they can learn and change: master new experiences, improve as the result of feedback, be more like a role model, or apply a skill learned in a training program.

One way to ensure a high level of ability to learn is to select and retain individuals who naturally have this ability. Thanks to personal predisposition and early life experiences, these people tend to have both a learning orientation and the skills to learn effectively from experience. Some organizations do look for ability to learn when they are hiring at entry management positions. They may ask specific questions in interviews that provide insight into the individual as a learner—for example: When was the last time you faced an unfamiliar task, and how did you handle it? Tell us about a recent significant learning experience.

Selecting individuals on the basis of their ability to learn is attractive because managers early in their career have not had the opportunity to learn the skills and abilities they will need as senior managers. They do not have miniature versions of strategic thinking, or the ability to coordinate multiple units, or political negotiation skills. But if they do have high learning ability and are exposed to a variety of learning opportunities, then they are more likely to develop executive competencies.

One potential problem with the selection approach is that estimates of the percentage of managers who naturally have high ability to learn are quite low—in the range of 10 to 15 percent (Bunker & Webb, 1992; Perkins, 1994). Without sophisticated selection techniques and with fierce competition for managerial talent, an organization's chances of having the talent pool they need for senior positions are quite low. Thus, the second approach—helping managers improve their ability to learn—is an attractive alternative.

The strategies to develop the ability to learn are much like those used to develop any other competency. Managers should be educated about learning strategies, should get feedback about their own learning skills and behaviors, should have the opportunity to practice—in both skill-building formal programs and job assignments—and should be able to observe and learn from senior managers who have well-developed learning capacity.

Organizational Context

Three aspects of the organizational context are particularly important for leadership development: a leadership development strategy with a strong link to the organization's business goals and strategy, human resource management practices that support development, and an organizational culture that reinforces the importance of learning.

Link to Business Goals and Strategy

The reason for developing executive talent is to serve the goals of the organization. Thus, a clear link needs to be established between business goals and strategies and the desired outcomes of leadership development (Seibert, Hall, & Kram, 1995). An important way to guide leadership development strategy is to determine what kinds of executive capabilities are particularly needed to implement organizational strategies. For example, the organization may be changing in ways that call for more executives who can work globally, manage partnerships and alliances, or facilitate temporary teams that quickly resolve customer issues. Or the organization may have goals to improve its performance on particular dimensions, such as innovation, speed to market, customer service, or diversity. Organizational support for leadership training and development will be stronger when it is designed and framed in the context of the business strategy it supports (Dalton & Hollenbeck, 1996). However, this link between business strategy and leadership development strategy is often missing or not well articulated in organizations (Seibert et al., 1995). The link can be strengthened in a number of ways (Hall, 1995; Ready, Vicere, & White, 1994; Seibert et al., 1995; Zenger, Ulrich, & Smallwood, 2000):

- Starting the formal training and development program design processes by articulating the strategic imperatives to be served by the program
- Putting together top management teams that communicate the direction for the business and the executive capacities needed to support those directions
- Developing close partnerships between key senior line managers and human resource staff who design, implement, and support developmental interventions
- Avoiding the oversystematization of development initiatives to allow for more responsiveness to emerging business needs
- Using the new types of job assignments created by new organizational strategies as natural executive development opportunities
- Clearly articulating the link between leadership capacities and the business results that managers are asked to achieve
- Evaluating how the outcomes of leadership development support business strategy

Human Resource Management Practices

Leadership training and development initiatives are part of a larger human resource management system that includes development planning, reward systems, succession planning, and personnel tracking processes. These components need to align with and support efforts to develop executive leadership capabilities within the organization.

Development Planning

Development planning is a process by which managers routinely take a look at their strengths and weakness and set goals for skills they want to improve or behaviors they want to change in order to be more effective. In many organizations, bosses are expected to engage in development planning with their direct reports annually. But in reality, this is often a haphazard process highly dependent on the skills and motivation of the boss. Human resource professionals in the organization need to provide the tools, training, and support for engaging in development planning with direct reports. This includes tools for identifying development needs, choosing appropriate development strategies and opportunities, and assessing progress toward goals; training in giving feedback and in coaching others; and support through the providing of resources and being the "coach's coach."

Reward Systems

Reward systems send a clear signal about what is important and valued in the organization. Thus, organizations need to examine whether their reward systems actually encourage learning and development. Are bosses held accountable for their subordinates' development? Are they rewarded for being a good developer of staff? Are people rewarded for setting and reaching developmental goals? Are there rewards for learning new skills or taking on new responsibilities?

Succession Planning

The most traditional approach to succession planning is one in which candidates are identified who are ready to move into a key job should it become vacant. The desire is to find the candidate whose skills and abilities best fit with the job so that he or she can immediately work efficiently and effectively in the job.

Increasingly organizations are using succession planning as a system for developing senior leaders. This requires identifying candidates who would benefit from a key assignment rather than those who already have all the knowledge and skills needed to handle the demands of the job. In one study, 31 percent of executive promotion decisions were developmental in nature (Ruderman & Ohlott, 1994). In these promotions, executives were being prepared for advancement, groomed for key positions, or given the opportunity to improve in order to prevent derailment. As part of its succession planning strategy, Citicorp places high-potential managers in developmental assignments for which they are only 60 to 70 percent qualified (Clark & Lyness, 1991). Looking across a number of organizations, Friedman (1986) found that incorporating individual development needs into succession planning decision is related to improved organizational reputation and financial performance.

Tracking Individual Development

Most organizations do not systematically track how their managers develop over time. They may keep records of jobs held and training programs attended. They may have personnel files with development plans. But they usually know little about how developmental any of these experiences were for their managers, whether they made progress on developmental plans, or what capacities they have developed over time. So they have little sense of the development history of their managers. If they more systematically tracked development, they would have a better sense of whether their managers are getting a variety of developmental experiences, what kinds of experiences appear to be most developmental in their organization, and if there is evidence that a manager has a high ability to learn from experience. They would also be communicating that development is an important enough aspect of managerial careers to be tracked and monitored.

Organizational Culture

The values, expectations, and norms shared by organization members define an organization's culture. Thus, the culture represents the shared mind-set that allows organization members to perceive and understand events and activities in similar ways. There are various shared mind-sets that encourage and support leadership development in an organization. Three are key: learning is a necessary part of work, feedback is a responsibility, and senior managers have responsibility for leadership development.

Learning Is a Necessary Part of Work

In a learning culture, the key mind-set is that individual, team, and organizational learning is a necessary part of the work of the organization (Tracey, Tannenbaum, & Kavanaugh, 1995; Wilson, McCauley, & Kelly-Radford, 1998). In other words, to be successful, the organization must not only produce high-quality products or services that meet needs in the marketplace, but must do so in a way that allows for continuous learning and improvement. Organizations with a strong learning culture see flexibility and adaptability as key to maximizing their performance in an increasingly complex and uncertain environment. In such a culture, ongoing learning and development are expectations. Managers are not reluctant to coach employees or allow them to attend training programs. Development budgets are not the first ones cut during financial uncertainty.

Feedback Is a Responsibility

Cultures in which giving feedback is a chore, receiving feedback a threat, and mistakes or deficiencies are hidden or downplayed will not encourage leadership development. Yet many organizations fall into this pattern because it is easier to believe that smart people will figure things out for themselves. But managers cannot learn, develop, and improve if they do not know how they are doing. They need input from others to make these assessments.

When managers are expected to seek out feedback and coworkers are expected to provide it in a constructive way, continuous learning is possible. And how mistakes are handled is a clear signal of an organization's orientation toward feedback. If they are hidden or mean the end of a career, then they are to be avoided at all costs and not to be examined for potential learning. The trial-and-error learning that makes work experiences a powerful source of development becomes impossible if "errors" are avoided or never surfaced. Morrison (1989) relates the story told by one manager who had just lost his company $10,000 and asked his boss if he were to be fired. "Why should I fire you now?" his boss replied. "I've just invested $10,000 in your development!"

*Senior Managers Have Responsibility
for Leadership Development*

A survey of management development practices in Fortune 500 companies revealed a strong belief that responsibility for the development of managers must rest at the highest levels of the organization (Conference Board, 1996). Leadership development is more likely to be linked with business strategy if senior managers play a key role in designing leadership development processes in the organization. They must also play an active role in developing others through informal mentoring and coaching or through taking on visible roles in formal development efforts. The culture at ServiceMaster Company encourages managers to coach and teach others, as noted by the company's chairman: "If a manager is too busy to teach, then he or she is probably too busy to be a manager at ServiceMaster. We are all involved in the teaching process" (Conference Board, 1996, p. 25). Visibility in formal development efforts is a key practice at Pepsico, where the CEO regularly teaches a leadership course for up-and-coming managers.

Development at the Executive Level

Development does not stop once managers reach the executive level, but it may become more difficult. Kaplan, Drath, and Kofodimos (1985) studied the factors that inhibit development at senior levels in organizations. First, the power, isolation, and autonomy afforded senior executives discourage feedback and criticism from others. Second, the complex and fast-paced nature of their jobs allows little time for reflection, introspection, or attending formal training. Third, the high degree of competence and success that propelled them into senior management roles can create too much self-confidence, or even arrogance, leading to beliefs that they no longer need to develop or to change anything about their behavior. So without the awareness of weaknesses brought about through feedback and introspection, or the motivation to change what already appears to be a winning formula, development at the senior levels can become stalled.

But it is unlikely that managers arrive at the executive suite with complete mastery of executive work or with no flaws. And senior managers are surrounded with opportunities for continued development. Recent surveys indicate a growing investment by companies in executive education ("Learning to Lead," 1999; Vicere & Fulmer, 1997). Bolt (1989) reported that the most senior executives are expected to spend about a week in executive education programs, with executives just below them spending one to two weeks in programs. The data in Table 11.2 indicate that more than three-fourths of U.S. corporations use 360-degree feedback and executive coaching at their top management levels. In addition, job assignments at the executive level are more likely to have the characteristics of developmental jobs (McCauley et al., 1994). Executives are also sought out as coaches and mentors and increasingly are serving in teaching roles in training programs for others in the organization (teaching others can be a powerful learning experience).

Despite the wide variety of developmental opportunities available at the executive level, executives need to be encouraged to take advantage of these opportunities. There is a tendency for leaders at this level to think they are already "developed." In addition, the demands of their positions create more of a task or performance orientation than a learning orientation. And executives have more discretion over whether they will pursue a developmental opportunity. Ongoing executive development can be supported by a CEO who continues to teach and coach his senior team and be a role model for ongoing development, development plans at all levels in the organization and rewards for continued development, and a climate that allows senior managers to be open with one another about their strengths and developmental needs. Whether preparing managers for executive leadership roles or supporting the ongoing development of executives, the same factors are important: the availability of a variety of developmental experiences that provide assessment, challenge, and support; the ability to learn; and an organizational context that encourages and supports learning.

Leadership training and development initiatives at the executive level are more likely to be tied closely to implementing business strategies or organizational change efforts (Bolt, 1989) rather than to developing general leadership capacities. For example, the Executive Leadership Institute at ARAMARK was created to address the core strategic imperatives of the organization; its objectives included creating a shared vision for growth and embracing change in order to have continued success as an organization (Vicere & Fulmer, 1997). Second, the content of training and education programs at this level reflects the tasks of the executive: formulating and implementing strategy, creating and managing change, and developing a broader business perspective. In addition, the learning styles of the typical executive and the time pressures that executives normally feel force these programs to be highly pragmatic, challenging, fast paced, and full of questioning and debate (Rose, 2000).

Executive development programs tend to fall in one of two categories: external programs conducted primarily by major business schools, which usually last several weeks, and short, highly customized internal programs (Bolt, 1989; Vicere & Fulmer, 1997). External programs provide outside perspective, network-building opportunities, a broader vision, the latest management information, a chance for renewal, and self-esteem enhancement (Vicere, Taylor, & Freeman, 1993). Customized internal programs can be more closely tied to business strategies, reach more executives more quickly, build internal cohesiveness, and target the organization's specific development needs. Customized programs have generally been designed and delivered by consultants or by internal training and development staff, but a growing trend is to bring together several providers with differing areas of expertise to partner in the design and delivery of a broader developmental initiative ("Learning to Lead," 1999). For example, the World Bank commissioned five graduate schools to design and deliver an executive education program targeted to improve capabilities as diverse as improving client relationships, financial analysis, and developing a culture committed to performance (Vicere & Fulmer, 1997). A third approach, the consortium model, is a hybrid, combining aspects of the external and customized programs (Lawler, 2000). In this approach, an education provider organizes a small group of noncompeting companies to share the cost and collaborate in the design of a developmental program for their executives.

A final difference in the developmental opportunities at executive levels is related to job experiences. Certainly executive-level jobs are more likely to have some of the job characteristics identified as developmental: experiences building relationships and creating change, high responsibility, and high latitude. What they may have less opportunity for are job transitions. There may be less lateral movement at these levels and fewer opportunities to continue to move upward. Greyhound Financial Corporation offers a strategy to overcome this obstacle (Northcraft, Griffith, & Shalley, 1992). Top-rated executives in this company are offered the opportunity to be placed in jobs doing tasks different from those in their background and experience by swapping jobs for several years with another executive in the organization. In addition to developing the talents of individual executives, the company has found that this strategy helps prevent career gridlock, fosters management diversity, and provides for top management succession.

Future Research Directions

Although a great deal is known from research and practice about preparing managers throughout their careers for executive leadership positions, there are noticeable gaps in our knowledge. The largest gaps may be in the area of organizational context. First, although we have some initial ideas of the kind of culture that encourages development at all levels of an organization, more insight is needed on how ongoing assessment, challenge, and support become embedded in the day-to-day values, processes, and systems of an organization. Also, are there specific aspects of organizational systems that encourage continued development once managers reach the executive ranks? Finally, as organizations themselves change in response to a changing external environment characterized by increased globalization, more diverse workforces, and increased demand for customization, how executives exercise leadership and the developmental path to the executive level will likely be reshaped.

Knowledge about developmental experiences in managerial careers has relied heavily on retrospective reports of executives and case studies of developmental interventions in specific companies. There is a need for more longitudinal studies of executive development, more systematic study of the impact of formal developmental interventions, and examination of the impact of these interventions across organizations. Also, much more is known about naturally occurring experiences and formal interventions than is known about self-directed learning activities.

In terms of knowledge about the ability to learn, what is perhaps most needed is an overarching framework or theory that integrates and helps explain the individual difference variables that have been associated with learning ability. Most research has tended to focus on a limited number of variables, chosen for inclusion in a particular study based on a hodgepodge of theories. A more well-developed construct grounded in broader learning theory could serve as a springboard for future research.

Organizational investment in leadership training and development for executives and for high-potential employees on the path to executive positions continues to grow. These organizations are developing approaches and interventions, with or without the benefit of research-based knowledge. It is an area where research cannot seem to keep up with the pace and demand of practitioners and is thus a fruitful area for research-practitioner collaborations.

References

Argyris, C. (1991). Teaching smart people to learn. *Harvard Business Review, 69*(3), 99–109.

Atwater, L. E., Roush, P., & Fischthal, A. (1995). The influence of upward feedback on self- and follower ratings of leadership. *Personnel Psychology, 48*, 35–60.

Bolt, J. F. (1989). *Executive development: A strategy for corporate competitiveness.* New York: HarperBusiness.

Bonoma, T. V., & Lawler, J. C. (1989). Chutes and ladders: Growing the general manager. *Sloan Management Review, 30*(3), 27–37.

Bunker, K., & Webb, A. (1992). *Learning how to learn from experience: Impact of stress and coping.* Greensboro, NC: Center for Creative Leadership.

Carden, A. D. (1990). Mentoring and adult career development: The evolution of a theory. *Counseling Psychologist, 18,* 275–299.

Chappelow, C. (1998). 360-degree feedback. In C. D. McCauley, R. S. Moxley, & E. Van Velsor (Eds.), *The Center for Creative Leadership handbook of leadership development.* San Francisco: Jossey-Bass.

Clark, L. A., & Lyness, K. S. (1991). Succession planning as a strategic activity at Citicorp. In L. W. Foster (Ed.), *Advances in applied business strategy* (Vol. 2). Greenwich, CT: JAI Press.

Conference Board. (1996). *Corporate practices in management development: A research report.* New York: Conference Board.

Conference Board. (1999). Developing leaders. *Human Resources Executive Review, 7,* 1–19.

Conger, J. A. (1992). *Learning to lead: The art of transforming managers into leaders.* San Francisco: Jossey-Bass.

Dalton, M. A. (1998). Developing leaders for global roles. In C. D. Mc-Cauley, R. S. Moxley, & E. Van Velsor (Eds.), *The Center for Creative Leadership handbook of leadership development*. San Francisco: Jossey-Bass.

Dalton, M. A., & Hollenbeck, G. P. (1996). *How to design an effective system for developing managers and executives*. Greensboro, NC: Center for Creative Leadership.

Dechant, K. (1990). Knowing how to learn: The "neglected" management ability. *Journal of Management Development, 9*(4), 40–49.

Dixon, N. (1994). *The organizational learning cycle: How we can learn collectively*. New York: McGraw-Hill.

Dotlich, D. L., & Noel, J. L. (1998). *Action learning: How the world's top companies are re-creating themselves and their leaders*. San Francisco: Jossey-Bass.

Douglas, C. A. (1997). *Formal mentoring programs in organizations: An annotated bibliography*. Greensboro, NC: Center for Creative Leadership.

Friedman, S. D. (1986). Succession systems in large corporations: Characteristics and correlates of performance. *Human Resource Management, 25*, 191–213.

Froiland, P. (1994). Action learning: Taming real problems in real time. *Training, 31*(1), 27–34.

Gardner, H. (1993). *Frames of mind: The theory of multiple intelligences*. New York: Basic Books.

Goodge, P. (1991). Development centres: Guidelines for decision makers. *Journal of Management Development, 10*(3), 4–12.

Gray, W. A. (1988). Developing a planned mentoring program to facilitate career development. *Career Planning and Adult Development Journal, 4*(2), 9–16.

Guthrie, V., & Kelly-Radford, L. (1998). Feedback intensive programs. In C. D. McCauley, R. S. Moxley, & E. Van Velsor (Eds.), *The Center for Creative Leadership handbook of leadership development*. San Francisco: Jossey-Bass.

Hall, D. T. (1995). Executive careers and learning: Aligning selection, strategy, and development. *Human Resource Planning, 18*(2), 14–23.

Hall, D. T., Otazo, K. L., & Hollenbeck, G. P. (1999). Behind closed doors: What really happens in executive coaching. *Organizational Dynamics, 27*(3), 39–53.

Henderson, I. (1993). Action learning: A missing link in management development? *Personnel Review, 22*(6), 14–24.

Kaplan, R. E., Drath, W. H., & Kofodimos, J. R. (1985). *High hurdles: The challenge of executive self-development*. Greensboro, NC: Center for Creative Leadership.

Kram, K. E. (1985). *Mentoring at work*. Glenview, IL: Scott, Foresman.

Kram, K. E., & Isabella, L. A. (1985). Mentoring alternatives: The role of peer relationships in career development. *Academy of Management Journal, 28,* 110–132.

Lawler, W. (2000). The consortium approach to grooming future leaders. *Training and Development, 54*(3), 53–57.

Lazarus, R. S., & Folkman, S. (1984). *Stress, appraisal, and coping.* New York: Springer.

Learning to lead. (1999, October 18). *Business Week,* pp. 76–80.

Lepsinger, R., & Lucia, A. D. (1997). *The art and science of 360-degree feedback.* San Francisco: Pfeiffer.

Levinson, (1978). *Seasons of a man's life.* New York: Knopf.

Little, D. M. (1991). *How executives learn: The demographic impact on executive development in the public service.* Unpublished doctoral dissertation, University of Southern California.

Marsick, V. J. (1990). Experience-based learning: Executive learning outside the classroom. *Journal of Management Development, 9*(4), 50–60.

Marsick, V. J., & Watkins, K. E. (1990). *Informal and incidental learning in the workplace.* New York: Routledge.

McCall, M. W., Jr. (1994). Identifying leadership potential in future international executives: Developing a concept. *Consulting Psychology Journal, 46,* 49–63.

McCall, M. W., Jr., Lombardo, M. M., & Morrison, A. M. (1988). *The lessons of experience: How successful executives develop on the job.* San Francisco: New Lexington Press.

McCauley, C. D., & Brutus, S. (1998). *Management development through job experiences: An annotated bibliography.* Greensboro, NC: Center for Creative Leadership.

McCauley, C. D., & Douglas, C. A. (1998). Developmental relationships. In C. D. McCauley, R. S. Moxley, & E. Van Velsor (Eds.), *The Center for Creative Leadership handbook of leadership development.* San Francisco: Jossey-Bass.

McCauley, C. D., Ruderman, M. N., Ohlott, P. J., & Morrow, J. E. (1994). Assessing the developmental components of managerial jobs. *Journal of Applied Psychology, 79,* 544–560.

McCauley, C. D., & Young, D. P. (1993). Creating developmental relationships: Roles and strategies. *Human Resource Management Review, 3,* 219–230.

McCrae, R. R., & Costa, P. T. (1990). *Personality in adulthood.* New York: Guilford Press.

McDonald-Mann, D. (1998). Skill-based training. In C. D. McCauley, R. S. Moxley, & E. Van Velsor (Eds.), *The Center for Creative Leadership handbook of leadership development.* San Francisco: Jossey-Bass.

Morrison, A. M. (1989, July). On-the-job training for managers. *Small Business Reports,* pp. 62–67.

Morrison, A. M., White, R. P., & Van Velsor, E. (1992). *Breaking the glass ceiling: Can women reach the top of America's largest corporations?* (Updated ed.). Reading, MA: Addison-Wesley.

Moxley, R. S. (1998). Hardships. In C. D. McCauley, R. S. Moxley, & E. Van Velsor (Eds.), *The Center for Creative Leadership handbook of leadership development.* San Francisco: Jossey-Bass.

Munchus, G., & McArthur, B. (1991). Revisiting the historical use of the assessment center in management selection and development. *Journal of Management Development, 10,* 5–13.

Murray, M., & Owen, M. A. (1991). *Beyond the myths and magic of mentoring: How to facilitate an effective mentoring program.* San Francisco: Jossey-Bass.

Newby, T. J., & Heide, A. (1992). The value of mentoring. *Performance Improvement Quarterly, 5*(4), 2–15.

Noe, R. A. (1988). An investigation of the determinants of successful assigned mentoring relationships. *Personnel Psychology, 41,* 457–479.

Noer, D. M. (1996). *Breaking free: A prescription for personal and organizational change.* San Francisco: Jossey-Bass.

Northcraft, G. B., Griffith, T. L., & Shalley, C. E. (1992). Building top management muscle in a slow growth environment: How different is better at Greyhound Financial Corporation. *Academy of Management Executive, 6*(1), 32–40.

Perkins, A. G. (1994). The learning mind-set: Who's got it, what it's good for. *Harvard Business Review, 72*(2), 11–12.

Ready, D. A., Vicere, A. A., & White, A. F. (1994). Linking executive education to strategic imperatives. *Management Learning, 25,* 563–578.

Reuber, A. R., & Fischer, E. M. (1993). The learning experiences of entrepreneurs. In *Frontiers of Entrepreneurship Research.* Proceedings of the Babson Entrepreneurship Research Conference, Houston, TX.

Revans, R. W. (1980). *Action learning: New techniques for management.* London: Blond & Briggs.

Rose, I. (2000, March 13). *Innovative techniques in executive development: A study by IBR Consulting Services.* E-mail summary of unpublished study.

Ruderman, M. N., & Ohlott, P. J. (1994). *The realities of management promotion.* Greensboro, NC: Center for Creative Leadership.

Seibert, K. W., Hall, D. T., & Kram, K. E. (1995). Strengthening the weak link in strategic executive development: Integrating individual development and global business strategy. *Human Resource Management, 34,* 549–567.

Smither, J. W., London, M., Vasilopoulos, N. L., Reily, R. R., Millsap, R. E., & Salvemini, N. (1995). An examination of the effects of an upward feedback program over time. *Personnel Psychology, 48,* 1–34.

Spreitzer, G. M., McCall, M. W., Jr., & Mahoney, J. D. (1997). Early identification of international executive potential. *Journal of Applied Psychology, 82,* 6–29.

Tornow, W. W., & London, M. (Eds.). (1998). *Maximizing the value of 360-degree feedback: A process for successful individual and organizational development.* San Francisco: Jossey-Bass.

Tracey, J. B., Tannenbaum, S. I., & Kavanaugh, M. J. (1995). Applying trained skills on the job: The importance of the work environment. *Journal of Applied Psychology, 80,* 259–232.

Van Velsor, E., & Guthrie, V. (1998). Enhancing the ability to learn from experience. In C. D. McCauley, R. S. Moxley, & E. Van Velsor (Eds.), *The Center for Creative Leadership handbook of leadership development.* San Francisco: Jossey-Bass.

Van Velsor, E., McCauley, C. D., & Moxley, R. S. (1998). In C. D. McCauley, R. S. Moxley, & E. Van Velsor (Eds.), *The Center for Creative Leadership handbook of leadership development.* San Francisco: Jossey-Bass.

Vicere, A. A., & Fulmer, R. M. (1997). *Leadership by design.* Boston: Harvard Business School Press.

Vicere, A. A., Taylor, M., & Freeman, V. (1993). *Executive education in major corporations.* University Park, PA: Institute for the Study of Organizational Effectiveness.

Wick, C. W., & Leon, L. S. (1993). *The learning edge: How smart managers and smart companies stay ahead.* New York: McGraw-Hill.

Wilson, P. O., McCauley, C. D., & Kelly-Radford, K. (1998). 360-degree feedback in the establishment of learning cultures. In W. W. Tornow & M. London (Eds.), *Maximizing the value of 360-degree feedback.* San Francisco: Jossey-Bass.

Witherspoon, R., & White, R. P. (1997). *Four essential ways that coaching can help executives.* Greensboro, NC: Center for Creative Leadership.

Yukl, G. (1998). *Leadership in organizations* (4th ed.). Upper Saddle River, NJ: Prentice Hall.

Zemke, R. (1985, August). The Honeywell studies: How managers learn to manage. *Training,* pp. 46–51.

Zenger, J., Ulrich, D., & Smallwood, N. (2000). The new leadership development. *Training and Development, 54*(3), 53–57.

CHAPTER 12

Assessment of Leadership Outcomes

David V. Day

*The interchange of action and structure occurs in time
and is cumulative, such that the legacy of the past is
always shaping the future.*
PETTIGREW (1992)

What we call results are beginnings.
RALPH WALDO EMERSON, *NATURE* (1836)

The word *outcome* implies some natural end state. In attempting to assess leadership outcomes, however, a much better description would be that of a "search to catch reality in flight" (Pettigrew, 1992, p. 10). Furthermore, the effects associated with leadership—especially at top organizational levels—are varied in nature, typically encompassing multiple levels as well as internal and external stakeholders; reciprocal, given that leaders directly and indirectly shape the structure and performance of an organization, but structure and performance also determine the appropriate type of leadership; and not immediately detectable, yet identifying the proper lag time for leadership effects is critical.

Considering the ongoing nature of leadership and leadership effects in organizations, along with noted methodological problems associated with leadership research at top levels (Day & Lord, 1988), gives some indication of the seemingly overwhelming task of trying to understand how to assess top-level leadership outcomes better. What we call results indeed are just beginnings. But Emerson also said, "I hate quotations. Tell me what you know." So perhaps the best place to begin is with a brief summary of what we know about the effects of top-level leaders.

It was popular for a time to argue that who occupied the executive suite was of little consequence to an organization's performance (Pfeffer, 1977). Compared with historical, environmental, and industry factors, there appeared to be minuscule remaining performance variance to be explained by individual difference variables such as leadership (Lieberson & O'Connor, 1972; Salancik & Pfeffer, 1977). More recently, Meindl and associates proposed that leadership is an overly romanticized concept and associated with effects that can be described as ephemeral at best (Meindl & Ehrlich, 1987; Meindl, Ehrlich, & Dukerich, 1985).

Subsequent research has been more optimistic about the importance of leadership. When properly interpreted and methodologically sound, the research on leadership succession, for example, has demonstrated a consistent effect for leadership that explained 20 to 45 percent of the variance in relevant organizational outcomes (Day & Lord, 1988; Thomas, 1988). Executive failure is not uncommon either, with some estimates reaching as high as 50 to 75 percent (Hogan, Raskin, & Fazzini, 1990; White & De Vries, 1990). Individual high-profile failures such as Robert Stempel at General Motors have been associated with contributing to the loss of billions of dollars in a single organization. To be more exact, because of his lack of a new vision for GM as well as his emphasis on management rather than leadership, Stempel and his top management team were held accountable for a total loss of more than $12 billion in 1990 and 1991 in GM's North American operations (Tornow, 1992). Put simply, leadership, like personality, matters in the real world (Hogan, 1998; Hogan, Curphy, & Hogan, 1994).

There has been a long-running debate in both the academic and popular press literatures on the overlap between leadership and management. Most authors agree that they are different constructs, but disagree as to the degree of difference. Some try to capture the distinction in a pithy saying, such as, "Managers are people who do things right and leaders are people who do the right thing" (Bennis & Nanus, 1985, p. 21). This is not very helpful. The approach today requires a more radical perspective, perhaps in the tradition of Zaleznik (1977), who argued that managers and leaders are qualitatively different kinds of people. Although managers and leaders may not be fundamentally different species, their roles are quite different. According to Kotter (1990), management is primarily about producing order and consistency, whereas leadership is responsible for adaptive and constructive change. Put somewhat differently, management is concerned with outcomes related to efficiency and preserving the status quo; leadership is an imperative for transformation.

Leaders at any level, and especially top levels, should address themselves to initiating and sustaining lasting organizational change. In terms of assessing leadership outcomes, we need to understand the range of possibilities with regard to relevant outcomes for top-level leaders, especially those related to organizational effectiveness. We also need to consider how such indicators might be changed through leadership, given that change is the fundamental outcome by which to gauge leadership, especially at top levels. Finally, we need to determine how best to measure these prospective changes.

Strategic Leadership Outcomes

The primary focus here is on executives who have overall responsibility for an organization—what has been termed *strategic leadership* (Finkelstein & Hambrick, 1996). A fundamental assumption of the strategic leadership approach is that an organization's strategy is a result of individual choice (Child, 1972) and that the choices of those in upper-echelon positions have the most influence on company performance. However, responsibility for strategic leadership does not reside solely with a single individual such as the chief executive officer. There are potentially many executives with responsibility for the overall well-being of an organization, including (but not necessarily limited to) the board of directors, members of the top management team, business unit general managers, and other senior executives (Finkelstein & Hambrick, 1996). Some elaboration is needed as to what the key responsibilities of these potential leaders are. One approach is to examine common indicators of business performance used in strategy research. That is, a general understanding of the basic kinds of organizational performance measures is needed to appreciate fully what the important change outcomes are that can be linked with strategic leadership.

It is an understatement to note that business performance is a multidimensional criterion. At a minimum, strategic leadership entails internal as well as external targets (Day & Lord, 1988) and incorporates direct and indirect tactics (Brewer, 1983). An overall classification scheme for business performance proposed it as a subset of the overall concept of organizational effectiveness (Venkatraman & Ramanujam, 1986). More specifically, outcome-based financial indicators reflect the attainment of the economic goals of the company yet provide the narrowest perspective on business performance. Typical indicators of financial performance include:

- Gross, unadjusted indexes, such as sales, income, and revenue
- Profitability measures, such as return on investment, return on equity, return on sales, and return on assets
- Value-based indexes, such as stock price and earnings per share

At the next broadest level is operational (that is, nonfinancial) performance, which subsumes financial performance. Such indicators include the following:

- Market share
- New product introduction
- Product quality
- Marketing effectiveness
- Measures of technological efficiency

One way to think of these indicators is as mechanisms that contribute to overall financial performance (Venkatraman & Ramanujam, 1986) or the economic health of an organization. Interestingly, Chakravarthy (1986) was unable to differentiate empirically between effective and ineffective firms in the computer industry using traditional financial and operational measures of strategic performance. However, measures based on estimated quality of the firm's transactions (not just outcomes) and satisfaction of all stakeholders (not just shareholders) were significant discriminators of strategic performance. These two measures could best be characterized as types of organizational effectiveness indexes.

At the broadest, most subsuming level is organizational effectiveness. The literature on effectiveness indicates a number of difficulties in attempting to study it empirically, including multiple constituencies (Connolly, Conlon, & Deutsch, 1980), multiple theoretical models (Cameron & Whetten, 1983), and measurement difficulties (Steers, 1975). In attempting to provide some direction in the assessment of organizational effectiveness, Cameron and Whetten (1983) proposed seven guidelines that would "provide an itinerary for mapping the construct space of effectiveness" (p. 270):

- From whose perspective is effectiveness being judged?
- On what domain of activity is the judgment focused?
- What level of analysis is being used?
- What is the purpose of judging effectiveness?
- What time frame is being employed?
- What types of data are being used for judgments of effectiveness?
- What is the referent against which effectiveness is judged?

These guidelines in no way define organizational effectiveness, but merely serve as a means of cataloguing the various assessment approaches. As such, they are useful questions to keep in mind when assessing strategic leadership outcomes.

An important consideration in assessing organizational effectiveness (as well as financial and operational performance) is that there are multiple influences on these outcomes and that top-level leaders are often constrained in their ability to change them (Hambrick & Abrahamson, 1995; Hambrick & Finkelstein, 1987; Salancik & Pfeffer, 1977). These constraints can be imposed by actions from other top managers and the board of directors or through general limits on managerial discretion. Choosing the appropriate type of data and the proper level of analysis for a particular industry and organization are two critical concerns with regard to appreciating the potential constraints on strategic leaders.

A somewhat different perspective on organizational effectiveness can be found by considering what leaders at the strategic apex are ultimately responsible for. In this regard, an interesting metaphor for organizational effectiveness is health. When the health of an organization is impaired, much as with any biological organism or open system (Katz & Kahn, 1978), its survival is potentially threatened. Thus, it could be argued that survival is the ultimate criterion by which to gauge organizational success. Threats to the health or survival of any organization can take many forms, including those of an external nature (for example, regulatory, environmental, technological, market based) or internal nature (poor human resource practices, inefficiency, dysfunctional climate). Trying to understand how strategic leaders respond to these threats gets at a central nexus, but risks collapsing of its own weight, given the myriad of possible actions and reactions. In addition, such a listing of possible reactions to strategic threats provides no general framework for the assessment of leadership outcomes (that is, change). What, if anything, is key to the health of an organization? For those leaders at the highest organization levels in which a systems perspective is imperative for successful performance (Katz & Kahn, 1978), it may be primarily a function of an organization's identity, image, and reputation.

Key Strategic Leadership Functions

Hogan (1998) makes an important point that individual personality varies naturally as a function of perspective: the actor's and the observer's. Both perspectives are critically important, but may be only modestly related in an empirical sense. How do such perspectives relate to identity and reputation? Furthermore, what do these concepts have to do with organizations and, more important, strategic leadership outcomes? Consider the following quotation from Hogan (pp. 7–8):

> We think about ourselves in terms of our identities. We think about others in terms of their reputations. Other people turn our social behavior, which is guided by our identities, into our reputations. It is clearly in our best interest to think about this. Being a criminal, being homeless, being an addict is as much an identity choice as being a psychologist. Why do people make self-defeating identity choices? Again, we see the continuing relevance of Freud, who originally highlighted the problem of self-deception. Mostly we are not very mindful or insightful about our goals, projects, or choices—our identities—which means that we lose control of our reputations.

Hogan's basic point (1998) is that personality is a function of identity and reputation, and both are defined through social behavior. The points Hogan raised also have organizational relevance and relevance for the assessment of leadership outcomes at the strategic apex of organizations. Selznick (1957) first noted that the study of organizations is comparable to the clinical study of personality, because both entities are inherently concerned with self-preservation, and "self-presentation has to do with the maintenance of basic identity, with the integrity of a personal or institutional 'self'" (pp. 141–142).

There also is an irrational side of self to consider. Like individuals, organizations make self-defeating identity choices—or those who have responsibility for overall functioning make such apparently irrational strategic choices. Consider the example of the now-defunct Pan American Airways, which sold off most of its profitable ventures to concentrate on its floundering airline business (Lord & Maher, 1991). Pan Am thought about itself as an airline (its core identity), not a hotel or real estate business. It is possible that before being able to bring about successful strategic change through the acquisition of nonairline businesses, the top leaders at Pan Am needed to change the organization's identity. Because the leadership could not or would not make such changes, strong organizational identity contributed to strategic rigidity, which ultimately contributed to Pan Am's demise. A failure to change identity can threaten the survival of an organization.

Organizational Identity and Image

It has been suggested that the best top-level leaders are able to answer three simple questions, and do so in an engaging manner: Who am I? Who are we? Where are we going? (Tichy, 1997; Weil, 1998). The first two questions deal with identity (individual and organizational, respectively), and the third pertains to envisioned organizational identity. So what is the nature of organizational identity, and how does it differ from the individual kind? Furthermore, what is envisioned identity?

Organization identity is what members believe to be the central, enduring, and distinctive character of an organization (Albert & Whetten, 1985). There is a parallel with individual identity, in that both types of identity provide for the ability to experience one's self or one's organization as something that has continuity and sameness and to act accordingly (Erikson, 1950). At either the individual or organizational level, loss of identity poses a serious threat to the health of a system. As with individual identity, organizational identity is reflected in the goals, projects, and choices that are made—primarily the strategic choices made by those at top levels (Child, 1972; Donaldson & Lorsch, 1983; Finkelstein & Hambrick, 1996). Identity reflects an organization's biography (Greenwood & Hinings, 1993) and comprises core organizational values as well as modes of performance and types of products (Elsbach & Kramer, 1996). Interpretive schemes, or those shared, fundamental (but implicit) assumptions that guide how members make sense of events and how people act in different situations (Bartunek, 1984; Ranson, Hinings, & Greenwood, 1980) are also important components of identity.

Several recent studies have demonstrated the significance of organizational identity in enacting effective strategic change. In examining strategic change in higher education, Gioia and Thomas (1996) suggested that successful change is preceded by a change in identity. In particular, identities need to be changed to be more fluid and flexible. Albert and Whetten (1985) discuss the issue of "identity drift" (p. 276), specifically, the drift or evolution from mono- to multiple identities. Over time, successful organizations develop, through the vision and behavior of top-level leaders, multiple identities to exploit the opportunities provided by an increasingly complex and changing environment and to adapt to increases in environmentally imposed constraints (that is, adaptive instability; Gioia, Schultz, & Corley, 2000).

Dutton and Dukerich (1991) demonstrated how organization identity guided individuals' interpretations of increased numbers of homeless people at the Port Authority of New York and New Jersey. Initially, identity constrained interpretations of the large number of homeless at its facilities as a police security issue, and thus as a threat. Eventually the issue came to be seen as more than just a business problem—as a moral issue and ultimately an issue of regional competitiveness (and thus opportunity). The change in identity at the Port Authority was driven by a change in the interpretive schemes of upper management, who came to accept the organization's responsibility for dealing with the issue and acknowledged that it was more than a police problem. Another important point was that the change in organization identity was not one of substitution but of addition. Specifically, the Port Authority identity came to encompass a sort of resigned ownership of the issue, in addition to its core mission of delivering effective service to transportation agency clients.

Fox-Wolfgramm, Boal, and Hunt (1998) provide another view on the role of identity in organizational change efforts. Those authors used a grounded theory approach in examining the strategic adaptation of banks to increasing regulatory pressure to comply with the Community Redevelopment Act. Their results suggested that organizations can change without changing their identities (Gioia & Thomas, 1996); however, a key aspect in successful change was the level of plasticity in identity. Similar to the results reported by Dutton and Dukerich (1991), this suggests that organization identities need to be malleable and expansive to address change best. But to sustain organizational change, there should be some change or plasticity in an organization's envisioned identity and envisioned image.

Organization image has been conceptualized in numerous ways, including how organization members believe others see the organization (that is, construed external image; Dutton, Dukerich, & Harquail, 1994), the way key internal stakeholders would like outsiders to see the organization (Whetten, Lewis, & Mischel, 1992), and the desired future perception of the organization that is held by internal members and external others (that is, the desired future image; Gioia & Thomas, 1996). Image is a way to gauge how outsiders are judging the organization and, by association, their members. Of particular importance to organization members is maintaining some level of congruence between identity and image (Fox-Wolfgramm et al., 1998).

Incongruence or dissonance between identity and image is salient and motivating to organization members because it involves a cognitive discrepancy (Carver & Scheier, 1981; Gioia et al., 2000). Thus, aligning identity and image should be primary motivational concerns of top-level leaders. Without some level of acceptable congruence or alignment, an organization could be considered dissonant, unbalanced, unhealthy, or deceptive. However, organizational identity is not static, nor is the interrelationship between organizational identity and image likely to be perfectly consistent in so-called healthy organizations; rather, the interplay between organizational identity and image is a dynamic, mutual-influence process that can help align "an organization's sense of self-definition with its environment" (Gioia et al., 2000, p. 74). Thus, if environments are turbulent and rapidly changing, then identities are likely to be characterized by Gioia and others' notion of adaptive instability to guard against the development of an overly rigid identity. From this perspective, an organization's self-definition encompasses its strategy. As such, the current approach to strategic leadership is connected to earlier strategy theories, which proposed that the most appropriate structure, technology, and levels of integration and differentiation (that is, strategy) depend on the characteristics of the environment in which an organization operates (Lawrence & Lorsch, 1967).

Another prominent concern is with how identity and image align with envisioned future identity and image. The need for, and communication of, a future vision on the part of an organization's strategic leadership becomes apparent when cast in identity and image terms (Gioia & Chittipeddi, 1991). This represents only part of the mandate of strategic leadership, because it is internally focused. To be effective, top leadership also must be keenly attuned to their organization's external reputation.

Organizational Reputation

Image generally pertains to how organization members think others perceive them; reputation is how others actually do see them. Reputation is complicated because of the number of different constituencies. An interesting question to ponder is whether organizations have one reputation or many (Fombrun & Shanley, 1990). Regardless of the answer to that particular question, it is clear that a positive reputation is an organizational asset that can generate future "rents" in the economic sense (Weigelt & Camerer, 1988; Wilson, 1985). Specifically, a positive reputation can enhance the competitive ability of an organization by attracting more investors, lowering the cost of capital, providing an attractive target for alliance partnerships, maintaining customers, attracting new ones, and improving labor market position (Fombrun & Shanley, 1990; Saxton, 1997; Seiders & Berry, 1998). One popular manifestation of reputational importance is *Fortune*'s annual report of the so-called most admired corporations.

Reputations are fragile commodities, "oft got without merit, and lost without deserving," says Shakespeare in *Othello*. Often external threats bring issues of reputation to the forefront. How these threats are handled clearly demonstrates the importance of competent executive leadership. For example, consider the difference between the *Exxon Valdez* fiasco and Johnson and Johnson's successful handling of the Tylenol crisis. Shakespeare was right in that it takes very little for a positive reputation to be sullied through gossip or ineffectual action with a single critical incident. It is unclear as to the economic utility of an organization's reputation, but organizations are willing to spend millions in the form of advertising dollars in the attempt to build a positive one. At the individual level, reputations are vastly consequential. People will take strong actions to protect their reputations; indeed, they will kill for the sake of their reputations (Hogan, 1998). It does not take a great leap of faith to imagine organizations arranging to do the same.

The manner by which those in strategic leadership positions influence the internal concerns of organization identity and image, as well as the external issues of reputation, is an interesting topic but beyond the scope of this chapter. Suffice it to say that any comprehensive understanding of strategic leadership needs to consider that there are multiple constituencies to consider in both the internal and external environments. Of particular relevance to this book, however, is how these proposed strategic concerns relate to the seven leadership imperatives: cognitive, social, personal, political, technological, financial, and staffing. These key points of integration will be explored before turning to how changes in organization identity, image, and reputation might be assessed.

Relevance to Leadership Imperatives

It has been argued that individuals charged with the responsibility for overall organizational health need to be concerned with the fundamental missions of aligning organizational strategy with image and identity and building a positive organizational reputation. To accomplish these missions successfully, effective use of all seven leadership imperatives is necessary. Some of these imperatives may be more relevant to one or the other mission; some are relevant for both.

With regard to the cognitive imperative, leaders need a relatively high level of cognitive complexity to infer present organizational identity ("who we are") and envision future identity ("where we are going") appropriately. Previous work on the topic of leadership derailment (McCall & Lombardo, 1983; Van Velsor & Leslie, 1995) suggests that those who arrive at top levels, as well as those who derail before reaching the strategic apex (or fail after arriving), are incredibly bright. In other words, it does not appear that cognitive ability differentiates effective from ineffective leaders at the top. Levinson (1994) disagrees with this assessment, but emphasizes that the majority of problems come about because those in strategic leadership positions experience difficulty grasping the degree of complexity that must be confronted. These difficulties are exacerbated when organizations take on new and different markets. That is, some leaders cannot envision the appropriate organization identity (or identities; Albert & Whetten, 1985) to keep pace with changes in environment or market. Rather than conceptualizing the cognitive imperative in terms of general intelligence (on which there is likely a restricted range), it may be more useful to think about differences in sense-making complexity. With increasing environmental complexity, there is a tendency to search for and rely on habitual, routine cues (Weick, 1988), which may be misleading. Effective strategic leaders have the sense-making complexity to notice and understand quickly such external changes and envision their relevance for existing and future identity.

The implications for the social imperative with regard to organization identity and reputation are profound. Besides envisioning a future identity, effective leaders must communicate this vision to others in the organization and persuade them of the need to change. It is easy to say but difficult to do. Indeed, one invariant with regard to implementing change is resistance. Thus, top-level leaders need to rely extensively on charisma and referent power (Katz & Kahn, 1978) in effecting strategic change. The use of appropriate symbolism, metaphor, and storytelling is also important. Before people are willing to change, they must be able to envision it, and one of the best ways to get people to venture into the unknown is to make it safe by taking them there in their imaginations through storytelling (Tichy, 1997; Weil, 1998). On the external side of the picture, reputations are bolstered or deflated based on how well those at the top persuade external constituencies of their honesty and integrity, possibly their remorse, or certainly the attractiveness of an envisioned identity. Often this responsibility falls on the shoulders of a single individual such as the CEO. The stories are legendary, for example, of how Lee Iacocca was able to persuade the U.S. Congress of Chrysler's future vision and bankable reputation.

Going hand-in-hand with the social imperative is the personal one. With regard to identity, a leader must have a clear sense of self ("who I am") before gaining credence in communicating and building a cohesive organization identity (explaining "who we are" and "where we are going"). This is also important internally because organizations are a reflection of those at top levels (Hambrick & Mason, 1984), especially if they are founders. In other words, the identity of an organization is often an extension of the identities of powerful strategic leaders. From an external perspective, the role of impression management—both individually and collectively—is important in building reputation. Leadership often involves dealing with paradoxes and competing values, which requires a certain degree of behavioral complexity (Denison, Hooijberg, & Quinn, 1995). This is similar to the notion of organizational plasticity (Fox-Wolfgramm et al., 1998). Both behavioral complexity and organizational plasticity are needed to satisfy stakeholders, who often have multiple and conflicting criteria for organizational effectiveness.

The political imperatives are thought to relate primarily to external reputation management, but they can also be related to important factors in how conflict is managed. Attempts to change an organization's identity will likely be met by resistance in the form of disagreement with the envisioned future identity (for example, "Why do we want to be like that? Haven't we been plenty successful as who we are?"). These types of commonly faced issues illustrate how the political and personal imperatives are closely related. To lead change effectively, a leader must be able to pry organization members loose from the status quo (Lawrence, 1998). Attempts to do this often bring issues of resistance and conflict to the surface, which a top-level leader must expect and handle with political and personal acumen.

Technological imperatives are required simply to do one's job as a leader of a contemporary organization; more important, these imperatives are needed to understand and anticipate technological changes. Tushman and Anderson (1986) discuss the impact of competence-enhancing and competence-destroying technological breakthroughs. technological shifts that either destroy or enhance the competence of existing firms in an industry. Both kinds of technological changes have implications for strategic leadership and organizational identity. In particular, if competence-destroying breakthroughs are expected (that is, those that represent a new way of manufacturing), it is a competitive advantage to incorporate these new processes early on. Doing so will require preparing an organization for the identity changes associated with manufacturing (or conducting a part of the business) in an entirely new manner. Simply imposing a change without addressing its impact on identity increases the likelihood of overt and covert resistance to its ultimate acceptance.

The good news is that most managers who experience early success are characterized as technically "brilliant" (McCall & Lombardo, 1983, p. 3) and that technical deficiencies are not the typical causes of leader derailment (Van Velsor & Leslie, 1995). The bad news is that issues of cognitive complexity are compounded when people who do not know the business are placed in top leadership roles (Levinson, 1994). In addition, it is highly unlikely for an organization to have a positive external reputation without some level of technological sophistication. But it is also important to point out that even the most technically brilliant managers are unlikely to be effective strategic leaders without also having high levels of social, personal, and political skills.

Specific performance problems with the business and the failure to meet business objectives (typically financial in nature) are primary reasons for leader derailment (McCall & Lombardo, 1983; Van Velsor & Leslie, 1995). These kinds of financial imperatives can lead to severe short-term pressures to perform. In a more strategic and long-term manner, it is necessary to link organizational identity with financial outcomes. That is, by changing who we are in these specific ways, it should make us financially healthier as judged by this set of specific financial outcomes. Designing a strategic plan that links identity changes with financial indicators should help obtain the buy-in of key stakeholders, as well as build a positive external reputation.

A leader's choices for top management positions are critically important. Failing to staff effectively (McCall & Lombardo, 1983) or to build and lead a team effectively (Van Velsor & Leslie, 1995) are primary factors associated with leader derailment. Staffing imperatives are a key component to identity because the people make the place (Schneider, 1987). Who is chosen for key organizational positions says a great deal about an organization's identity (for example, "We are a firm that emphasizes growth through product innovation, so we place a premium on creative engineers"), as well as its desired future image (for example, "We want to be seen as a cutting-edge, innovative firm"). Furthermore, who is chosen to fill key leadership positions (for example, the top management team and board of directors) has reputational implications for an organization. Individuals with demonstrated records of prominent accomplishments are selected not only for their expected contributions to the organization, but also for symbolic purposes. Such high-profile hiring signals to both internal and external stakeholders that the organization is concerned with attracting the best possible intellectual talent.

All seven organizational leadership imperatives are needed to support what are seen as the fundamental leadership concerns of those charged with ensuring the health of an overall organization. It has been proposed that leadership effects (that is, outcomes) can be organized internally around identity and image and externally around reputation. Despite the clarification of these two primary outcomes, assessment issues need to focus on change. After all, leadership in general, and strategic leadership in particular, are characterized by concerns with growth and change (Tichy, 1997). Thus, the fundamental assessment questions focus on how best to measure changes in organizational identity and image, as well as organizational reputation. Given the notorious difficulties associated with measuring change (Cronbach & Furby, 1970), this is no easy task. Nonetheless, considering recommendations on how to use 360-degree feedback to assess change (Martineau, 1998) provides for specific suggestions as to how researchers and practitioners might be better able to document the effects of strategic leadership. What must be kept in mind is that there is an overarching consideration that these approaches are nothing more than attempts to "catch reality in flight" (Pettigrew, 1992, p. 10).

Assessment of Leadership Outcomes: Identity, Image, and Reputation Change

Assessing strategic leadership outcomes is a delicate undertaking. Of foremost concern are the number of possible criterion variables that vary as a function of the relevant stakeholder and as an amount of managerial discretion. Financial performance is the most typical criterion used in strategic leadership research (Finkelstein & Hambrick, 1996); however, financial indexes are susceptible to issues of contamination and deficiency. Furthermore, research indicates that they may not reliably differentiate effective from less effective firms (Chakravarthy, 1986). Another problem with using financial outcome variables is that they are static, providing only a snapshot of economic prosperity, and do not address the fundamental nature of leadership. As a means of overcoming these stated limitations, principles from 360-degree feedback will be used as the foundation for a general methodology in assessing organizational identity, image, and reputation changes associated with strategic leadership.

Traditionally, 360-degree feedback has been used for individual appraisal and development. Individuals receive performance ratings from several coworker sources (supervisors, peers, and subordinates) as well as external customers (London & Tornow, 1998). Although the primary uses of 360-degree feedback are for management and leadership development (Tornow & London, 1998), it is also effective for motivating behavioral change (Waldman, Atwater, & Antonioni, 1998). And this feedback can also be used as part of an organizational transformation effort, targeted at assessing macrolevel change and improvement (Nadler, 1977; Tornow, 1998). It is at this organizational level that 360-degree feedback could be a valuable tool in the assessment of strategic leadership outcomes.

A difference between the recommended approach here, as compared with more typical 360-degree feedback interventions, is that it proposes using feedback surveys to measure change instead of driving it (Martineau, 1998). Before elaborating on the specifics of the proposed methodology, a caveat is in order about change measurement in general. Cronbach and Furby (1970) noted that the measurement of change has been "a persistent puzzle in psychometrics" (p. 68), primarily because of the intractable nature of difference scores. Although there have been subsequent theoretical advances on this issue (Bedeian, Day, Edwards, Tisak, & Smith, 1994; Edwards, 1995; Rogosa & Willett, 1983), the measurement of change remains a delicate issue, especially when it is assessed from multiple perspectives. Three fundamental questions must be addressed: the content of the assessment (What should be measured?), the appropriate informants and time frame (Who should be surveyed and when?), and drawing appropriate inferences (What does it all mean?). These three questions are subsumed under the previously discussed guidelines for mapping the construct space of organizational effectiveness (Cameron & Whetten, 1983).

Content Issues

The content of the proposed assessments should incorporate the three areas that together can provide information on the overall health or effectiveness of an organization: identity, image, and reputation. The central question of interest in assessing organization identity is, "Who are we?" The questions of issue with organization image are, "How do we think others see us?" and "How do we want others to see us?" The issue of organization reputation is gauged through the eyes of external constituents in terms of the question, "How do we see you?" Thus, image and reputation are perceptually based phenomena that differ primarily in terms of the locus of perspective (internal organizational members or external stakeholders). For effective assessment, especially in terms of identifying discrepancies, the content of the adopted measures should be highly similar for assessing image and reputation. However, the specific instrument content depends on the particular industry, relevant possible strategic orientations, and ultimately what really matters to an organization (or what might matter).

Gioia and Thomas (1996) provide examples from the domain of higher education, which included in the identity domain the importance of symbols and ceremonies, competition for students, degree of focus on academic quality, and the importance of economic performance. From the responses to these questions, Gioia and Thomas classified identities as utilitarian (that is, economic) or normative (that is, ideological or value based). They also developed questionnaire items to measure identity strength (such as having a strong sense of institutional history, pride, and identification) and image (for example, how peer institutions would rate the organization on various aspects of quality, climate, innovativeness, financial and economic status, goals, and overall reputation and prestige). The image items could be used in almost their exact form to assess reputation if external stakeholders were surveyed. In addition, other authors have used qualitative techniques based on grounded theory approaches to the assessment of organizational identity and image (Dutton & Dukerich, 1991; Fox-Wolfgramm et al., 1998) and should be considered by anyone interested in alternative approaches to the assessment of leadership outcomes.

Respondents, Scope, and Time Frame

There are at least four major stakeholder groups with different perspectives on any organization: employees, stockholders, customers, and community (Chakravarthy, 1986; Makin, 1983). Some of these stakeholders are completely internal to the organization (employees), whereas others are primarily external, although there may be a mixture of both perspectives (internal customers; stockholders or community members who are also employees). Each of these stakeholders has a somewhat different perspective as to what is most important for an organization. In general, employees are the most relevant source for assessing organization identity and image, whereas stockholders, customers, and community members are most suited for providing assessments of company reputation.

With regard to time frame, leaders at top levels are unlikely to have immediate results on an organization (with the possible exception of stock prices); thus, choosing an appropriate lag time is critical. A review of the leadership succession literature suggests a minimum of a two-year lag before the effects of strategic leadership can be reliably assessed (Day & Lord, 1988). From a research design standpoint, it would strengthen the interpretation of results to use a pre- and postcontrol group design (Cook & Campbell, 1979; Waldman et al., 1998); however, this level of rigor may not be possible in most applications. Complicating matters is the difficulty of obtaining responses from the same set of individual raters over a two-year interval or longer. Without this control, the meaning associated with any noted change is likely to be uninterpretable (Is it due to actual change, or merely a differences in respondents' understanding of what is to be rated?). An innovative approach that has been used to some success with individual 360-degree feedback involves a retrospective methodology (Martineau, 1998).

A necessary condition for empirically comparing pretest and posttest scores is that there is a common metric (Cronbach & Furby, 1970). In many applied assessments, however, what is being measured comes to be redefined by respondents. This can occur through changes in respondents' expectations of the target or through the development of a new understanding of the construct of interest. A technique that has been used with some success is based on retrospective methodology. Although there are various versions of this methodology (Martineau, 1998), it generally includes gathering two unique ratings at the same point in time after an intervention (such as leadership succession or implementation of a new strategic plan). Another promising method, retrospective degree of change (Peterson, 1993), uses a single measure of the degree of change made on a single dimension over a specified time period. Research on these retrospective methods has demonstrated greater validity than traditional (pretest-posttest) self-report measures (Howard & Dailey, 1979; Howard et al., 1979; Peterson, 1993). Similarly, Martineau reports greater success with 360-degree feedback retrospective methodology in terms of assessing individual change associated with leadership development interventions than with traditional pretest-posttest assessments.

A 360-degree approach in conjunction with a retrospective methodology can be used to assess organization changes associated with strategic leadership. The target to be rated would be organization identity, image, or reputation (depending on the particular constituency), and a stratified sample of respondents would be selected from each of the most relevant stakeholder groups: employees, stockholders, customers, and community members. The content of the assessment instrument could be cast widely in terms of what the various stakeholders see in terms of general identity, image, and reputation or could be focused on a particular form of envisioned identity change. An example might be an organization's attempt at moving from having customer service as a small part of the business to having it as a central aspect of an envisioned identity. In that case, a 360-degree instrument specifically designed around customer service would be recommended (Martineau, 1998). This type of focused assessment could incorporate employees' perceptions of the importance of customer service to the organization (identity) and how employees think customers perceive their service (image), as well as a customer-based survey based on the organization's reputation for service fairness (Seiders & Berry, 1998). Another example would be envisioned strategic change from primarily a "defender" organization that emphasizes specialization and efficiency to more of a "prospector" type that takes advantage of new market opportunities (Miles & Snow, 1978). This is a potentially more fundamental change in identity, requiring a much longer implementation period for change to occur. It would necessitate an assessment instrument that was broader in scope than the previously discussed example of an envisioned customer service change.

Inferences, Uses, and Overall Meaning

As proposed, the retrospective 360-degree method could be used as a way of assessing the ongoing changes associated with leadership as well as a needs assessment to identify where more intensive strategic action should be directed. If conducted comprehensively across stakeholder groups, the proposed assessment method would help answer questions of what needs attention (identity, image, or reputation), which stakeholder groups are most problematic (that is, what combination of employees, stockholders, customers, and community members should be attended to), and what is the consistency of agreement among the various groups. The last could be empirically estimated by means of an interrater agreement statistic such as r_{wg} (James, Demaree, & Wolf, 1993). Significant heterogeneity within a particular stakeholder perspective could indicate a need to bring about greater consistency in communicated identity or reputation.

Another possible use of the proposed method could be in drawing inferences regarding the type of change that has occurred.

Bartunek and Moch (1987) differentiated among first-, second-, and third-order change in organization development. First-order change concerns incremental modifications within an established identity (see Fox-Wolfgramm et al., 1998, for an example of this type of change in the banking industry). Second-order change represents a modification to identity in a particular, specified direction, such as a new strategic orientation. And third-order change represents a move toward identity flexibility (or plasticity), such that modifications can occur in response to environmental threats and opportunities, which would allow an organization to maximize its adaptation or health. In conjunction with an assessment of the specific content areas in which changes in identity, image, or reputation are desired, a retrospective method of the type of experienced change could be assessed. Thus, the overall assessment of organization changes associated with strategic leadership can be tailored to understand what has changed and how.

Conclusion

This chapter has proposed an overarching framework for understanding and assessing leadership outcomes. As discussed, *outcomes* is a bit of a misnomer given that leaders are responsible for change, and change is ongoing and always incomplete. Further complicating matters is that multiple constituencies have different perspectives on organization effectiveness (Cameron & Whetten, 1983; Connolly et al., 1980). Nonetheless, leaders at the strategic apex are ultimately responsible for the overall health or effectiveness of an organization, which involves attending to organization identity, image, and reputation. These general responsibilities are proposed to underpin financial and operational performance (Venkatraman & Ramanujam, 1986), and to be the source of sustained change in organizations (Gioia & Thomas, 1996).

The proposed content (identity, image, and reputation) and method (retrospective 360-degree) address the central questions posed by Cameron and Whetten (1983) as guidelines for understanding organization effectiveness. Specifically, the recommended approach addresses the issues of whose perspective is used to judge effectiveness (internal and external stakeholders), the domain of activity (identity, image, and reputation), level of analysis (macro-organizational), purpose (needs assessment as well as criterion data for research), time frame (minimum of two years), type of data (primarily aggregated survey responses), and referent against which effectiveness is judged (same organization over time). It was also shown how the seven leadership imperatives proposed as the organizing framework for this book relate to the overarching concerns of top-level leaders in terms of an organization's identity, image, and reputation.

Much like individual personality (Hogan, 1998), these specified concerns addressed from a macro-organizational perspective are ongoing and continually being constructed and negotiated. Ultimately, strategic leadership that is unconcerned with aligning organization identity, image, and reputation is at risk for contributing to a "self-deceptive" organization. And as with individuals, self-deceptive organizations are inherently unhealthy.

References

Albert, S., & Whetten, D. A. (1985). Organizational identity. *Research in Organizational Behavior, 7,* 263–295.

Bartunek, J. M. (1984). Changing interpretive schemes and organizational restructuring: The example of a religious order. *Administrative Science Quarterly, 29,* 355–372.

Bartunek, J. M., & Moch, M. K. (1987). First-order, second-order, and third-order change and organization development interventions: A cognitive approach. *Journal of Applied Behavioral Science, 23,* 483–500.

Bedeian, A. G., Day, D. V., Edwards, J. R., Tisak, J., & Smith, C. S. (1994). Difference scores: Rationale, formulation, and interpretation. *Journal of Management, 20,* 673–698.

Bennis, W. G., & Nanus, B. (1985). *Leaders: The strategies for taking charge.* New York: HarperCollins.

Brewer, G. D. (1983). Assessing outcomes and effects. In K. S. Cameron & D. A. Whetten (Eds.), *Organizational effectiveness: A comparison of multiple models.* Orlando, FL: Academic Press.

Cameron, K. S., & Whetten, D. A. (1983). Organizational effectiveness: One model or several? In K. S. Cameron & D. A. Whetten (Eds.), *Organizational effectiveness: A comparison of multiple models.* Orlando, FL: Academic Press.

Carver, C. S., & Scheier, M. F. (1981). *Attention and self-regulation: A control-theory approach to human behavior.* New York: Springer-Verlag.

Chakravarthy, B. S. (1986). Measuring strategic performance. *Strategic Management Journal, 7,* 437–458.

Child, J. (1972). Organization structure, environment, and performance: The role of strategic choice. *Sociology, 6,* 1–22.

Connolly, T., Conlon, E. M., & Deutsch, S. J. (1980). Organizational effectiveness: A multiple constituency approach. *Academy of Management Review, 5,* 211–218.

Cook, T. D., & Campbell, D. T. (1979). *Quasi-experimentation: Design and analysis issues for field settings.* Boston: Houghton Mifflin.

Cronbach, L. J., & Furby, L. (1970). How we should measure "change"— or should we? *Psychological Bulletin, 74,* 68–80.

Day, D. V., & Lord, R. G. (1988). Executive leadership and organizational performance: Suggestions for a new theory and methodology. *Journal of Management, 14,* 453–464.

Denison, D. R., Hooijberg, R., & Quinn, R. E. (1995). Paradox and performance: Toward a theory of behavioral complexity in managerial leadership. *Organization Science, 6,* 524–540.

Donaldson, G., & Lorsch, J. W. (1983). *Decision making at the top.* New York: Basic Books.

Dutton, J. E., & Dukerich, J. M. (1991). Keeping an eye on the mirror: Image and identity in organizational adaptation. *Academy of Management Journal, 34,* 517–554.

Dutton, J. E., Dukerich, J. M., & Harquail, C. V. (1994). Organizational images and member identification. *Administrative Science Quarterly, 39,* 239–263.

Edwards, J. R. (1995). Alternatives to difference scores as dependent variables in the study of congruence in organizational research. *Organizational Behavior and Human Decision Processes, 64,* 307–324.

Elsbach, K. D., & Kramer, R. M. (1996). Members' responses to organizational identity threats: Encountering and countering the *Business Week* rankings. *Administrative Science Quarterly, 41,* 442–476.

Erikson, E. H. (1950). *Childhood and society.* New York: Norton.

Finkelstein, S., & Hambrick, D. C. (1996). *Strategic leadership: Top executives and their effects on organizations.* Minneapolis, MN: West.

Fombrun, C., & Shanley, M. (1990). What's in a name? Reputation building and corporate strategy. *Academy of Management Journal, 33,* 233–258.

Fox-Wolfgramm, S. J., Boal, K. B., & Hunt, J. G. (1998). Organizational adaptation to institutional change: A comparative study of first-order change in prospector and defender banks. *Administrative Science Quarterly, 43,* 87–126.

Gioia, D. A., & Chittipeddi, K. (1991). Sensemaking and sensegiving in strategic change initiation. *Strategic Management Journal, 12,* 443–448.

Gioia, D. A., Schultz, M., & Corley, K. G. (2000). Organizational identity, image, and adaptive instability. *Academy of Management Review, 25,* 63–81.

Gioia, D. A., & Thomas, J. B. (1996). Identity, image, and issue interpretation: Sensemaking during strategic change in academia. *Administrative Science Quarterly, 41,* 370–403.

Greenwood, R., & Hinings, C. R. (1993). Understanding strategic change: The contribution of archetypes. *Academy of Management Journal, 36,* 1052–1081.

Hambrick, D. C., & Abrahamson, E. (1995). Assessing the amount of managerial discretion in different industries: A multimethod approach. *Academy of Management Journal, 38,* 1427–1441.

Hambrick, D. C., & Finkelstein, S. (1987). Managerial discretion: A bridge between polar views of organizations. *Research in Organizational Behavior, 9,* 369–406.

Hambrick, D. C., & Mason, P. A. (1984). Upper echelons: The organization as a reflection of its top managers. *Academy of Management Review, 9,* 193–206.

Hogan, R. (1998). Reinventing personality. *Journal of Social and Clinical Personality, 17,* 1–10.

Hogan, R., Curphy, G. J., & Hogan, J. (1994). What we know about leadership: Effectiveness and personality. *American Psychologist, 49,* 493–504.

Hogan, R., Raskin, R., & Fazzini, D. (1990). The dark side of charisma. In K. E. Clark & M. B. Clark (Eds.), *Measures of leadership*. West Orange, NJ: Leadership Library of America.

Howard, G. S., & Dailey, P. R. (1979). Response shift bias: A source of contamination of self-report measures. *Journal of Applied Psychology, 64,* 144–150.

Howard, G. S., Ralph, K. M., Gulanick, N. A., Maxwell, S. E., Nance, D. W., & Gerber, S. R. (1979). Internal invalidity in pretest-posttest self-report evaluations and re-evaluations of retrospective pretests. *Applied Psychological Measurement, 3,* 1–23.

James, L. R., Demaree, R. G., & Wolf, G. (1993). r_{wg}: An assessment of within-group interrater agreement. *Journal of Applied Psychology, 78,* 306–309.

Katz, D., & Kahn, R. L. (1978). *The social psychology of organizations* (2nd ed.). New York: Wiley.

Kotter, J. P. (1990). *A force for change: How leadership differs from management*. New York: Free Press.

Lawrence, D. M. (1998). Leading discontinuous change: Ten lessons from the battlefront. In D. C. Hambrick, D. A. Nadler, & M. L. Tushman (Eds.), *Navigating change: How CEOs, top teams, and boards steer transformation*. Boston: Harvard Business School Press.

Lawrence, P. R., & Lorsch, J. W. (1967). *Organization and environment.* Boston: Harvard Business School Division of Research.

Levinson, H. (1994). Why behemoths fell: Psychological roots of corporate failure. *American Psychologist, 49,* 428–436.

Lieberson, S., & O'Connor, J. F. (1972). Leadership and organizational performance: A study of large corporations. *American Sociological Review, 37,* 117–130.

London, M., & Tornow, W. W. (1998). Introduction: 360-degree feedback—more than a tool! In W. W. Tornow & M. London (Eds.), *Maximizing the value of 360-degree feedback: A process for successful individual and organizational development.* San Francisco: Jossey-Bass.

Lord, R. G., & Maher, K. J. (1991). *Leadership and information processing: Linking perceptions and performance.* Boston: Unwin-Hyman.

Makin, C. (1983, January 10). Ranking corporate reputations. *Fortune,* pp. 4–44.

Martineau, J. W. (1998). Using 360-degree surveys to assess change. In W. W. Tornow & M. London (Eds.), *Maximizing the value of 360-degree feedback: A process for successful individual and organizational development.* San Francisco: Jossey-Bass.

McCall, M. W., Jr., & Lombardo, M. M. (1983). *Off the track: Why and how successful executives get derailed.* Greensboro, NC: Center for Creative Leadership.

Meindl, J. R., & Ehrlich, S. B. (1987). The romance of leadership and the evaluation of organizational performance. *Academy of Management Journal, 30,* 91–109.

Meindl, J. R., Ehrlich, S. B., & Dukerich, J. M. (1985). The romance of leadership. *Administrative Science Quarterly, 30,* 78–102.

Miles, R. E., & Snow, C. C. (1978). *Organizational strategy, structure, and process.* New York: McGraw-Hill.

Nadler, D. A. (1977). *Feedback and organization development: Using data-based methods.* Reading, MA: Addison-Wesley.

Peterson, D. B. (1993). *Measuring change: A psychometric approach to evaluating individual training outcomes.* Paper presented at the eighth annual conference of the Society for Industrial and Organizational Psychology, San Francisco.

Pettigrew, A. M. (1992). The character and significance of strategy process research. *Strategic Management Journal, 13,* 5–16.

Pfeffer, J. (1977). The ambiguity of leadership. *Academy of Management Review, 2,* 104–112.

Ranson, S., Hinings, C. R., & Greenwood, R. (1980). The structuring of organization structures. *Administrative Science Quarterly, 25,* 1–17.

Rogosa, D. R., & Willett, J. B. (1983). Demonstrating the reliability of the difference score in the measurement of change. *Journal of Educational Measurement, 20,* 335–343.

Salancik, G. R., & Pfeffer, J. (1977). Constraints on administrator discretion: The limited influence of mayors on city budgets. *Urban Affairs Quarterly, 12,* 475–498.

Saxton, T. (1997). The effects of partner and relationship characteristics on alliance outcomes. *Academy of Management Journal, 40,* 443–461.

Schneider, B. (1987). The people make the place. *Personnel Psychology, 40,* 437–453.

Seiders, K., & Berry, L. L. (1998). Service fairness: What it is and why it matters. *Academy of Management Executive, 12*(2), 8–20.

Selznick, P. (1957). *Leadership in administration: A sociological interpretation.* New York: HarperCollins.

Steers, R. M. (1975). *Organizational effectiveness: A behavioral view.* Santa Monica, CA: Goodyear.

Thomas, A. B. (1988). Does leadership make a difference to organizational performance? *Administrative Science Quarterly, 33,* 388–400.

Tichy, N. M. (1997). *The leadership engine.* New York: HarperBusiness.

Tornow, W. W. (1992). Comment on D. L. De Vries's "Executive selection but no progress." *Issues and Observations, 12*(4), 1.

Tornow, W. W. (1998). Forces that affect the 360-degree feedback process. In W. W. Tornow & M. London (Eds.), *Maximizing the value of 360-degree feedback: A process for successful individual and organizational development.* San Francisco: Jossey-Bass.

Tornow, W. W., & London, M. (Eds.). (1998). *Maximizing the value of 360-degree feedback: A process for successful individual and organizational development.* San Francisco: Jossey-Bass.

Tushman, M. L., & Anderson, P. (1986). Technological discontinuities and organizational environments. *Administrative Science Quarterly, 31,* 439–465.

Van Velsor, E., & Leslie, J. B. (1995). Why executives derail: Perspectives across time and cultures. *Academy of Management Executive, 9*(4), 62–72.

Venkatraman, N., & Ramanujam, V. (1986). Measurement of business performance in strategy research: A comparison of approaches. *Academy of Management Review, 11,* 801–814.

Waldman, D. A., Atwater, L. E., & Antonioni, D. (1998). Has 360-degree feedback gone amok? *Academy of Management Executive, 12*(2), 86–94.

Weick, K. E. (1988). Enacted sensemaking in crisis situations. *Journal of Management Studies, 25,* 305–317.

Weigelt, K., & Camerer, C. (1988). Reputation and corporate strategy: A review of recent theory and applications. *Strategic Management Journal, 9,* 443–454.

Weil, E. (1998, June-July). Every leader tells a story. *Fast Company,* pp. 38–40.

Whetten, D. A., Lewis, D., & Mischel, L. J. (1992, August). *Toward an integrated model of organizational identity and member commitment.* Paper presented at the annual meeting of the Academy of Management, Las Vegas.

White, R. P., & De Vries, D. L. (1990). Making the wrong choice: Failure in the selection of senior-level managers. *Issues and Observations, 10*(1), 1–6.

Wilson, R. (1985). Reputations in games and markets. In A. E. Roth (Ed.), *Game-theoretic models of bargaining.* New York: Cambridge University Press.

Zaleznik, A. (1977). Managers and leaders: Are they different? *Harvard Business Review, 55*(5), 67–78.

PART 3

Conclusion

CHAPTER 13

The Nature of Organizational Leadership
Conclusions and Implications
Robert G. Lord

At the start of this book, editors Zaccaro and Klimoski noted that despite thousands of studies and almost a century of work, the leadership literature remains disconnected and directionless. They suggested that for the field to advance, researchers need to view leadership as a situated rather than context-free process, and seven key imperatives in the life space of top-level leaders (cognitive, social, personal, political, technological, financial, and staffing imperatives) needed to be incorporated into leadership theories. The chapters in this book were organized around six of these seven imperatives, with the technological imperative receiving only tangential attention. This chapter takes stock of the progress made in describing and understanding these imperatives. Thus, it is organized in terms of cognitive, social, personal, political, financial, and staffing imperatives.

Before moving to this systematic coverage of material offered in this book, I briefly suggest an alternative reason for the slow progress in developing systematic theory in the leadership field: the basic paradigmatic approach that has dominated the leadership field seems backward when applied to top-level leadership. Researchers and practitioners generally see leaders as proximal causes of favorable organizational outcomes and consequently have tried to build theories of how this causal process develops from individual aracteristics of leaders. However, top-level executives often have indirect, long-term effects that occur through a variety of internal or external social systems (Day & Lord, 1988) rather than direct, short-term effects. Moreover, a leader's actions may be intertwined with many environmental factors rather than the leader being a unitary cause. Causality lies in a confluence of systems factors, not in the traits or behaviors of a single individual (Lord & Smith, 1999).

This social systems view on leadership is reflected in Zaccaro and Klimoski's functional perspective, which suggests that executive leadership is merely a part, albeit an important part, of a comprehensive group or organizational theory. To be most useful, attempts to understand leadership should be integrated with a comprehensive theory. For example, the enduring value of Katz and Kahn's ideas about leadership (1978) occurs in part because they are integrated with the much broader perspective of systems theory. In their theory, the traits, behaviors, or strategies of top-level leaders can be understood in terms of mediating systems factors such as the creation of structure rather than as direct determinants of organizational performance. In addition, Katz and Kahn's theory articulates very different functions for leaders at top, middle, and lower levels, as noted in several chapters in this book.

One value of this book and the variety of approaches described in the chapters is that it has the potential to create a more fundamental grasp of executive leadership theory by embedding it in a broader, collective understanding of how Zaccaro and Klimoski's seven imperatives affect leadership processes. What is needed, and is provided by the chapters in this book, is an integration of these imperatives into a comprehensive framework for understanding leadership. It is against this backdrop that the variable role of leaders in specific contexts will be clearest. My goal in this discussion of each imperative that Zaccaro and Klimoski raised is to broaden the perspective of individual chapters and highlight their contribution to developing a comprehensive basis for understanding executive leadership theory.

Cognitive Imperative

Leader cognitions are important because executive leadership occurs in response to nonroutine and ill-defined events, involves the anticipation of environments many years in the future, and requires the construction of abstract systems that shape both internal and external processes. The cognitions of others are also an important part of the leadership process, because followers or stakeholders respond to the internal meaning of a leader's direct actions and of the systems he or she puts in place. Leadership perceptions, organizational cultures and identities, collective models of environments, and underlying values all reflect the direct and indirect effects of effective executive leadership. Such collective constructs also define and create, at least in the short run, the internal environment that top-level leaders face.

Cognitions are important from another perspective. What distinguishes humans most from other species is our ability to represent reality in terms of abstractions or symbols and operate on these symbols in a systematic manner to create new meanings. This is accomplished with a neural technology that has been elaborated through evolution into a complex, multifaceted system that involves both symbolic processing capacities and the ability to use networks of subsymbolic processes. I will focus here only on symbolic capacities (subsymbolic capacities and their role in leadership have been discussed elsewhere; Hanges, Lord, & Dickson, 2000; Lord, Brown, & Harvey, in press). Human cognitive architectures create, organize, store, retrieve, and operate on symbol structures to construct individualized meanings and invent adaptive responses or retrieve them from memory. Leadership and other social and organizational processes ultimately operate through such cognitive processes. Hence, grounding our understanding of executive leadership in the cognitive imperative is a logical beginning for this book.

Jacobs and McGee in Chapter Two contribute several ideas that are central to the cognitive imperative and reflect broad trends in cognitive and personality research. Three ideas—time span and complexity, recognition-primed decision making, and network-like mental models—will be discussed in this section.

Time Span and Complexity

Jacobs and McGee maintain that an organization's competitive advantage accrues from the conceptual skills and abilities of executive leaders. Reasoning from Jaques's stratified systems theory (1989), they discuss the need for executive-level leaders to handle increased complexity and abstractness in their activities and to deal with the uncertainty involved in creating actions for which the consequences may take several decades to occur. Such processes may afford only minimal guidance from external feedback and instead are highly dependent on the internal symbolic representations by which leaders represent key environments. One might expect, then, that the capacity for using abstract systems as a means of understanding environments, or as a means to communicate this understanding, would be the hallmark of top-level executives. But this is only one aspect of a more complex process. As Hooijberg and Schneider noted in Chapter Four and Brass in Chapter Five, leaders are part of networks of individuals who collectively develop an understanding of organizational processes. Thus, social intelligence as well as symbolic ability is required.

Jacobs and McGee raise the issues of defining cognitive capacity and potential capacity and hint that part of the answer comes from the difference between experts and novices. They note that experts use "patterns" that permit the rapid assessment of situations. Curiously, however, they do not address the extensive literature on expertise as a guide to their theorizing. Several points regarding expertise should be made. First, experts do things differently than novices do, because they have highly organized and complex knowledge structures that are specific to their domain of expertise (Chi, Glaser, & Farr, 1988; Lord & Maher, 1991). This knowledge is gained through experience—typically ten years or more of extensive attempts to acquire a high degree of skill in a domain (Ericsson & Charness, 1994). Second, expert executives understand strategic problems at multiple levels, using both deep and surface levels (Day & Lord, 1992). Surface levels reflect physical features, and deeper levels reflect underlying principles, which are often abstract. Third, experts often move directly from an understanding of problems to the choice of potential solutions that exist in memory, rather than having to construct solutions on the spot. Thus, experts substitute domain-specific knowledge for on-the-spot computation. Such trade-offs underlie many types of intelligent behavior (Newell, 1989). Rather than being concerned with cognitive capacity as a general ability to manage abstract symbols or as academic intelligence, Jacobs and McGee's observation implies that leadership researchers might better focus on factors that affect the development of expertise. A critical issue according to Ericsson and Charness (1994) is the personality and motivational factors that keep one engaged in specific domains for decades. The capacity to manage complexity in leadership domains, then, might be understood in terms of factors that maintain engagement in leadership positions and leadership development activities over one's lifetime (see Chapter Eleven).

Recognition-Primed Decision Making

Jacobs and McGee suggest that the growth of executive capacity is associated with the development of frames of reference, which are integrated sets of constructs that impart meaning. They argue, with some merit, that frames of reference are needed to extend from past experience into the future. They illustrate the role of frames of reference by describing recognition-primed decision making (RPDM), a form of decision making that emphasizes the diagnosis rather than the choice phase of decision making (Durso & Gronlund, 1999). According to Durso and Gronlund, RPDM is common among experts "when the current situation is similar to typical situations from the past" (p. 300) and thus seems to depend on the capacity of experts to categorize a situation appropriately. Such capacities can simplify processing and allow executives to handle greater complexity, but when applied by collectives (Porac, Thomas, & Baden-Fuller, 1989), categorization processes also can be a source of rigidity that retard development and adaptation. Thus, although RPDM is important in maintaining situational awareness in contexts like battlefields that change quickly, it does not seem to be a process that is well matched to the complexity and foresight demands of top-level executives in constructing long-term visions. However, it may be that the use of RPDM in areas where executives have considerable expertise creates sufficient slack so executives can devote more deliberative thought to issues that have long-term payoffs.

Mental Models

Jacobs and McGee point out that growth capacity requires the integration of multiple frames with all their inherent contradictions. This point rings truer than reliance on RPDM, and it is well illustrated by Hooijberg and Schneider's description of how top executives use networks of stakeholders to build a complex view of the future and their organization's role within it. In short, complexity arises from mental models of an organization and its role in future society that are jointly constructed by executives through activities involving networks of individuals with multiple perspectives. Jacobs and McGee seem to have such mental models in mind when they describe decision support systems as being network-like entities that allow the generation of independent perspectives on the strategic environment. Rather than being grounded in individual cognitive skill or ability, such models seem to be built from extensive social interactions, and thus they illustrate the interplay between social and cognitive factors.

Because the Jacobs and McGee chapter is so closely tied to stratified systems theory (SST) and its view on the cognitive requirements of top-level leadership, it is important to note the limitations of this view of managerial cognitions. SST does a nice job of conceptualizing rational, forward-thinking cognitions, but it underemphasizes the cybernetic quality of much organizational decision making at the executive level. For example, Hambrick, Cho, and Chen (1996) note that many strategic actions are reactions to competitor moves rather than being proactive. At a more aggregate level, Tushman and Romanelli (1985) argue that many organizational processes gradually drift out of fit with environments, and dramatic reorientations, often spearheaded by new leaders, are required to restore fit. Again, this is a reactive, feedback-driven process.

SST also emphasizes the cognitions and capacities of individual CEOs, yet top management teams generally extend the cognitive capacities and knowledge base of CEOs. Heterogeneous teams allow the use of expert processing to create multiple meanings for environmental events, which are then worked out through team processes. Thus, greater cognitive complexity accrues through expert processing in multiple domains, and flexibility develops from effective team processes.

Emotions and Social Processes

Johnson, Daniels, and Huff discuss in Chapter Three sense making and mental models and make several important points. Foremost is the connection between cognitions and actions. Following Weick (1985), these authors note that it is the meaning created by cognitive schema or mental models that allows individuals to act. This is particularly true for executive leaders, because the effects of some actions may be indirect or years downstream, so actions are gauged in terms of reference to mental models, not in terms of immediate effects. Yet this is not the only way that actions and cognitions are related. Executive leadership teams often must make decisions pertaining to environmental factors that are unknown. Here, as Weick (1979) has noted, actions and cognitions can be intertwined across time, and environments can be discovered only through actions. This is because future environments are created by the collective actions and reactions of individuals (Astley & Van de Ven, 1983).

Johnson, Daniels, and Huff also note that studies of the content of managerial cognitions are limited in their value because content reflects context-specific effects. Context is akin to focusing on surface structure. They argue that it is more useful to examine the structure of knowledge in order to understand the linkage between cognitions and action. Following Walsh (1995), they suggest that part of the structure for cognitions is social, in that collective—not individual—mental processes are involved in leadership. They maintain that interpersonal processes also have an emotional quality that is often overlooked when the focus is on cognitions.

Such recommendations have merit but sidestep two important issues. First, collective cognitions are still the aggregation of individual cognitive processes. Individual cognitive architectures limit the nature of collective cognitive processes and constrain the means by which individuals integrate information or emotions derived from multiperson processes. Although individual cognitions are not the whole story, they are an important component of collective processes. For example, individual-level research shows that experts are especially good at recognizing and understanding the meaning of patterns within their domain of expertise. When generalized to top management teams made up of experts in heterogeneous domains, this principle implies that multiple and conflicting meanings will be created precisely because each individual is understanding environments in terms of his or her own domain-specific experience and knowledge base. These conflicting individual cognitions set the stage for the construction of collective cognitions through group processes.

The second issue concerns the interplay between emotions and cognitions. Emotions are not independent of cognitions but interact with cognitions, particularly when they unfold in group contexts. For example, Gross (1998) illustrates several points at which cognitive processes affect the display of emotions, which include antecedent-focused (situation selection, situation modification, attention deployment, and cognitive change) and response-focused emotional regulation. Others note that perceptions must be imbued with meaning to produce emotions, and this meaning comes from cognitive appraisals. For example, an individual's perceived capacity to manage a situation can differentiate fear from challenge as an emotional response to difficult situations.

In sum, rather than undercutting the cognitive imperative, Johnson, Daniels, and Huff illustrate the need to integrate cognitions and social-emotional processes to provide a basis for understanding top-level leadership. With this need in mind, we turn to the social imperative.

Social Imperative

Zaccaro and Klimoski note that leaders are required to fulfill many organizational roles and maintain relationships with individuals in many units. Further, they need to integrate these units, even though these units may have conflicting goals and demands. Others go even further toward linking leadership with the social realm, arguing that leadership is defined by social perceptions (Lord & Maher, 1991), that it is a social construction (Meindl, 1995), or that it is an emergent process involving a leader and networks of followers and tasks in a specific temporal and organizational context (Lord & Smith, 1999). Thus, leadership is a situated social perception in which the accessibility of the leadership construct for perceivers depends on situational cues, perceivers' schemas, target characteristics, and behaviors. Self-perceptions are also situated constructions, which depend on dyadic and group-level leadership processes, since self-knowledge depends in part on reflected social reactions. Crucial issues are the meaning of social processes to individuals (for example, whether leadership processes enhance the self-esteem of others and communicate inclusion into a group and whether social processes foster or limit skill development). Leaders are central in such processes to the extent that their actions have an impact on individual and organizational identities (see Chapter Twelve of this book).

The social aspects of leadership also extend beyond the personal reactions of followers because there are many systems aspects of leadership that depend on the ability of leaders to maintain linkages in social networks. The nature and pattern of such linkages have important effects on the development of a leader's mental models of an organization and its environment as Hooijberg and Schneider explain. Social networks also affect the social capital of organizations as Brass points out, influencing both the flow of knowledge and the strength of norms and collective values. A leader's social and cognitive skills develop and maintain the linkages that comprise such networks. As Daily and Dalton explain in Chapter Six on organizational governance, leaders can sometimes affect their own power in an organization by changing the form of governance networks. Thus, a leader's cognitive, social, and political skills, as well as the ability to regulate emotions for instrumental purposes in social exchanges, have an impact on the nature of organizational networks in which the leader is embedded.

Effective top-level leaders must master and manage these sociological aspects of leadership networks. Although they are still social-cognitive in nature, such leadership skills may be very different from the skills required for leaders of smaller work groups with frequent face-to-face interactions, which have more personal rather than systemic orientations. Due to the multifaceted nature of the many network linkages compared to leadership at other levels, top-level leadership becomes more cognitively complex and requires a longer time perspective, as suggested by Jaques's stratified system theory (see Chapter Two). Executive-level leadership also requires behavioral complexity and social intelligence to use such networks as a basis for the creation of structure, which is the central point that Hooijberg and Schneider make.

Behavioral Complexity and Social Intelligence

Hooijberg and Schneider make an important contribution to the theory of executive-level leadership by describing how personal qualities pertaining to the behavioral and social intelligence of leaders allow them to create needed structure. Thus, they extend the application of these personal qualities, which have previously been applied to lower- and middle-level leadership (Zaccaro, Gilbert, Thor, & Mumford, 1991).

Behavioral complexity is required of top-level leaders because they must adjust their behavioral repertoire to fulfill a variety of roles in different organizational contexts. Since the role set of top-level leaders extends to many stakeholders outside the organization (suppliers, competitors, government agencies, and others), the basis for such interactions differs widely, and different forms of influence are required. Hooijberg and Schneider stress that social intelligence and the ability to convey appropriate emotions are critical components of leaders' interactions with diverse internal and external stakeholders. Such interactions convey underlying values and help build the social capital that allows leaders to establish trust, enforce norms, and accomplish instrumental objectives.

Hooijberg and Schneider's model posits that three processes mediate between the personal qualities of behavioral complexity and social intelligence and the creation of structure: co-option, foresight, and systems thinking. Co-opting involves absorbing new elements into the leadership and decision-making structure of organizations to increase stability and avoid threats. Many stakeholders of organizations, such as union representatives and suppliers, are co-opted by including them on the board of directors. Foresight accrues through the exploration of long-term agendas with a wide variety of stakeholders. By understanding these stakeholders' views of their organization's future environments, executive leaders gradually build mental models of the environments that their own organization will encounter in the future, and they learn how to function successfully in such environments. In other words, they build symbolic representations on which they can operate to produce new, unique understandings of how their organization can operate in the future. This is an inherently cognitive process, yet it is also social in that leaders' symbolic representations have a social origin. Also, as Hooijberg and Schneider point out, tentative ideas are often shared with trusted external parties, providing a "peer review" of insights and conclusions. In this sense, foresight is socially constructed and can be thought of as the type of collective cognitive process that Johnson, Daniels, and Huff advocate as a domain for leadership inquiry.

Importantly, such collective processes extend the time perspective of top-level leaders. They also help develop systems thinking, which is the ability to understand an organization's role within the larger industry and society. Thus, they help develop an executive's vision of what an organization could be in the future. Systems thinking also helps an executive to see how an organization's reputation among diverse constituencies constrains its potential strategies, fostering direct attempts to manage one's reputation (for example, charitable and philanthropic activities). Systems thinking also is the basis for political activities that attempt to influence future environments.

These three mediating processes provide the basis for the design of organizational structures that can guide an organization into the future, as Hooijberg and Schneider note. Effective executives do this before their competitors do because their understanding of the future is more developed, but also because they are able to articulate a vision that has internal support and because they can initiate required actions. Day points out in Chapter Twelve that changing organizational identities may be required to support substantial changes, which is a clear example of the structure creation on which Hooijberg and Schneider focus. In addition to changing identities, structure can be created by altering organizational cultures or articulating specific values—all indirect means by which top-level leaders can influence performance (Day & Lord, 1988). Hooijberg and Schneider's important contribution is to show how the basis for such far-reaching changes lies in the understanding of organizations and environments that executive leaders develop through skillful interaction with diverse networks of stakeholders. Personal qualities of executive leaders related to cognitive complexity, behavioral complexity, and social intelligence are fundamental to such social-cognitive leadership processes.

Social Capital

Brass's chapter connects social capital to leadership by articulating the role of a leader as a linkage in complex social networks. He notes that a variety of types of networks create social capital, which is defined as "social relationships that can potentially confer benefits to individuals and groups." Leaders help build such networks. He stresses that the social capital perspective focuses on relationships rather than actors (links rather than nodes in networks). Yet Hooijberg and Schneider suggest that the ability to build a variety of linkages also reflects qualities of actors.

Brass notes that the social capital created by networks can involve factors such as obligations and expectations, norms and sanctions, or needed information. Social networks act as conduits to the information and human capital provided by others, augmenting the limited perspectives and information processing capacities of individual leaders. This is particularly true for top management teams. Alternatively, networks (or teams) can also constrain leaders and create liabilities as well as social capital, depending on the types and structure of relationships.

The distinction between weak and strong ties that Brass describes is particularly interesting. Weak ties, which are often developed through relatively infrequent contacts with external stakeholders or divergent groups, "are key sources of novel, divergent, nonredundant information or resources." They correct strategic myopia and help develop an understanding of an organization's role in broader systems. Brass notes that transformational leaders use such networks in developing visions and that such networks have been shown to relate to organizational performance. Strong ties, in contrast, are typically internal. They are based on more frequent contact, have higher emotional intensity, and may be the primary medium for social influence. Strong ties also require more maintenance, so there are limits to the number of strong ties a leader can maintain.

Networks also differ in structural qualities, with centrality in networks being another source of power for leaders. Effective leaders not only build networks to others; they are often hubs around whom others gather and collectively create social capital. Brass points out that centrality in networks also allows leaders to transmit visions and values created through networks of weak ties. Thus, Brass shows us that effective executive leadership involves the social capital created through a variety of types of linkages and network structures, providing another illustration of the complexity of the social systems used by top-level leaders.

Personal and Political Imperatives

Zaccaro and Klimoski point out that top executives need to manage their careers and reputations as well as develop internal and external networks. Such networks are important for the use of political power and are required to assimilate diverse perspectives into a comprehensive mental model. As Daily and Dalton discuss, whether political power is centralized in management or in boards of external stakeholders is an emerging leadership issue, particularly as institutional investors attempt to exert more control over organizations.

Corporate Control

Daily and Dalton address a variety of governance issues organized around the contrasting philosophies underlying agency and stewardship theory. They note that boards can be used as a source of motivation and control, which is emphasized by agency theory, or they can be used as a linkage with critical environments of the firm, a view more consistent with a stewardship or resource-dependence perspective. Board composition is a critical parameter that determines both the relative power of insiders and outsiders, as well as the boundary-spanning function of corporate boards. Daily and Dalton note that there is inconsistent evidence supporting the linkage of the agency and stewardship perspectives to organizational performance. Some studies find that a having a majority of outside directors is associated with superior firm performance, which is consistent with agency theory; other studies show that inside directors and CEO duality (that is, the CEO is also the board chair) are positively associated with performance, a view more consistent with stewardship theory.

One resolution of such issues is suggested by the contingency theory notion of fit. Where environments are turbulent or developing appropriate long-term visions is crucial, the boundary-spanning aspects of outside directors may be critical, as Zhang, Rajagopalan, and Datta note in Chapter Nine. These authors also suggest that governance issues like board composition may need to be considered in conjunction with specific types of strategies to understand organizational effectiveness.

Executive Vision

The nature of executive vision and its impact on organizational performance reflect the combined effects of a number of imperatives:

personal, political, social, cognitive, and technological. Zaccaro and Banks note in Chapter Seven that visions can be differentiated in terms of three factor analytically derived dimensions: vision formulation, which refers to whether the vision has a short- or long-run orientation; implementation, which refers to whether the vision is widely understood and communicated throughout the organization; and innovative realism, which pertains to the innovativeness of the vision. The relation between these dimensions and aspects of networks discussed in prior chapters is unmistakable. We would expect innovative realism and long-run vision formulations from individuals who developed systems thinking and foresight through external networks with other top-level executives. Such networks allow the development of mental models of future environments according to Hooijberg and Schneider's theory. Brass also notes that vision is collectively constructed by individuals with diverse, and typically weak, external relations. Whether visions are widely understood and communicated (the vision implementation factor) likely reflects the nature of the internal networks of top executives. As Brass notes, when leaders are central in networks and are strongly connected to other central individuals, they provide an efficient basis for communicating vision. Such internal networks also provide a basis for shared norms and a collective orientation.

Network approaches to vision development complement the more traditional leadership approach that Zaccaro and Banks discuss, which emphasizes the behavioral styles of leaders, particularly transformational leadership. This complementarity can best be seen in the notion of collective identities, which could be created by transformationally oriented leaders or could result from extensive internal networks of centrally connected top-level executives. Our preference (Lord & Smith, 1999) is to view vision as being a social construction of systems of individuals rather than merely the consequence of one leader's experience and values.

One means of integrating individually oriented and network-based ideas is to see the personal qualities of executives that Zaccaro and Banks discuss as affecting the type of networks they develop. Executives who are high on dimensions such as openness may be comfortable with linkages to diverse, external individuals. Individuals with more of a power orientation may become central in internal networks (see Chapter Five) or may develop structures with boards of directors that enhance a CEO's power as Daily and Dalton discuss. As Hooijberg and Schneider already noted, social intelligence is related to the development of networks used in co-option, foresight, and systems thinking. Thus, the effects on vision of a variety of leader qualities may operate through the types of social networks in which leaders function best.

Zaccaro and Banks also make an important contribution by emphasizing the value basis of visions. Here again, though, values can be thought of as being an individual factor that reflects an executive's personal value structure, or they can also be conceptualized as reflecting cultural constraints on a leader's actions. Lord and Brown (in press) suggest that leaders mediate between culturally based systems of values and subordinates' individual identities. Leaders use specific types of values to prime individual versus collective identities, which then set up means of self-regulation in individuals that are consistent with broad sets of value constraints inherent in cultures. As Schwartz (1999) noted, cultures tend to be organized around either individual or collective values.

Top Management Teams

In Chapter Eight, Klimoski and Koles address the interface between top management teams and CEOs, identifying both aspects of top management teams (TMT) that have been investigated and the challenges for CEOs in structuring and working with TMTs. Despite covering considerable literature, these authors lament the lack of systematic research on this interface and its relation to organizational performance. One undercurrent in this chapter, which echoes concerns in other chapters, is the nature of causal processes related to this interface. A predominant view is that TMTs are structured by CEOs, reflect a CEO's concerns, and function to protect and leverage a CEO's influence and visions. An alternative view is that these factors have more of an emergent systems quality, with the structure, processes, and functions of TMTs developing in response to systems constraints on TMTs and their own internal dynamics. This is a critical issue for understanding top management functioning, and as Zhang, Rajagopalan, and Datta suggest, many systems factors (nature of environment, type of compensation factors) may be critical moderators determining the type of TMT-CEO interface that exists and the type of interface that leads to superior organizational performance. One might expect, for example, that emergent TMT structures would work better with organizations in high-velocity or turbulent environment, with networks that involve diverse and weak linkages, and where organizational cultures emphasize growth and long-run orientations.

Financial Imperative

Zaccaro and Klimoski maintain that the financial imperative is "perhaps the most fundamental source of pressure on organizational leaders." They note that a substantial aspect of this pressure stems from the short-run need to demonstrate continually adequate financial performance to shareholders, which may conflict with the long-term orientation required for developing and implementing strategic visions.

Both Daily and Dalton and Zhang, Rajagopalan, and Datta address issues related to CEO compensation and financial performance. Such issues are both causes and results of power distributions between CEOs and boards of directors, and they have important implications for understanding how leadership activities are translated into organizational effects. For example, adequate financial performance is required to have the monetary resources to implement an organization's strategic vision. But it is also required for CEOs to have the personal power to motivate change.

Much of the research and theorizing on corporate board structures concerns compensation systems and a CEO's potential influence on compensations. Daily and Dalton reviewed evidence indicating that a CEO's influence and managerial discretion were positively related to CEO compensation and that the relation of discretion to CEO compensation was stronger among high-performing firms. They explain this result by suggesting that part of the ability to influence organizational processes accrues from having led a financially successful corporation. This conclusion is consistent with extensive experimental leadership research that shows leadership perceptions, a source of potential influence, to be dependent on feedback about group or organizational performance provided to subjects (see Lord & Maher, 1991).

Zhang, Rajagopalan, and Datta discuss another aspect of compensation, arguing that it is the type rather than the amount of executive compensation that is critical. They note that executive compensation systems interact with firm strategies, with long-term incentive systems encouraging both risk taking and increased capital expenditures. Other research indicates that high-performing organizations had compensation systems that matched environmental characteristics, the nature of a firm's dominant technology, or the overarching strategic orientation of the firm. This research strongly suggests that top-level executives need to consider the effects of compensation systems on a wide variety of organizational processes. While this aspect of leadership has not received much attention, the research that Zhang, Rajagopalan, and Datta review suggests that it should be explored more fully in the future. Compensation has both motivational and symbolic value in organizations, which directs attention and legitimizes activities, and thus it can be a crucial mechanism for leadership effects.

Staffing Imperative

Zaccaro and Klimoski note that senior staffing issues affect the sets of skills, dispositions, and capabilities possessed by top management. Traditional strategies for addressing such issues are recruitment, selection, and training and development, which are critical leadership concerns. Such techniques are normally focused at the individual level, but research covered in this book, such as Klimoski and Koles's focus on the CEO-TMT interface, indicates that more systematic, aggregate treatment of these concerns is needed as well. For example, as Zhang, Rajagopalan, and Datta note, the heterogeneity of TMTs provides a potential resource that can facilitate strategy development, particularly in high-velocity environments. However, heterogeneity can also create process losses as conflict is addressed and worked through, which can slow strategic responses (Hambrick et al., 1996). Zhang, Rajagopalan, and Datta also note that superior organizational performance may require a fit between the traits of new managers and the strategic orientation of a firm, again illustrating the interaction between individual-level factors like traits and macroissues like strategy.

Leadership Training and Development

McCauley's chapter on leadership development (Chapter Eleven) discusses several means of developing leaders, after first making the excellent point that the most effective developmental experiences combine three elements: assessment, challenge, and support. Assessment helps leaders develop a self-regulatory basis for learning by providing comprehensive feedback, which often is not otherwise be available. Challenge puts leaders in situations where they must learn new skills to perform well, and support helps leaders turn extreme challenge or failure experiences into enhanced skills rather than reduced self-confidence. As McCauley notes, alternative types of development experiences have different emphases in these three domains, with optimal development requiring many different types of experiences throughout a leader's career.

An important observation of McCauley that did not receive much emphasis is that in order to meet the multiple imperatives demanded of top-level leaders, executives develop needed capacities over many years and through a variety of developmental experiences. Such extensive skill development has been discussed by cognitive psychologists in terms of expert processing (Ericsson & Charness, 1994). Expert processing is knowledge driven in that experts substitute domain-specific knowledge for brute processing (computational) capacity, yielding superior performance with much less sensitivity to stress or cognitive load. When performance is knowledge based, the key issue becomes accessing relevant knowledge, which often requires context-specific cues. This is one reason that learning through experience rather than just through formal means is a necessary component of developing expertise. As Anderson (1987) stresses, context-specific, proceduralized skills develop by constructing productions (if-then rules), which are the building blocks of skills. The "if" component or cue for productions involves patterns of situational cues and internal goals, so for learning to generalize to real-world situations, proceduralization needs to occur in contexts that are similar to application contexts in terms of both environmental cues and internal motivational factors.

In discussing the individual qualities or abilities required for effective leader development, McCauley notes that three types of individual qualities are necessary: conceptual and analytic, social, and intrapersonal intelligence. The needs for conceptual and analytic and social skills have been discussed previously. Intrapersonal intelligence involves the ability to develop accurately and use a model of oneself. Certainly this requires meta-monitoring skills, which Zaccaro and Banks discussed. Intrapersonal intelligence also involves developing an accurate model of the self or an accurate self-identity. Self-identities, then, are also tied to the meta-monitoring component needed for long-term development of leadership skills. Influencing self-identities of others can be a powerful means by which top-level leaders help others develop leadership skills, which McCauley notes is an important activity of effective top-level leaders.

Leadership Assessment

Chapter Twelve by Day, on assessment of leader outcomes, raises a number of issues regarding defining and measuring the effect of leaders on organizations. The critical insight is that organizations and relevant outcomes are constantly changing, and the key function of executive-level leaders is to foster such change. Thus, measuring leadership outcomes by necessity requires the definition, measurement, and interpretation of change. Building on ideas from the personality literature, Day argues that the key strategic functions of top-level leaders are to help define identity, image, and reputations for organizations. He then shows how 360-degree feedback techniques could be used to measure such constructs. Finally, Day argues that for leaders to produce substantial change, they must also change organizational identities.

The notion that leaders manage identities as a means of fostering change is a fundamental insight that applies at the organizational level, as Day has noted, and with respect to leader-follower interactions (Lord, Brown, & Freiberg, 1999). Borrowing from individual-level theory, Markus and Wurf (1987) emphasize that identities serve key self-regulatory functions, being direct determinants of motivation and also cues for the scripts and plans that actually guide behaviors. Such reasoning helps us understand why, as Day proposed, changes in identities need to precede organizational change. Identities are the source of relatively automatic self-regulatory processes that counter random deviations and restore stability. Self-regulatory processes do this by matching sensed feedback to internal standards derived from identities and then altering behavior so as to reduce detected discrepancies (Carver & Scheier, 1998). Without prior identity change that resets the desired standard, the actions of leaders to promote change will simply provoke self-regulatory responses aimed at reconfirming prior identities. Thus, Day's perspective helps us understand resistance to change as the result of ongoing, identity-based self-regulation. However, when identities change first, self-regulation can become a factor precipitating change rather than a process that absorbs change attempts.

Markus and Wurf (1987) also suggest two other identity-related constructs that can help us understand the implications of Day's perspective. One is the construct of possible selves—images of whom we desire to become in the future or seek to avoid becoming. Possible selves can be both a rationale for current striving and a support for learning and development. For example, Lord and others (1999) maintain that resiliency in the face of adversity stems from focusing on possible rather than current selves. It seems likely that by emphasizing possible future organizational identities, executive leaders can both motivate growth and development on an organization-wide basis and engender resilience in coping with current challenges. Movement toward desired possible selves is also likely to be part of the leader's own meta-monitoring processes, which McCauley maintains are required for effective leader development. Comparison of actual to desired selves can help executive leaders define areas where they need development.

The second idea borrowed from Markus and Wurf is the notion of working-self concepts, which is the portion of one's identity that is currently highly active and engaged in self-regulatory activities. Identities are rich, multifaceted, and often inconsistent cognitive structures. Only a part of one's identity, the working self-concept, is active at any one time. Applied to organizations, this idea implies that operating identities are not uniform but rather are subject to continual change based on internal and external factors. Leaders can make components of existing identities more or less salient as a means of adaptation to short-run change, or they can prepare the organization for long-run challenges by creating new identities. These are quite different strategic functions and should not be confused.

While it has many advantages, Day's focus on identities, images, and reputations as a means of assessing leadership has some disadvantages as well. One disadvantage for the use of identities, images, and reputations as an assessment device is that they are tied to indirect effects of leadership that operate through an aggregation of individual self-definitional processes. As such, they are contaminated by many individual-level processes within perceivers. Identities, images, and reputations are contaminated by more aggregated processes as well. For example, many industry-level factors may substantially affect the identities of constituent organizations (Gordon, 1991; Porac et al., 1989). Thus, assessment of leadership based on identities is likely to be contaminated by influences from higher-level units as well as from individual respondents.

Another disadvantage is that we are moving the assessment of leadership very far from individual qualities of leaders. The value of such assessments for leader selection or training may therefore be reduced substantially, though the value of assessment for evaluating or guiding organizational change may be enhanced. This is not necessarily bad for organizations, but it reflects a choice in orientations that needs to be made explicit.

Progress Toward a Systematic Theory of Executive Leadership

At the outset of this chapter, I suggested that a comprehensive theory of executive leadership was needed as a backdrop for understanding the variable role of top-level leaders in specific contexts. One might then ask whether this book has helped develop such a systematic theory. Although various chapters and imperatives were covered individually, I believe that as a whole they provide a wealth of insights concerning the complexity of top-level leadership. By bringing together many diverse scholars to address the topic of executive leadership, this book creates a much deeper understanding of the process than prior attempts, which reflect narrower perspectives (Lord & Maher, 1991; Zaccaro, 2001). Yet because each chapter discusses a particular topic from the unique perspective of the authors, the collective value of this work in creating a more systematic theory can be easily overlooked. These chapters provide a sound beginning for a new theoretical approach to executive leadership. Like executive vision, it is a collective construction rather than an individual enterprise. Further, this collective vision draws on individual expert knowledge in many diverse areas to create a deeper structure for understanding top-level leadership. Collectively, I believe these chapters represent a promising start toward theory building in the area of executive leadership.

Such a theoretical approach would stress the emergent, systems aspects of executive leadership by viewing it as being embedded in a variety of social networks. It would also clearly recognize that executive leadership involves multiple imperatives, all grounded in social and cognitive capacities. Also critical is the recognition that while individual qualities and behaviors are important, their effects are likely to be indirect and distributed over time, being mediated through networks of internal or external individuals or through collective cognitive processes like developing organizational structures, cultures, identities, and visions.

References

Anderson, J. R. (1987). Skill acquisition: Compilation of weak-method problem solutions. *Psychological Review, 94,* 192–210.

Astley, W. G., & Van de Ven, A. H. (1983). Central perspectives and debates in organizational theory. *Administrative Science Quarterly, 28,* 245–273.

Carver, C. S., & Scheier, M. F. (1998). *On the self-regulation of behavior.* New York: Cambridge University Press.

Chi, M.T.H., Glaser, R., & Farr, M. J. (1988). *The nature of expertise.* Mahwah, NJ: Erlbaum.

Day, D. V., & Lord, R. G. (1988). Executive leadership and organizational performance: Suggestions for a new theory and methodology. *Journal of Management, 14,* 111–122.

Day, D. V., & Lord, R. G. (1992). Expertise and problem categorization: The role of expert processing in organizational sense-making. *Journal of Management Studies, 29,* 35–47.

Durso, F. T., & Gronlund, S. D. (1999). Situation awareness. In F. T. Durso (Ed.), *Handbook of applied cognition.* New York: Wiley.

Ericsson, K. A., & Charness, N. (1994). Expert performance: Its structure and acquisition. *American Psychologist, 49,* 725–747.

Gordon, G. G. (1991). Industry determinants of organizational culture. *Academy of Management Review, 16,* 396–415.

Gross, J. J. (1998). The emerging field of emotion regulation: An integrative review. *Review of General Psychology, 2,* 271–299.

Hambrick, D. C., Cho, T. S. & Chen, M. J. (1996). The influence of top-management team heterogeneity on firms' competitive moves. *Administrative Science Quarterly, 41,* 659–684.

Hanges, P. J., Lord, R. G., & Dickson, M. W. (2000). An information processing perspective on leadership and culture: A case for connectionist architecture. *Applied Psychology, 49,* 133–161.

Jaques, E. (1989). *Requisite organization.* Arlington, VA: Cason Hall.

Katz, D., & Kahn, R. L. (1978). *The social psychology of organizations* (2nd ed.). New York: Wiley.

Lord, R. G., & Brown, D. J. (in press). Leadership, values, and subordinate self-concepts. *Leadership Quarterly.*

Lord, R. G., Brown, D. J., & Freiberg, S. J. (1999). Understanding the dynamics of leadership: The role of follower self-concepts in the leader/follower relationship. *Organizational Behavior and Human Decision Processes, 78,* 167–203.

Lord, R. G., Brown, D. J., & Harvey, J. L. (in press). System constraints on leadership perceptions, behavior and influence: An example of connectionist level processes. In M. A. Hogg & R. S. Tindale (Eds.), *Blackwell handbook of social psychology. Vol. 3: Group processes.* Oxford: Blackwell.

Lord, R. G., & Maher, K. J. (1991). *Leadership and information processing.* New York: Routledge.

Lord, R. G., & Smith, W. G. (1999). Leadership and the changing nature of work performance. In D. R. Algin & E. D. Palaces (Eds.), *The changing nature of work performance: Implications for staffing, personnel decisions, and development.* San Francisco: Jossey-Bass.

Markus, H., & Wurf, E. (1987). The dynamic self-concept: A social psychological perspective. *Annual Review of Psychology, 38,* 299–337.

Meindl, J. R. (1995). The romance of leadership as a follower-centric theory: A social constructionist approach. *Leadership Quarterly, 6,* 329–341.

Newell, A. (1989). *Unified theories of cognition.* Cambridge, MA: Harvard University Press.

Porac, J., Thomas, H., & Baden-Fuller, C. (1989). Competitive groups as cognitive communities: The case of Scottish knitwear manufacturers. *Journal of Management Studies, 26,* 397–416.

Schwartz, S. (1999). A theory of cultural values and some implications for work. *Applied Psychology, 48,* 23–47.

Tushman, M. L., & Romanelli, E. (1985). Organizational evolution: A metamorphosis model of convergence and reorientation. In B. M. Staw & L. L. Cummings (Eds.), *Research in organizational behavior* (Vol. 7). Greenwich, CT: JAI Press.

Walsh, J. P. (1995). Managerial and organizational cognition: Notes from a trip down memory lane. *Organizational Science, 6,* 280–312.

Weick, K. E. (1979). *The social psychology of organizing.* Reading, MA: Addison-Wesley.

Weick, K. E. (1985). Sources of order in under organized systems: Themes in recent organizational theory. In Y. S. Lincoln (Ed.), *Organizational theory and inquiry.* Thousand Oaks, CA: Sage.

Zaccaro, S. J. (2001). *Executive leadership.* Alexandria, VA. American Psychological Association.

Zaccaro, S. J., Gilbert, J. A., Thor, K. K., & Mumford, M. D. (1991). Leadership and social intelligence: Linking social perceptiveness and behavioral flexibility to leader effectiveness. *Leadership Quarterly, 2,* 317–347.

CHAPTER 14

"Into the Box" Thinking About Leadership Research

John E. Mathieu

Developing a better understanding of what constitutes and influences effective leadership has been a topic of inquiry as long as there has been recorded history. Whether the specific concern has focused on leading armies during the crusades or leading multinational e.coms, the question has remained the same: What makes for effective leadership? At one level, the answer to this question is easy. Effective leadership is the ability to use resources and mobilize the efforts of others toward goal accomplishment. At a deeper level, however, the answers get far more complicated. What constitutes effective leadership? It depends. It depends on a complex combination of who the leader is, what he or she does, who the members are (what their relative knowledge, skills, abilities, and other characteristics are), what the situation affords in terms of resources and constraints, what is occurring in the larger environment, and what historical events led up to the current situation. In other words, there is a confluence of a multitude of factors that collectively set the stage for episodes of effective or ineffective leadership to occur. A brief review of notably effective leaders, such as Caesar, Napoleon, Rommel, Gandhi, Martin Luther King, Vince Lombardi, Lee Iacocca, Golda Meir, Bill Gates—name your favorite— will inevitably reveal that they would not have been nearly as successful in different historical times or in leading a different array of people. Given this complex phenomenon, how can we better understand the primary drivers that crystallize into instances of effective leadership?

Here at the dawn of the twenty-first century, scholars have at their disposal roughly eighty years worth of scientific research on the factors leading to effective leadership. Numerous theories have been advanced, and thousands of studies have been conducted. Much has been learned. Still, we are faced with a myriad of explanations for our findings. This chapter advances a perspective for how previous leadership research can be interpreted and future research designed and implemented.

Cattell's Data Box

Any research investigation essentially boils down to an effort to model the relationship between variance of Xs on variance of Ys, as indexed by sets of observations, gathered through some means, on some sample of units of inquiry, over some duration, in some context, and at some point in time. Therein lies the complexity of trying to understand cause-and-effect relationships. Cattell (1966) articulated a "data box" concept whereby he observed that variance in observations in classic psychological research was thought to have stemmed from the following factors:

- Stimulus, that is, attributes of the predictor variables
- Particular patterns of responses in the ongoing behavior process, that is, the outcome variables
- Organisms in question, that is, the sample (for example, people, animals, or, organized groups)
- Background attributes, that is, the general context of the study
- The observer—more generally, the method of measurement

These facts can be mapped to that of traditional leadership investigation (see Table 14.1). The "stimuli" in leader research are, in fact, the leaders themselves, whereas the responses would be the outcome variables in question, such as organizational or subunit effectiveness, members' reactions, and behaviors. The organisms in question translate to the sample of followers, or the targets of leader influences and their attributes, such as organizational units. The background and observer facets (respectively, the larger con-

Table 14.1. Cattell's Data Box and
Leadership Research Facets

Cattell's Dimensions	Leadership Research Parallel Facets
Stimulus and predictor variables	Leader attributes
Response patterns and outcome variables	Outcome variables
Organisms in question and sample	Follower and unit attributes
Background attributes and general context	Local and macro context
Observer and measurement methods	Measurement methods

text and the methods of measurement) apply directly to the leadership research context.

Cattell (1966) further observed that each of these five facets could vary along a temporal dimension. That is, stimuli, including leaders, have stable (trait) and transient (state) aspects. Patterns of behaviors (outcomes) will also likely evolve over time and exhibit unstable patterns. Organizations, subsystems, and members all develop, stagnate or grow accustomed to certain influences, and otherwise change. Organizational contexts are dynamic entities and are becoming particularly fluid in recent times. Measurement systems are also sensitive to time-based effects, whether that is simply random variability or more insidious effects such as response biases (primacy and recency effects) or other instrumentation confounds (Cook & Campbell, 1979).

Even in the simplest situations where, for example, researchers collect measures of leaders' behaviors and relate them to members' reactions, a myriad of questions arise. What influenced the observed indexes of leader behaviors? It depends. It depends on which leaders we chose to sample, in what situations, over what durations, on what dimensions, and by what means. What influenced the observed indexes of outcomes variables? It depends. It depends on what we conceive of as being influenced by leaders (for example, systems, units, or individuals), how we sample those entities, in what situations, over what durations, on what dimensions, and by what means. The covariation between these two sets of observations is also likely to be influenced by how temporally proximal they are to one another, a slew of other third variables, and a host of psychometric concerns. Notice that thus far I have been discussing leadership as though it emanates from "one person" and is directed uniformly toward a system or multiple members. What happens when we think about leadership as creating and shaping organizational systems rather than guiding individual members? What happens if a leader deals with different units or with different people in different ways? What happens to the question if leadership is shared in a self-directed team or among a top management group? Answering these questions is the challenge for leadership researchers.

Theoretical Foundations

Modern leadership theories advanced in the previous forty years are almost invariably contingency based, and each of the prominent approaches considers at least two, and usually three or more, facets as codetermining leader effectiveness (Hughes, Ginnett, & Curphy, 1996; Yukl & Van Fleet, 1992). For example, path-goal theory (House & Dressler, 1974) formally considers the combination of member and situational characteristics, in conjunction with group processes, as specifying the most effective profile of leader behaviors for a given situation. Vroom and Yetton's leader decision-making model (1973) suggests that leaders should adopt the particular decision-making style that is best suited for their situation on the basis of the time that is available, members' relative expertise, and the importance of their accepting the outcome. Fielder's theory (1971, 1978) suggests that attributes of the situation, such as task structure and leader position power, dictate which style of leadership will be most effective. Hersey and Blanchard (1977), Blake and Mouton (1964), and scores of others have argued that the effectiveness of leader behaviors such as initiating structure or consideration will depend on characteristics of followers (such as maturity) and aspects of situations (such as task ambiguity). Dechant and Altman (1994), Gupta (1984, 1988), and several other authors have argued that top-level leadership effectiveness hinges on the extent to which executives can maintain an alignment between their organizational systems and environmental forces.

In one of the more comprehensive approaches advanced recently, stratified systems theory suggested that the nature of effective leadership behavior varies by organizational level (Jacobs & Jaques, 1987, 1991). More specifically, they argue that lower-level leaders should focus on fairly concrete internal matters related to task accomplishment and member reactions, whereas upper-level leaders should concentrate more on visionary activities, sense making, and sense giving and have an external focus (see Zaccaro, 1996, for more details). Work in the tradition of charismatic and transformational leadership (see Bass & Avolio, 1990, 1993) echoes the points about the effectiveness of visioning and symbolic efforts of high-level leaders. Still other studies in this line of research reflect a contingency style and incorporate situational attributes (Keller, 1992; Leavy & Wilson, 1994). In short, there is no paucity of thinking about leadership effectiveness as a confluence of effects. At issue is the extent that such effects are managed and articulated in various research investigations so that their impact on the interpretation and generalization of findings can be articulated.

In the following sections, I consider each of these facets more specifically. The general theme, however, is that some combination of all of these factors is at play whenever one studies leader effectiveness. The theoretical frame that is guiding an investigation will highlight which sources of variance are of interest and which ones are potential sources of confounds. My point is that researchers should articulate, a priori, how they have decided to deal with each source of influence. These matters cannot be ignored or somehow left to chance; to do so simply relegates them to error variance or, worse yet, serious confounds that cannot be modeled in the analysis stage or appreciated in the interpretation stage of research investigations. In effect, this strategy sets the stage for the interpretation of effects and the boundary conditions, or breadth of generalizations, associated with any given investigation.

Managing Variance

Researchers faced with the decision about how to deal with each potential influence in the data box can either rely on randomization or attempt to control variance in one of three ways. First, one could experimentally hold constant or manipulate factors of interest. For example, one might hold situational factors constant by having a sample of leaders respond to the same hypothetical situation in a simulation exercise. Alternatively, one might choose to manipulate situational effects and have the sample of leaders respond to a number of situations that have been crafted and controlled by the researcher. In either case, the variance of the facet (or lack thereof) has come under direct control of the researcher.

A second form of "control" available to researchers may be garnered by systematically sampling either a limited range of a facet or intentionally sampling a wide range along the facet. For example, if a researcher believes that the impact of leader-structuring behaviors on member performance will be moderated by members' ability levels, then one alternative would be to sample only members who have ability falling within a "sensitive zone." This approach would focus the investigation squarely on those followers thought to be most influenced by the leader behaviors in question. Alternatively, a researcher might choose to sample members who vary widely in terms of relevant abilities, assess those abilities, and then use the measures as a moderator variable and model such effects. The third option is to assess potential confounding variables and then model their effects in analyses. Commonly referred to as "controlling for, blocking, or covariates," the idea is that by applying statistical techniques, a researcher can isolate effects of interest as if "all else being equal" caveats applied (see Cook & Campbell, 1979, and Pedhazur & Pedhazur-Schmelkin, 1991, for commentaries highlighting the shortcomings of this strategy).

The common theme among all three research strategies is that the researcher somehow gains control over the variance of potential confounds by managing the situation, selecting the makeup of the samples, or applying statistical techniques, and then attempts either to minimize the influence of such effects or formally model them as moderators. At issue is the fact that these decisions should be articulated a priori so as to maximize their likelihood of success at achieving their intended goals. In other words, if, for example, a researcher is studying leader effects in a field study with limited opportunities to control the situation, then care should be exercised a priori to identify the relevant sources of influence that could contaminate the interpretation of results. Then such factors should either be sampled in such a way as to minimize or to specify their effects, or they should be assessed and modeled empirically. Notably these recommendations are not on the surface revolutionary, but when one begins to consider the myriad of influences on the effectiveness of leadership and then reviews the substantive literature, one finds that they are rarely articulated or considered (see Day & Lord, 1988, for similar sentiments). Below I review what some of these influences may be, as organized by the general facets listed in Table 14.2. Then I consider some additional temporal and methodological factors that may well play a role in the interpretation of leadership research findings.

Table 14.2. Examples from the Domain
of Leadership Research Facets.

Leadership Research Facets	Examples from the Domain
Leader attributes	*Fixed:* Drive and motivation, personality, task-based intelligence and ability, physical characteristics, social intelligence
	Variable: Motivational and affective states, tacit knowledge, decision-making style, behavioral orientation
Follower attributes	*Fixed:* Drive and motivation, personality, task-based intelligence and ability, departmentalization
	Variable: Motivational and affective states; tacit knowledge; group processes, development, affective tone; organizational processes
	Compositional: Unit/plant or member homogeneity or heterogeneity, stability over time, developmental stage
Outcome variables	Tangible performance (quality and quantity); members' attitudes, motivations, and reactions; member longevity
Context	*Proximal:* Task structure, complexity, and interdependence; situational constraints and resources; reward systems; group size; members' and leader's hierarchical levels
	Distal: Organizational strategy, structure, policies, and culture; technology and environmental influences
Measurement methods	Archival traces, performance ratings, surveys, interviews, observations, critical incidents

The Leaders

Obviously the focus of leadership research is on the leaders: who they are, what they do, and how they do it. As the research has matured over time, it has expanded to consider formally the role of followers, the immediate situation, and larger contextual factors, including organizational systems and the environment. Nevertheless, the focus of leadership research remains squarely on the leaders themselves. Leader characteristics can be viewed in terms of relatively stable "traits" and more variable factors such as moods, attitudes, and behaviors.

Trait-Based Approaches

Trait theories of leadership essentially suggest that certain characteristics of leaders, such as their personality attributes, task competence, and values, render some leaders more effective than others. Embedded in this logic is that leader traits will give rise to certain patterns of leader behaviors and that these behaviors will be fairly consistent across members and situations (Kenny & Zaccaro, 1983; Kirkpatrick & Locke, 1991). Invariably, more modern research and theorizing have adopted a contingency-type approach that refines this thinking and suggests that leaders who possess certain traits will be more effective in some situations than others. The underlying logic of this approach is that leaders are "fixed effects" and cannot readily change. They will exhibit a fairly consistent pattern of behaviors across situations and people. Should their style be "right" for the situation and times, such leaders will be quite effective.

To test trait-based theories of leadership adequately, one needs to "cross" leaders, followers, and situations. One way that this can be accomplished is to track the influence of a given set of leaders, each operating in a number of different situations that vary in terms of situational demands and follower ability. For example, one could study the influence of a leader in her organizational context, as a leader in her religious group, and as the coach in a youth soccer league. An alternative way to study such effects would be to sample a diverse number of people who lead similar followers in situations that are fairly comparable. For example, one might study the effects of leader traits among managers of national or international franchises who deliver the same product or services in a wide variety of settings. Alternatively, studying coaches and managers of professional sports teams may offer another forum (mainly because abundant information is available to control statistically for influences such as relative team talent and difficulty of schedule).

On the surface, these two alternatives appear fairly easy to implement, and each would provide informative testing grounds. However, one does not often find leaders randomly distributed in situations. Stated differently, Schneider (1987) and others have described an attraction-selection-attrition (A-S-A) process whereby certain kinds of people are drawn to particular organizations, organizations tend to select only a subset of people who are deemed suitable matches, and the people who remain in an organization are indeed the ones who "fit." Schneider argues that over time, this yields a fairly homogeneous set of people who comprise an organization and that it then becomes impossible to distinguish "person effects" from "situational effects" clearly. In the current context, this means that the two research designs described above will be very difficult to implement. In the first case, because leaders largely choose the situations that they operate in, tracking leader behaviors across situations will still yield a shortsighted view of potential interactions. This follows because leaders will choose a limited number of all possible situations to operate in. The second design is also constrained because A-S-A processes will limit the extent to which different kinds of leaders appear in any given situation that is being focused on. In sum, the application of A-S-A logic suggests that the variance of combinations of leader trait sets in different situations and with different members is likely to be seriously limited. In effect, then, the observed covariances of leader traits and outcomes of interest are likely to be restricted and effects attenuated. The limiting forces of A-S-A process will be a continual concern throughout this chapter.

Behavior-Based Approaches

Other theories of leadership assume that leaders can modify their behaviors and act differently as circumstances warrant. For example, vertical dyad theory (Dansereau, Graen, & Haga, 1975) suggests that leaders may act in one way toward some members, while simultaneously acting in different ways toward others. Similarly, other theories suggest that given a particular set of circumstances, leaders should share decision making fully, partially, or not at all (Vroom & Yetton, 1973; Vroom & Jago, 1974). Hitt and Tyler (1991) argued that top-level managers need to scan the environment and make choices about how best to position their organization. In effect, these theories suggest that leader behaviors are not fixed but may vary from one circumstance to another. Such theories differ in terms of whether the circumstances are demarcated by situational events or member characteristics, but the point remains the same: leaders can (or should) adopt different behaviors under different circumstances.

Measurement issues aside for a moment, modeling this kind of leadership theory requires that a researcher differentiate when leaders act uniformly—the "average leadership approach"—and when they modulate their behaviors in response to circumstances—a "differentiated approach." To test these theories adequately, we need to sample or create situations where, for example, leaders lead a given set of employees in different situations that vary systematically along continuums of interest, such as task structure. Alternatively, we might examine leader-member exchanges in instances where situations sampled remain fairly consistent in terms of demands but the followers vary in terms of needs, perhaps because a given set of employees are developing rapidly or because different employees occupy the positions. In either instance, one could systematically track leaders' behaviors in response to changing demands that are not contaminated by follower-situation confounds. Stated differently, attempts to model how leaders act by sampling them in different situations where they are leading different employees will provide insight as to whether they are consistent or vary their behaviors. What it cannot tell us, however, is what any variance that is observed is in response to. And when we sample leader-follower dyads from real organizational settings, we are dealing with a constrained set of options. A-S-A processes have served to limit the kinds of leaders who occupy those positions, as well as the variety of followers whom they influence. There are some organizational designs, however, that may provide unique windows of opportunity for testing these types of theories. For example, in a matrix-designed organization, leaders may simultaneously be managing multiple project groups, each with its unique array of members and its particular goals, context, time frame, and so forth. Similarly, instances where executives lead different units, plants, and so forth that produce similar products but are organized in different fashions offer good opportunities to track such influences. Although these situations are still susceptible to the potential sources of confounds, they create opportunities to focus attention on the natural crossings of leaders, situations, and followers in a real organizational setting.

The Followers

Follower characteristics have profound influences on the effectiveness of various leader behaviors. Some follower characteristics can be considered to be fairly stable over time—for example, knowledge, skills, and abilities (KSAs)—whereas other factors, such as mood states and affective reactions, often vary from one instance to another. In other instances, the organization system may be fairly stable (as in functionally differentiated designs) or have a more fluid design (say, a matrix or team-based design). In Cattell's terms, this suggests that some follower facets are "fixed effects" while others are "variable effects." Thus, prescriptions emanating from theories such as path-goal that suggest particular combinations of leader and follower characteristics optimize effectiveness become complex to implement. For example, once a follower's KSAs are taken into account, the extent to which a leader should structure the environment becomes a fairly consistent matter. Subordinates with lower KSAs will, all else being equal, benefit from structuring, whereas the same activities would be redundant, and a potential source of alienation, for followers with greater KSA levels. However, the extent to which supportive leader behaviors will be seen as beneficial will likely be a more transitory relationship tied to the followers' mood and affective states. Stated differently, the extent to which a leader can best align his or her behavior with the needs of a subordinate will in some instances be a consistent pattern and in other instances vary from one occasion to another—for any particular subordinate.

As if the above "combination rules" were not difficult enough to assess, model, and understand, the homogeneity and heterogeneity of followers complicate matters further. What are the implications of leading a uniformly skilled and similarly oriented group of subordinates—say, a special-forces military unit? Contrast such a situation to one in which a manager leads a group of employees who vary markedly in educational background, KSAs, full- and part-time status, and other characteristics—say, a regional food co-op. At the executive level, the comparison would be between leading a national franchise that places a premium on uniformity throughout their system (as with fast food restaurants) versus one that intentionally varies from one site to another (such as a radio media executive who has different types of stations catering to different audiences throughout the country). In the former cases, one could adopt a fairly consistent leadership style and reach nearly all subordinates or units, whereas in the latter cases, an effective leader would have to modulate his or her behavior for every employee, clusters of employee types, or different subunits. Clearly these considerations drive variance in terms of whether leaders operate in a consistent fashion or adopt a more differentiated approach. Considered from another angle, the average subordinate KSA level (in the case of members) or organizational design (in the case of subunits), *together* with the homogeneity around that average, has clear implications for whether a leader would behave consistently over time and across subordinates and units will be deemed effective. In sum, it is not enough to say that follower or unit characteristics interact with leader behaviors to influence effectiveness. We need to consider which characteristics, of which subordinates or units, at what times, are important and whether these same combinations pertain to their teammates or to other units. Only then can we fully model how leaders' behaviors come into play.

The Situation

Prominent contingency theories of leadership also take into account attributes of the leader-follower situation. For example, Fiedler's theory (1967) considers the role of task structure and leader position power. Vroom and Yetton's theory (1973) emphasizes the time that is available to make a decision. Path-goal theory has explored the role of several features, including task structure and more social psychological aspects such as group cohesion (House & Dressler, 1974; Schriesheim, 1980; Schriesheim &

Schriesheim, 1980). Zaccaro (1996) and Katz and Kahn (1978) have argued that effective top-level leaders must be responsive to external forces and interorganizational relations. As discussed in regard to follower attributes, the level and distribution of the task environment will limit the extent to which leader behavior and out-come relationships can be adequately tested. In an ideal test bed, one would sample instances where individuals lead similar follow-ers who happen to work in different situations. For example, the leaders would guide a group of salespersons who work with single customers and have stable long-term working relationships, while simultaneously leading a group of salespersons who manage mul-tiple accounts in a very fluid environment. In this fashion, one could isolate the impact of situational factors from leader attributes and follower characteristics. Again, given the operation of A-S-A type processes, such opportunities will likely be few and far be-tween. But the issue is that if we are to interpret the results of re-search, we need to account formally for such effects. And if the primary purpose of an investigation is to feature the role of situa-tional factors, then we need to sample or create instances where they vary in such a manner as to be tested.

Situational influences may include factors that go far beyond the immediate leader-member exchange environment. The larger subunit or organizational culture, industry, and other "macro" fea-tures will likely place a premium on certain leadership styles. What works for a National Football League (NFL) head coach will not likely be effective for a leader of a community social services cen-ter or a virtual e.com. In effect, the dynamics here can be seen as a large-scale version of the A-S-A processes in that the work culture of various industries virtually precludes certain leadership styles from even occurring; examples are an NFL coach who emphasizes interpersonal support and an overly task-focused leader of a women's resource center.

Several variables cannot be neatly sorted into leader, follower, or situational categories but nonetheless play a role in leader ef-fectiveness research. Included here are variables such as the rela-tive hierarchical levels of leaders and their followers, their relative organizational tenure, salaries, and other factors that are really by-products not only of the situation but also of the individuals in-volved (see Roberts, Hulin, & Rousseau, 1978, for further discussion of this notion). For example, stratified systems theory (Jacobs & Jaques, 1991; see also Chapter One of this book) suggested that what constitutes the most effective leader behaviors and orientations differs markedly between those at the lower levels of an organization as compared to those near the apex. Yet lower-level leaders are generally younger, have a larger span of control, interact with less-skilled employees, and deal with much more concrete issues than do higher-level leaders. Are the differences in such relationships attributable to different leaders, followers, or the situation? The question cannot be unequivocally answered, because the factors involved are inextricable.

Temporal Issues

The influence of time on substantive relationships can be viewed from three different perspectives: stage of development, historical context, and cause-and-effect lags. Each of these issues has implications for when one might best investigate a particular relationship of interest and how the sampling of leader, members, and measures should best be orchestrated.

The stage of development issue suggests that leader-follower relationships evolve over time and may qualitatively change depending on when one investigates them. The most effective leadership style for mentoring newly hired employees will differ drastically from the best style for leading well-seasoned veteran employees. Similarly, the most effective executive leadership style will differ for organizations working through a merger and acquisition process versus operating in a steady state, versus experiencing a decline in their product life cycle. This type of phenomenon formally acknowledges the follower (or organizational) maturation process (Cook & Campbell, 1979), which places a premium on different leader behaviors at different times in the developmental sequence.

The historical context issue is akin to what Cook and Campbell (1979) refer to as a history threat to internal (and external) validity. The larger notion here is that something beyond the immediate context helped to account for the outcomes observed. For example, the scary rise to power and influence of an Adolf Hitler, or the notable rise to power and influence of a Martin Luther King Jr. can both be largely attributable to the larger historical context of their times. No doubt both possessed attributes that enabled them to occupy the roles that they did—but neither would likely have been so influential in other historical settings. Less profound examples, such as Lee Iacocca's leadership during the Chrysler turn-around of the early 1980s or Bill Gates's rise to power with Microsoft during the 1990s, reflect the same type of dynamic. They were effective not just because of who they were, what they did, and who they led; they were effective because of the times that they operated within.

Day and Lord (1988) have made similar observations about historical and methodological problems in executive succession studies. They argued that previous conclusions about the limited influence of top-level leaders on organizational performance (Lieberson & O'Connor, 1972; Salancik & Pfeffer, 1977) were methodologically questionable. For example, Day and Lord (1988) argued that when contextual issues such as organizational size and year effects (larger economic concerns as reflected in cost-of-living adjustments), along with different time lags are taken into consideration, top-level leader succession could account for as much as 45 percent of the variance of organizational performance.

Day and Lord's insights are important to recognize, although I believe that their conclusions may be overly optimistic. A normal succession study is equivalent to a classic pretest-posttest design, with the change of leadership being the intervention. And while many executive leadership changes are merely evolutionary as retirements and deaths occur, many others are revolutionary and designed to signal an organizational transformation. Is it the change in leadership or the larger organizational transformation that is responsible for souring profits, return on equity, and so on? This is simply a variation of the classic "third variable" problem in behavioral science research. On one hand, if an organization decides to acquire another, drastically downsize, introduce new technology, change markets, or modify its culture and brings aboard new leadership to guide the transformation, it is impossible to disentangle how much of the net result is attributable to leadership changes versus the other efforts. On the other hand, any of these organizational changes may stem from the vision of the new leader and his or her efforts to transform the organization. In this sense, perhaps some of these "other effects" *are* attributable to leadership.

Day and Lord (1988) discuss this distinction in terms of direct and indirect influences of top-level executives on organizations. At issue here is that as one moves up the organizational hierarchy, it becomes more and more difficult to disentangle leadership effects from organizational effects. This follows because the target of influence shifts from leading members through well-defined tasks to creating and shaping organizations and aligning them with the external environment (Katz & Kahn, 1978; see also Chapter One of this book). As the target of influence grows larger and more diffuse, the role of leadership versus other factors becomes much more difficult to disentangle. In this sense, leadership becomes more of a systems phenomenon and less of a person phenomenon.

The third temporal-based effect is cause-and-effect lags. This is a classic research design matter that concerns the likely time between when a stimulus (the cause) occurs and when its effects will likely be manifest. For example, if a leader were to become more supportive as a consequence of some intervention, how long would it take for team cohesion to crystallize? At a more macrolevel, if a leader articulates a clear vision and well positions an organization in its environment, how long will it take to see changes in stock values? In brief, specifying this ideal temporal window for assessing the effects of some relationship or interventions becomes a critical matter. Done too early, before the causal relationship can take root, one runs the risk of falsely concluding that no relationship exists. Wait too long, and extenuating circumstances will likely obscure any relationship that existed. Obviously these matters are particularly salient in cross-sectional designs where time-based relationships cannot be untangled. For example, Day and Lord (1988) noted that adopting a three-year time lag rather than a cross-sectional analysis (and controlling for organizational size) changed the variance in organizational performance attributable to leadership succession in the Lieberson and O'Connor (1972) study from 7.5 to 32.0 percent. But merely employing a longitudinal design is not a panacea for the concerns. In sum, it is not enough to use longitudinal designs to address time-related issues; the lags between when a hypothesized causal event occurs and when we assess its effects must be carefully thought through and articulated. This will also likely vary as a function of the dependent variable that is focused on (Day & Lord, 1988; see also Chapter

Twelve of this book). Combining that with the fact that we need to consider the development stage of the exchange context, as well as outside historical events that may enhance or constrain certain relationships, means that extracting valuable inferences from any kind of study becomes a tricky endeavor, to say the least. Certainly using longitudinal designs, particularly ones with multiple assessment periods, is a step in the right direction. But the timing of those assessments is critical.

Measurement Issues

It is beyond the scope of this chapter to detail the variety of measurement tools and approaches that are employed in leadership research. They certainly run the gamut from simply gathering survey responses from subordinates, to ethnographic accounts of leader behaviors, to clever use of archival indexes, to macro-organizational effectiveness models. Nevertheless, at a coarser level, one must consider the nature and source of measures commonly employed in leadership research, and whether they might be deficient or contaminated. Because Day has done an excellent job in Chapter Twelve at highlighting the issues related to outcome measures of leader effectiveness. I will focus primarily on the predictor or leader side of the equation.

In terms of assessing leaders' traits, the traditional array of measurement of knowledge, skills, abilities, and other characteristics (KSAOs) has been employed, ranging from structured and unstructured paper-and-pencil tests, interviews, and surveys, on up through quite elaborate assessment center approaches. Evaluating the quality of these measures follows the same rules that pertain to any construct validity assessment in applied psychology and organizational behavior (Cook & Campbell, 1979; Pedhazur & Pedhazur-Schmelkin, 1991). For example, there has been much debate over the construct validity of Fiedler's Least Preferred Co-Worker scale (Rice, 1978; Schriesheim & Kerr, 1977). On the other hand, there has been no more controversy about the assessment of leaders' "Big Five" (conscientiousness, extraversion, agreeableness, emotional stability, and openness to experience) than there has in any other domain interested in the role of personality. Similarly, the assessment of outcome measures is comparable to other applications that focus on individual and group-level criteria. Perhaps the most controversy has surrounded assessments of leaders' behaviors. In part, some debate has centered on the construct validity of particular measures, such as the Ohio State Forms (Schriesheim & Kerr, 1974; Schriesheim & Stogdill, 1975), or more recently on the nature of Bass's measures of transformational and transactional leader behaviors (Bass & Avolio, 1993). Clearly this work is worthwhile and serves to enhance the construct validity of such measures and consequently our understanding of leadership phenomenon.

Equally important, however, is the matter of how measures of leader behaviors are used. Mathieu and Klein (2000) have demonstrated that the referents used in otherwise identical survey measures (individual versus group versus organizational) account for significant variance in responses, and that these differences are not uniform across levels of analysis. For example, researchers interested in deciphering whether leaders tend to behave uniformly toward all subordinates versus whether they adopt a more differentiated dyadic style usually have subordinates individually complete surveys of leader behaviors. They then proceed to contrast variance within versus between leaders, using these measures as dependent variables. But let us look closely at the nature of the items on which these contrasts are made. Assuming for the sake of argument that a leader *does* behave in a differentiated manner with subordinates, when faced with the task of agreeing or not on a 1–5 scale with the statement, "Our leader treats his or her subordinates with respect," how should a person respond? If the leader respects some followers but not others, what should the response be? Should the respondent offer the middle "3" point as a compromise or averaging logic? Should he or she simply respond in terms of how the leader behaves toward himself or herself and ignore the group referent? I suspect that these ambiguous types of situations would be the ones most susceptible to implicit leadership rating biases where respondents project their stereotypical conceptions of ineffective or effective leadership in their ratings (Lord & Maher, 1993; Rush, Thomas, & Lord, 1982). If some respondents adopt the averaging strategy, some the individual experience strategy, and still others project their implicit theories of leadership in this situation, what is the meaning of subsequent analyses based on their combined scores?

Perhaps this dilemma would be minimized if leader behavior measures employed an individual-level referent such as, "My leader treats me with respect." This would yield a less confounded analysis if one contrasts within and between variance using such measures; but does it allow one to aggregate clearly individual-based responses to represent average leader behavior? If a leader works closely with each of three subordinates and structures their work in unique ways and thereby receives uniformly high ratings on initiating structure measures, does the average of the subordinates' ratings imply that the leader structured a group activity well? It would if, and only if, we believe that an isomorphism exists for leader behaviors across levels of analysis (see Rousseau, 1985, for more on this concept). This remains an issue for future theorists and researchers, but my position is that isomorphism is not likely to hold in many circumstances. For example, if a leader is uniformly high on individualized consideration behaviors, I do not believe that the average of the followers' ratings well reflects a leader who emphasizes group morale and collective affect (George, 1990). Indeed, by using individualized consideration, a leader might well end up driving wedges between teammates who believe that their treatments are not equitable. In sum, I believe that efforts to separate average and differentiated leader behaviors from analyses of responses to a single set of measures will lead to equivocal results. My recommendation is for researchers to collect measures simultaneously of both how a leader treats individual followers, as well as how he or she behaves in general toward all subordinates. Comparisons of the relative within- and between-variance residing in the two measures therefore would shed light on this issue. Unfortunately using this approach, there is still no way to disentangle unequivocally respondents' personal implicit theories of leadership from true individualized interactions with their leaders because there is a single source of measurement. Perhaps this could be addressed somewhat by having leaders also complete such measures for each employee that they guide, but such efforts have previously yielded quite low interrater reliabilities (yet another sign that something is amiss). It is also the case that the diversity of the other facets of the data box will drive or constrain variance related to these measures. Again, we must consider the larger context within which the questions are posed and think through how the sampling of followers and their KSAOs, situations, and timing issues influence the question at hand.

Analysis Issues

Analyzing leadership research represents a difficult challenge that is well representative of the evolving "meso" tradition in I/O psychology and organizational behavior. Meso research seeks to link constructs that operate at different levels of influence (and analysis) into a unified framework (House, Rousseau, & Thomas-Hunt, 1995). The logic of this approach is that variances between outcomes of interest are likely to be products of multiple influences that may emanate from different levels. In the context of leadership, we can envision relationships between leaders' actions and consequences at the same level of analysis (such as leader behaviors and unit effectiveness). We could also think about downward cross-level effects, such as the impact of leader behaviors on members' reactions. In a similar vein, we could examine contextual influences on the leadership style that individuals choose to adopt. Cross-level relationships may also compile and exhibit upward influences. For example, the average follower ability levels (and their distribution) may influence the behavioral style that a leader adopts. Similarly, a particularly effective middle-level leader may act to transform an organization's culture by setting a vivid example. Moreover, the meso approach suggests that any given influence may operate at multiple levels simultaneously. For example, a leader might behave in a consistent manner with all subordinates on some matters (for example, exhibit a common task focus), yet simultaneously operate in a more dyadic fashion on other matters (for example, exhibit individualized consideration), and all this might vary as a function of contextual demands.

While the meso approach and some advanced statistical techniques (WABA, HLM, and others) do open up new opportunities for thinking about and testing multilevel leadership phenomena, they also put pressure on researchers to articulate clearly the underlying nature of hypothesized relationships. Is leadership defined in terms of a given exchange or a pattern of exchanges over time? Is how a leader behaves on average the independent variable, or how she behaves with each individual the variable? What are the outcomes of effective leadership, and at which levels do they operate? Are they individual-level outcomes, such as satisfactions or motivations; group-level outcomes, such as morale or performance; or organizational-level outcomes, such as culture or return on investment?

Although statistical techniques such as WABA and HLM can dissect overall variance into that which occurs or is predictable within and between units of inquiry (for example, leaders), the answers to the level-based questions listed above are not statistical issues per se. That is, one cannot simply cast data into an analysis and determine from it that some phenomenon is a group, individual, or some combination of relationships. It is precisely the "data box" framework that makes such conclusions tenuous. For example, a typical leadership "levels study" (Yammerino & Dubinsky, 1994) gathers multiple assessments of a sample of leader behaviors and associates them with outcome measures at or below the leader—for example, group morale or individual satisfactions, respectively. However, if we sample leaders from relatively few levels of a single organization, what is the likelihood that between-leader variance will be observed? To the extent there are any pervasive organizational norms, common situational demands, A-S-A process operative, or something else, such an investigation will be hard pressed to find differences between leaders. Gather the same measures about a sample of leaders from different hierarchical levels and different organizational contexts, and the between-leader variance is likely to be far more pronounced. Gather such observations during particularly lean versus bull market conditions, vary the lag between when leader behaviors are assessed and when the consequences are indexed, or use slightly different outcome measures, and it becomes exceptionally difficult to draw definitive conclusion.

I do not mean to berate researchers who have attempted to disentangle the variance of leader behaviors and their consequences. Many of these efforts are among the best examples of meso-based research investigations that exist. My point is more of a cautionary one about inferences, in that when researchers seek to investigate the impact of various cell combinations in the multidimensional data box, they must formally consider what the impact of the other facets may be and then take steps to manage them as most appropriate for their intended purposes. This may involve systematically controlling for such effects through design, sampling, or statistical means or formally incorporating variance of such facets into the substantive part of the study. Once addressed, these decisions then provide a valuable frame within which to interpret results.

A Few Caveats

What I have said in this chapter pertains mostly to empirically driven research of the effectiveness of formally designated leaders. For example, my discussion has been focused on the impact of "the leader"; this implies that we are talking about a single leader who is clearly recognized—most likely formally assigned. Yet in many instances, and in particular in more modern team-based organizations, leadership is a shared phenomenon (Manz & Sims, 1991; Sims & Lorenzi, 1992; Mohrman, Cohen, & Mohrman, 1995). What implications does this have for what I have said? It complicates it tremendously. Consider the fact that rather than dealing with a single leader, his or her traits, behaviors, and so forth, the data box gets a new vector represented by different people, any one of whom may occupy the leadership role. In designs where the designated leader role is formally acknowledged yet rotated among members, leader effectiveness can continue to be studied in the traditional fashion. One merely needs to know exactly when different people occupied the leadership role and yoke data collection and analytic efforts accordingly. In fact, these organizational designs provide a unique opportunity to overcome some of the limitations of more traditional designs (for example, some of the leader self-selection, A-S-A type processes), yet introduce new or more pronounced challenges (for example, deciphering cause-and-effect relationships that are temporally lagged and may not surface until long after the leader position has rotated).

As if the rotating leader role did not present enough challenges for researchers, many team-based organizational designs use empowered teams that do not have any formally designated leader (Fishman, 1999). While some individual may emerge as a universal leader within a group in such situations, the leadership functions are much more likely to be distributed and shared by multiple members in the group. Moving back to the data box framework, this means that we not only have to add a "person vector" to represent the fact that the leader is not a "fixed effect," but we must cross it with a "task functions vector" that depicts the different critical tasks that need to be performed in the group. One can imagine the chaos of trying to discern the simultaneous effects of Person A leading Task Q, Person B leading Task R, Person C leading Tasks S and T, and Person D not initially leading any task but taking over for Persons A and B when they were temporarily reassigned, and so forth.

I do not believe that the relatively neat and tractable data streams of traditional empirical leadership designs can be stretched so far as to incorporate such phenomena. Two alternatives appear evident in response. One strategy is to study leadership at the team level and consider it to be a team property. This would then transform some of the data box facets to new yet related constructs. Rather than focusing on leader traits, team composition would be the issue. This would include not only the average level of various leader-related KSAOs in the team, but also their distributions. It also means that follower characteristics get co-mingled into this facet. The "leader behaviors" facet would get transplanted by an emphasis on team design and processes. Other facets may have to be reconceptualized as well. Nevertheless, the traditional role of formally designated leadership does not entirely disappear in team-based organizations. For example, even in a jet engine plant that employs more than 170 people arranged into eleven self-directed teams with only one formal leader (the plant manager), the influence of that plant manager's leadership style was considered to be a primary determinant of overall effectiveness (Fishman, 1999). Indeed, due to their heightened salience, one might argue that the relatively few formal leaders in team-based organizations have an even larger impact on organizational effectiveness than would their counterparts in traditionally designed organizations.

My second caveat relates to my emphasis on empirically based research investigations. Clearly there have been several notable qualitative studies that have provided unique insights into the leadership phenomenon (Bryman, Bresnen, Beardsworth, & Keil, 1988; Gioia & Chittipeddi, 1991; Smircich & Morgan, 1982). My comments about the role of the data box and its implications for the design and interpretation of qualitative studies readily apply. In fact, most qualitative researchers readily acknowledge that they are investigating the confluence of a number of influences in a particular time, place, and manner. Stated differently, whereas large-sample, empirically oriented leadership researchers typically try to focus on relatively few columns and rows of a data box while minimizing the influence of other facets, qualitative researchers take a different track. They articulate a particular cell of the larger set of matrices and seek to bring to life in its entirety. Whereas the generalizability of any particular cell is of course limited, the insights afforded by such a detail investigation better serve to reveal the richness of leader effectiveness. Thus, although my comments about the variance of the leader and follower samples, the nature of the situations, the applicability of analytic techniques, and so forth hardly apply to the qualitative investigation, the foundation of my thesis remains. The insights that a qualitative study can provide are driven in large part by researchers' a priori decisions about which leaders and followers to study, in what settings, over what time periods, and using particular data collection techniques. And the inferences that can be drawn from such work also become clearer when viewed within the box.

References

Bass, B. M., & Avolio, B. J. (1990). The implications of transactional and transformational leadership for individual, team, and organizational development. In R. W. Woodman & W. A. Passmore (Eds.), *Research in organizational change and development*. Greenwich, CT: JAI Press.

Bass, B. M., & Avolio, B. J. (1993). Transformational leadership: A response to critiques. In M. M. Chemers & R. Ayman (Eds.), *Leadership theory and research*. Orlando, FL: Academic Press.

Blake, R. R., & Mouton, J. S. (1964). *The managerial grid*. Houston, TX: Gulf.

Bryman, A., Bresnen, M., Beardsworth, A., & Keil, T. (1988). Qualitative research and the study of leadership. *Human Relations, 41,* 13–30.

Cattell, R. B. (1966). The data box: Its ordering of total resources in terms of possible relational systems. In *The handbook of multivariate experimental psychology*.

Cook, T. D., & Campbell, D. T. (1979). *Quasi-experimentation: Design and analysis issues for field settings*. Boston: Houghton Mifflin.

Dansereau, F., Graen, G., & Haga, W. J. (1975). A vertical dyad linkage approach to leadership within formal organizations. *Organizational Behavior and Human Performance, 13,* 46–78.

Day, D. V., & Lord, R. G. (1988). Executive leadership and organizational performance: Suggestions for a new theory and methodology. *Journal of Management, 14*, 453–464.

Dechant, K., & Altman, B. (1994). Environmental leadership: From compliance to competitive advantage. *Academy of Management Executive, 8*, 7–28.

Fiedler, F. E. (1967). *A theory of leadership effectiveness.* New York: McGraw-Hill.

Fiedler, F. E. (1971). Validation and extension of the contingency model of leadership effectiveness: A review of the empirical findings. *Psychological Bulletin, 76*, 128–148.

Fishman, C. (1999, October). Engines of democracy. *Fast Company,* pp. 174–202.

George, J. M. (1990). Personality, affect, and behavior in groups. *Journal of Applied Psychology, 75*, 107–116.

Gioia, D. A., & Chittipeddi, K. (1991). Sensemaking and sensegiving in strategic change initiation. *Strategic Management Journal, 12*, 433–448.

Gupta, A. K. (1984). Contingency linkages between strategy and general managerial characteristics: A conceptual examination. *Academy of Management Review, 9*, 399–412.

Gupta, A. K. (1988). Contingency perspectives on strategic leadership: Current knowledge and future research directions. In D. C. Hambrick (Ed.), *The executive effect: Concepts and methods for studying top managers.* Greenwich, CT: JAI Press.

Hersey, P., & Blanchard, K. H. (1977). *Management of organizational behavior: Utilizing human resources.* Upper Saddle River, NJ: Prentice Hall.

Hitt, M. A., & Tyler, B. B. (1991). Strategic decision models: Integrating different perspectives. *Strategic Management Journal, 12*, 327–351.

House, R. J., & Dressler, G. (1974). The path-goal theory of leadership: Some post hoc and a priori tests. In J. G. Hunt & L. L. Larson (Eds.), *Contemporary approaches to leadership.* Carbondale: Southern Illinois University Press.

House, R. J., Rousseau, D. M., & Thomas-Hunt, M. (1995). The meso paradigm: A framework for the integration of micro and macro organizational behavior. In L. L. Cummings & B. M. Staw (Eds.), *Research in organizational behavior* (Vol. 17). Greenwich, CT: JAI Press.

Hughes, R. L., Ginnett, R. C., & Curphy, G. J. (1996). *Leadership: Enhancing the lessons of experience.* Burr Ridge, IL: Irwin.

Jacobs, T. O., & Jaques, E. (1987). Leadership in complex systems. In J. Zeidner (Ed.), *Human productivity enhancement.* New York: Praeger.

Jacobs, T. O., & Jaques, E. (1991). Executive leadership. In R. Gal &

A. D. Manglesdorff (Eds.), *Handbook of military psychology*. Chichester, England: Wiley.

Katz, D., & Kahn, R. L. (1978). *The social psychology of organizations* (2nd ed.). New York: Wiley.

Keller, R. T. (1992). Transformational leadership and the performance of research and development project groups. *Journal of Management, 18,* 489–501.

Kenny, D. A., & Zaccaro, S. J. (1983). An estimate of variance due to traits in leadership. *Journal of Applied Psychology, 68,* 678–685.

Kirkpatrick, S. A., & Locke, E. A. (1991). Leadership: Do traits matter? *Academy of Management Executive, 5,* 48–60.

Leavy, B., & Wilson, D. (1994). *Strategy and leadership*. London: Routledge.

Lieberson, S., & O'Connor, J. F. (1972). Leadership and organizational performance: A study of large corporations. *American Sociological Review, 37,* 117–130.

Lord, R. G., & Maher, K. J. (1993). *Leadership and information processing*. New York: Routledge.

Manz, C. C., & Sims, H. P. (1991). Super leadership: Beyond the myth of heroic leadership. *Organizational Dynamics, 19,* 18–35.

Mathieu, J. E., & Klein, S. R. (2000). Measuring climate at multiple levels in organizations: Use of appropriate referents.

Mohrman, S. A., Cohen, S. G., & Mohrman, A. M., Jr. (1995). *Designing team-based organizations: New forms of knowledge work*. San Francisco: Jossey-Bass.

Pedhazur, E. J., & Pedhazur-Schmelkin, L. (1991). *Measurement, design, and analysis: An integrated approach*. Mahwah, NJ: Erlbaum.

Rice, R. W. (1978). Construct validity of the least preferred co-worker score. *Psychological Bulletin, 97,* 274–285.

Roberts, K. H., Hulin, C. L., & Rousseau, D. M. (1978). *Developing an interdisciplinary science of organizations*. San Francisco: Jossey-Bass.

Rousseau, D. M. (1985). Issues of level in organizational research: Multi-level and cross-level perspectives. *Research in Organizational Behavior, 7,* 1–37.

Rush, M. C., Thomas, J. C., & Lord, R. G. (1982). Implicit leadership theory: A potential threat to the internal validity of leader behavior questionnaires. *Organizational Behavior and Human Performance, 20,* 93–110.

Salancik, G. R., & Pfeffer, J. (1977). Constraints on administrator discretion: The limited influence of mayors on city budgets. *Urban Affairs Quarterly, 12,* 475–498.

Schneider, B. (1987). The people make the place. *Personnel Psychology, 40,* 437–454.

Schriesheim, C. A., & Kerr, S. (1974). Psychometric properties of the Ohio State Leadership Scales. *Psychological Bulletin, 81,* 758–765.

Schriesheim, C. A., & Kerr, S. (1977). Theories and measures of leadership: A critical appraisal of current and future directions. In J. G. Hunt & L. L. Larson (Eds.). *Leadership: The cutting edge.* Carbondale: Southern Illinois University Press.

Schriesheim, C. A., & Stogdill, R. M. (1975). Differences in factor structure across three versions of the Ohio State Leadership Scales. *Personnel Psychology, 28,* 189–206.

Schriesheim, J. F. (1980). The social context of leader-subordinate relations: An investigation of the effects of group cohesiveness. *Journal of Applied Psychology, 65,* 183–194.

Schriesheim, J. F., & Schriesheim, C. A. (1980). A test of the path-goal theory of leadership and some suggested directions for future research. *Personnel Psychology, 33,* 349–370.

Sims, H. P., & Lorenzi, P. (1992). *The new leadership paradigm.* Thousand Oaks, CA: Sage.

Smircich, L., & Morgan, G. (1982). Leadership: The management of meaning. *Journal of Applied Behavioral Science, 18,* 257–273.

Vroom, V. H., & Jago, A. G. (1974). Decision making as a social process: Normative and descriptive models of leader behavior. *Decision Sciences, 5,* 743–769.

Vroom, V. H., & Yetton, P. W. (1973). *Leadership and decision making.* Pittsburgh, PA: University of Pittsburgh Press.

Yammerino, F. J., & Dubinsky, A. J. (1994). Transformational leadership theory: Using levels of analysis to determine boundary conditions. *Personnel Psychology, 47,* 787–811.

Yukl, G., & Van Fleet, D. D. (1992). Theory and research on leadership in organizations. In M. D. Dunnette & L. M. Hough (Eds.), *Handbook of industrial and organizational psychology.* Palo Alto, CA: Consulting Psychologists Press.

Zaccaro, S. J. (1996). *Models and theories of executive leadership: A conceptual/empirical review and integration.* Alexandria, VA: U.S. Army Research Institute for the Behavioral and Social Sciences.

Name Index

Subject Index